THE WIRE®

TRUTH BE TOLD

RAFAEL ALVAREZ

WITH AN INTRODUCTION BY

DAVID SIMON

WITH CONTRIBUTIONS BY

Victor Paul Alvarez	Laura Lippman
Michael A. Fletcher	Ann LoLordo
Greg Garland	George Pelecanos
Nick Hornby	Deborah Rudacille
Joy Lusko Kecken	Tom Waldron
Scott Kecken	Anthony Walton

William F. Zorzi

HOME BOX OFFICE®

CANONGATE

Edinburgh · London · New York · Melbourne

Published by Canongate Books in 2009

1

Parts of this book were first published in the United States in 2004 by Pocket Books, a
division of Simon & Schuster, Inc., 1230 Avenue of the Americas, New York, NY 10020

Revised edition first published in Great Britain in 2009 by Canongate Books Ltd,
14 High Street, Edinburgh EH1 1TE

www.meetatthegate.com

British Library Cataloguing-in-Publication Data
A catalogue record for this book is available on request from the British Library

ISBN 978 1 84767 653 5

Designed and typeset in Minion and Trixie by Cluny Sheeler, Edinburgh

Printed and bound in the UK by CPI Mackays, Chatham ME5 8TD

Dedicated to the memory of
Bob Colesberry
1946 to 2004

CONTENTS

INTRODUCTION

by David Simon

"We're building something here ... and all
the pieces matter."

DETECTIVE LESTER FREAMON

Swear to God, it was never a cop show. And though there were cops and gangsters aplenty, it was never entirely appropriate to classify it as a crime story, though the spine of every season was certain to be a police investigation in Baltimore, Maryland.

But to say so nearly a decade ago, back when *The Wire* first premiered on HBO, would have been to invite certain ridicule. It would have sounded comically pretentious to have invoked Lester Freamon's claim.

As a medium for serious storytelling, television has precious little to recommend it – or at least that has been the case for most of its history. What else can we expect from a framework in which the most pregnant moment in the story has for decades been the commercial break, that five-times-an-hour pause when writers, actors, and directors are required to juke the tale enough so that a trip to the refrigerator or bathroom does not mean a walk away from the television set, or, worse yet, a click on the remote to another channel.

In such a construct, where does a storyteller put any serious ambition? Where are the tales to reside safely and securely, but in the simplest paradigms of good and evil, of heroes, villains, and simplified characterization? Where but in plotlines that remain accessible to the most ignorant or indifferent viewers. Where but in the half-assed, don't-rattle-their-cages uselessness of self-affirming, self-assuring narratives that comfort the American comfortable, and ignore the American afflicted; the better to sell Ford trucks and fast food, beer and athletic shoes, iPods and feminine hygiene products.

Consider that for generations now the cathode-ray glow of our national campfire, the televised reflection of the American experience – and, by extension, that of the Western free-market democracies – has come down to us from on high. Westerns and police procedurals and legal dramas, soap operas and situation comedies – all of it conceived in Los Angeles and New York by industry professionals, then shaped by corporate entities to calm and soothe as many viewers as possible, priming them with the idea that their future is better and brighter than it actually is, that the time is never more right to buy and consume.

Until recently, all of television has been about selling. Not selling story, of course, but selling the intermissions to that story. And therefore little programming that might interfere with the mission of reassuring viewers as to their God-given status as indebted consumers has ever been broadcast – and certainly nothing in the form of a continuing series. For half a century, network television wrapped its programs around the advertising – not the other way around, as it may have seemed to some.

This is not to deny that HBO is a large and profitable piece of Time Warner, which itself is a paragon of Wall Street monolith. *The Wire*'s 35mm misadventure in Baltimore – for any of its claims to iconoclasm – is nonetheless sponsored by a media conglomerate with an absolute interest in selling to consumers. And yet, on that conglomerate's premium cable cannel, the only product being sold is the programming itself. In that distinction, there is all the difference.

Beginning with *Oz* and culminating in *The Sopranos*, the best work on HBO expresses nothing less than the vision of individual writers, as expressed through the talents of directors, actors, and film crews. For a rare window in the history of television, nothing much gets in the way of that. Story is all.

If you laughed, you laughed. If you cried, you cried. And if you thought – and there is actually no prohibition on such merely because you had a TV remote in your hand – then you thought. And if you decided, at any point – as many an early viewer of *The Wire* did – to change the channel, then so be it. But on HBO, nothing other than the stories themselves was for sale and therefore – absent the Ford trucks and athletic shoes – there is nothing to mitigate against a sad story, an angry story, a subversive story, a disturbing story.

The first thing we had to do was teach folks to watch television in a different way, to slow themselves down and pay attention, to immerse themselves in a way that the medium had long ago ceased to demand.

And we had to do this, problematically enough, using a genre and its tropes that for decades have been accepted as basic, obvious storytelling terrain. The crime story long ago became a central archetype of our culture, and the labyrinth of the inner city has largely replaced the spare, unforgiving landscape of the American West as the central stage for our morality plays. The best crime shows – *Homicide* and *NYPD Blue*, or their predecessors, *Dragnet* and *Police Story* – were essentially about good and evil. Justice, revenge, betrayal, redemption – there isn't much left in the tangle between right and wrong that hasn't been fully, even brilliantly explored by the likes of Friday and Pembleton and Sipowicz.

By contrast, *The Wire* had ambitions elsewhere. Specifically, we were bored with good and evil. To the greatest possible extent, we were quick to renounce the theme.

After all, with the exception of saints and sociopaths, few in this world are anything but a confused and corrupted combination of personal motivations, most of them selfish, some of them hilarious. Character is essential for all good drama, and plotting is just as fundamental. But ultimately, the storytelling that speaks to our current condition, that grapples with the basic realities and contradictions of our immediate world – these are stories that, in the end, have some chance of presenting a social, and even political, argument. And to be honest, *The Wire* was not merely trying to tell a good story or two. We were very much trying to pick a fight.

To that end, *The Wire* was not about Jimmy McNulty. Or Avon Barksdale. Or Marlo Stanfield, or Tommy Carcetti or Gus Haynes. It was not about crime. Or punishment. Or the drug war. Or politics. Or race. Or education, labor relations or journalism.

It was about The City.

It is how we in the West live at the millennium, an urbanized species compacted together, sharing a common love, awe, and fear of what we have

rendered not only in Baltimore or St. Louis or Chicago, but in Manchester or Amsterdam or Mexico City as well. At best, our metropolises are the ultimate aspiration of community, the repository for every myth and hope of people clinging to the sides of the pyramid that is capitalism. At worst, our cities – or those places in our cities where most of us fear to tread – are vessels for the darkest contradictions and most brutal competitions that underlie the way we actually live together, or fail to live together.

Mythology is important, essential even, to a national psyche. And Americans in particular are desperate in their pursuit of national myth. This is understandable, to a point: coating an elemental truth with the bright gloss of heroism and national sacrifice is the prerogative of the nation-state. But to carry the same lies forward, generation after generation, so that our collective sense of the American experiment is better and more comforting than it ought to be – this is where mythology has its cost, and a cost not only to the United States but to the world as a whole. In a young and struggling nation, a moderate degree of self-elevating bullshit has a certain earnest charm. For a militarized, technological superpower –

overextended in both its economic and foreign policy impulses – it begins to approach the Orwellian.

We began writing *The Wire* when certain narratives were playing out within the American culture: the shocking frauds at the heart of Enron and Worldcom, outlying harbingers of the economic implosion that was still to come, as well as the institutional scandal of sexual abuse by priests and the self-preservation of the American branch of the Catholic Church. It seemed to us, back in 2002, that there was something hollow and ugly at our institutional core, and from what Ed Burns understood of the Baltimore police department and school system, and from what I had witnessed at the heart of that city's newspaper, the institutional and systemic corruptions of our national life seemed near universal. In practical ways, America was becoming the land of the juked statistic – the false quarterly profit statement, the hyped school test score, the non-existent decline in crime, the impossible campaign promise, the hyped Pulitzer Prize.

We were observant, but not as prescient as the state of our nation now makes us seem. Or at least, we don't now count ourselves as prescient; the enormity of the mortgage security scandal and the Wall Street pyramid schemes that wrecked the world economy were too shameless and absurd for even our fevered imaginations. We saw that there were elements in the culture that were parasitic and self-aggrandizing, that the greed and rapaciousness of a society that exalted profit and free markets to the exclusion of any other social framework would be burdened by such a level of greed. We understood that throughout our national culture, there was a growing inability to recognize our problems, much less deal honestly with them. But, forgive us, we had no idea that the greed had become policy, that the rogue elements were not being carried by corrupted systems, but were in command of those systems. We could not have imagined Katrina and the hollow response to that tragedy. We could not have fathomed the empty lies and self-delusions that brought about the senseless misadventure in Iraq. We had a good argument, as far as we knew; but in the beginning we didn't know how good.

To state our case, *The Wire* began as a story wedged between two American myths. The first tells us that in this country, if you are smarter than the next man, if you are shrewd or frugal or visionary, if you build a better mousetrap, if you get there first with the best idea, you will succeed beyond your wildest imaginations. And by virtue of free-market processes, it is entirely fair to say that this myth, more than ever, happens to be true. Not only is this accurate in America, but throughout the West and in many emerging nations as well. Every day, a new millionaire or three is surely christened. Or ten. Or twenty.

But a supporting myth has also presided, and it serves as ballast against the unencumbered capitalism that has emerged triumphant, asserting as it does for individual achievement to the exclusion of all societal responsibility, and thereby validating the amassed wealth of the wise and fortunate among us. In America, we once liked to tell ourselves, those who are not clever or visionary, who do not build better mousetraps, have a place held for them nonetheless. The myth holds that those who are neither slick nor cunning, yet willing to get up every day and work their asses off and come home and stay committed to their families, their communities and every other institution they are asked to serve – these people have a portion for them as well. They might not drive a Lexus, or eat out every weekend; their children might not be candidates for early admission at Harvard or Brown; and come Sunday, they might not see the game on a wide-screen. But they will have a place, and they will not be betrayed.

In Baltimore, as in so many cities, it is no longer possible to describe this as myth. It is no longer possible even to remain polite on the subject. It is, in a word, a lie.

In my city, the brown fields and rotting piers and rusting factories are testament to an economy that shifted and then shifted again, rendering obsolete whole generations of union-wage workers and their families. The cost to society is beyond calculation, not that anyone ever paused to calculate anything. Our economic and political leaders are dismissive of the horror, at points even flippant in their derision. Margaret Thatcher's suggestion that there is no society to consider beyond the individual and his family speaks volumes in the clarity of its late-20th-century contempt for the ideal of nation-states offering citizens anything approximating a sense of communal purpose and meaning.

From Sparrows Point at the southeastern approaches to my city, the corporate remnant of the once-great Bethlehem Steel informs thousands of retirees that money is no longer available for their pensions. Men who

worked the blast furnaces and shipyards – the very men who built Liberty ships to beat Hitler and Mussolini – are told that while they may suffer from asbestosis, they no longer have health benefits or life insurance.

From the piers of what was once Maryland Ship & Drydock, luxury condominiums and townhomes now rise in place of industrial cranes, while the yachts and powerboats of Washingtonians speckle an inlet where the world's great shipping lines once maneuvered. And, as predicted, the grain tower and pier that Frank Sobotka tried to salvage in *The Wire*'s second season did indeed fall to the developers, who have transformed it into something called Silo Point, featuring luxury housing rather than union-wage jobs.

From Johns Hopkins University – now, by default, the city's largest employer – comes the news that the remaining families who survived generations of poverty, neglect, and addiction in the barren ghetto just north of the East Baltimore Hospital would be moved out entirely, allowing the university to bulldoze their blocks into a biotechnology park. For most of the last century, Hopkins and city officials could find no meaningful way to connect the great research institution with surrounding communities; finally, they destroyed what remained of the village in order to save it.

From the city school system comes year after year of failure and decay, with graduation rates of no more than 30 percent as we prepare Baltimore's children to join an economy that has no real need for them. And with each passing election, the test scores magically rise at the third and fifth grades, before collapsing entirely two years later when the same students – having been taught both the test and the Orwellian perfection of the slogan, "No Child Left Behind" – finally opt out and disappear from the classrooms, choosing the corners instead. From the police department, the arrest rates go ever higher as raw statistics dominate actual police work, and the numbers game ensures that the most incompetent commanders are promoted over those actually capable of investigating crime. The clearance rate for homicides – in the 80 percent range 20 years ago – is now below 35 percent.

And from the city's last remaining daily newspaper, a string of buyouts and attritions now leaves Baltimore's premiere watchdog institution with 140 reporters to report on a city once covered by 500 souls. And the *Baltimore Sun* is not alone in its collapse; from Martin-Marietta to Koppers to Black & Decker to General Motors comes a seemingly endless string of layoffs, reductions-in-force, half-shifts and idle assembly lines. And the city empties; drive through East or West Baltimore and behold a world of boarded-up rowhouses and vacant lots.

The new Baltimore? The Baltimore reborn?

It is here, too, at points, certainly: new technologies, tourism, an ever-expanding service economy. And yet this Baltimore is distant from too many people, heard only as a rumor in the east and westside ghettos, in Pimlico and Brooklyn and Curtis Bay and Cherry Hill. For too many in those neighborhoods, the new Baltimore exists as vague talk about a job at a computer screen well beyond the county line, where mice scrape on pads and cursors ticktack through data streams. If you sensed the sea change and caught the wave – if you were smart enough to tear up your union card and walk away from your father's local to start over at a community college somewhere – then you are there in that world, perhaps, and not here in this one, and maybe it is all for the better.

But so many were left in the shallows – men and women on the streets of Baltimore who are, every day, reminded that the wave has crested, and that now, with the economic tide at an ebb, they are simply worth less than they once were, if they are worth anything at all in a post-industrial economy. Unemployed and under-employed, idle at a West Baltimore soup kitchen or dead-ended at some strip-mall cash register – these are the excess Americans. The economy staggers along without them, and without anyone in this society truly or sincerely regarding their desperation. Ex-steelworkers and ex-longshoremen, street dealers and street addicts, and an army of young men hired to chase and jail the dealers and addicts, whores and johns and men to run the whores and coerce the johns – and all of them unnecessary and apart from the New Millenium economic model that long ago declared them irrelevant.

This is the world of *The Wire*, the America left behind.

Make no mistake: a solitary television drama cannot – and would not – claim to be all of Baltimore, or by extension, all of America. *The Wire* does not claim to represent all of anything as large, diverse, and contradictory as the American experience. Our storylines and our cameras rarely ventured to Roland Park or Mount Washington or Timonium, and the lives misspent and misused in our episodes are not the guarded, viable lives of private schools and county tax-bases and tree-lined business parks. *The Wire* is most certainly not about what has been salvaged or exalted in America. It is, instead, about that portion of our country that we have discarded, and at what cost to our national psyche we have done so. It is, in its larger themes, a television show about politics and sociology, and, at the risk of boring viewers with the very notion, macroeconomics. And, frankly, it is an angry show, but that anger comes honestly.

I used to work at a great gray newspaper in Baltimore until Wall Street found the newspaper industry and eviscerated it for short-term profits, and out-of-town chain ownership proved that they could make more money producing a mediocre newspaper than a good one. The worship of the bottom line, coupled with the venalities of transplanted, prize-sniffing editors, sucked all joy from the place. My co-creator and fellow writer, Ed Burns, worked at a police agency in Baltimore, until organizational politics and Peter-Principled, self-preserving commanders undermined the best police work. On the writing staff of the show since the first season, George Pelecanos sold shoes and tended bar, and then spent years researching and writing novels about that portion of the nation's capital that remains virtually invisible to the nation's leaders, the Shaws and Anacostias where black life is marginalized in the very shadow of the great edifices of American democracy. A fourth writer, Rafael Alvarez, saw his father's career on Baltimore's harbor tugs end on the picket line outside McAllister Towing and was himself working as an ordinary seaman on a cable-laying ship when HBO came calling for an episode or two. A fifth, Richard Price, spent hour after hour, day after day in the Jersey City housing projects to find his lost and tragic voices, just as a sixth, Boston's Dennis Lehane, brought to the page the working-class hurt and hunger of the rough-and-tumble Charlestown and Dorchester neighborhoods. And don't leave out Bill Zorzi, who spent years covering the smoky backrooms of Baltimore politics before joining the staff to help create and guide the show's political dynamic.

These are professional writers, of course. It would be a pompous fraud to claim that those of us who inhabited *The Wire*'s writing room are perfectly proletarian. It is one thing to echo the voices of longshoremen and addicts, detectives and dealers, quite another to claim those voices as our own. The D'Angelo Barksdales and Frank Sobotkas live in their worlds; we visit from time to time with pens poised above splayed notepads.

But neither would it be fair to categorize *The Wire* as a television show written and produced by people who were intent on writing and producing television. None of us is from Hollywood; soundstages and backlots and studio commissaries are not our natural habitat. Hell, never mind Los Angeles, with the exception of Price – and his great Dempsey books speak to the worn Jersey cities across the river – we are not even from the literary capital of New York.

Instead, *The Wire* and its stories are rooted in the ethos of a second-tier city, of a forgotten rust-belt America. No, it isn't as if the angriest and most alienated souls in West Baltimore or Anacostia or Dorchester actually hijacked an HBO drama series and began telling tales. But, at this point, it's as close as television has come to such an improbability.

Which credits HBO as well, for giving us the chance to voice something other than the industry's standard fare. *The Wire* could not exist but for

HBO, or, more precisely, a pay-subscription model such as HBO. Nor could *Oz* or *The Sopranos* or *Deadwood* or *Generation Kill*. These are stories that can entertain and amuse, but also disturb and nettle an audience. They can, at their best, provoke viewers – if not to the point of an argument, then at least to the point of a thought or two about who we are, how we live, and what it is about our society and the human condition that makes it so.

The first season of *The Wire* was a dry, deliberate argument against the American drug prohibition – a Thirty Years' War that is among the most singular and comprehensive failures to be found in the nation's domestic history. It is impossible to imagine pitching such a premise to a network television executive under any circumstances. How, he might wonder, do I help my sponsors sell luxury sedans and pre-washed jeans to all the best demographics while at the same time harping on the fact that the American war on drugs has mutated into a brutal suppression of the underclass?

The second season of *The Wire* was even more of a lighthearted romp: a treatise about the death of work and the betrayal of the working class, as exemplified by the decline of a city's port unions. And how exactly do we put Visa-wielding consumers in a buying mood when they are being reminded of how many of their countrymen – black, white and brown – have been shrugged aside by the march of unrestrained, bottom-line capitalism?

Season Three? A rumination on our political culture and the thin possibility of reform, given the calcified oligarchy that has made raw cash and simple soundbites the mother's milk of American elections. And having established our City Hall, the stage is set for viewers to coldly contemplate the state of public education and, by extension, the American ideal of equality of opportunity and what that might mean for the likes of Michael, Namond, Randy, and Duquan in the drama's fourth season.

Finally, for anyone who has come as far as season five, a last reflection on why these worlds endure, why the crime stats stay juked and the test scores stay cheated and the majors become colonels while the mayors become governors – a depiction of what remains of our media culture, a critique that makes plain why no one is left to do the hard work of explaining the precise nature of our national problems, so that we have become a nation that comfortably tolerates failing schools and corrupting drug wars, broken levees and bought politicians.

And through all of this, how can a television network serve the needs of advertisers while ruminating on the empty spaces in American society and informing viewers that they are a disenfranchised people, that the processes of redress have been rusted shut, and that no one – certainly not our mass media – is going to sound any alarm?

The decoupling of the advertising construct from a broadcast entity was the key predicate for the political maturation of televised drama. It made it possible for writers such as Burns, Price, Lehane and Pelecanos to work in television without succumbing to shame and self-loathing. And again, HBO was smart enough to simply let it be.

As I learned on my earlier experience in network television, the NBC executives used to ask the same questions every time they read a first-draft *Homicide* script:

"Where are the victories?"

Or better still:

"Where are the life-affirming moments?"

Never mind that the show was called *Homicide*, as head writer and executive producer Tom Fontana liked to repeatedly point out, and never mind that it was being filmed in a city struggling with entrenched poverty, rampant addiction, and generations of de-industrialization.

Brave soul that he is, when Fontana wanted to write three successive episodes in which a violent drug trafficker escaped all punishment, he was told he could do so only if the detectives shot and killed the villain at the end of a fourth episode.

Good one, evil nothing. Cut to commercial.

To bring it all the way back, *The Wire* had its actual origins in the main Baltimore County library branch in Towson, where I went as a police reporter to schmooze a city homicide detective named Ed Burns.

It was 1985, and I was working on a series of newspaper articles about a career drug trafficker whom Burns and his partner, Harry Edgerton, had managed to bring down with a prolonged wiretap investigation. Edgerton, or at least his facsimile, would later become known to NBC viewers as Detective Frank Pembleton. But Burns? Too implausible a character, even for network.

When I first met Ed, he was sitting by the checkout desk, a small pile of books atop the table in front of him. *The Magus* by John Fowles. Bob Woodward's *Veil*. A collection of essays by Hannah Arendt.

"You're not really a cop, are you?"

Seven years later, when Burns – having alienated many of his bosses in McNulty-like fashion with his sprawling investigations of violent drug gangs in the Westside projects – was contemplating retirement and life as a city schoolteacher, I approached him with an alternative.

If he could delay his teaching career for a year and a half or so, we could venture together to one of Baltimore's one hundred or so open-air drug markets, meet the people, and write a book about the drug culture that had consumed so much of our city. Which corner? Pick a corner, any corner, at random.

The idea appealed to Ed, who had spent 20 years watching the city police department win battle after battle with individual drug traffickers, yet continue to lose the war. As a patrolman in the Western District, a plainclothesman assigned to the escape squad, and finally a homicide detective, Burns was impressed by the organizational ethos of the West Baltimore drug trade. Amoral and brutal they might be, but the true players were committed – more committed, perhaps, than much of the law enforcement arrayed against them. It was not unlike Vietnam, he acknowledged, and it is fair to say that as a veteran of that losing effort as well, Ed Burns was more entitled than most to render the comparison.

We chose Monroe and Fayette streets in West Baltimore and spent 1993 and much of the ensuing three years following the people there. *The Corner* was published in 1997, and by then – with my newspaper increasingly the playground of tone-deaf, out-of-town hacks – I had moved across town to the writing staff of *Homicide*, hired by Barry Levinson and Tom Fontana.

As a day job, it was a great one. And I found that the artifice of film and the camaraderie were enough to offset my exile from the *Sun*'s city desk, where I had long imagined myself growing old and surly, bumming cigarettes from younger reporters in exchange for back-in-the-day stories about what it was like to work with Mencken and Manchester.

Script by script, Tom shaved my prose style until the pacing and dialogue began to show muscle. Then he slowly began adding fresh responsibilities, sending me to set calls and casting sessions and editing. Jim Finnerty, the production manager and line producer who has long played Stringer Bell to Fontana's Avon Barksdale, offered lessons of his own in practical filming, crew management, and, most of all, making the day.

"You become a producer to protect your writing," Fontana explained.

By the time *The Corner* was published, Tom was already locked down in Oswald Penitentiary, proving to HBO and the world in general that even the most discomfiting drama now had a place on American television. Perhaps, I thought to myself, there was room at HBO or some other premium channel for something as dark as life on an open-air drug corner.

Tom and Barry didn't see *The Corner* as material for a continuing series, but Fontana was good enough to call Anne Thomopoulos at HBO on my behalf. At the resulting meeting, it became clear that the cable channel was willing to take a shot, provided I could pair myself with a black writer.

It didn't matter to me one way or the other – I knew I had those Fayette Street voices in my head – but the other white folk in the room were not about to let a lone pale scribbler produce a miniseries about black drug addicts and dealers.

"How about David Mills?" I ventured.

One of the HBO execs in the room, Kary Antholis, startled. "Do you know David Mills?"

"We're friends. I worked on my college newspaper with him. We wrote our first script together." And so we had. A second-season *Homicide* episode in which Robin Williams had guest-starred. Mills had taken that outcome as an omen, quitting his reporting job at the *Washington Post* and moving to Los Angeles, where he had spent five years making a name for himself in network television. Kary had known about Mills for a long time.

"If you can get Mills on this, that would be great."

I volunteered him as an executive producer, no problem. And upon leaving the HBO offices, I used a cell phone to catch the man at home: "Hey, David. I know what you're doing for the next year."

On the production side, Jim Finnerty volunteered a protégé, assuring me I could do no better for myself. Nina Noble had been first assistant director on the premiere season of *Homicide* and had worked her way up in the Fontana organization. Of course, I immediately agreed to the partnership: a recommendation from Finnerty is enough for such things.

Mills, Noble, myself – that was all the producing we needed for a six-hour miniseries, or so I thought. But HBO had doubts aplenty, and the execs wanted a visual producer in the mix. Antholis arranged interviews in New York with several candidates.

Enter Bobby Colesberry, whose résumé of nearly two decades producing high-end features made me nervous. I saw myself and David fighting with Feature Boy over the down-and-dirty scripts, and over the rough-and-tumble, handheld manner in which we wanted to shoot the drug corners. I saw Nina, too, fighting with him to keep the budget down, to make him realize that series television was not a place for two-page days and arcing crane shots.

So there was little trust in Kary's office that day, particularly when we walked in and saw a copy of *The Corner* splayed open in front of this Colesberry fellow, its pages already marked up in two different colors of ink. A healthier soul might have taken this as a good sign: here was a producer, a veteran of an industry where studio suits reduce all stories to single-sentence concepts, endeavoring to read a 550-page tome and then begin charting scenes and shots in his head. Instead, I'm embarrassed to say, I trusted him not at all.

"We'll take your script notes, but the last pass is ours."

Bob agreed.

"And we don't want to be frozen out of production. We're not as experienced as you, but David and I know how to put film in the can."

No problem.

Months later, with *The Corner* beautifully cast and crewed, and with Charles "Roc" Dutton turning in magnificent dailies as the director of all six hours, I thought back to that first meeting with Bob Colesberry and realized I did not want to put anything to film ever again without him. For something that had begun as a shotgun wedding, it was turning out to be quite a marriage.

Looking past *The Corner* even before it aired, I thought about what it was that I still wanted to say about the drug war, about policing, and, ultimately, about what was happening in the city where I lived.

The Corner was the diaspora of addiction brought down to microcosm – a single, broken family struggling amid the deluge in West Baltimore. The scripts had allowed us to probe the human dimension of the tragedy; the failure of policy, however, could only be implied with something so intimate.

And so back to Mr. Burns, who was by now getting the full dose of the Baltimore public educational system as a middle-school teacher of social studies. There were days, Ed assured me, when a Western District patrol shift felt safer and more manageable than a tour of duty at Hamilton Middle School.

We turned in the pilot script a few months after HBO had collected a trio of Emmys for *The Corner*, and, so, the timing felt right. After all, had we not delivered on that previous project? Just write some checks and send us back to Baltimore where we belong.

But Carolyn Strauss and Chris Albrecht were unconvinced. The show's emphasis on surveillance would be new, and the tone of the piece was different from network fare, but *The Wire*, as it began to be called, still appeared to be a cop show. And HBO's primary concern became apparent: if the networks do cop shows, why are we doing one? The nightmare was to imagine critics across the country finally declaring that this was not in fact HBO, but TV.

I asked Carolyn for a chance to write two additional scripts, if only to show that the pacing, arc, and intention of this drama would be decidedly different from anything on a network. She agreed, and I went back to work as *The Corner* team drifted away, looking for fresh work elsewhere.

Nina Noble produced and managed the HBO movie *Shot in the Heart* for Fontana-Levinson, then headed home to North Carolina. Dave Mills went back to Los Angeles and began banging his head against the network wall, working on a series of pilots and producing a promising gangster epic, *Kingpin*, which, in true network fashion, would be canceled after six episodes. Bob Colesberry returned to features, producing the science fiction film *K-Pax* with Kevin Spacey.

In the end, it took HBO more than a year to agree to shoot even a pilot. There was a second pass of the three scripts, followed by a begging-ass memo to Chris Albrecht by yours truly, followed by an ingathering of *The Corner* crew – save only for David Mills, who could not be budged from a fat development deal. I remember picking up the phone to call Colesberry in Los Angeles, catching him as he was just completing post-production on the Spacey film.

"I bet you thought that HBO show was dead," I remember saying to him.

"Very dead," he admitted.

Asked what I had done to get the green light on the pilot, I confessed that other than begging Chris Albrecht, I was not entirely sure. I read Bob the memo over the phone, and in his own gentle, Bob-like way, he affirmed that it was pathetic, and that, ever after, I should consider myself Mr. Albrecht's bitch.

"Also, no one likes the name Jimmy McArdle."

Bob considered this for a moment. "How about McNulty?"

"Jimmy McNulty."

"It's my grandmother's family name."

"McNulty it shall be."

By November 2001 we were back on the streets of West Baltimore. The scripts were in many ways the same ones that I had originally turned in, albeit with some scenes added to the pilot that hinted at the surveillance

techniques that would be employed later in the season, once the detail had slowly earned the probable cause to secure a wiretap.

The casting by Alexa Fogel in New York and Los Angeles, and the redoubtable Pat Moran in Baltimore, surpassed all expectations. Only the role of McNulty gave us fits, until a bizarre videotape landed in Baltimore, shipped from a London address. On it, an actor was tearing through the orange-sofa scene in which Bunk and McNulty jack up a reluctant D'Angelo, search him, find his pager, then walk him away in handcuffs.

Unlike every other casting tape ever made, however, this one seemed to be the merest suggestion of a scene. The actor, a square-jawed, Jack-the-Lad sort named West, was reading the McNulty lines, then pausing in silence, reacting to emptiness where the responding lines should have been.

With several weeks of fruitless searching for a lead actor weighing on our souls, the tape caught us off guard. Bob and I watched this weird half-scene for a long moment, then fell out of our chairs, laughing uncontrollably. Hearing us, Clark Johnson, the *Homicide* veteran who was directing the pilot, entered the room, watched a few moments of tape, then joined us on the floor.

"What the hell is this goofy motherfucker doing?"

The audition tape may have been comic, but the performance itself – when we gathered our wits and began to concentrate on what the actor had going – was impressive. A week later in New York, Dominic West explained that he couldn't get anyone in London to read the scene with him, and he didn't have access to a casting office to put himself on tape. His girlfriend had tried to help, but her full English accent kept making him laugh, throwing off the scene. Best she could do was keep quiet and hold the video camera steady.

"I didn't know what else to do," our McNulty confessed, "except say my lines and leave spaces where the other lines are supposed to be."

By the time we returned to shooting the remainder of the first season, Ed Burns and I had drafts of the first six episodes in hand, as well as elaborate beatsheets that brought us all the way to the final episodes. Deliberate planning and overarching professionalism had exactly nothing to do with it, but rather a sense that a story so intricate, with so many characters and so much plotting, had to be considered a single entity.

An early script note from HBO execs – who, by and large, were gentle and discerning with their input – argued that an early-episode robbery by Omar and his crew should be omitted, primarily because the robbery was perpetrated on random street dealers who had no value to the central plot.

Our counterargument was basic: wait.

Omar seemed an aside early on, just as Lester Freamon and Wallace seemed to be mere hangers-on. But in time, they would prove themselves essential to the story. And we needed the street robbery to hold Omar's place in the tale, to remind viewers that he and his crew were still in the world, so that by the fifth episode, when McNulty and Greggs try to pull him up for information, we are still aware of who, exactly, this much-talked-about Omar is and what it is he does for a living.

After all, we had it in mind that we would not explain everything to viewers. The show's point of view was that of the insider, the proverbial fly on the wall – and we had no intention of impairing that point of view by pausing to catch up the audience. Consequently, all of the visual cues and connections would need to be referenced fully and at careful intervals.

Perhaps the first fundamental test of our willingness to forgo exposition and an end-of-every-episode payoff came in the fourth episode of that first season, when D'Angelo Barksdale first claimed responsibility for the murder of a woman in an apartment out near the county line. Fronting for the boys in The Pit, D'Angelo describes the murder in some detail and suggests that he was the shooter. Later in the episode, McNulty and Bunk Moreland are in an emptied garden apartment, examining old crime-scene photos of a slain young woman and reworking the geometry of the murder.

The five-minute scene offers no explanation for itself beyond the physical activities of the detectives as they address the crime scene and the almost continuous use of the word 'fuck' in all its possible permutations – an insider's homage to the great Terry McLarney, a veteran Baltimore murder police who once predicted that Baltimore cops, in their love of profanity, would one day achieve a new and viable language composed entirely of such.

A casual viewer could watch the scene and ascertain that the detectives had figured out the murder scenario. They conclude, in fact, by locating a rusting shell casing outside the kitchen window.

But what exactly is that scenario? And does it match the murder that D'Angelo spoke of earlier? And what were the white speckles on the floor in the crime-scene photo – the droplets that Bunk pointed to? And how did that lead McNulty to open the refrigerator door, then slam it closed? And why, for Chrissakes, will no one explain what the hell is going on?

For the answers, viewers would not have to merely wait out the episode, but all of them. Only during D'Angelo's interrogation at the season's end does he corroborate the crime scene details in a way that convinces Bunk and McNulty of his authenticity. And, even then, the exposition is at a minimum.

When D'Angelo explains that he had brought cocaine to the woman, who told him she would put it "on ice," the detectives acknowledge the connection to their crime scene with a single word:

"Refrigerator," says Bunk.

And McNulty nods casually.

Such calculating restraint offered viewers a chance to do something that television rarely, if ever, allows its audience: they were free to think hard about the story, the different worlds that the story presented, and, ultimately, the ideas that underlie the drama. And the reward for such committed viewers would come not at the end of a scene or the end of an episode, but at the end of the season, indeed, at the end of the tale.

As storytelling, it seemed like the best way to do business. But, even so, we had to acknowledge that this much plotting from episode to episode was an extraordinary risk, even for HBO. We would certainly lose some viewers: those who did not devote enough effort to follow the intricate story, those who gave it their all but were confused nonetheless, and those who, expecting an episodic television drama, would be bored to death by the novelistic pace of The Wire.

Bob Colesberry and I told ourselves repeatedly that we were making the drama for those remaining. A couple dozen or so hard cases, at least.

Before the first season aired in June 2002, HBO made sure to send as many as five consecutive episodes to critics – all of those we had edited. The hope was that by seeing more episodes, those being asked to consider the show would understand that while the pilot episode violated many of the basic laws of episodic television, it was at least an intentional affront.

To that same end, in a series of press interviews, I began referring to the work as a "visual novel," explaining that the first episodes of the show had to be considered much as the first chapters of any book of even moderate length.

"Think about the first few chapters of any novel you ever liked, say, *Moby-Dick*," I told one reporter in a phone interview. "In the first couple chapters, you don't meet the whale, you don't meet Ahab, you don't even go aboard the *Pequod*. All that happens is you go with Ishmael to the inn and find out he has to share a room with some tattooed character. Same thing here. It's a visual novel."

All of which sounded great to me until I hung up the phone and turned to confront a certain Baltimore writer by the name of Lippman, who has penned and published nine actual novels and with whom I share quarters. Her lifework is replete with hardback covers, actual chapter breaks, and descriptive prose that goes a good deal further than "INT. HOMICIDE UNIT/HEADQUARTERS – DAY."

"First of all," she informed me, "you just compared yourself to Herman Melville, which even by your egotistical standards is a bit over-the-top. And second of all, if *The Wire* is really a novel, what's its ISBN?"

A mouthy broad; clever, too. But, fortunately, a lot of critics were less exacting with my hyperbole, and, more important, they actually put four or five tapes into their machines before writing reviews. At least in the hinterlands they did. In New York, where time runs faster than elsewhere and critics can give you no more than an hour to make your case, *The Wire* suffered poor reviews in every single newspaper. We went oh-for-four in The Big Apple, feeling much like the Orioles on a long weekend at Yankee Stadium.

Ratings dipped, too, but HBO – being HBO – did not panic.

"We love the show," Carolyn Strauss said repeatedly, reassuring us. "We don't care about ratings, so you shouldn't care about ratings."

For his part, Chris Albrecht called to say he had just watched the cut of Episode Five and "it's getting better with every episode."

I hestitated to argue that I thought they were all good episodes, that they were paced precisely for the maximum payoff over 13 hours. Instead, I took the comment to heart, reminding myself that when you read a good book, you are more invested with every chapter. What Chris was sensing was our intention.

By the last third of the season, the tide had slowly turned. Viewers were fully committed and there were more of them; ratings began to rise amid some healthy word of mouth. A couple of New York critics revisited the show and affirmed its worthiness. The actors, too, began to sense that we were building a different kind of machine. One Monday on set, Andre Royo, who owned the role of Bubbles, sauntered over to a pair of writers to say he had watched the previous night's episode:

"Every time I start to wonder what you all are doing with a scene, I just wait a couple episodes, and, sure enough, there's a reason for it."

Other actors, notably those on the wrong side of the law, began to wonder what we would do if we were picked up for a second season, what with Avon and D'Angelo Barksdale heading to their respective prison cells.

Corey Parker Robinson, who played the role of Detective Sydnor, thought he had it figured: "They're gonna get out on a technicality, right?"

It was an understandable assumption, given that we were standing on a film set in the West Baltimore projects, where we had thus far filmed much of our story. But in our heads, the writers were already elsewhere, and, as a finishing touch, we made sure to deliver McNulty to the police boat at the end of the last episode.

By then, a lot of viewers had forgotten Sergeant Landsman's prophecy in the pilot episode, that McNulty would ride the boat if he didn't stop provoking the departmental brass. As far back as the pilot, we had decided on the substance of a second season, should there be one.

And when McNulty shipped out with the marine unit, it happened – typically – without dialogue, with nothing more than Bunk Moreland and Lester Freamon walking to the edge of the dock and tossing him a fifth of Jameson's beneath the roar of boat motors.

If you got the joke, great. Thanks for staying with us.

If not, hey, sorry. It's what we do.

It's Laura Lippman, again, who gets a mention for making me read George Pelecanos. Not that I hadn't been given fair warning of what George had been doing with his D.C. novels – half a dozen other writers had urged me to check him out, comparing his voice and material to that of *The Corner*. But we Baltimoreans have this chip on our shoulders about Washington, and though I'd grown up in the same D.C. suburbs as George, I had long ago taken my allegiances north, embracing every stereotype about those tie-wearing, GS-rated, lawyer-assed sonsabitches down I-95.

When I finally cracked *The Sweet Forever* and saw that Pelecanos had been mining a different Washington altogether, it made perfect sense. And, later, upon encountering George at the funeral of a mutual friend, I tried to explain what we were trying to do with *The Wire*, and why he might want to be a part of it.

"It's a novel for television," I said, but under my breath, for fear that my consort, also in attendance at the memorial, would overhear.

Like many writers, George had suffered the slings, arrows and indignities of trying to get so many of his own worthy stories to film, and he immediately grasped the possibilities. In the feature world, after all, it's the studios, if not the directors and stars, who have the drag. In episodic television, by virtue of the continuing storylines, it's the writer with the suction. And at HBO, this is more so.

During the first season, George was given the penultimate episode – particularly because it included the stark, horrifying death of Wallace. The drama of that singular moment required a writer who had built so many of his novels toward similar crescendos. And George, true to form, nailed it.

Would he come back for Season Two? Would he commit to working as a story editor and producer? He certainly didn't need the money; his day job of drop-kicking genre fiction into the literary ether was enough without the hassle of a television gig.

But George, who loves film and can't resist a story well told, not only signed on, he set about enlisting other novelists who were doing much the same kind of work.

We could promise Richard Price and Dennis Lehane no reward commensurate with the talent. The best we could offer was that, unlike any other film project with which they might become involved, *The Wire* would not compromise story for the sake of a studio, a director, or a movie star.

"If you get fucked over, at least it'll be another writer doing it to you."

And while both Lehane (*Mystic River*) and Price (*Clockers*) are masters of a strain of crime fiction that long ago rendered the presumed boundaries of genre meaningless, the addition of Price to the writing staff seemed especially appropriate, if not at all probable.

Anyone who has ever read *Clockers* – which is to the cocaine epidemic of the early 1990s as *The Grapes of Wrath* is to the Dust Bowl – understands the debt owed to that remarkable book by *The Wire*. Indeed, the split point-of-view that powers *The Wire* is a form mastered first in the modern novel, and Price, in his first Dempsey book, proved beyond all doubt how much nuance, truth, and story could exist between the world of the police and the world of their targets.

On learning that the Season Three lineup of writers would include Price and Lehane, Bob Colesberry was beside himself with glee. And whom,

I teased him, did he want Pelecanos to bring us for a fourth season? Elmore Leonard? Philip Roth? How about this Melville fuck I keep mentioning? He hasn't worked in a while, has he?

And Bob would laugh at the effrontery of it, though in his own way, he, too, was expanding the show during the second season, transforming it from a limited cops-and-dealers saga into something larger, something panoramic enough to justify all the writing and acting talent.

The rotting piers and rusting factories of the waterfront – and, most of all, those Gothic cranes at Seagirt and Locust Point – gave Colesberry the visuals he needed to show just what could be done with a television series shot on location.

His standards had always been those of the directors he had worked with in his long feature career – Scorsese, Parker, Benton, Forsyth, Ang Lee – and Bob had learned well, rising from location manager to first AD to line producer. He was not a deskbound executive. He was instead a set rat, familiar with every aspect of filmmaking and committed to serving story.

His elegance, and that of Uta Briesewitz, the show's director of photography in those early years, found subtle ways into the film throughout the first season. In the pilot episode, note the decision to stay wide, filming from across the street as Wee-Bey berates D'Angelo for talking about business in a car. As Bey dresses the less experienced player down, he stands outside a carryout and beneath a neon sign that reads BURGERS.

D'Angelo, humiliated, is framed beneath a second sign: CHICKEN.

The camera stays wide as Wee-Bey starts back to the parked SUV, only to pause as two police cars, blue lights flashing, wipe frame and wail away, seemingly after those, unlike Bey, who fail to take the lessons of the street to heart.

Film such as that, conceived and edited with intelligence and restraint, was Bob's stock-in-trade. The projects of West Baltimore and the taut, credible precinct sets of production designer Vince Peranio guided the show's first year to an appropriately claustrophobic look, just as the rogue fashions of costume designer Alonzo Wilson suggested a violent and stunted street world. All of it was creativity with absolute context.

As the show began to grow – carving off fresh slices of Baltimore – so, too, did Colesberry expand the show's visual sense of a working city. And even as Season Two was underway, Bob and I were contemplating a third season in an altogether different locale, and a fourth elsewhere, too. With each season, by showing a new aspect of a simulated American city in all its complexity, we might, by the end of the show's run, have a chance to speak to something more universal than Avon Barksdale or Jimmy McNulty or drugs or crime.

To do the same show over, season after season – this was never an option. And Bob – who was once made to concede that the last pass on *The Corner* scripts would be writers-only – had become a partner in every aspect of the storytelling. He was never happier about the show's plotting than during the writers' meetings for the third season – meetings at which he was a full and welcome participant.

Midway through the meeting on the second episode, in fact, Richard Price expressed surprise on learning that the man sitting to his immediate right was not actually a fellow writer.

"Bob's an executive producer."

A title which, in Hollywood terms, is often synonymous with asshole. Price was truly thrown, later confessing out of Colesberry's earshot that this was the only production he knew in which you could not discern someone's job title by the way he behaved.

For all of us who worked with him, part of the fun was pushing Bob out of the background – where he had long labored as the right arm of so many talented and noted directors – and bringing him into the light, where he belonged.

When *The Corner* won an Emmy for best miniseries, Nina, David, and I were determined that Bob should accept the award. And on *The Wire*, we pressed him into a small cameo as Detective Ray Cole, a shambling, hapless sort who symbolized the workaday ethos of the homicide unit.

Bob assumed he was on the hook for maybe a line or two of dialogue, but with great delight the writers began churning out more moments for Ray Cole, most of them comic and at the character's expense.

Finally, and most importantly, we pressed Bob to do the one thing for which he had seemingly spent a lifetime preparing: the last episode of the second season was not only produced, but directed, by Robert F. Colesberry. Among other moments, he is the true author of that ending montage of dying industry seen through the eyes of Nick Sobotka – all that spare, brutal imagery, edited together in such a way as to imply the anger of the story as a whole.

When Bob, only fifty-seven, died in February 2004 from heart surgery complications, it seemed to all of us on the show nothing less than an outrage. His best was yet to come, or so we had all assumed.

In the ensuing three years, we did the best we could to maintain the template that Bob Colesberry brought to *The Wire*. And to that end, we continued forward with many of the same veteran directors that Colesberry chose in those first two seasons, and indeed, with Bob's wife Karen Thorson handling post-production duties, familiar as she is with what Colesberry would want the film to be. Whatever we got wrong in Seasons Three, Four, and Five, he was unable to prevent, and whatever we got right can safely be credited to the man.

Lastly, we meant no offense.

We staged *The Wire* in a real city, with real problems. It is governed and policed and populated by real people who are every day contending with those problems. The school system we depict is indeed the school system in which Ed Burns taught. The political infrastructure is that which Bill Zorzi covered for two decades. The newspaper on which we centered some of the final season's story is indeed the newspaper at which I labored and learned the city.

The mayor does not love us. Nor does the police commissioner, nor the school superintendent, nor the publisher of the *Baltimore Sun*. Nor should they. If I had their jobs, I would regard *The Wire* and its antecedents – *Homicide* and *The Corner* – as a necessary evil. And, ignoring for a moment the film industry that burgeoned here over the last decade, I would more often than not wonder what is so damned necessary.

In our defense, the story is labeled as fiction, which is to say we took liberties in a way that journalism cannot and should not. Some of the events depicted in the 60 hours of *The Wire* actually occurred, a few others were rumored to have occurred. But many of the events did not occur, and perhaps the only distinction worth making is that all of them could have happened – not only in Baltimore, but in any major American city contending with the same set of problems.

Certainly, we do not feel that the shots taken were cheap ones. The police department in Baltimore really did cook the crime stats so that the mayor could become governor. The school system truly does fail to graduate the vast majority of students, and faculty are, in fact, teaching the standardized test rather than attempting to educate children. Unionized labor and the dignity of work are disappearing from the city's landscape, and the war against the only industry remaining in many neighborhoods – the drug trade – has indeed become a brutal farce. And, yes, Baltimore's surviving newspaper spent the last two decades reducing its staff and content, and concentrating its remaining resources on the petty frauds of "impact" journalism and the prize culture. They actually did abandon comprehensive coverage of the city and now miss nearly every story that actually matters to the life of Baltimore.

It is a harsh critique, no doubt. But for the most part, we live in this city. By choice. And living here, we see what is happening in Baltimore for better and for worse, and we speak to such things as those with a vested interest in the city's improvement and survival. Speaking as Baltimoreans, we quite naturally found it appropriate to reference our known world in these stories.

But, in fairness, the stories are more universal than this; they resonate not just in West Baltimore, but in East St. Louis, North Philadelphia, and South Chicago. And judging from the continuing reaction to this drama overseas, it seems these stories register as well in cities the writers were in no way contemplating when we began the journey. Perhaps Baltimore isn't any more screwed up than some other places. If it were the case, then these stories would only have meaning for people here.

The Wire depicts a world in which capital has triumphed completely, labor has been marginalized and monied interests have purchased enough political infrastructure to prevent reform. It is a world in which the rules and values of the free market and maximized profit have been mistaken for a social framework, a world where institutions themselves are paramount and every day human beings matter less.

"World going one way," says Poot, reflective, standing on his corner. "People going another."

Many may regard these stories, in their universality, to be cynical and despairing of humanity as a whole. I am not so sure. The problems of this new and intimidating century are worthy of some genuine despair, certainly. And a supposedly great nation that cannot keep a single low-lying city behind functional levees hardly seems capable of grasping the challenge of, say, global warming. Considering that the Netherlands has for generations successfully kept most of itself out of the North Sea, the American institutional response to its problems thus far seems to justify a notable degree of cynicism.

But in all of these Baltimore stories – *Homicide*, *The Corner* and *The Wire* – there exists, I believe, an abiding faith in the capacity of individuals, a careful acknowledgment of our possibilities, our humor and wit, our ability to somehow endure. They are, in small but credible ways, a humanist celebration at points, in which hope, though unspoken, is clearly implied.

True, the stories themselves don't exalt the bricks and mortar and institutions of Baltimore; nor do they spare American policing, or education, or politics or journalism much in the way of criticism. But they at least reckon with the city honestly, and they are written with a homegrown affection that should be readily apparent even to viewers in London, or Mexico City, or Beijing. Watching *The Wire*, true citizens of my city will smile when they see the mallet hit a crab claw, or when an a-rabber's cart trundles past in the background; those foreign to Baltimore will miss many a reference, but not, I believe, the overall sense that they are learning about a city that matters.

If the stories are hard ones, they are at least told in caring terms, with nuance and affection for all the characters, so that whatever else a viewer might come to believe about cops and dealers, addicts and lawyers, longshoreman and politicians, teachers and reporters, and every other soul that wanders through *The Wire* universe, he knows them to be part and parcel of the same tribe, sharing the same streets, engaged in the same, timeless struggle.

David Simon
Baltimore, Md.
July 2009

LETTER TO HBO

Date: June 27, 2001
To: Chris Albrecht, Carolyn Strauss
From: David Simon
Re: The Wire

So, why do this?

Let me be direct about addressing what I believe to be HBO's predominant concern, to wit: HBO has succeeded in the past by creating drama in worlds largely inaccessible to network television, worlds in which dark themes, including sex and violence, can be utilized in more meaningful and realistic ways than in standard network fare. So, why do a police show when the networks trade in such? And if we are to do a police show, how does *The Wire* differ from what viewers have before encountered?

The past is a prescription for the past only. What HBO has accomplished with *The Sopranos*, *Sex and the City*, *Six Feet Under*, and *Oz* is to seize a share of the drama market by going to places where no network could compete. This was sound programming and it has achieved, for HBO, a cultural resonance and viewership.

But, creatively, I would argue that you guys are at a crossroads now: either you continue to hew to this formula to the exclusion of other ideals, or you find a different – perhaps even more fundamental – way to differentiate your programs. If you continue to seek worlds inaccessible to other networks, it will, creatively, become a formula of diminishing returns. The networks can't or won't do sex, serious, thoughtful violence (now there's an oxymoron I like), and character-based dramas in which characters are fundamentally, or drastically, flawed. Having achieved with prisons, drug corners, criminality, and the young and sexually active, HBO has, I would argue, gone about as far as it can in bringing fresh worlds to television.

At the same time, this formula has – by default – ceded the basic dramatic universe of politics, law, crime, medicine, to the networks. In the past, this was wise. These things were the networks' bread and butter, and they are at their most competitive in the hour-long ensemble drama.

But *The Wire* is, I would argue, the next challenge to the network logic and the next challenge for HBO. It is grounded to the most basic network universe – the cop show – and yet, very shortly, it becomes clear to any viewer that something subversive is being done with that universe. Suddenly, the police bureaucracy is amoral, dysfunctional, and criminality, in the form of the drug culture, is just as suddenly a bureaucracy. Scene by scene, viewers find their carefully formed presumptions about cops and robbers undercut by alternative realities. Real police work endangers people who attempt it. Things that work in network cop shows fall flat in this alternative world. Police work is at times marginal or incompetent. Criminals are neither stupid nor cartoonish, and neither are they all sociopathic. And the idea – as yet unspoken on American TV – that no one in authority has any reason to care what happens in an American ghetto as long as it stays within the ghetto is brought into the open. Moreover, within a few hours of viewing, the national drug policy – and by extension our basic law enforcement model – is revealed as calcified, cynical, and unworkable.

In the first two episodes, the impulse to assert control over one housing project in one city – a microcosm for what America is trying to do in every one of its cities – results in threatened careers, murdered witnesses, a near-riot in which a fourteen-year-old child is nearly killed. All of this brings no one any closer to a solution. These are costs paid for their own sake, and, slowly, viewers discern that unlike every other cop show that they have been raised on, this one refuses to play the card of good versus evil. We want McNulty to succeed, yes. But we also feel for D'Angelo, trapped by an equally malevolent bureancracy. We feel, too, for Daniels, leading an investigation no one wants, but resent his unwillingness to commit. And though we have been taught to despise someone like Bubbles, no one consistently shows more fundamental humanity.

The argument is this: it is a significant victory for HBO to counterprogram alternative, inaccessible worlds against standard network fare. But it would, I will argue, be a more profound victory for HBO to take the essence of network fare and smartly turn it on its head, so that no one who sees HBO's take on the culture of crime and crime fighting can watch anything like *CSI*, or *NYPD Blue,* or *Law & Order* again without knowing that every punch was pulled on those shows. For HBO to step toe-to-toe with NBC or ABC and create a cop show that seizes the highest qualitative ground through realism, good writing, and a more honest and more brutal assessment of police, police work, and the drug culture – this may not be the beginning of the end for network dramas as industry standard, but it is certainly the end of the beginning for HBO. The numbers would still be there for *CSI* and such; the relevance would not. We would be stepping up to the network ideal, pronouncing it a cheap lie, and offering instead a view of the world that is every bit as provocative as *The Sopranos* or *The Corner.* But because that world of cops and robbers is so central to the American TV experience, *The Wire* would stand as even more of a threat to the established order than a show that was marginalized because it offered a world (prison, gangsters, sex) where some viewers are reluctant to tread on any terms.

I know the basic fear and I share it: some critic somewhere watches ten minutes of *The Wire* and says, it's good, but it's a cop show. Guess what: it's not HBO. It's TV.

It's for that reason that I have spent so long thinking about the exacting structure and the inherent message of these episodes. The journey through this one case will ultimately bring viewers from wondering, in cop-show expectation, whether the bad guys will get caught, to wondering instead who the bad guys are and whether catching them means anything at all. This could be a remarkable journey and a brave one for HBO. But the payoff is enormous. You will not be stealing market share from the networks only by venturing into worlds where they can't, you will be stealing it by taking their worlds and transforming them with honesty and wit and a darker, cynical, and more piercing viewpoint than they would ever undertake. You leave them the warm fuzziness of *West Wing* and *Providence* and little else.

I also know that there is concern that because the full maze of the wire and electronic surveillance scenes is not employed up front (it is far better that the best police work – rather than a given as in all other cop shows – must be first earned by the struggle to merely identify and isolate the Barksdale gang in the first episodes), a less than discerning critic might wonder how this is different from other police shows. I can only answer: go scene by scene. Read this dialogue. These cops are behaving, thinking, surviving, and struggling with issues as no predecessors on TV ever have. These drug dealers are more complex than anything the networks can imagine. An example: from Episode Two, as additional manpower is brought into the case and we learn that it is not only a gathering of menials and incompetents – but is meant to be such. Has any such scene occupied the screen time of *CSI* or *NYPD Blue*? Or the drug dealers discussing chicken nuggets, until their own sense of their stunted place in the world overtakes them: have criminals ever been allowed this kind of sadness or complexity on a network show?

As with *The Corner*, most critics will be discerning if the quality is there. But, more than that, I would argue that we can eliminate the risk entirely by filming the full season, so that all the ironies and all of the darkness and the entire point of the undertaking is utterly apparent. And for this first season at least, we can offer the critics the entire package or most of the package at the premiere so that no one could possibly miss the point. This strategy worked on *The Corner*. Anyone armed with only the first ten minutes of that miniseries could have concluded that it was a stereotypic ghetto drama. Instead, the critics had four episodes before the first one aired – and with that much material to see that we were after fresh ideas and bigger game, they did not turn away. If we do this right – and we will – the critical response will be that HBO has turned its gaze to a standard of television fare: the cop show. And the cop show can never be the same.

Episode Three should be polished by week's end. I wish I could have sent it with Two, but I had some personal circumstances that prevented me from finishing last week. Indeed, I am concerned that because Two contains much of the setup for what follows, the full sense of what Three does in terms of upending this universe may not be clear. If you still have doubts, wait until Three arrives and then scan the first three. And if that doesn't convince you, Four and Five will follow. I'm going to keep honing this story until you admit that it needs to be told and that HBO, for obvious reasons, is the place to tell it.

This is a smart series. It is good storytelling. And it could be the best work on television that I've done so far. Pull the trigger, guys. As with *The Corner*, you will only be proud.

David Simon

BARACK OBAMA: WIRE FAN

Barack Obama's march into history has been as unconventional as it has been unlikely. It began on a seven-degree day in front of the Old State Capitol in Springfield, Illinois, the place where Abraham Lincoln delivered one of his most famous speeches against slavery. Here he was, less than a century and half later, a first-term senator, a black first-term senator, announcing his candidacy for presidency of the United States.

Thousands of supporters braved the cold to cheer Obama that frigid February morning in 2007, but there was also an abiding sense that his journey seemed a bit quixotic. How did a man who had been a US senator for just over two years, a state senator for seven years, a law school instructor, a civil rights lawyer, and a community organizer, find the audacity to run for president of the United States?

Even now that he occupies the White House, many people remain slightly dazed by his victory. Not just that he won, but also how he won.

All along, Obama promised to bring change to Washington. It was an annoyingly vague declaration, which he nonetheless demonstrated throughout his campaign and now as president. In ways big and small he flouted old political conventions and dared to do things on his own terms, rewriting the rules as he moved along.

He shattered fundraising records, using the Internet to build an army of grassroots supporters and take in more contributions than any presidential candidate before him. Born to a white mother and Kenyan father, Obama self-identified as an African American. It is safe to say that is not the best brand for winning elections in a country where fewer than one in nine citizens is black and polls find significant numbers of people who still hold negative racial stereotypes.

But Obama confidently operates as a man impervious to stereotype.

Asked what his favorite sport is, he answers basketball. On one level that seems simple enough. It even has the virtue of being genuine: the 6'2" Obama played basketball for his high school in Hawaii. He continues to run ball with his friends, and from the presidential podium he occasionally brags about the accuracy of his left-handed jump shot. He even installed a basketball hoop on an outdoor tennis court at the White House where he occasionally takes guests "to school."

But in America, basketball is seen as a black sport, an urban sport, and one that some people say too many black youngsters are obsessed with, sometimes to the detriment of their studies. In short, it's a sport vulnerable to stereotype.

But Obama holds it close, swishing three-pointers for the troops in Afghanistan, casually sitting courtside with a beer in hand as he talked trash with a playfully heckling fan at a National Basketball Association game in Washington, and going on ESPN to reveal for the world his picks for the closely watched NCAA collegiate basketball tournament.

It is safe to say that no conventional political adviser told Obama to identify with basketball. In the old days, that would be considered bad politics. But somehow Obama eclipsed the negative views of basketball while embracing all its coolness and hipness, transforming it into good politics. Clearly, it is a new day.

So it was when he was asked about his favorite television show during the heat of the presidential campaign. That can be a tricky question. Someone who wanted to flaunt their national security credentials might cite *24*, the television show that focuses on the daring-do of fictional counterterrorism agent Jack Bauer.

Or perhaps someone interested in health care might lift up *Grey's Anatomy*, which would have the added benefit of being in line with mainstream American viewing habits. That show was Hillary Clinton's choice.

But Obama chose *The Wire*. Not only did he choose *The Wire*, but he also went on to say that his favorite character was Omar, the gay stick-up man who tormented the drug dealers with his bold robberies.

"That's not an endorsement," Obama has explained. "He's not my favorite person, but he is a fascinating character." Obama went on to call Omar, "the toughest, baddest guy on the show."

Obama continued to be a close fan of *The Wire* even after the show faded from television. During his first European visit as president, Obama was in Prague to deliver a speech laying out his vision for nuclear non-proliferation, when he spotted the actor Andre Royo, who was in town filming *Red Tails*, about the racial trials faced by America's first black military pilots, the Tuskegee airmen.

In *The Wire*, Royo had played the part of "Bubbles," the heroin addict turned recovering heroin addict with a sweet personality and an encyclopedic knowledge of the underside of the drug game.

Obama turned up at the filming locale, and immediately recognized Royo.

"I was standing on a podium and Obama points to me and says, 'My dude from *The Wire*! Keep up the good work!'" Royo recalls. "And I'm like, the president of the United States just shouted me out."

America is a nation where many presidents have been mythologized as rural outdoorsmen. Ronald Reagan had a ranch in beautiful Santa Barbara, California. George W. Bush had a few thousand acres in Crawford, Texas, where he would retreat to ride his mountain bike and "clear brush" during 100-degree August days. Jimmy Carter was a peanut farmer from Plains, Georgia.

By contrast, Obama is an urban president, America's first urban president since John F. Kennedy. Obama may have been raised in Indonesia and sunny Hawaii, but his political identity was forged in Chicago, known as America's "Second City" – behind New York; the City of Big Shoulders, as Lincoln's biographer Carl Sandburg called it.

Obama is not the only political leader who has shown love to *The Wire*. Michael Nutter, mayor of Philadelphia, America's 6th largest city, is also a huge fan of the show. The mayor brought together about 100 city leaders and ordinary citizens (who were chosen by raffle) for a City Hall screening of the series finale.

So Obama's love of *The Wire*, while maybe politically risky under the old rules, makes sense. He's an urban guy. And the show appeals to urban sensibilities. While it never had huge ratings, *The Wire* enjoyed a loyal, urbane, informed following, drawn by the show's great writing, gritty realism, and complex, morally ambiguous storylines.

If *The Wire* helped change the conventions of television by altering the good–bad moralism that inhabits much of popular entertainment, Obama's presidency is also all about the oft-mentioned change.

During the campaign, he was cautious and never fully explained what "change" meant. But, as president, Obama has been boldly setting about changing how the US government operates.

He wants to expand health care coverage in the world's wealthiest nation, where 46 million people go without insurance. He wants to cap carbon emissions, in a nation that is the world's largest emitter of ozone-producing carbon (even if China is closing fast).

In a country where the cost of higher education has increased far faster than the salaries of most workers in recent decades, he wants government-sponsored college grants and loans to be more available.

In a nation that for a generation worshipped at the altar of small government and free-market capitalism, even as fewer workers had pensions, job security, and pay increases outpacing inflation, he wants government to do more to lift the take-home income of average Americans.

On the international stage, he is winding down the war in Iraq, even as he is stepping up the fight in Afghanistan. He has sought to engage America's antagonists. He heartily shook hands with leftist Venezuelan President Hugo Chavez, who the Bush administration had clashed with, even as his oil-funded brand of socialism and friendship with Fidel Castro made him popular in many parts of Latin America.

He has reached out to Iran and opened his administration to talks with North Korea. He has tried to arrest the drift in relations with a newly assertive Russia. He has made a few cautious overtures to Cuba, where a US trade embargo has held firm for more than four decades, without anything resembling an effect.

All of this has happened in the first few months of the Obama presidency, even if much of it remains work in progress.

Obama likes to say that his presidency has a chance to be transformative. That opportunity, he acknowledges, comes because the nation is at an inflection point caused by anger over the war in Iraq and an economic meltdown that has caused many Americans to rethink the "rugged individualism" and distrust of government that has long been an American hallmark.

Looking back, Obama says, not many presidents have confronted crises of a similar scale. And the ones who did are best remembered by history. Lincoln faced down a civil war. Roosevelt steered the nation out of the Great Depression. LBJ helped drive a stake in the heart of American apartheid.

And Reagan brought an end to an alleged American "malaise," (attributed to Jimmy Carter for a 1979 speech in which he never used the word) that Reaganites called a product of liberalism's excesses.

Now Obama is leading a kind of restructuring of America. He is working to remake government, just as *The Wire* changed television.

Michael A. Fletcher

SEASON ONE

SEASON ONE OVERVIEW

"It's more about class than race."
DAVID SIMON

When John Waters was filming *Hairspray* in Baltimore in 1988, Pia Zadora reportedly complimented the filmmaker on the extraordinary authenticity of the set.

"This isn't a set, Pia," Waters chuckled. "People *live* here."

People live here.

"Like any other American city," said Doug Olear, who played FBI Agent Terrence Fitzhugh on *The Wire*, "it has places that are amazing and beautiful, but a couple of miles in any direction and you can be fearing for your life . . . you can't build that in a studio."

Of the many storytelling goals pursued by David Simon – from journalism at the *Baltimore Sun*, to the books *Homicide* and *The Corner*, and, finally, creating *The Wire* from all that came before it – a priority was to humanize the underclass.

To show that people don't just die in West Baltimore, lower Park Heights, or Belair-Edison, that they often navigate extraordinary circumstances in order to live.

Like the teenage Wallace running a half-block length of extension cord to bring electricity to the abandoned shithole where he plays grown-up to a gaggle of virtual orphans.

Touching?

As far as it goes – certainly in light of the fate awaiting Wallace – but some corner dealer will soon enough take an interest in the potential labor pool of un-parented children.

Or Omar robbing drug dealers of product and profit with a shotgun he doesn't mind using; yet a soft touch for a young mother desperate for a fix, respectfully addressing her request for heroin to "Mr. Omar."

A twisted act of corporal mercy, but no skin off the stickup man's ass.

How about Bubbles applying an ingenuity that would make him a star at any enterprise even approaching legitimacy – subprime loans, anyone? – to the Sisyphean pursuit of scoring dope?

What was it Black Sabbath said?

Killing yourself to live.

Just beneath the drama, *The Wire* is making a case for the motivations of people trying to get by in a society in which indifferent institutions have more rights than human beings.

That includes bureaucracies on both sides of the law; the cultures of addiction – to power, ambition, and dope – and the maw of raw capitalism.

What is it about this epoch in which, if one commits to anything larger than oneself, one will regret it?

Since Zadora's comment some 21 years ago, the gentrification of neighborhoods adjoining Baltimore's waterfront has continued with good-life gusto. Though the pace slowed during the busted housing bubble recession of 2009, it pushes on.

At the same time, the Monster That Ate Baltimore City (perhaps the real star of *The Wire*, a mutant drawing strength from human despair) continued to devour neighborhoods two generations removed from the days when people with living-wage jobs resided there.

In 1992, Mother Teresa of Calcutta marched her saints into Baltimore not to fight the dragon but to provide succor to its victims, dispatching her Missionaries of Charity to the slums of East Baltimore to work with the HIV population.

You see these nuns in white robes with blue piping, coming and going from their Gift of Hope convent at St Wenceslaus Church on Collington Street at Ashland Avenue.

"What we bless today is not a hospice in the technical sense, but [the] sisters' home," said then-Archbishop of Baltimore William H. Keeler at the dedication, ". . . the home the Missionaries of Charity are sharing with the sick poor."

Not the sick and the poor. The sick poor.

In 2004, during a Los Angeles panel for the 21st Annual Museum of Television and Radio's Television Festival, Sonja Sohn, who played Detective Kima Greggs, said she was often self-conscious making entertainment, however serious, out of such material.

"I felt guilty, especially the first season," said Sohn, who grew up in subsidized housing at the south end of Newport News, Virginia. "It reminded me too much of home.

". . . to go into it playing a cop when I grew up seeing the cops as an oppressive force who never brought order . . . who I never saw help anybody . . . that's where my resentment comes from.

"I grew up torn between watching some pretty fucked-up shit go down in my own house or calling the cops, who calmed things down and left."

To make TV out of a plague struck Sohn as somewhat exploitative.

"This stuff needs to be divulged, but it still ends up being entertainment, and that bothers me," she said, adding that the show was her first real break in the business. "If it's going to be entertainment, *The Wire* is the best choice for it."

The parcel of Baltimore central to Season One was a fictional housing project, the Franklin Terrace high-rises, modeled on the actual Lexington Terrace and George B. Murphy Homes that once ringed the western edge of downtown.

The eight towers and adjoining low-rise buildings were addresses for some of the worst bloodletting in the city's storied criminal history.

[An early municipal nickname – Mobtown – stuck to the city after pro-Southern locals fired upon Union troops from the 6th Massachusetts Regiment moving through Baltimore at the start of the Civil War.]

Many plotlines from *The Wire*'s first year are rooted in a case from the 1980s investigated by writer/producer Ed Burns when he was a city homicide detective.

"Most of Season One came from the Little Melvin Williams and [Lamont] 'Chin' Farmer case," said Burns. "The murder that left the girl [answering a tap at the window] dead in Episode Four – that all came out of the Williams investigation."

The original target in the state and federal prosecution was a cocaine trafficker named Louis "Cookie" Savage, suspected of ordering the murder of a jealous girlfriend who'd threatened to turn the player in.

A nearly two-year investigation led not only to Savage, but through cloned pagers and wiretaps, the legendary Williams, one of the most significant wholesale narcotics brokers in Baltimore history, particularly in the 1960s and 1970s.

A line was also drawn to Williams's elusive, Stringer Bell-like lieutenant, Lamont "Chin" Farmer.

[Released from his last prison term in 2003, Williams played a preacher called "The Deacon" in Seasons Three through Five. His casting angered many in Baltimore, who found it the ultimate and perverse glorification of a drug lord responsible for countless deaths.]

As in Season One's investigation of the Barksdale gang, a federal wiretap compromised the Williams organization. Detectives carrying pagers took to rooftops with binoculars to watch specific payphones.

A key break came when Burns and his partner Harry Edgerton figured out the beeper codes.

The moment is delivered in Episode Five – "The Pager" – by Detective Roland "Prez" Pryzbylewski. Stuck on desk duty, Prez applies a passion for supermarket "word find" puzzles to the telephone keypad.

In the drama and in real life, the dealers were sending numbers that could be decoded by jumping over the five at the center of the keypad.

"It dawns on you: 'Motherfuckers, isn't this brilliant!'" said Burns. "Figuring it out was one thing, but creating it was a stroke of genius."

By the time informants were engaging principal targets in attempted transactions, detectives were ordered to prematurely close out what Burns called "a gem" of an investigation.

In December of 1984, a city narcotics detective, Marcellus "Marty" Ward, was killed when an unrelated undercover operation went awry.

Authorities responded by immediately using evidence from the Williams probe to stage a series of

raids, an angry and emotional response to Ward's death that prevented the wiretap from revealing additional facets of the organization helmed by Williams and Farmer.

Williams was sentenced to 34 years on a combination of drug charges and parole violations, while Savage – caught cutting cocaine on a pinhole wall camera similar to that used by detectives to spy on Avon Barksdale – got 30 years.

Chin Farmer, who Burns regards as one of the true geniuses in the history of Baltimore's drug trade, skated on the likelihood of a seven-year sentence because the case shut down too early.

In the wake of the convictions, Baltimore's relatively stable drug culture was turned upside down in the 1980s by the arrival of cheap cocaine, soon followed by the crack epidemic.

The Terrace and the Murphy Homes became 24/7 drug markets beyond the capacity of the city to police. The Eastside high-rises – Lafayette Courts and Flag House – were equally impenetrable.

By the time a cop chased a kid across an open courtyard, the kid was inside the tower taking the stairs three at a time. By the time that same officer followed up the stairwell, bolts would begin locking on doors, the drugs would disappear, and both the suspect and contraband could be in one of a hundred apartments on more than a dozen floors.

The value of the high-rises to the drug trade became public in the mid-1980s in a turf battle over Lexington Terrace and the nearby Edgar Allan Poe Homes that was known as the War Against the Downers.

Waged throughout the summer of 1986 by a 24-year-old dealer named Warren Boardley against brothers Alan and Spencer Downer, the battle left seven dead and twice as many wounded before Boardley had control of the Terrace and Poe.

While Avon Barksdale and Stringer Bell are fictional composites, Avon Barksdale bears more than a passing resemblance to Warren Boardley.

Once an adolescent boxer, Boardley was sentenced to a 43-year prison term after a two-year investigation by Burns, Edgerton, and federal agents.

Having fought brutally to secure the towers as his own, Barksdale is loath to give the territory up, even when Stringer Bell reasons convincingly that product, and not territory, is the key to success.

Boardley also staked his reputation on primacy in the high-rises, and, much like the Barksdale crew, his organization attracted police attention not for drug traffic but the bodies that fell over his insistence on monopoly.

After Boardley's arrest in late 1988, Burns and other cops walked through Lexington Terrace talking to the myriad dealers still working the stairwells and courtyards.

They let it be known that Boardley did not go down for drugs but for the murders which revealed his business. For two years after the Boardley investigation, said Burns, the Terrace remained an open-air drug bazaar while violence fell dramatically.

And thus the argument behind Season One: law enforcement can only make a ripple upon the baser human appetites. And not even the best police work can stem the traffic of illegal drugs.

In the origin of Baltimore's public housing lies a sad irony of the entrenched underclass: one generation's attempt to provide good housing becomes a later generation's nightmare.

In the late 1940s and 1950s, government housing projects of steel and brick with indoor plumbing and central heating replaced wooden shacks dating to the 19th century. They went up in every quadrant of Baltimore.

Some 40 years later, the city razed the towers and replaced them with suburban-styled townhomes.

Under the Clinton Administration, Baltimore was the first American city to tear down all of its high-rise projects. By the time *The Wire* began production in 2002, none remained to film.

To get the look, a two-tower apartment complex for senior citizens in West Baltimore was dressed to look like the old projects. On each side of the city, the towers have been replaced by good-looking homes on streets with names like New Hope Circle.

The new configuration houses less than half of the 4,000 or so people who once lived in the towers; the poverty and attendant problems once defined by the high-rises are dispersed throughout the city and the near and aging suburbs of Baltimore County.

Said former city homicide detective Oscar Requer, whose nickname and general demeanor inform the character of Detective Bunk Moreland, "The problem just moved somewhere else."

"We have a culture of violence made up of kids two generations removed from people who worked and neighborhoods that were viable," added Burns. "Now, we're seeing the limits of what teachers and police can do."

In the new housing developments, low- and middle-income home-owners are sprinkled in with families living on federal housing vouchers.

Homeowners complain that renters and their "ghetto" ways bring down property values. Renters resent homeowners – their private property is built on land once housing folks too poor to own anything – who look down on them.

Strict lease agreements tell renters what they can and cannot do in regard to visitors, noise, and tidiness. The regulations have helped create an environment that poor folks in the city have long imagined exists in that over-the-rainbow land called "the county."

Having chronicled the time when the high-rises defined the rampancy of Baltimore's drug trade, *The Wire* would follow the natural progression of the story once they came down.

Said David Simon: "The demolition of the projects was, I think, a tactical solution to a strategic problem."

By depicting the tactical approach as a mere salve, Simon hoped that attempts at social reform would become public debate. The inherent contradictions of America's war on drugs would stand throughout the five-year run of *The Wire*, even though the Terrace towers did not.

It took a mere 20 seconds for several hundred pounds of dynamite to implode Murphy Homes, Lexington Terrace, and Lafayette Courts. But nearly a decade after the bricks fell, the children of those projects were naming gangs after the lost world.

In April of 2004, a US district court found two West Baltimore gang members guilty of conspiracy in a crack cocaine business supported by homicide near the projects where they grew up.

The gang, ten of whom went to jail on various federal charges, were known as the Lexington Terrace Boys Prosecutors won convictions against all ten, claiming that the victory also cleared more than two-dozen open West Baltimore murder cases.

After the trials, then US Attorney General John Ashcroft ordered federal prosecutors in Baltimore to seek the death penalty. Defense attorneys argued otherwise, describing for federal jurors – many from distinctly rural and suburban counties in Maryland – what it was like to grow up in the projects.

Among witnesses testifying for the defense during the penalty phase was *The Wire* producer Ed Burns. Burns spoke successfully against putting the Lexington Terrace boys to death because, he said, Americans have the right to be judged by a jury of their peers.

"You cannot be a peer to these defendants if you don't understand what that world was like and what it meant to grow up in that world."

THE WOMEN OF THE WIRE
(No, Seriously)

Certain biases must be acknowledged: I have always loathed the tokenism that prevails in most television shows about cops and courts. According to the unscientific survey conducted with my remote control, this alternative universe teems with a rainbow coalition of female professionals – cops, attorneys, coroners, lab techs, judges, maybe even dogcatchers.

They occasionally butt their pretty heads against primitive attitudes about women and their capabilities, but these ceilings prove to be more gossamer than glass, allowing our plucky gals to shimmy through with no effort greater than a furrowed brow.

There are no institutional biases, just a backward individual here or there who needs his consciousness yanked sternly upward, an atomic wedgie for the sexist soul. The argument is not that entertainment should function as documentary; anyone who writes, as I do, about homicide-solving private investigators has obviously embraced the power of fantasy. The problem with these frictionless utopias is their numbing complacency.

The Wire, by contrast, offers a world so starkly masculine that the very title of this essay requires defensive clarification. *What* women? The dancers bumping and grinding in what my sister once dubbed "the obligatory HBO tittie bar shot"?

The bodies on the dock in Season Two, a veritable pile of double-X chromosome MacGuffins? The first season of *The Wire* had only two female actors billed in the opening credits; Season Two, just three.

Yet the full list of *Wire* women is, in fact, long and varied. And while the roster may appear yawningly familiar at first glance – the cop, the prosecutor, the wife, the ex-wife, the mother, the girlfriend, the stripper, the corpse – *The Wire*'s writers have provided some welcome subtlety within these archetypes.

Take Shakima Greggs, the narcotics detective played by Sonja Sohn, the most prominent female in *Wire*-world. Smart, tough, and hardworking, Greggs seemed almost *too* admirable in the early going – it's a bird, it's a plane, it's Super-Lesbian!

One cynical critic even predicted that the writers would make Greggs the show's heroine, allowing her to crack the case while her less competent partners were undone by their het-male peccadilloes. Instead, she ended up sidelined by a gunshot wound well before the Barksdale case reached its climactic anticlimax in Season One. The last glimpse we had of Greggs was on a walker, thumping her way down a hospital corridor, far from the action she craved.

When the second season began, Greggs was deskbound against her will – and on the receiving end of some surprising advice. "If you were a man – and in some ways, you're a better man than most of the men I know – a friend would take you for a beer and tell you the truth," advised Herc, a colleague not usually known for his interpersonal insights. "You're *whipped*."

It turned out that Greggs's relationship problems, while superficially not as severe as those of her male colleagues, were slowly catching up with her, exacerbated by tensions rooted in temperament, class, and ambition. Greggs might not have been pussy-whipped, but her partner, Cheryl, sure wanted a house cat.

Greggs's opposite number is Beatrice "Beadie" Russell, the transportation cop portrayed by Amy Ryan, who played a pivotal role in Season Two. No one would ever call Russell a good police, to use the Baltimore vernacular. When first sighted, she was cruising through her days literally and figuratively. Her only concern appeared to be getting to the end of her shift and rushing home so she wouldn't have to pay the babysitter overtime.

Yet Russell proved an eager acolyte when the situation demanded that she step up, readily admitting what she didn't know and learning on the fly.

The scene that cemented my Russell–Ryan love, however, was the character's tentative attempt to transform a would-be boyfriend into a confidential informant. No femme fatale, Russell struggled with the assignment, torn between being a good police and a good person.

The resulting exchange was rueful, elliptical, painfully real. We're used to watching men and women smolder on-screen, reciting blocks of brittle, hyper-knowing dialogue. It's more unusual to watch two recognizable humans tiptoeing around a subject that is seldom discussed past seventh grade: *Do you like me? Check "yes," "no," or "as a friend."*

Of course, there are women on *The Wire* who enjoy a more conventional chemistry with the men around them. A partial list would have to include Assistant State's Attorney Rhonda Pearlman, the redhead with the bad Jimmy McNulty habit that she can't quite break. McNulty's ex-wife, Elena, who has kicked her Jimmy Jones, but dabbles just often enough to keep him off-balance; Shardene, the nearsighted stripper who is saved by the love of a good man; and the deliciously pragmatic Donette, who understands that her body is the only capital she has, so it must be invested wisely.

The actors who play these roles embrace the flaws and contradictions, not worrying about seeming foolish or – in the case of Elena – even shrewish and manipulative.

There are false notes here and there – a line of dialogue that clanks because it's better suited to a eunuch as opposed to a woman, some notable failures to explore why some of the women behave as they do.

Pearlman – as written, not as played by Deirdre Lovejoy – strikes me as especially problematic. While utterly convincing as a driven prosecutor, she is an enigma when it comes to her love life – or, more correctly, her lust life.

It's baffling to me that the same show that probes the conflicts between Greggs and her upwardly mobile girlfriend doesn't want to explore the self-destructive dynamic between Pearlman and McNulty.

We know why McNulty sleeps with Pearlman; he'll sleep with pretty much anyone. But Pearlman's willingness to pursue this doomed romance is never explained. Lonely? Horny? Self-loathing?

McNulty is clearly not marriage material for a striver such as Pearlman, who steps so adroitly around the minefields in her professional life. He's not even particularly reliable as a friend-with-benefits, unless one interprets "benefits" as falling into a dead-to-the-world stupor before anything happens.

On the other hand, the motivations of Marla Daniels, wife of Lieutenant Cedric Daniels, are abundantly clear. In terms of screen time, it's a small part, but Baltimore actor Maria Broom wrings a lot out of it.

[To appreciate just how good she is in *The Wire*, it's helpful to go back to *The Corner* and her equally strong performance as a drug addict.]

Marla is no Lady Macbeth, but she has definite ideas about her husband's career, counsel that he once sought regularly. Alas, he also rejected her shrewd advice, which is good for *The Wire* as a drama, but not so good for the Danielses' marriage.

In fact, for those keeping score at home, few romantic relationships have flourished in *The Wire*, except for the surprising alliance between Lester Freamon and Shardene, the former stripper who didn't need contact lenses to see what a catch this detective was.

True, William "Bunk" Moreland is still with his yet-to-be-seen wife, but that could change if he continues to pursue his hobby of waking up in other women's bathrobes. Herc and Carver? Well, if you're going to liken two characters to Batman and Robin, no matter how irreverently, you have to own all the implications of that comparison.

It has been said that we can judge cultures by how they treat their dead. Similarly, *The Wire*'s attitude toward women can be evaluated via its treatment of female corpses. Again, the number is even higher than one might recall – not only the fourteen Jane Does in Season Two, but three female victims in Season One as well.

The characters may be cynical and benumbed about all these bodies, but *The Wire* never is.

Consider Season One, when McNulty and Bunk attempted to reconstruct the scene of a botched homicide that they hoped to pin on the elusive Avon Barksdale. To the detectives, the dead woman was a means to an end, one factor in their equation of trajectories. To D'Angelo Barksdale, who exaggerated his role in her murder, she was a "shortie" with a great body and the hubristic notion that she could make an amoral killer into a faithful boyfriend. Yet the Polaroid of her corpse kept reminding the viewer of death's indignity and, consequently, its horror.

Through the first two seasons, only one woman, Joy Lusco Kecken, wrote for *The Wire*, and only three episodes were directed by women.

There are strong women behind the scenes every day – most notably executive producer Nina Kostroff Noble, director of photography Uta Briesewitz, and producer Karen L. Thorson – but no women are involved in hammering out the stories, even as *The Wire* has continued to add first-rate novelists to its staff.

So, like it or not, we must credit men with these human-scale portraits. Yes, many of the women in *The Wire* appear in secondary roles, but that is a simple truth about the world it portrays – and the point of view through which it is filtered. Instead of giving us Women with a capital *W*, it showcases flawed human beings who happen to be women. It may be frustrating, but it is never boring or unbelievable.

Laura Lippman

SEASON ONE EPISODE GUIDE

"Where's it all go? The money, where's it go?"
D'ANGELO BARKSDALE

The debut of *The Wire* on the first Sunday in June of 2002 introduced the world to the first chapter of a visual novel – a singular, interlocking narrative played out over 13 programming hours on cable television.

In this tale, no good deed goes unpunished, reason and morality are impaired by a mother lode of economic imperatives and institutional loyalties, and the first character to take residence in our consciousness is a freshly murdered crapshooter with an elegant Baltimore street name.

Snotboogie.

The detective investigating Snotboogie's demise – the amiable, self-absorbed Jimmy McNulty – would appear to be more interested in how the victim got his moniker than how he became a victim.

"You called the guy Snot?"

"Snotboogie, yeah."

"Snotboogie? He like the name?"

If Season One did not make its plotlines immediately clear, it was obvious that what someone does or does not like, about themselves or the world in which they are trapped, makes little difference. *The Wire* would be a universe where hoped-for escapes to places that value individual desires do not exist – whether Jimmy McNulty, for all his intellectual vanity, wants to admit it or not.

Among the multiple versions of Baltimore that pulse along the banks of the Patapsco River, the only exit from this one is via an exit wound.

The first season concentrated on parallel corridors: the drug market of the West Baltimore housing projects and the police department charged with containing it.

Over the pilot and a dozen subsequent episodes, the cops began pulling the threads of Avon Barksdale's drug empire and its attendant murders. The work led to a complicated investigation with wiretaps and old-fashioned surveillance mixed with ancient themes of betrayal, corruption, and luck, both good and bad.

The characters who would bob along that investigation included the kingpin Barksdale, his corporate-inspired lieutenant, Stringer Bell, and their primary muscle, Wee-Bey and Stinkum.

Below this tier is Avon's nephew D'Angelo, a reluctant gangster who acts as foreman on a narcotics plantation in which the man-child Bodie labors with his running buddy, Poot, and a handful of outright children such as Wallace, who now and then is seen playing with toys amidst the open-air trafficking.

On the other side is McNulty and his homicide partner, Bunk Moreland, who report to the Gleasonesque Detective Sergeant Jay Landsman. In turn, Landsman reports to a humorless, sexually-conflicted, statistics-will-keep-my-tit-out-of-the-wringer colonel named William A. Rawls.

Down the hall from the homicide unit, Lieutenant Cedric Daniels heads a shift of the CID narcotics section, which includes hard-as-any-man Detective Kima Greggs; a lovable knucklehead called "Herc" (Detective Thomas Hauk); and his rip-and-run partner, the ambitious Detective Ellis Carver.

When the investigation gets going, with nominal support from an embarrassed and indifferent department, all are tossed together with a handful of broken-down career cops who only have eyes for overtime and a pensive detective from the pawn unit by the name of Lester Freamon.

And then there's Omar Little, the wild-card homo-thug at the broken edge of both worlds, robbing drug dealers for a living without uttering a foul word or otherwise violating his personal code of ethics, in which law-abiding citizens and other taxpayers are spared.

And Bubbles, part informant and part court jester, who parlays the chump change he gets from the cops and every other dollar he can snatch into a speedball habit that promises only a pauper's grave.

Said Andre Royo, who played Bubbles with grace and depth: "Just doing whatever he has to do to get high."

episode
one

THE TARGET
"When it's not your turn ..." — MCNULTY

Directed by Clark Johnson
Story by David Simon & Ed Burns; teleplay by David Simon

The story begins with the late-night shooting to death of the aforementioned Snotboogie, whose habit of shooting craps until the pot gets big and then running off with the cash eventually proves lethal.

McNulty asks: "If Snotboogie always grabbed the pot and ran away with it, why would you even let him play?"

The lone witness to the murder is talking because it pissed him off that Snot would be murdered rather than simply beaten for his thieving ways. He looks at McNulty as if the question has come from another world and explains that they had to let him play.

"This is America."

Besides being a true anecdote right down to that three-word declaration of patriotic faith (the murder of Snotboogie was recounted by Baltimore Detective Terry McLarney and first appeared in David Simon's book *Homicide*), the vignette launches *The Wire* with a simple premise.

This is America. And to the extent that its institutions manage to exclude or diminish its people, they will nonetheless find a way to play. In the Baltimore ghetto, and, ultimately, in those working-class neighborhoods decaying into the 'hood for lack of opportunity, there are souls who will not be denied a turn. And this: whatever is excluded from the mainstream will eventually surface as a separate society complete with its own economy and systems of justice and education. The Snotboogies of the world may be comical and doomed and they are often dangerous. But as citizens of a parallel world under the same Stars and Stripes as the legitimate America, they must be allowed to play.

Snotboogie's is a simple murder, easily handled. The next day, McNulty goes to the courthouse to watch D'Angelo Barksdale – on trial for having panicked and killed a man in a drug-related dispute in the projects – beat a seemingly solid prosecution when a key witness backs up on her testimony. In the courtroom, Stringer Bell and other members of the Barksdale crime family celebrate the moment. Disgusted, Judge Phelan, hearing the case, calls McNulty back to chambers, where the detective gives the true story of the acquittal. The Barksdale organization has beat a string of killings in the projects, McNulty tells Phelan, by rewarding perjury and intimidating witnesses.

And who in the police department, the judge inquires, is working on Barksdale?

"No one," says McNulty.

Has he tipped his hand to the judge on impulse alone, or is McNulty manipulating the system to get something going that he can sink his teeth into? In what will become typical McNulty behavior, the detective has happily stirred the shit.

The judge begins battering the police command staff with questions about the unpunished drug murders. McNulty soon finds himself in his commander's office, where Colonel Rawls rips him robustly for talking out of turn and orders a report on the Barksdale murders for the following day.

Here the drama becomes thematic and parallel as D'Angelo returns home after months in pre-trial detention only to have his ass chewed by the boss, his uncle Avon Barksdale.

The murder case may have collapsed, but the need for the murder in the first place was clearly dubious; D'Angelo is not the hardest soldier in his uncle's army, and the project killing – half self-defense but mostly panic – proved this. D'Angelo is home, but he will not be returning to the family drug business in the high-rise towers. Instead, he is demoted to the low-rise projects, The Pit.

McNulty writes his report, as does Lieutenant Daniels, who is also ordered to provide some intelligence on the previously unknown Barksdale, as the bureaucracy begins to churn. McNulty is warned that such behavior will surely stunt his career as a detective. Detective Sergeant Jay Landsman, his boss in homicide, tells him that more shenanigans will see him walking a beat in the Western District. McNulty claims not to care, and Landsman asks where it is he doesn't want to go.

"The boat," laughs McNulty, meaning the marine unit.

Keep it up, says Landsman, and that's what you'll get – on the midnight shift. The well-tailored Bunk Moreland, McNulty's partner, having earlier blamed McNulty for "giving a fuck when it ain't your turn to give a fuck," affirms Landsman's judgment.

The reports get kicked upstairs. What comes back is a special detail to investigate Barksdale, but in the most halfhearted manner. Daniels is given command of the unit, and brings his people with him. McNulty comes from homicide with another homicide detective, the hapless Santangelo, who wants little to do with the project.

Daniels is ordered to put a charge on Avon Barksdale quickly and not to let the investigation sprawl. McNulty is dubious. Barksdale is too clever, too insulated, and too serious a trafficker to be caught so easily.

McNulty wants to do the case properly – to follow it where it leads – but so far has few allies.

And the violence continues. When a snitch named Bubbles sees his running buddy, a white addict named Johnny, beaten to within an inch of his life over a two-bit scam, he offers his services to Detective Kima Greggs, with whom he has worked in the past.

Finally, a witness bold enough to testify against D'Angelo Barksdale during the trial before Judge Phelan, a project maintenance worker named William Gant, is shot to death in the low-rises.

Avon Barksdale's reach in the projects is unquestioned.

Even D'Angelo, watching from behind the crime scene tape, seems stunned by a murder that amounts to nothing more than sending a message. After all, the trial was over: He'd beaten the charge.

episode
two

THE DETAIL
"You cannot lose if you do not play."
— MARLA DANIELS
Directed by Clark Johnson
Story by David Simon & Ed Burns; teleplay by David Simon

The tale resumes at the medical examiner's office, where the open murder of citizen Gant has become Bunk Moreland's problem. McNulty surmises that it was most likely a hit ordered by Avon Barksdale.

To test the theory, he and Bunk pick up D'Angelo for a chat that offers an extraordinary window into the younger Barksdale's soul: while admitting nothing, the young gangster feels so bad for the dead man's family that he begins to write them a letter of apology.

D'Angelo's genuine, if ill-considered act of regret is interrupted only when the drug organization's lawyer, Maurice Levy, arrives to gather him up.

Daniels reaches out to add more manpower to his detail after realizing that Deputy Commissioner Ervin Burrell – the No. 2 man in the department, who handpicked Daniels for the detail and urged him not to allow the case to sprawl – has saddled him with fools and also-rans.

The message is clear: if they give you good police, they expect good police work. But little is expected or desired from this detail, a point further hammered home by the unit's off-site offices in the basement of the courthouse.

Meanwhile, Greggs begins to harvest street-level information about the projects from her on-retainer snitch Bubbles. Herc and Carver, accompanied by new detail member Roland "Prez" Pryzbylewski – notorious for shooting up his squad car, which might have gotten him tossed out of the department if he weren't the son-in-law of a certain district major – sit in the courthouse basement feeling neglected.

After a half dozen beers each, they decide to solicit information in the high-rise projects in a very irregular manner. The trio's two a.m. visit to the towers ends up in a near riot.

Air conditioners and old televisions are tossed out of high-rise windows and a 14-year-old project kid loses an eye when Prez, a loose cannon beyond even the few boundaries that Herc and Carver recognize, knocks him cold with the butt of his gun. Daniels is reluctantly forced to cover for the brutality.

When Daniels refuses to bring the Gant murder (the slain witness from the recent Barksdale acquittal) to the attention of the bosses as leverage for more resources, the information surfaces in the news. Though McNulty denies being the leak, Daniels knows he will have trouble with this detail both from within and without.

THE BUNK AND THE BUNK

"Being a good cop is in line with Bunk's social point of view; being a good cop is not being unfair. I think that's why he's a cop."
— WENDELL PIERCE

Wendell Pierce is so good at portraying the Baltimore City homicide detective on which his character is based that *The Wire* credits might read, "Starring 'The Bunk' as Himself."

"I'll never forget the first time I saw *The Wire*," Pierce told New Orleans writer Noah Bonaparte Pais. "We saw a screening, and we said, 'OK, I guess that's it. Nobody's going to get into this.'

"You never know. It's a fragile thing. But it will be authentic."

Indeed.

Both Pierce and the real-life Bunk – cigar-chomping Oscar "Rick" Requer – have roots that go back to Louisiana. Though the actor is about 20 years younger than the original, both are African-Americans from strong families. Each man's father served in the military, and both might kindly be described as portly.

And although Requer grew up in segregated, post-World War II Baltimore and Pierce came of age at the beginning of integration in the New South, both see the vast wasteland of West Baltimore as a tragedy so pronounced they feel it personally.

"I was raised in West Baltimore, my mother still lives up there on Westwood Avenue, near North and Pulaski," said Requer, who came on the Baltimore department as a patrolman in 1964.

"There used to be black schoolteachers and nurses and doctors living all around there. My father worked at the post office. It's terrible now, and a lot of the people who couldn't get out are stuck. My mom is in her eighties, but she won't leave."

Wendell Pierce, who won the role of a New Orleans trombone player in David Simon's *Treme* series when *The Wire* went dark, grew up in a suburban-styled, middle-class subdivision of New Orleans called Pontchartrain Park, a post-war oasis built on the dreams of black war veterans with GI Bill benefits.

So peculiar to the early 1950s was the "Negro" development that Dixieland tour buses filled with white tourists would cruise by for a peek.

Compared to the respite of Pontchartrain Park – by God, there was even a golf course in the middle of it – the neighborhoods where *The Wire* is filmed came as a shock to the Juilliard-trained Pierce.

"West Baltimore is so small and the concentration of poverty and destruction of the educational infrastructure [so intense] that it's a mass of clinical depression just now being diagnosed," said Pierce.

"My parents never came right out and talked racism, but they always alluded to it this way: 'Son, there are people in this world who do not have your best interest at heart.'"

And such people, in Pierce's view, do not have the best interest of a neighborhood or the city itself at heart when it comes to squeezing a buck from a system that needs people at the bottom in order to prosper.

"Once you destroy the educational infrastructure – remember, during slavery you risked death if you learned to read – it takes just a few years for the impact to spread through a family and then the neighborhood," said Pierce.

Throw drugs and their attendant violence in the mix, he added, "and it's the icing on the cake.

"I'm not absolving personal responsibility – the people of Baltimore are the descendents of Frederick Douglass, and there's still plenty of examples of folks who have come from those neighborhoods and have done well – but when those in the community become those who help to destroy the community, you know that people who don't have your best interest at heart come in all colors."

Drugs were unheard of in West Baltimore back when Oscar Requer, a 1958 graduate of Frederick Douglass High School, was known as Obbie in the Gilmore projects before his father bought the house on Westwood Avenue.

Around the corner stood rows of derelict wooden shacks on Bruce Street. By comparison to what once passed for African-American housing in Baltimore, the Winchester Homes projects were, in the beginning at least, an oasis not unlike Pontchartrain Park.

"In the projects we had radiators and gas stoves," said Requer. "Before that, you'd never lived in a brick house or had a daggone radiator."

Time changed the Winchester Homes, much as it did all of Baltimore's public housing projects. Eastside and Westside, the drug trade devoured neighborhoods whole. And the radiators of Requer's memory can occasionally be seen in metal shopping carts, being pulled by the addicts to scrapyards for blast money.

Requer served as a homicide detective for 20 years, ending in 1998. His nickname, acquired in the department, came from his habit of addressing all he met with the simple, all-purpose moniker Bunk.

"Solving a homicide is one of the most gratifying moments an investigator can have," said Requer.

Among the most notable cases of his long career, the Bunk hung a drug murder on a suspect without learning the identity of the victim, no piece of cake when you consider that a murder investigation invariably begins with the victim.

In the early 1990s case, Detective Requer received information from a snitch that a particular gangster was responsible for a drug-related robbery and shooting of a New York drug courier. Further, the body of the courier had been rolled in a rug and left in an East Baltimore dumpster.

The victim's name? No clue, except that he was supposedly from the Bronx and had come to Baltimore with a delivery of cocaine.

Requer checked the year's case files and found something that seemed to match – a John Doe who had been discovered in an Eastside dumpster, rolled in carpeting. Working the case hard, Requer eventually found an eyewitness who corroborated the informant. When the detective finally got a line on the shooter, he learned that he was in a New York State prison near the Canadian border.

Requer got a road car from the motor pool and made the drive, arriving at the prison and confronting his suspect with the facts as he knew them. The guilty man went slack-jawed.

"You came all the way up here, damn near to Canada, to charge me with a murder and you don't even know who it was that I killed?"

Requer allowed that this was the case, and that the charging documents would allege that the man had murdered a John Doe in the City of Baltimore.

"Not my day, is it?" the suspect replied.

The real-life Bunk was also notable for his dry, off-the-cuff humor. On midnight shifts, he was known to favor a smoking robe and slippers, padding around the darkened homicide unit as if it were his den.

Watching late-night westerns and gangster films on the television, he had a habit of announcing happily, whenever a shooting occurred among multiple witnesses, that the case could be easily solved with a minimum of police work.

"There's a dunker," he once declared after watching Clint Eastwood shoot three men dead on a dusty main street. "Put cuffs on 'em, Bunk."

Requer left the homicide unit in 1998 and began working with the department's retirement office. He worked with widows and other survivors of officers, making sure all benefits were properly paid. Not a few of the recipients are the widows or children of cops who took their own lives.

"The job can be stressful and you always have the instrument of your own destruction right at hand," he says.

Pushing 70, Requer often has fishing and cold beer on his mind. He met his on-screen impersonator after Wendell Pierce had already been cast.

On set during the filming of *The Wire* pilot, Detective Requer expressed some surprise that David Simon, a police reporter during a portion of Requer's tenure in the homicide unit, had not only named a character in his honor, but had found an actor of similar stature and gruff charm. Right down to the cigar.

episode
three

THE BUYS

"The king stay the king." — D'ANGELO

Directed by Peter Medak

Story by David Simon & Ed Burns; teleplay by David Simon

By Episode Three, D'Angelo Barksdale is entrenched in The Pit, monitoring the youngest and least experienced of the Barksdale drug crews while trying to improve their performance. In a succinct metaphor played out in The Pit, we get a sense of the drug hierarchy and everyone's place within that world.

D'Angelo, finding Wallace and Bodie playing checkers with chess pieces, is incredulous that they don't know the better game. Bodie couldn't give a fuck, but Wallace, perhaps the last innocent on the untethered planet that is Baltimore, wants to learn.

Piece by piece, D'Angelo catalogs how everyone in "the game" has a role and how few, if any, transcend their assigned roles. Bodie, ignorant of chess but not without pride and self-interest, is fixated on the pawns. If they make it across the battlefield to the other side, they become royalty.

"The king stay the king. Everyone stay what they is 'cept the pawns," says D'Angelo. "They get capped quick. They be out of the game early . . ."

"Unless they some smart-ass pawns," says Bodie, correcting him.

[Bodie, with heart and wit, will play out the string of a smart-ass pawn for many episodes to come.]

The tension between D'Angelo and Bodie is exacerbated when D'Angelo appears halfhearted and weak in the eyes of his underlings. Notably, D'Angelo is blamed when he is on a food run at the moment that Omar and his stickup crew roll into The Pit to take an entire drug delivery – the "re-up" – from a stash house.

Tension is also evident in the opposing bureaucracy, where the presence of so many weak investigators brings out McNulty's contempt. Only Detective Freamon shows any initiative at all – locating a photo of Avon Barksdale on an old boxing poster – though for the most part, he sits at his desk sanding antique dollhouse miniatures.

McNulty is dubious of Daniels' insistence on trying to go up the ladder to Bell and Barksdale through street-level hand-to-hand sales via Bubbles while a detective – Leander Sydnor – comes over from the auto theft squad to go undercover on drug buys.

The buys only implicate the lowest rungs of the organization, and the ensuing raids on the projects leave the detail empty-handed, save for the enigmatic Freamon, who uses the opportunity to look over the locations carefully, going so far as to write down phone numbers scratched on stash house walls.

During the raids, Bodie knocks one of the detailed officers on his ass, dropping an aging alcoholic cop with a single punch, earning himself the respect of his peers and a beating at the hands of responding police, including Greggs.

McNulty's doubts intensify when his FBI source, Agent Fitzhugh, warns that Daniels is a dirty cop. The Bureau had looked into Daniels a few years before and found he had too much unexplained money banked away.

The Feds informed Deputy Commissioner Burrell about it, says Fitzhugh, and nothing happened.

episode
four

OLD CASES
"Thin line 'tween heaven and here" — BUBBLES
Directed by Clement Virgo
Story by David Simon & Ed Burns; teleplay by David Simon

Fallout from the raids includes the disability retirement of Detective Mahone, who uses Bodie's solitary punch to end his career with pay, leaving his equally alcoholic partner, Detective Polk, abandoned and lonely.

Meanwhile, Herc and Carver journey down to lower Prince George's County to try to interrogate Bodie at the juvenile facility where he is locked up after the melee. Bodie defeats them by simply walking away from the facility, stealing a car, and returning home to Baltimore.

He arrives in time to hear D'Angelo recount his apparent involvement in the earlier murder of a young woman – a girlfriend of his uncle's who, angry at Avon's inattention, had threatened to expose him to the authorities. D'Angelo describes the murder in detail – a recounting motivated as much by the disrespect of his underlings in The Pit as by the horror of the story itself.

Meanwhile, Detectives Greggs and McNulty reluctantly find each other as allies, agreeing that they are eventually going to need a wiretap to make the case – a conclusion that Daniels has been loath to accept, having promised Deputy Commissioner Burrell that he would contain the case.

Greggs hears secondhand about the stash house robbery from Bubbles, who identifies Omar as the stickup artist. She brings that information to McNulty, along with a plan to jack up Omar, perhaps catch him with a gun and pull whatever information Omar can give them on the Barksdale crew.

Together, McNulty and Greggs pitch Daniels and the rest of the detail, whereupon Freamon chimes in: he has done his own police work, discovering that in addition to the pagers the Barksdale dealers carry, they are communicating via payphones around the projects. Watch the payphones, Freamon says, and put together probable cause for a wiretap.

Great idea. But do they even have a pager number? Freamon pulls his notes on a number written on the stash house wall during the earlier raids, a number that had *D* written next to it. It's D'Angelo's pager. He checked.

McNulty regards Detective Freamon as if for the first time. He had thought him to be another piece of deadwood dumped on the detail. Not so.

At the same time, McNulty and Bunk are obliged to look into an unsolved murder as Landsman dumps old cases on the Barksdale detail, hoping for a murder clearance or two.

The case file in question is the murder of a young woman; a witness called in months earlier to claim that a "D" had been present on the night the victim was slain. McNulty and Bunk work a scene similar to one that D'Angelo described in The Pit earlier and discover fresh evidence, though nothing that yet suggests Barksdale's involvement.

episode
five

THE PAGES
"A little slow, a little late."
– AVON BARKSDALE
Directed by Clark Johnson
Story by David Simon & Ed Burns; teleplay by Ed Burns

In the wake of the recent raids and stash house robbery, Avon Barksdale and Stringer Bell fear a snitch among D'Angelo's crew in The Pit. Bell tells D'Angelo to cut the pay for his people and see who is still holding cash at the end of the week.

Arguing in court papers that nothing else has worked, the detail gets the green light to clone D'Angelo's pager. The clone works, with the detectives receiving the same pager numbers as D'Angelo, but the numbers that come back do not, indicating that the Barksdale crew is utilizing a code.

McNulty and Greggs get on Omar and his young lover, Brandon, attempting to follow

them and pull them up on weapons charges. Instead, Omar leads them into a cemetery, then gets out of his car to confront the police. A parley ensues in which Omar refuses to snitch on Barksdale or anyone else.

Only after McNulty surprises Omar with the news that the third member of his crew, Bailey, was murdered overnight does Omar offer anything in return, telling the detectives that if they want to know who killed the workingman – Gant – they need to look at another Barksdale shooter, who goes by the name Bird.

Help then comes from an unlikely source as Prez, consigned to desk duty since the near riot, fiddles with a pager code and discovers how the Barksdale dealers are working the code: jumping over the five in the middle of the keypad.

Now, the detectives can begin collecting payphone numbers, even as Daniels remains resistant to a wiretap.

The episode concludes with two of The Pit underlings, Wallace and Poot, spotting Omar's lover – the stickup boy Brandon – in a downtown greasy spoon and video arcade. Communication leading to Brandon's subsequent ambush and abduction by a truckload of Barksdale muscle is all recorded on the pager logs.

episode
six

THE WIRE
"And all the pieces matter." — FREAMON
Directed by Ed Bianchi
Story by David Simon & Ed Burns; teleplay by David Simon

The tale resumes with the image of Brandon's tortured body – at the hands of Stinkum and other Barksdale assassins – lying across the roof of an abandoned car in a Westside alley near the projects, a message to all about the cost of challenging Avon Barksdale. The "trophy" is on display near the vacant rowhouse where Wallace and Poot live, acting as surrogate parents to a crew of even younger waifs.

After viewing the body, and knowing that he not only contributed to the death but profited from it when he earns the bounty for Brandon's head, Wallace is never the same again. He begins to brood and worry.

Back downtown, Freamon takes Prez under his wing and together they begin to monitor the pager traffic in earnest. At headquarters, Rawls gets around to reading the follow-up reports that McNulty wrote on the open Barksdale cases, including the fresh but weak evidence on the slaying of the young woman in the apartment.

Realizing there is enough to charge D'Angelo Barksdale with the murder (but not enough to convict), Rawls wants to bring whatever charges he can, which would cause Barksdale's crew to change their patterns, jeopardize any chance at a wiretap, and end the detail.

Daniels asks Rawls to hold back. Rawls refuses and the struggle goes before Burrell, where Daniels fights for his detail – more aggressively, perhaps, than Burrell had expected when he gave the posting to Daniels.

As Daniels turns a corner and fights for the importance of the case beyond simple drug busts, Omar gets in touch with McNulty.

Brandon's brutal torture and murder has persuaded him to offer what he knows about the Barksdale organization – to the point of lying about being an eyewitness to the Gant murder and naming Bird as the shooter.

And a promise to avenge his lover's death through means that will not involve the police.

episode seven

ONE ARREST

"A man must have a code." – BUNK

Directed by Joe Chappelle

Story by David Simon & Ed Burns; teleplay by Rafael Alvarez

With probable cause established, the wiretaps on several project payphones are up. Coupled with surveillance on those phones, the detectives are able to monitor midlevel communications of the Barksdale organization. They do so to the point of catching a resupply of drugs to The Pit, supervised by Stinkum, whom they let go in the hope he will lead them up the ladder.

The move raises Avon's suspicions and Stringer Bell decides to change the pattern, disabling the payphones closest to The Pit, where the arrest occurred, and ordering D'Angelo to use phones some distance away.

Bunk and McNulty find another witness to the Gant murder, while the other homicide investigator assigned to the detail, Detective Santangelo, is told by an angry Rawls – jilted by McNulty and embarrassed by Daniels – to bring him dirt on McNulty.

When Santangelo objects that it is not his job to destroy another cop, Rawls notes that Santangelo has done piss-poor police work in homicide and gives him an ultimatum: bring back dirt on McNulty or clear one of his many open cases.

Bunk and McNulty, with Omar as a "witness," arrest Bird as the shooter of Gant, at the same time clearing an additional murder given up by Omar almost as a casual favor, a murder in which Santangelo was the primary detective.

His ass saved by his fellow detectives, Santangelo resists Rawls and tells McNulty that the commander is out to destroy him.

episode
eight

LESSONS

"Come at the king, you best not miss." – OMAR

Directed by Gloria Muzio

Story by David Simon & Ed Burns; teleplay by David Simon

As Stinkum and Wee-Bey prepare to murder a rival dealer to extend Barksdale territory onto fresh corners, Omar emerges from the shadows with a shotgun blast, killing Stinkum and wounding Wee-Bey to avenge Brandon's death.

The whole point of letting Stinkum walk away from the re-up bust in the previous episode is now moot, his murder weakening the case built so far against the Barksdale group.

The hit by Omar comes after a wild party among the crew, at which one of the dancers from a Barksdale-owned club overdoses. When her body is found in a back room, it is rolled in a rug, a death that will work to the advantage of detectives when they are ultimately able to turn another dancer – D'Angelo's lover, Shardene – into an informant.

Using the wiretap, the detectives target what they believe will be another re-up. Instead, they catch the aide to West Baltimore state senator Clay Davis taking a bag of cash from a project dealer. The reaction from police HQ is swift and virulent.

Called to the deputy commissioner's office by Burrell, who seems to know everything that happens inside the detail as it occurs, Daniels is ordered to return the cash to the aide and write up the car stop as unfounded.

He does so, and McNulty again challenges him, asking if Burrell has anything on Daniels himself, angering the lieutenant as it hits home. When Burrell presses harder, ordering Daniels to take down the wire, Judge Phelan – McNulty's original patron – intervenes, threatening the deputy commissioner with contempt of court.

Back on the street, Wallace sinks into depression and addiction, unwilling to work The Pit or leave his bedroom as gossip about whether he's cracking up buzzes along the wiretap.

episode nine

GAME DAY
"Maybe we won." – HERC
Directed by Milcho Manchevski
Story by David Simon & Ed Burns; teleplay by David H. Melnick & Shamit Choksey

As Barksdale and a rival Eastside dealer, Proposition Joe Stewart, are gathering ringers for an annual Eastside-Westside neighborhood basketball game, the detectives press their investigation.

Freamon sends Prez and Sydnor in search of the paper trail on Barksdale's assets and influence, and they bring back information on front companies and real estate holdings west of the downtown. There are also a number of political contributions to incumbent state officials.

Detectives, using the overdose death of her friend as emotional leverage, press Shardene into service as an informant inside Barksdale's club. At the same time, McNulty overhears talk on the wiretap about Wallace being upset and distant since Brandon's murder – a weak link to be exploited.

As Herc and Carver take in the basketball game, it dawns on them that Barksdale, thus far unseen by police since the investigation began, may be in attendance. Daniels calls for surveillance, but Barksdale is quickly onto them.

There is further trouble within the detail when Herc and Carver, having seized money from Wee-Bey in an earlier car stop, fail to turn in all of the cash. They luck out when sloppiness and not corruption is suspected.

Finally, Omar robs another stash from a Barksdale crew and uses it to pay Proposition Joe for a pager number for Avon Barksdale. He uses that number to ambush Barksdale outside the strip club. If not for Wee-Bey's timely return from a food run, it would have been curtains for Avon.

A SNITCH FROM A SOUTH BALTIMORE ALLEY

"PROPERTY OF BUBBLES"

In March of 1992, a peculiar obituary appeared in the *Sun* newspaper of Baltimore.

No services were listed. Nor survivors. And certainly not a worthy charity to which the bereaved might send donations. The dead man wasn't even identified by the name his mother gave him.

It was the obit of a 48-year-old police informant who went by "Bubbles" if you knew him in Baltimore, "Possum" if you ran across him in New York, and "Larry Johnson" if you were the police department payroll clerk processing vouchers.

The obit was written by the paper's cop reporter, David Simon, who stood on his head to get such unorthodox fare in the paper. To get Bubbles to tell his life story, all he had to do was cough up $20.

For the better part of three decades – when he wasn't shooting dope, running hustles, or stealing outright – Bubbles collected $50 to $100 of taxpayers' money for each felon he gave to the police, all of them wanted on warrants and many of them escapees. Sometimes the cops paid him out of their own pockets.

Back in his prime in the 1970s, Bubbles was the best police informant in Baltimore, working on commission for the Feds, state authorities, and street cops. He is the con who perfected the red hat trick that his cinematic alter ego, played by Bronx-born-and-raised Andre Royo, would perform with élan on *The Wire*.

Royo wanted to act from the time he was a kid and saw the power that comedy and drama had on his no-nonsense father, a bongo-playing, Cuban-American construction worker named Louie.

"He loved Fred Astaire," said Royo, "and he'd act out John Wayne scenes. I wanted to be involved in anything that could make this serious dude emote."

As for Bubbles, Royo said: "I was intimidated when they asked me to play a street junkie; when you've never done drugs like that, you don't want to be a cliché.

"At first I was a little superior to the role, thinking a junkie was different from people addicted to other things, thinking they were bad people . . . When I'd see junkies begging on the subway in New York they got on my nerves.

"But I went out of my way to meet some of them . . . to try and find a common thread I could hang on, but I found there isn't one. The drug affects everyone in different ways; they're human beings and most of them were just happy to talk to someone trying to depict them as human beings."

Over the course of *The Wire*'s five seasons, junkies in Baltimore – where heroin has been entrenched since as far back as the 1930s – came to see Bubbles as their very human hero.

Enjoying a dinner of meatloaf and mashed potatoes at a restaurant co-owned by his wife Jane – Canele in the Atwater Village neighborhood – Royo said street addicts hanging around the on-location sets of *The Wire* often came to his trailer between shots.

"They'd give me pointers, like how a junkie would *never* throw a half-smoked cigarette away. So I went to the director and said, 'We gotta do that one again.'"

After the day's shooting was over, however, Andre would clean up, change his clothes and hop in a car. A Teamster would drive him back home, leaving Bubbles behind until the next day's call.

"The junkies would see that and it would hurt them," said Royo. "One of them said, 'I wish it was that easy.'"

By Season Five, after years of pushing stolen scrap metal through the streets of Baltimore, Bubs managed to shake out the junk for the last time in his sister's basement.

"I didn't think living in the basement carried that much weight [for the story] until I saw it on the screen," said Royo, finishing off the meatloaf special with an ice cream sundae.

"But in the end, he got to walk up the stairs. Bubbles earned the right to sit down at the dinner table . . . a little hope."

•

The real Bubbles carried his role with pride.

"I'm a watcher," said Bubbles a month before his death from AIDS, gaunt face bobbing, one of his dark, stick legs stretched over a table in a rowhouse apartment on Harlem Avenue in Northwest Baltimore.

"I can watch people and tell things about them. I can look at a face and remember it. I would go round a-rabbing, or in my truck, or I'd ride my bicycle even, and all the time, I'd be seeing what's up."

When Bubbles sussed that something was up, it was up. His information led some 500 escapees back to prison.

"Always dead-on," said a homicide detective at the time. "If he told me right now to go kick in a door, I'd kick in that door."

Bubbles was born on an alley street in South Baltimore where Oriole Park at Camden Yards has stood since the year of his death. He tried heroin for the first time at 15, got sick, and tried it again.

By 17, he was shooting dope just about every day and working as an *a-rabber*, the Baltimore term for men who sell produce on the streets from a horse-drawn cart.

Before he turned to snitching, Bubbles was a "sneak-thief," shimmying through roof caps and skylights of stores in South Baltimore and Pigtown, grabbing what he could and breaking out through a window to confuse police as to how he got in.

One night in the late 1950s, a crew Bubbles had trained and worked with broke into a pawnshop on South Charles Street. They came down through the skylight but forgot to break a window on the way out to distract attention from the point of entry. A detective noticed the open skylight.

"He asks around and finds out that I'm always coming down the skylights," remembers Bubbles. "So he comes by my house and I tell him it ain't me, and he says to me, 'Okay, but then you know who it was.'"

The choice was to give up names or take the charge.

"I gave him the names," said Bubbles. "And he paid me a few dollars."

Soon enough the retired sneak-thief was churning out information on burglaries, robberies, and fugitives, making enough to keep his habit going, and no one on the street was ever the wiser.

"I was careful," he said.

In 1976, Bubbles found himself playing the escapee, having walked away from a state work camp for convicts and a seven-year sentence on drug charges.

A cop familiar with Bubbles's usefulness arranged to have the drug sentence commuted and the escape charge dropped. That's when he went to work more or less full-time for the Baltimore Police Department's escape unit.

Bubbles was loyal, but not without testing his new employer's commitment.

At an early meeting with the escape squad, Bubbles showed up with a baby in his arms, his son. The whole time he was talking with the cops outside of police headquarters on Fayette Street, he held the infant tight.

Later, after the working arrangements had proved satisfactory, Bubbles explained the baby's presence.

"I figured they were just going to lock me up . . . so if it was going to be this way, I was going to hand the baby to the cop that looked the fastest. Then I was gonna outrun the others."

Bubbles was the guy with the photographic memory who always blended in with the action, whether selling cantaloupes from the back of a wagon or stealing new copper downspouts. No one paid much attention to him while he was paying attention to everything.

At first, he'd turn guys in by name. In time, he'd memorized the escape unit's mug-shot binder and was turning in wanted men by their faces.

Because he only got paid when the mark was caught, he complained when the cops failed to show on the right corner at the right time. Like the time he was working a section of Amsterdam Avenue in Upper Manhattan, called Little Baltimore for the surplus of Crabtown gangsters who'd go there when sought by authorities back home.

As they'd done many times before, detectives put their best informant on a bus to the Big Apple, hoping to fill their quota from the Amsterdam Avenue corners. Once, however, with a high-profile escapee in view, the New York Feds kept grabbing the wrong guy.

Eventually, Bubbles gathered up a bunch of hats, hit the hot corner, and went to work. Pretending to be selling stylish lids, he put a red cap on the right man and drifted into the scenery as the agents finally grabbed their fugitive.

Introduced by Baltimore homicide detective Ed Burns, who had worked with Bubbles for many years, Simon was able to sit and talk with Bubbles only twice.

On a third visit to the West Baltimore walk-up, the reporter, hoping to write a magazine article on Bubbles and his notable career, encountered an empty apartment. The landlord confirmed that Bubbles had died in his bed a few days prior.

Although proud of having fashioned a career that avoided direct violence, Bubbles told Simon in their last interview, somewhat sheepishly, that he'd "killed two people once."

There was a stickup man in the projects who kept taking dope from him when he was trying to make a little bit on the side.

"Every week he robbed me," said Bubbles. "And every time, he would take not only what I was selling, but the couple bags I kept in my pocket up here for myself."

After the third or fourth robbery, Bubbles switched the heroin in his pocket with battery acid.

"Eventually [he] fired it and got dead then and there. Another someone died because they fired it with him . . . I felt bad for that person, but, hey, it's all in the game."

·

There was so much in the game meticulously diagrammed by *The Wire* that Royo and some of his fellow actors had doubts that the pilot would be picked up as a series, much less last five seasons.

"We always thought *The Wire* would never fly," said Royo. "It's long, it's low and it has too many characters."

But it flew in such a graceful, feathered arc that Royo – who by the show's end was pestering the producers for a Bubbles love scene, "a little cardboard box make-out session," – found plenty of work when *The Wire* left the air.

"I was getting arrested on *Law & Order* and I saw that the hallway was clear and was going to make a run for it," said Royo, who in May 2009 was filmed in George Lucas's remake of the *Tuskegee Airmen* story in Prague.

"The [*Law & Order*] producers said, 'This isn't *The Wire*, Andre. When you see our cops coming you just put out your hands and let them cuff you.'"

Royo says he will carry Bubbles with him forever, having come to see the character "as someone trying to hold onto his goodness through all of it.

"Drugs are destroying his mind and his body and his ego, but not his good spirit."

And apparently not his legs, favored limbs of addicts once they've blown through all of the veins in their arms.

In a scene where his shopping cart dents a car owned by Marlo's muscle, Bubbles and his sidekick Johnny are facing the gun until the kingpin tells his men to either "do it or don't" but he's got to roll. The thugs extract humiliation as payment, and Bubbles and Johnny are next seen pushing the grocery cart in their underwear.

"The producers never saw me without my pants," said Royo, without irony regarding the casting couch. "My legs are in good shape and huge.

"I told [the director] that if a junkie is carrying around radiators all day, he might have some legs on him, but they still didn't think it looked right so I just walked through the scene fast."

The beauty of Bubbles plays across Royo's face through large, tired eyes; in the subtle "Are you fucking kidding me?" look he gives a fellow junkie when he realizes the man can't read.

"Ed Burns told me I had a Chaplinesque quality. That's the sort of thing you don't hear in this business," said Royo, who in one memorable scene takes in the world from a park bench without saying a word.

Like Michael Kenneth Williams, who played Omar, Royo was told early on that his character may not survive more than seven or eight episodes.

But both proved to be of service to the story from beginning to end.

"The first time in my acting career that I got to follow a [true] journey," said Royo. "Bubbles wakes up every day with a big, big wish-list. He needs his dope, but he still tries to complete the rest of the list, maybe one day get around to seeing his kid, seeing his sister.

"He finds pleasure in helping the cops. It ain't just about the $20 to get high. If you really want money for dope, you can do it a million different ways for a lot more money than snitching."

And then there was the day that Royo won the kind of prize they don't award in Hollywood.

"We were filming on the street; I was in makeup but away from the cameras," he said. "This guy comes up to me and handed me some drugs. He said, 'Here, man, you need a fix more than I do.'

"That was my street Oscar."

episode
ten

THE COST

"And then he dropped the bracelets . . ." — GREGGS

Directed by Brad Anderson

Story by David Simon & Ed Burns; teleplay by David Simon

McNulty catches up with Wallace and breaks him down in the interrogation room, implicating Wee-Bey and Stringer Bell in Brandon's murder. Without money for witness protection, Daniels stashes Wallace at his grandmother's house on the Eastern Shore, more or less the Mississippi of Maryland.

An unrelated Maryland State Police undercover investigation nabs Wendell "Orlando" Blocker – the frontman for Barksdale's nightclub and a gangster hanger-on – for attempting to buy narcotics.

Cut loose by Barksdale and with no other protection, Orlando tries to avoid jail by making a controlled drug buy from the Barksdale organization. Detectives are dubious that Orlando can get anyone above a lower-level lieutenant in the room for a buy, but Burrell, seeing a quick end to the case, approves the operation.

Bubbles, worn down by the suicide-by-sandpaper life of the street, resolves to get clean and prevails on his estranged sister to let him shake it out in her basement. He appeals to a sympathetic Greggs for help.

At the same time, Omar is approached – through Proposition Joe – about a possible truce with the Barksdale group. McNulty and Greggs put a wire on Omar, hoping to get Stringer Bell talking about drugs and/ or murder in the ensuing meet with Omar. Stringer proves too smart for that.

Having used Omar as much as possible, McNulty puts him on a bus to New York, if only to keep one of his two witnesses in the Gant murder alive.

The detectives plan their controlled buy with Orlando carefully. The buy proves to be a setup, and both Orlando and Detective Greggs, who is with him as a "club girl," are ambushed in a darkened alley. Orlando is killed, Greggs severely wounded.

episode
eleven

THE HUNT

"Dope on the damn table . . ." — DANIELS

Directed by Steve Shill

Story by David Simon & Ed Burns; teleplay by Joy Lusco

Working back from the scene of Orlando's murder and info from the continuing wiretap, detectives are able to identify two possible shooters. Greggs, unconscious in the hospital, cannot help.

Daniels is now all-in with the investigation in the wake of Greggs's shooting and fends off political interference as best he can, even as Deputy Commissioner Burrell orders premature raids. When Daniels tries to hold out one location for further investigation – the main Barksdale stash house – he is again ordered to do otherwise by Burrell.

Who is the leak in the detail providing top brass with day-by-day info?

The raids put dope and cash and some guns on the table, but the wiretap is now useless as the Barksdale organization has changed its method of communication.

Bubbles, now without Greggs's help, stumbles in his effort to stay clean, particularly when he is pushed back into the project world as an informant.

As the investigation into Greggs's shooting progresses, Wee-Bey is forced to flee to Philadelphia with D'Angelo's help. Barksdale's nephew fears that his uncle's efforts to clean up the organization may include more executions, including his own.

In the end, the department congratulates itself on the successful raids in response to the shooting of an officer while Daniels and his officers know the job is far from finished.

episode
        twelve

CLEANING UP

"This is me, yo, right here." – WALLACE

Directed by Clement Virgo
Story by David Simon & Ed Burns; teleplay by George Pelecanos

Bored with the country and unsure of his place in the world, Wallace returns to The Pit – much to the consternation of D'Angelo, who knows that his uncle, having learned of the wiretaps, is cleaning house.

D'Angelo is ordered to go to New York on a resupply mission as the Barksdale organization struggles to maintain its hold on the projects in the wake of the police raids. Though the wiretap is now useless, detectives manage – with the help of Shardene – to place a hidden camera and microphone into the back room of Barksdale's club. They then overhear the conversation between Avon Barksdale and his nephew, implicating both.

New Jersey troopers catch D'Angelo dirty on the turnpike, but he refuses to cooperate. McNulty leaves him with this to consider: Wallace has been found shot to death in the projects.

Alienated by the hit on Wallace, D'Angelo argues with Stringer Bell and the lawyer Levy when they arrive in New Jersey, repeatedly asking Stringer about Wallace's whereabouts. Stringer, who ordered Bodie and Poot to murder their friend, will not answer.

As Deputy Burrell tries to put the case down for good, Daniels is summoned to meet state senator Clay Davis, who assures him that he is neither corrupt nor profiting from Barksdale drug money.

With Greggs still clinging to life, Daniels will not be deterred, even at the risk of his career. Burrell orders the arrest of Avon Barksdale on a charge connected to D'Angelo's arrest in New Jersey.

McNulty and Daniels go to the club and cuff Barksdale. But they are forced to leave Stringer Bell on the street – he has not implicated himself on the wire – and the death of Wallace has made it impossible to charge him in the murder of Brandon.

episode
thirteen

SENTENCING

"All in the game..." — TRADITIONAL, WEST BALTIMORE

Directed by Tim Van Patten

Written by David Simon & Ed Burns

Frustrated by their department's unwillingness to pursue the case beyond the arrest of Avon Barksdale on a minor charge, Daniels, McNulty, and Freamon try to take the investigation to federal agents.

They quickly realize that the US attorney is more interested in political corruption than inner-city murder and drug trafficking, particularly since Freamon has connected the Barksdale ring's political contributions to real estate holdings in a government-funded redevelopment area downtown.

The detectives back away from the Feds, but their approach is soon known to Rawls, and, ultimately, Burrell.

Greggs regains consciousness and can identify the heavy-set Little Man (played by Micaiah Jones) as one of her shooters, but not the second, even though Bunk gives her the heavy thumb on Wee-Bey's mug shot.

The case breaks wide open when D'Angelo begins to cooperate in New Jersey, consenting to a meeting with Assistant State's Attorney Rhonda Pearlman and the detectives in which he recounts the violence, including Brandon's murder, the slaying of the young woman in the apartment, and other brutalities.

D'Angelo wants immunity and a new life and the detectives, seeing both Barksdale and Bell vulnerable to weighty charges, are ready to agree.

It falls apart when D'Angelo's mother – Avon's sister, Brianna - arrives to make it clear to her son what he owes to his family. She succeeds and D'Angelo backs off from the promised cooperation.

Barksdale's lawyer arranges a structured plea agreement in which all of those arrested plead guilty instead of subjecting themselves to further investigation via a trial. While Avon faces a minimum sentence, D'Angelo gets 20 years for the New Jersey bust and Wee-Bey takes life without parole for owning up to a number of murders, some of which he clearly did not commit.

Now the number one man on the street, Stringer Bell sets up business in a funeral home as the drug dealing continues unabated. Bodie is put in charge of a tower and Poot runs The Pit.

Greggs is left to recover from her wounds. Freamon, rescued from oblivion by the case, is reassigned to the homicide unit. Burrell's informant in the detail unit proves to be Detective Carver, who is rewarded with a promotion to sergeant and the contempt of Daniels.

And McNulty?

Go back to the pilot episode, the scene in which Detective Sergeant Landsman holds up $20 and declares: "I'll go this against ten, you're riding the boat, midnight shift."

Q&A WITH LITTLE MELVIN WILLIAMS

In March of 2004, David Simon and Ed Burns – the former reporter and the ex-cop whose adventures with bureaucracy and bad guys pumped stranger-than-fiction blood into *The Wire* – sat down with one of the legendary kingpins in the annals of Baltimore narcotics, Melvin D. "Little Melvin" Williams.

Williams, then 63, had spent more than a third of his life in prison when he met with Simon, Burns, and a tape recorder at *The Wire* offices on South Clinton Street along the southeast Baltimore waterfront.

He was less than a year out of prison – and a year away from making his debut as "The Deacon" on *The Wire* – after a federal judge had reduced a 22-year sentence on a 2000 handgun charge because it did not meet certain technicalities.

Simon, who in 1987 chronicled Melvin's criminal career in a five-part series in the *Baltimore Sun*, described the meeting as one of the more "wonderfully bizarre" moments of his career.

As a city homicide detective, Burns had a lead role in the 1984 federal wiretap case that had resulted in Williams' spending 16 years in federal prisons. For his part, Simon cemented his reputation as a crime reporter at the *Baltimore Sun* with the aforementioned series.

When the trio got together for the first time, taking lunch several months earlier, Williams passed out a business card with his phone number on it.

"What I wouldn't have given to have had that more than 20 years ago," quipped Burns, who had spent hundreds of hours on dialed-number recorders and wiretaps before discerning exactly which phones were being used by Williams.

The 2004 meeting – taking place between Seasons Two and Three of the show – only occurred because of the mutual respect the unlikely trio have for one another.

Burns, the career cop, who played fair; Simon, the reporter who looked past the immediate details of the crime scenes for motivations more subtle than greed; and Williams, a survivor of a lifetime in the big leagues of organized crime, a man who prides himself on an unblemished reputation for loyalty and discretion.

"I wouldn't be in this room if Ed had shit in his blood," Williams said of the cop who locked him up. "He was as sincere about what he was as I was about what I was."

The Baltimore saga of Little Melvin goes back to the late 1950s, when, at the tender age of 14, Williams was being pulled out of Pennsylvania Avenue pool halls by the cops with hundreds of dollars in his pocket.

He learned to shoot dice – and, more importantly, to cheat at dice – before leaving grade school. By the time he entered Frederick Douglass High School, Williams was regarded as one of the best pool players in the city, if not the East Coast.

As a sharp young man on his way up in the world of 1950s gambling – he is fabled among a certain generation for hitting the three-digit number twice in a row on $100 bets – Melvin eventually became a protégé of Julius "the Lord" Salsbury.

A lieutenant of Meyer Lansky, Salsbury controlled the layoff for Baltimore's lucrative illegal lottery before jumping bail and disappearing in 1970, never to be seen again.

"You can't come in as a guy from West Baltimore and have any better break than to have Salsbury say, 'Respect this man,'" observed Burns.

A math prodigy specializing in games of chance, Melvin impressed Salsbury instantly, having cost the older man dearly with those successive lottery hits. In his first stretch in prison, where Williams earned his high school equivalency, he was accused of cheating because he'd scored so high on math tests.

"So [the teacher] made up another test right in front of me, and as fast as he would put up the problems. I would do them," recalled Williams. "He said, 'When did you learn that?' and I said, 'I don't know.' He said, 'How did you learn that?' And I said, 'I don't know.'"

To hear law enforcement authorities tell the tale, by the mid-1960s when the Avenue had changed and heroin had become the dominant criminal enterprise, Williams turned from gambler to drug trafficker and became one of the most successful in the city's history.

Williams says he did not get involved with narcotics until he was framed by federal drug agents and Baltimore narcotics detectives, who utilized the testimony of a corrupt informant and planted a small amount of heroin on Williams when he was arrested.

In his 1987 series of articles, Simon interviewed a former federal agent – long since fired from the job – who acknowledged that the probable cause to arrest Williams was manufactured and the drugs were likely planted by a Baltimore sergeant who later killed himself while under investigation for perjury.

This agent, as well as others, argues that the frame-up was motivated by the fact that Williams was a large-scale trafficker who could not be caught fair-and-square.

Williams returned to the streets in the early 1970s, built a larger and more insulated drug ring, but was again felled by a federal investigation and served another four years. Again he came home, this time caught up in Ed Burns's protracted wiretap probe of several interconnected West Baltimore drug crews.

Acknowledging that he had "not been a nice guy by any stretch of the imagination," Williams is pleased to have retired from a game that buries most of its players before they hit thirty.

Williams also nurtured and cherished a home life and the middle-class agenda that goes with it, including college for his kids.

"It's not easy buying your daughter's automobiles from the visiting room [of prison], even though you've got more than enough money," he said. "So you say to yourself, 'When did I not have enough money? Why did I continue to be involved when I long ago had too much money?'"

Because it's not about money.

"Calling the shots," Williams conceded, reflecting on his legendary status in the East Coast drug trade. "It's addictive, calling the shots."

Williams never drank or used drugs. He does not eat meat and has long maintained a personal discipline that made pursuing him a nightmare for investigators, who knew they would never catch him flashing money or openly associating or communicating with other suspects, much less ever being in the room with product.

"He's a very, very intelligent guy who knows how to listen, how to read between the lines and size people up," said Burns. "He was a nine-to-five drug dealer who never went out after dark, whose daughter went to college."

DAVID SIMON: The drug game has grown beyond the small, back-alley game that you might have known in the 1950s. Now, it's almost part of the pop culture. What are the people trying to play it now not seeing?

MELVIN WILLIAMS: That nobody got away. They're not seeing that at a time when I spent 26½ years in [some] of the world's worst penitentiaries, there was still a parole board and I only did one-third of every sentence I ever had.

But in 1987, the United States removed parole from off the planet. Now, the standard sentence they give young people for drug involvement is 30 to life, usually life.

These kids have been [deluded]. But there's so many of them on so many street corners that the big boys [federal agents] don't have a chance to go after all of them, as they did back in our day. The only thing they have going for them is numbers. As each one grows to be a shark, they're going to cut his head off.

And when one of them slips out of the Mickey Mouse drug-dealer [phase of the game] and buys the automobile that says "I have arrived," he identifies himself to the big boys. And the big boys are the big boys just because they are the big boys. They don't play and they don't miss and they're going after kids that study no law, know nothing about protecting themselves or their family, and the end result is so [inevitable] that you could make book on it.

DS: Ed, what do you think the players miss when they're in the game?

ED BURNS: I think it's a question of culture, this is all they have. You know what the scariest place in Baltimore is today? The middle schools. Go in there and see how damaged these kids are at the age of 11, 12, 13.

[But] when Melvin started, I'm sure he came in on a level several steps removed from the street. The kids starting out today start on the street.

The gangs in Baltimore are neighborhood gangs, and the clever kids use their little group as a vehicle [to work the game].

They're always going to have muscle around them and they're going to play the other kids, but they're hoping to get off the street, because you get killed out there. There's only very few people that have that intellectual capacity, that distance that allows them to marginally go up the ranks.

In West Baltimore, you might have 20,000 kids trying out, you might have five "winners," and by "winners" we mean people who move up the line. The difference between [Melvin's] generation and today is that before it was semi-controlled. Murders meant something. Now it's just your shoes are wrong, bang, you're dead.

Before cocaine came and changed everything, there was a certain amount of charm to it. I locked up a guy one time on an escape [warrant]. His name was Peacock, and when we rode downtown and got on the elevator, he says, "Maybe you can do me a favor?"

"Anything you want," I said, and he goes, "Can you take this out of my back?"

I reached around and he had a .45 in his back and I said, "Tell you what. We'll write this up as found property," and he said, "Thank you."

I was going to take him up to the office, take the handcuffs off him, and get him a coffee. If he was another type of guy, he would have pulled out the .45, blown us all away, and walked out of the goddamn building at two o'clock in the morning.

It's all ugly now, and ugly is not where you want to be.

DS: You remember Peacock?

MW: Of course.

DS: I don't think I ever met anybody from any side of the tracks that had as much personal discipline as you, Melvin. Where did it come from?

MW: I grew up in a martial arts environment and all of it was designed so that you defend yourself. It didn't have anything to do with attack. The discipline of doing push-ups on your knuckles and running after everybody else stopped – when your guts are falling out and you say, "I'm going to run for three more miles" – that's part of where the discipline came from. I started when I was around 15.

DS: Ed, what did the name Melvin Williams mean to you when you heard it the first time?

EB: Melvin is unique unto himself as far as his stature in the Baltimore drug world. There were other guys that got big, but they never really left the street. Melvin was the top of the pinnacle. He was the guy you would go for.

The drug game didn't interest me so much as the challenge [of the pursuit]. In any occupation, if you work with a second person, there's got to be communication. A prosecutor once told me, "You build a mousetrap. Every day you build a mousetrap because it's only got to work one time. That mouse can beat you 364 days of the year, but the one time it works, it's over."

So it became about building a better mousetrap and getting the department to give you the time to do it. Not all of my wars were fought on the street. A lot of my wars were fought inside the building, saying, "This guy over here is dangerous, truly dangerous people. Just let me have the time this time to get him," and they'd resist.

Once a police officer aspires to rank – you would think that stopping crime would be the number one priority – crime is so far down the list you can't find it.

DS: Is there a way to play the game where you're not vulnerable to enforcement?

MW: There are people that have sold boatloads of narcotics for the last 40 or 50 years. People who transfer narcotics in boats at ports where nobody's watching. That's what they do. And by the time it winds up in the city, it's been broken down eight million times.

The kind of credibility that you have to have to communicate with those kinds of organizations has to come from the kind of past that a Melvin would have. The kids [hustling] today are disenfranchised. They can never come from the street to be anything more than what is considered trivial in New York but is special here.

Tonight, tomorrow, and all the rest of your life, somebody is going to sell poppy illegitimately for a tremendous amount of money. Just like the New York Stock Exchange.

Once, someone called me way back when and said, "I want you to go to [New York], just be present and take a little money with you." I go, and I'm the only guy there who looked like me.

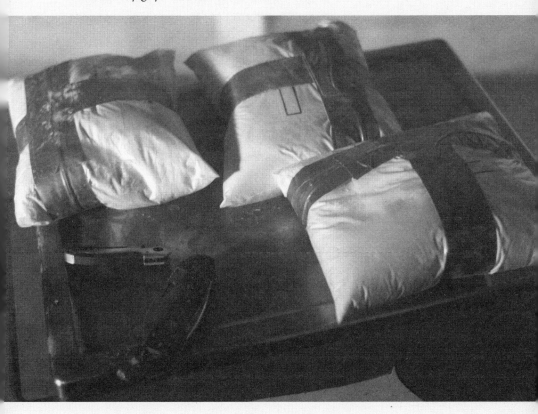

Everybody has on Turkish mohair suits, top-of-the-line, $3,000 or $4,000 suits. The alligators match perfectly – burgundy with burgundy, blue with blue, black with black. The ties were the very best of silk. You're at the top of your game.

One guy reaches [for something], another guy brings him a vial, he puts something into the vial and shakes it and it turns blue-black, and it's evident this is heroin.

The man says: "I got 3,842 kilograms of that, Melvin, and you're first because you're the newest guy here. I'm selling these for $75,000 a kilogram – China White – you cut it 40 times and it gets stronger."

I reach into my briefcase and I bring out $225,000 and he takes it and balls it back up and sticks it back in my case. He says, "I don't want to offend you because I understand you're a martial artist," and everybody laughs.

He says, "You have not understood the gravity of your being here. You have been accepted. Tell me the amount of these that you want, and two streets that cross any place on the planet, and in 24 hours I'll make it happen."

I told him, "I'll take 40,' and I gave him two streets in East Baltimore, and within 24 hours he did just what he said. He said, 'If the material is in a vehicle, the vehicle is yours. If it's in a U-Haul, take it out to the airport and turn it in." And the rest is history. You become a millionaire overnight. You don't have a choice.

I remember going into Julius Salsbury's office one evening, and he and three other men were sitting around talking about people that died 20 years ago, billions of dollars, people that would die 20 minutes from now, billions of dollars.

Two of those persons were present at the Appalachian mountain meeting when they [organized crime bosses] divided the country up. I walked in, and nobody ever looked around to see who this black guy was that had just sat down or changed his thoughts.

[Salsbury] had told them, "There's a black kid that's going to come in here that I love. Don't offend me, or him, by breaking conversation or stopping whatever the nature of this conversation is all about."

I have never been more proud in my life.

DS: But now, to work your way up that pyramid from the bottom?

MW: Can't happen. [The new guy of today] is never going to be accepted. The door is closed.

DS: No one on the planet can say that Melvin Williams had a conversation with law enforcement that was about anything beyond the weather. There were people who broke that code, much to your detriment. How much of the code is still intact?

MW: When I got into a federal penitentiary, somebody at the top of each of the [crime] families, at some point when I first come through the door, would kiss me in the proximity of everybody so that everybody can see, "We don't want this guy to have a problem."

There's just so little of that going on that that's what [an up-and-coming drug trafficker] aspires to. That's carte blanche in jail and they wouldn't trade that for nothing.

DS: What do you miss the most?

MW: In the game? I don't miss it.

DS: There's got to be something.

MW: The only reason I became involved in the drug game was I had a group around me, and the group didn't have the same kind of gambling, thinking, and charisma that I had, so I had to find something where everybody could earn that kind of money without really being that kind of person. And drugs was the only thing at the time.

DS: Was there nothing about it that had its charm?

MW: It was a headache. Every day you gotta worry about Joe making a mistake. You know you weren't going to make any, but Joe has gotten more money now than he's ever dreamed of in life, and [women], and everybody that's wise is always after him, so you've got to watch him all day, protect him all day long from his whores and his fantasies. Every day you've got to ride around and see who's trying to throw a curveball at him. That's a headache.

DS: Who do you miss, Melvin?

MW: When I was away, the old man that first taught me everything that I know about gambling passed away – Cherry Reds Franklin.

We met because I had devised a way to shoot the dice; it's called the turn down. I had found a way to shoot the turn down on every surface, including smooth concrete . . . to determine at least a high percentage of making my number.

I went around to see him the next day and I went around every day after that until I became an adult and went to the penitentiary. I missed that I wasn't there when that old guy died. He was a very light-skinned old man considered to be a grumpy old guy to everybody he had ever met.

He never worked a day in his life and sent all of his children to college. I was the only dark-skinned person that anybody had seen him with. And he used to call me his baby. He must have passed away sometime around 1970.

He told me, "Melvin, never place a bet – no matter how much better you are than your opponent – on something that you can't replace." I'll never forget that. He also asked me if I planned to have a lot of money and fame [and power], and I said, "Absolutely," and he said, "Then you're planning in reverse."

He gave me a week to figure that out, and after that week I said, "I don't know the answer."

So he told me, "Anytime you plan to have a blow job, a lottery hit, a windfall of astronomical dimension, you're gonna like that. And you don't never have to plan for something that you like because you'll be delighted.

"Plan [instead] to be going in the house in the middle of the night with your hands full of shopping bags and the stickup mob turn the corner. Plan to be sitting at the table, counting the amounts of different kinds of substances that will turn into millions of dollars and the door come off the hinge.

"Always plan for something that you don't like so you can stop it."

I never forgot that.

DS: Ed, who do you miss?

EB: I miss Bubbles. He was my informant and he was an amazing guy. When I left, I turned Bubbles over to guys who didn't respect him. They didn't like him because Bubbles made them work.

Bubbles would call and say, "There's an escapee out here," and they'd go, "Hey, it's lunchtime." I'd have to go out to Bubbles and take money out of my pocket because they'd been cheating him.

DS: Aside from the 26 years of lost time, are there other regrets?

MW: The way the script was written, that's just the way it is. That's a long time to be removed from your family, but I've had some days in the penitentiary that were so delightful, I wouldn't replace them with nothing. Sometimes the gates were opened and I was told, "See you," but there ain't nowhere that I could go.

I've had some dinners and some meals prepared by people from other parts of the world that own restaurants and villas, people I am certain have never been in the presence of an African-American before, who said, "Melvin's on a late detail and we're not going to eat one shred of this stuff until he gets here."

I consider that priceless. People who have conversations that can go from billions of dollars to murder and never worry that I might repeat it. That's the top of the line for me. I wouldn't substitute that for anything.

DS: There's been an American prohibition on drugs going back for most of the last century and increasing in its fervor. What do you think about that, what you've seen it do to the city?

MW: I see the country for what it is. This is a part of the world where they say, "Give us our piece and we basically don't care what you do." We have a lifestyle and grandkids that need to ride horses in fields that go as far as the eye can see. I need to have money that's going to be regular and often. That [culture] governs and determines things. The changes in the community, as ugly as it appears to be, are something that nobody has been able to overcome.

A junkie in England can go and get his shot for a dollar. Who the hell can compete with that? You want to stop drugs? Sell it legitimately.

Make a package that has the same amount every time, rather than let somebody that has no intellectual or chemical experience make something up in a bowl in his kitchen, and when he runs out of [thinners], he reaches up in his cabinet because he needs another hundred pills and dumps something white down in it.

He doesn't know what kind of negative chemical reaction it's going to have on anybody; he's interested in dollars and cents.

In Britain, they have determined that if we put this amount in this container over this period of time, the user will never OD. You want to do that, you don't have to worry about [anything else] because nobody can sell and make money below a dollar.

EB: In this society, as far as the legitimate economy goes, only a certain amount of people are productive. The ones who are not productive, you have to do something with them. You could be a nice guy and educate them and take care of them and make them part of your economy, or you could say, "Go get high."

The addiction rate is increasing – not only in the inner city, but all over the country – because the jobs are disappearing, and if I don't need you to work anymore, I'll just get rid of you.

I can't kill you, that would be bad, so I send you down the road of addiction, which is hideous, and I'm quite content to say, "It's your fault because you got addicted, not society's fault."

And that's the interesting thing – why don't we do something about drugs? This war's been going on for 30 years and they haven't begun to do anything about it. If drugs went away, law enforcement, as it's structured today, would take a terrible hit.

MW: No question.

SEASON TWO

SEASON TWO OVERVIEW

"Them days is gone ..."

HORSEFACE PAKUSA

It was exciting to be an eight-year-old kid in Baltimore in 1966.

The Orioles won their first World Series of the modern era behind the slugging of Frank Robinson, the defense of Brooks Robinson and the pitching of Dave McNally.

Every day, something new and strange came blaring out of WCAO, the AM pop station – red doors painted black sailing through the theremin vibrations of blossom worlds – while a blizzard dumped 20 inches of snow in the backyard.

And my father – Manuel Alvarez, a tugboat man on the South Broadway waterfront – went on strike with the Seafarers International Union.

Three local towing companies were hit, with picket lines going up outside of the City Recreation Pier in Baltimore where the tugs docked, a true seaman's village of brothels, pickle factories, coffee wharves, and evangelical soup kitchens.

Decades later, when the gentrification of the neighborhood was complete, NBC's *Homicide: Life on the Street*, would be filmed at the Rec Pier.

During the strike, bay pilots trying to dock ships without the aid of tugs damaged or destroyed several piers, although vessels carrying military cargo to and from Vietnam were serviced by the tugs.

The work was performed by all parties, from stevedores to management, out of patriotic pride. Tug crews accepted no pay for this work.

The strike of '66 lasted for six months.

"I remember Mom cleaning other people's houses for money and my parents agonizing over whether or not to apply for food stamps out of pride," said Gregory Lukowski, who followed his tugboat mate father down to the waterfront and eventually became a Chesapeake Bay pilot.

"Christmas was lean," said Lukowski of 1966. "And the winter seemed extremely cold."

The strike ended with basic hourly wages set from $2.71 for deckhands to $3.23 for captains.

Not much by 21st-century standards, even in the Great Recession. But it was a good buck when overtime, holiday pay – even a relic known as triple time – were factored into the crews' salaries.

"That strike guaranteed us a five-day workweek and put an end to the company using us as casual labor," Dad recalled.

"When that contract expired, we went on strike again and did better. Before it was all over, we killed the goose that laid the golden egg."

Today, none of the major tugboat firms in Baltimore are locally owned. When the out-of-town companies succeeded in defeating the union in the late 1980s, my father went to work in a hardware store until he was old enough to collect Social Security.

•

I grew up with the expectation that I would go to college and learn to do something that didn't involve shovels or wrenches or, as the old man often said when we were doing chores around the house, "picking 'em up and putting 'em down."

His skilled-labor wage put us in a brick rancher in a solidly middle-class suburb where most of the other fathers worked at Westinghouse and the moms more or less stayed home. My mother kept track of inventory in the shoe department at Sears and was home before we got out of school.

The same wage that put us in with the white-collar families paid tuition for my brothers and me at a Catholic high school. Mom still remembers "Seventy-five bucks out of every paycheck" going to the Xavierian brothers at Mount Saint Joseph High School.

That union wage had my back as I worked my way through Loyola College. And it bought the 1978 Ford Granada – bright green with white

Landau roof – I drove to the clerk's job I'd landed on the sports desk of the *Baltimore Sun* on my way to becoming a newspaperman.

And if all of our middle-class achievements went to hell, there was always that working-class safety net: the waterfront.

When the economy would go soft and things got tough at Bethlehem Steel or the Esskay meatpacking plant or even Westinghouse, work typically remained stable around the port.

"There's always something down the waterfront," Dad would say, even though the last thing he wanted was for his boys to be pulled into the labor pool, however plentiful, along the Baltimore harbor.

Always something has been something close to nothing for almost 20 years now.

.

Season Two of *The Wire* was about the last days of being able to follow in your old man's footsteps to make a living.

It was, said David Simon, a 12-episode wake for the "death of work."

Before HBO gave the green light to *The Wire*, Simon was considering this as a subject for his next non-fiction, fly-on-the-wall book: a narrative account of life on Baltimore's diminished waterfront.

The story could have been set amidst the ruins of any number of manufacturing plants that once made Baltimore one of the great producers of goods in the world: the mammoth carcass of Bethlehem Steel's Sparrows Point shipyard or the breweries that announced one's arrival in East Baltimore.

Once upon a time there were even factories that made umbrellas and hats and bread and licorice.

But the second season was set in the middle of the place that made so much of the other commerce possible: a commercial port dating back to the 17th century.

The harbor waterscape is the star of the very first scene when McNulty, banished, not just from homicide, but from terra firma itself, rides the police boat with Officer Diggins of the marine unit.

McNulty points out the Beth Steel Sparrows Point complex where his father worked until he was laid off in 1973. Diggins says his uncle was a supervisor there until he got the ax in 1978.

Some 30 years ago, the largest private employer in the Baltimore area was Beth Steel.

My grandfather, an immigrant from the Galicia region of Spain, was a shipyard worker during World War II when – to beat Hitler and Mussolini and a cat named Tojo – Liberty ships were launched almost daily.

To slide those gray ships out of the cradle and into the Patapsco River, three shifts of unionized workers, many of them recent transplants from Carolina tobacco fields and Appalachian coal mines, worked the Beth furnaces around the clock.

When Beth Steel went bankrupt in 2001, robbing several generations of pensioners and their widows of benefits thought to be good to the grave, my father was dumbstruck.

In my father's youth, it seemed as though Bethlehem Steel alone kept solvent the Highlandtown neighborhood where he grew up and a half dozen other communities around it.

A sausage factory might come and go, but no one could imagine no more Bethlehem Steel. When the steel mill was bought several years later by a Russian company, Pop was beyond disbelief.

Rooskies owning Bethlehem Steel?

For a while, and then they went belly-up too.

Today, the largest employer in the metro area is Johns Hopkins medical system and university. For the average Baltimorean, making beds and taking blood does not pay as well as making steel.

And while Hopkins helps their entry-level employees get high school equivalency degrees to train for better jobs, at "the Point" there was on-the-job advancement for smart workers without education.

When my grandfather started his career at Sparrows Point – some 40 years honored by a stainless steel plaque engraved with a picture of a ship, a testimonial that hangs today in the front room of his old rowhouse where I live – he was shoveling slag for a dollar a day.

At the time of his retirement in 1970, he was a skilled machinist with no more formal education than four or five elementary grades in the village where his father worked with oxcarts.

.

It's not long in the opening episode of Season Two before the harbor patrol finds a floater. The questionable death that gets McNulty worked up about being a detective again and will, in time, play a key role in the detail's new case.

But the investigation and eventual wiretap, which inevitably bleeds into the drug trade, doesn't begin with a mystery as simple as a dead body. It is launched from a stupid, ego-driven pissing match – one not far removed from the sandbox – between a pair of Locust Point Polish-Americans with bad blood between them.

Major Stan Valchek, commander of the Southeastern District, collected money to have a stained-glass window put into the local Polish-Catholic church, one that honored police officers. A longshoremen's union boss, Frank Sobotka, beats him to the punch with a window depicting men unloading a ship the old-school way, with brute strength.

When neither will back off, Valchek starts turning over rocks to find out how the financially struggling union, with less than a hundred men left, has the money to commission a gorgeous window, make fat contributions to the church, and hire a lobbyist to seduce the suits in Annapolis.

What Valcheck's detail discovers is that some economies never suffer recession: stolen goods, narcotics, and the international smuggling of human beings, especially highly-profitable young women.

Before filming began in early 2003, the writing staff interviewed dozens of stevedores and immigration officials, port personnel, customs inspectors, and steamship agents to get an idea of what moved through a modern port.

We heard about men who could steal the devil's pitchfork, others who could drink all night and work all day, and one particular dockworker whose matinee idol good looks had earned him the nickname "Horseface."

[The waterfront has always been a rich source of nicknames, most derived from the range of human imperfections, usually physical or otherwise. The men my father worked with on the boats had names like Ace and Pinhead; Frenchie, Din-Din, Ronnie Rotten Crotch, Joe Blow and Hercules.]

The man who brought Horseface to life was an actor named Charley Scalies, a child of South Philly who could have been raised in any one of Baltimore's working-class neighborhoods.

"The actors who comprised our fictional International Brotherhood of Stevedores needed no acting to demonstrate our closeness," said Scalies.

"Only men will understand what happens when a group of them 'hang out' for 10 to 12 hours a day, day after day, week after week, meal after meal, story after story, joke after joke, fart after fart and laugh after laugh."

The *esprit de corps* carried over when the real port workers upon whom Horseface and Ziggy and New Charles and Johnny Fifty were based mingled with the actors.

"From the stiletto cold winds of January to the hot and hazy days on the harbor in late May, we had camaraderie. Except for the fact that we were pretenders, there was no difference between us," said Scalies.

"In every bar scene, the directors had one hell of a time keeping us under control. We didn't need a script. We were the script."

Easy for an actor to say.

In the reporter-style interviews with people from all corners of the port, *The Wire* staff learned that what moves through a modern port – in Baltimore, mostly foreign automobiles – is less important than how it moves.

Machines, including robots in some foreign ports, have replaced thick arms and strong backs on the waterfront, moving more cargo more cheaply and efficiently, yet at a great cost in jobs.

This is the indifferent windmill against which Frank Sobotka tilts, believing that the money he's getting to smuggle containers of contraband off the docks can be used to save a way of life that has largely passed from the city, the port, his union, and his family.

He gets in bed with gangsters to do right by men who maybe stole a case of Scotch and a TV set now and again – sometimes a container of appliances – but who nonetheless have mortgages and car payments and remember a way of life that went back before their great-grandfathers' day.

It is a relationship, like virtually all in Sobotka's life – including the one with his half-ass son Ziggy – that spirals beyond his control.

With an anger that simmers and boils throughout his various ordeals, all geared toward turning back the clock on a story that only moves forward, Sobotka delivers a shoebox full of cash to a lobbyist named Bruce DiBiago.

With money from smuggling, Sobotka hired Bruce to get legislation passed to rebuild the port's grain pier and maybe get the Chesapeake & Delaware Canal dredged and widened.

He wants both for the same reason: more ships, more cargo, more work.

"Down here it's still 'Who's your old man?' till you got kids of your own and then it's 'Who's your son?' But after the horror movie I seen today – piers full of robots! – my kid will be lucky if he's even punching numbers five years from now.

"It breaks my fuckin' heart that there's no future for the Sobotkas on the waterfront."

Yet again, a fundamentally decent person – a mere human being – will have their heart cut out by giving it and their loyalty to an institution they believed would reward such fidelity.

The foolishness of such faith is twice shown in moments of reflection for Nicky Sobotka, Frank's nephew and cousin to Ziggy.

The first is when Nick has waded deep into the drug trade, delivering packages and getting paid on the white marble steps of an old woman who likely is a widow of a Beth Steel worker, a woman who could easily be his grandmother.

Though she is a stranger to Nick, she shames him with a look of disgust. Otherwise decent young men have gone to hell right along with a neighborhood where working people took pride in their homes

– particularly the well-scrubbed white marble steps where drugs are now being sold – and their families.

These are neighborhoods where the streetcar line shot straight to Sparrows Point, where houses rarely went on the market because they were handed down to a relative.

The next time we see the old lady's house, there's a For Sale sign on it.

At the very end, in the closing montage of Season Two, Nicky stares at an idle crane, closes his eyes, and sees visions of Baltimore's rusting and neglected industry interspersed with soft, slow-motion shots of people being tossed aside.

Black drug slingers and the addicts they service go about their business in the projects; the white sons of steelworkers and longshoremen, young men without union cards or those who have stopped paying dues to a union that no longer gets them work, emulate the project dealers and work their own neighborhood corners.

And the underworked stevedores, perhaps a year or less away from complete idleness, are lost in liquor and aimless talk of "them days" that are gone.

FRANK SOBOTKA: UNION MAN

"It was impossible for me to separate my character from the town. That's what I was trying to honor ..." — Chris Bauer

Some 65 years ago, Walt Benewicz was born into the life to which Chris Bauer paid tribute as a headstrong waterfront union boss.

The son of a stevedore and the grandson of a stevedore, Benewicz grew up in the Locust Point neighborhood of South Baltimore, hard by Fort McHenry, back when the port supported most of the families and businesses there.

Walt's father, a one-time boxer nicknamed Flash, died in an accident on the docks. His grandfather passed the same way, leaving Benewicz's grandmother to support the family – and send young Walt to Catholic school – on what she made running a grocery store on Locust Point's Hull Street.

In those days, when a stevedore died on the job, the neighborhood flag was flown at half-mast and the family got about $200, maybe a little more when the hat was passed at the local gin mill.

Before retiring a few years after Season Two of *The Wire* aired, Benewicz served as president of the "checkers" Local No. 953 of the International Longshoremen's Association, which has its offices on the same street where his grandmother's grocery once stood.

[On the show, the ILA became the IBA: the International Brotherhood of Stevedores.]

In waterfront parlance, a "checker" is a longshoremen responsible for documenting all cargo that is loaded and unloaded on a ship, a job once done with clipboard and pencil that is now fully computerized.

Benewicz and his union brothers provided many of the anecdotes that helped make Season Two of *The Wire* authentic. And it was a composite of the best traits of men like Benewicz – blended with a liberal dollop of their shortcomings and honest mistakes – that Chris Bauer drew upon in his portrayal of Frank Sobotka.

"There is a citizenry of Frank Sobotkas out there," said Bauer, cast in 2009 as small-town Louisiana cop Detective Andy Bellefleur on HBO's *True Blood* vampire drama.

"They want to be the best man they can be – Frank Sobotka was living a life of service – but sometimes the circumstances of their lives prevent them from seeing clearly who that best man is."

•

On hand when *The Wire* writing staff descended upon the neighborhood union hall in 2003 were longtime Local No. 953 business agent Richie Hughes and Steve "Steamboat" Markowski, the checkers delegate to the Baltimore district council of the ILA.

Veteran checkers dispatcher Steve Lukiewski played himself in a late episode where Sobotka goes to the hiring hall to grab a ship to work.

"No autographs," Lukiewski told friends when the episode aired. "You wanna talk to me, you gotta go through my agent."

From their life's work came the details of the ever-shrinking universe of Frank Sobotka and his men.

"Help my union?" Sobotka says to FBI agents when they want him to "name names" after the union is charged with racketeering and fraud when their smuggling comes violently to light at the end of Season Two.

"Twenty-five years we been dyin' slow down there," Sobotka rants. "Dry docks rustin', piers standin' empty. My friends and my kids like we got the cancer. No lifeline got throwed all that time.

"Nuthin' from nobody. And now you wanna help us. Help me?"

Ziggy Sobotka was partly based on a South Baltimore legend named Pinky Bannon, who was known to wear a tuxedo to the docks and did indeed bring his pet duck, replete with a diamond-studded collar, to various Locust Point bars, where the bird bellied up with the rest.

Pinky was also given to displaying his manhood with gusto: not only did Bannon dress up "Pretty Boy" in a green ribbon every St. Patrick's Day, he once introduced it into the bell of Al Bates's saxophone during a show. Bates never missed a beat.

On *The Wire*, Pinky became Sobotka's misguided, 20-something son.

"Nepotism is not a bad thing," conceded Benewicz, speaking of the generations-old tradition of bringing your boys to work alongside of you. "But sometimes it is to our disadvantage."

Some stories didn't make it into the show. Like the one about a stevedore named Scobie who got into a fistfight over an apple with a monkey that a sailor had brought back from South America.

Scobie was driving over the Francis Scott Key Bridge at the time. When a cop pulled him over for swerving, Scobie pointed to the monkey and complained, "I can't teach this monkey any manners."

Once, a shipload of Brazil nuts hit Baltimore, and a stevedore with a limp, charitably nicknamed "Hoppit," put some in his pocket to eat while he worked. It was the same pocket where he'd put his "keel," a black paint stick.

Before long, Hoppit's mouth was black and he was muttering that the nuts "taste like shit."

And so forth.

Though plenty of people throughout the Port of Baltimore helped writers and actors better understand their world, the heart and soul of Frank Sobotka bore no small resemblance to Walt Benewicz.

"The thing about Frank Sobotka that most blows me away is how much people *liked* him," said Bauer, who called the role the "pinnacle" of his long and busy career. "I was very conscious of not doing anything to solicit the audience's sympathy."

Time and again, when the writers were uncertain about a fine point of moving cargo through the port, staff researcher Norman Knoerlein would call Benewicz for the answer.

And in the small town that is big city Baltimore – "people here are loyal as dogs," said casting director and Crabtown native Pat Moran – Benewicz knew Knoerlein's mother from childhood.

And young Norman's calls were always returned.

"Sobotka was excellent," said Benewicz. "Not only did he look and act like a longshoreman, I've got to give him the ultimate compliment: he looked like a Polack."

Benewicz especially appreciated the scene in which Sobotka tried to use another man's union card to sweat out his felonious guilt with an honest day's work unloading a ship.

When dispatcher Lukiewski objects, Sobotka quips, "We're both bald and we're both Polish, what else you need to know?"

Bauer, an LA native unaware of any Polish heritage, didn't audition for the part.

Wire executive producer Bob Colesberry had produced *61**, an HBO film about Mickey Mantle and Roger Maris chasing Babe Ruth's home run record, and admired Bauer's work as the team's third outfielder.

Long before the union boss character was named or a word of dialogue put in his mouth, Bauer was the favorite to play him.

"I really felt like Frank Sobotka on the second or third day of filming. It was in the church when he goes to see the stained-glass window of the waterfront and he genuflects at the altar," said Bauer, who wore a "fat suit" and was cosmetically aged beyond his then 39 years.

"I spent a lot of time sitting on benches looking at the water and memorizing names of ships, getting used to the tempo of the harbor," he said. "As much as some things had changed, there was still a lot that hadn't, and you couldn't separate the people who lived there from it."

Often was the day when a local would stop Bauer on Thames Street in Fells Point (in Baltimore, the natives pronounce the "Th" in the fabled river's name) to tell him how much they loved "Franoosh" Sobotka.

"It created this weird, temporary intimacy," said the actor. "They'd invite me to their kids' baptisms and graduations. Once a guy drove by, rolled down the window, and yelled, 'Hey, Frank! ILA all the way!' That's quite a leap for one hour of television."

In an acting career begun at the age of four, Bauer has played Mitch in *A Streetcar Named Desire* on Broadway; a variety of psychotics, a prison inmate, a Confederate soldier, and the carpenter in a stage adaptation of William Faulkner's *As I Lay Dying*.

But the role of Frank Sobotka "was the closest I've come to playing someone who actually lived – real heartache, real suffering, real ecstasy.

"That's how I felt about Baltimore," he said, joking that he still has some harbor water in his ears from being dropped in the drink for his death scene. "I miss it."

Also dockside as Sobotka's right-hand was a foulmouthed little fat man with the nickname of Horseface, a role played by Charley Scalies.

"He had the strut of a longshoreman," said Benewicz of Scalies, who grew up as "Charley Boy" in South Philly in the late 1940s and early 1950s, when the area from Second Street east to the Delaware River was home to stevedores.

Scalies knew plenty of ethnic stevedoring families in the area; men who weren't always liked, but were respected for their strong union and living wage.

"They were hardworking, hard-drinking laborers who had lethal cargo hooks in their hands and expressions on their faces that told you they could just as easily use it on you as on a bale of whatever," said Scalies.

"When we first started shooting on the docks, I expected to meet men who fit that mold. They didn't oblige. Bulk cargo is all but gone. Pencil and paper have given way to handheld computers, and brute force is supplied by sophisticated machinery that takes skill and training to operate."

In the theater, said Scalies, one of the greatest compliments an actor can give a colleague is to say that he or she is "generous."

"Which means when you're working a scene together, he gives you everything you need to do your job," he said, noting that the real longshoremen he depended on to nail the part of Horseface were likewise generous.

"I asked how, they told me how. I asked why, they told me why. They even cared enough to tell me when I screwed up. First they did it quietly. But as we got to know each other better, they did it in loud, good-hearted fashion. Only a friend will do that to you!"

One of Horseface's shining moments came in retaliation for selective enforcement of traffic laws against union members when he steals Major Stan Valchek's surveillance van off the Southeastern police district's parking lot.

While some of the best thieves in the world are dockworkers, heads of other ILA locals in Baltimore took exception to the way the vocation was portrayed on *The Wire*.

"They said it depicted us as nothing but a bunch of thugs and dummies," said Benewicz.

While Benewicz noted that life on the docks is not as freewheeling as in the days of bulk cargo, it is also true that just before filming began, a few imported luxury sedans disappeared from the Dundalk marine terminal lot and were never seen again.

Similarly, another stevedore by the name of Champ, when asked by writers how a container might be made to disappear from the docks without leaving a paper trail, provided four different scenarios.

"Which," he added, "is not to say that we would do such a thing."

Benewicz reminded his ILA brethren that the HBO production "was bringing a lot of revenue [and union jobs] to the state of Maryland. And I reminded them that it was fiction."

Fiction except for the bedrock of the story: the slow, steady decline of a once-mighty port.

"It's always going to be a fight to keep work on the waterfront, a constant struggle," said Benewicz, who saw membership in the checkers' local shrink from 585 in the early 1990s to well under 200 by the time of his retirement.

"Baltimore's not a workingman's town anymore," said Benewicz. "You don't see stevedores 'shaping up' [waiting to be picked for work] on the corners in Locust Point like they used to.

"This was the port that built a city. You had so many working people. And it was Baltimore's work, things were made right here, but the work they did is gone.

"Look at what happened to [Bethlehem Steel at] Sparrows Point – they took away health plans from the poor guys who were retired. The people who are left over at GM on Broening Highway, they're depressed because it looks like it's just a matter of time there, too."

[Time caught up with the Broening Highway plant in May of 2005 when a white Safari van was the last to roll off the assembly line. Behind it, a gang of Sobotkas and Pakusas attached two small American flags and a cardboard sign that read: The End.]

On the *Wire* waterfront, just a mile or two from Baltimore's real GM plant, the writers focused on a collapsed CSX grain pier.

It was one of Frank Sobotka's many fevered dreams to have the grain pier up and working again before it could be developed into condominiums.

One of the final scenes of Season Two shows politicians and developers gathered at the site of a soon-to-be luxury high-rise known as The Grainery.

It was apt symbolism for a waterfront where mixed-use development had already conquered the Inner Harbor and was doing the same along the outer edges.

It was also make-believe.

Briefly.

Before filming ended for Season Two, local papers were announcing a proposed development for the idle CSX pier, one that would require the heavy industrial area to be rezoned.

For condos.

SEASON TWO EPISODE GUIDE

"On my docks this happened ..."
FRANK SOBOTKA

The first season of *The Wire* ended with drug lord Avon Barksdale going to prison; his lieutenant, Stringer Bell, moving the business from a strip club to a funeral parlor; Detective Kima Greggs recovering from a gunshot wound ...

And good money betting that Detective Jimmy McNulty's worst nightmare – a fate worse than being alone and sober on a Friday night – would come true.

That he would find his insolent ass riding the police boat. Naturally, Season Two opened with McNulty on harbor patrol in winter gear.

episode fourteen

EBB TIDE
"Ain't never gonna be what it was."
– LITTLE BIG ROY
Directed by Ed Bianchi
Story by David Simon & Ed Burns; teleplay by David Simon

In his debut as a law enforcement mariner, McNulty bitches about the cold weather as the police boat passes the rusting hulk of what is left of the Bethlehem Steel plant. He tells his partner, Officer Claude Diggins – played by real-life Baltimore marine police officer Jeffrey Fugitt, "My father used to work there . . . got laid off in '73."

Moments later, McNulty pockets a little cash from the host on a party boat in distress instead of dragging the yacht back to the dock.

The vessel, a yacht christened *Capitol Gains*, replete with black-tie partygoers from the salons of Washington, sparkles and sways long into the night as the rusting remnants of a working harbor stand idle witness.

At the same time, Detective Roland "Prez" Pryzbylewski is trying to tell his father-in-law – Major Stan Valchek of the Southeastern District – that the complexities of the Barksdale investigation made him feel like a real cop for the first time in his career.

"I wanna work cases," says Prez. "Good cases."

Valchek is only half-listening; he is entranced by pieces of a stained-glass window he has bought for the local Polish-Catholic church, an act of big-shotism masquerading as charity.

He finally tunes into Prez and shuts him up with a succinct plan of action: Do what you're told, in time you'll make lieutenant and have "a career in this department."

Bodie, looking like a man on his way up in the Barksdale organization, drives to Philly to pick up dope contracted through Dominicans in New York. The drugs, however, are not there.

Returning to Baltimore, Bodie is forced to go over every aspect of his trip in detail for Stringer Bell to make sure the fuck-up is not on his end.

Meanwhile, Bunk visits McNulty on the docks to ask for help in finding the stickup artist Omar, needed for the upcoming trial of Bird in the Gant murder.

And then, a first glimpse of the man at the center of the new investigation: Frank Sobotka, secretary-treasurer of the checkers' local of the International Brotherhood of Stevedores.

Sobotka is obsessed, to the point of blurring his own lines of conduct, with getting the C&D Canal dredged to get larger ships back into Baltimore. It's the only way, he argues, to save the beleaguered port and the union.

Sobotka greets his nephew Nick and tells him there is "one on the way" for The Greek. A moment later, Sobotka strides across the cargo terminal to deal with his son, Ziggy, who has lost a container of rush cargo, demonstrating that nepotism has its limits.

At police headquarters, Lieutenant Cedric Daniels is rewarded for pushing the previous investigation beyond what the brass wanted: he's buried in the basement evidence-control unit.

Visiting St Casimir Roman Catholic Church, Sobotka drops by with a generous donation to see the stained-glass window that he and the union have donated: a beautiful portrait of stevedores unloading a ship the old-fashioned way.

It is decidedly *not* the image of a noble police officer helping a child that Valchek had secured. Sobotka asks the priest's help in lobbying Maryland's veteran Senator – Barbara Mikulski, a Polish-Catholic – to support dredging the canal.

The priest obliges and asks when Sobotka last made confession.

Detective Kima Greggs is on desk duty in the property unit, having promised her girlfriend that she will stay off the street after being wounded. Herc calls her pussy-whipped and Greggs knows it's true.

That night, at a Locust Point gin mill called the Clement Street Bar, HQ for stevedore oldtimers, Ziggy makes fun of their fairy tales, ordering all hands starboard to prevent the bar from capsizing with its cargo of bullshit.

Finally, Ziggy climbs a stool and whips out his formidable cock, calling it bulk cargo that the graybeards could never have handled.

The next morning, McNulty finds the body of a woman floating in the harbor. He may not know the aft from the stern, but he is once again a "murder police."

When McNulty expresses skepticism that the dead woman jumped from the Francis Scott Key Bridge, The Greek's stray container is discovered by port police officer, Beatrice Russell.

It is stuffed with the bodies of an additional 13 women, all dead.

Season Two is launched.

episode
fifteen

COLLATERAL DAMAGE

"They can chew you up, but they gotta spit you out."
— MCNULTY

Directed by Ed Bianchi
Story by David Simon & Ed Burns; teleplay by David Simon

The show opens with Officer Beatrice "Beadie" Russell, a single mother working as a port police officer after bumping up from tunnel toll-taker, walking investigators through a warehouse of body bags: the women from the container.

No one from the various agencies present wants the case. The deaths are assumed accidental, that the stowaway women suffocated when the container's air pipe was accidentally crushed during the journey.

Russell gets the case by default.

At Little Johnny's on South Clinton Street, the waterfront diner that The Greek uses to conduct business, Frank Sobotka reads the riot act to The Greek's main lieutenant, Spiros "Vondas" Vondopoulos.

"I don't know what the fuck you people want and don't want. All I know is, I got a can full of young girls suffocating on my docks!"

Vondas: "*Now* you wanna know what's in the cans?"

Vondas explains that his driver did not take the can with the women off the dock because he never got the sign that no one was watching.

When that didn't happen, and Vondas doesn't know yet why, the driver was told to leave.

In prison, Avon Barksdale learns from his sister Brianna that their New York-based, Dominican drug connection was busted by the DEA. Which makes clear why the shipment that Bodie was supposed to mule down from Philadelphia was missing.

Until the Dominicans can be sure that their legal problems don't stem from Barksdale's earlier arrest – that Barksdale is not turning state's evidence – they will not do business.

Barksdale ponders where to go for product. At the same time, he's working to keep his nephew and fellow inmate, D'Angelo – who took a 20-year sentence for the family – within reach.

"D" has taken to getting high in prison and doesn't want anything to do with his uncle or his uncle's influence. Avon tells his sister to ensure that D'Angelo's girlfriend, Donette, brings their son to the lockup once a week to see D'Angelo and keep his spirits up.

On a nearby tier, heads are knocking between Wee-Bey – who copped to several life terms' worth of murders for the Barksdale crew – and a guard named Tilghman, kin to one of Wee-Bey's victims. Avon assures Wee-Bey that he will not have a problem with the guard for long.

Back at the homicide unit, McNulty and Bunk are washing down a sweet pile of steamed crabs with cold beer. Bunk congratulates McNulty on having dutifully checked time and tides to put the female floater inside the city line – and jurisdiction – at the time of her death.

That makes her the problem of city police Col. William Rawls, who already hates McNulty's guts for the Season One investigation.

Bunk reminds McNulty of the need to find Omar for the Gant case while McNulty notices a soiled headline in the traditional newspaper-as-tablecloth beneath the steamed crabs: 13 women found dead in a shipping container at the port.

McNulty puts 1 and 13 together and makes a trip to the warehouse where Beadie Russell is cataloging personal belongings found with the dead girls.

Examining the damage to the container's air pipe, McNulty quickly deduces that the suffocations were no accident. Soon, a medical examiner is telling Beadie: "You just bought yourself thirteen homicides."

Meanwhile, Sobotka's boys get a taste of Valchek's vengeance in the battle of the church windows: sheaves of parking tickets, soon to be followed by early-morning Driving While Intoxicated [DWI] checkpoints outside union watering holes.

The battle is on, especially once Valchek learns the International Brotherhood of Stevedores [IBS] has enough cash to hire a high-end lobbyist to work the state legislature on the dredging issue.

Calling in a favor from Deputy Commissioner Burrell, Valchek gets a detail to investigate Sobotka and the union.

Sobotka, in turn, has his people steal Valchek's expensive surveillance van from the parking lot of the Southeastern District. The stevedores roll the toy into a container and send it on an extended tour of seaports around the world.

And then an irony: thanks to McNulty's keen eye for police work and his desire to stick his nemesis Rawls with 14 unsolved murders, Bunk and his new partner in homicide, Lester Freamon, get stuck with the case.

The episode ends with an engineer (from the ship that carried the container with the smuggled women) bleeding to death.

Identified as the man who closed up the air pipe after having his way with one of them, the engineer's throat is cut by Vondas, who tells a subordinate to make sure that the corpse is dumped without hands or a face.

Vondas and The Greek calculate the loss of the women in money, but The Greek acknowledges that the loss can be made good.

There will be more women, The Greek assures his lieutenant.

episode sixteen

HOT SHOTS
"What they need is a union." – RUSSELL
Directed by Elodie Keene
Story by David Simon & Ed Burns; teleplay by David Simon

The episode opens on the streets of West Baltimore as Omar schools his new lover, Dante, in the art of the stickup.

They are watching money, hidden in a laundry basket, come and go from a drug house. Like clockwork – once in the morning, once at night – out comes a basket of clothes.

Watch and learn, says the old pro, when out of nowhere, a couple of girls hit the boys with the laundry basket first.

Omar is impressed, chuckling: "That something you don't see every day."

Bunk, still looking for Omar to testify in the Gant case, has bigger fish to fry: 13 stowaways, dead in a shipping container. He and Freamon head

to Philly to interview the crew of the freighter that carried the can. Beadie Russell tags along.

None of the sailors finds it convenient to speak English.

Back in Baltimore, Nicky Sobotka's girlfriend, Aimee – the mother of his young daughter – continues to nag him about living in a better place. Nick says there hasn't been enough work on the docks to make a move.

McNulty drops by the evidence unit to return a few things and encounters Daniels. They talk about the Barksdale case, how they did the best they could with what they had, and the shitty rewards for the effort.

Daniels tells McNulty he's leaving the force to make use of his law degree.

While the laundry basket stickup girls – Kimmy and Tosha – count their loot, they are surprised by Omar. He is there not to ambush, but recruit.

Informed that Bunk and Freamon let the *Atlantic Light* sail without doing much more than holding the gear of a crewmember who seemingly jumped ship, Sergeant Landsman is not happy: "Rawls is watchin' on this one . . . let's at least pretend we got a fucking clue."

Meanwhile, Barksdale boys Shamrock and Country follow prison guard Tilghman. When they discover where Tilghman buys heroin that he is selling inside the prison, Stringer Bell visits the supplier, a blind tavern owner named Butchie.

Noting that he speaks for Avon, Stringer prevails on the reluctant Butchie to set up Tilghman with a bad package of narcotics.

Stringer also reminds Donette of her obligation to visit her imprisoned baby's daddy regularly. And then he seduces her, perhaps out of genuine desire, perhaps to keep her close as a source of information about D'Angelo; most likely both.

[D'Angelo nearly became a state's witness once before, and he can easily tie Stringer Bell to murders should he choose to roll again.]

In prison, Avon visits D'Angelo and tells him to stop getting high, at least for a while.

"I'm askin' you, man, outta love . . ."

Shirking his marine unit duties, McNulty takes it upon himself to pursue the identity of the Jane Doe he found in the harbor.

He is determined to connect her to the 13 girls in the can. Breast implants in the dead women connect them to Budapest. Doc Frazier, the medical examiner, is also able to determine that all of the girls in the can had had intercourse within 14 hours of their deaths. The floater, however, turned up negative for semen.

On the docks, the cousins Ziggy and Nick, frustrated by the lack of work for guys like them with low seniority, decide to boost a container of digital cameras and fence them to a lieutenant of The Greek's.

At a dinner for his wedding anniversary, Valchek asks son-in-law Prez how his detail to find dirt on Sobotka is going. It's lame, answers Prez, nothing but deadwood on the case.

Again, Prez says that if the brass had let the Barksdale case go forward, they would have traced big money to many places.

Valchek is listening this time, then blackmails Deputy Commissioner Burrell, who is seeking to be named acting commissioner of the department. The ultimatum: assign a real team of detectives to look into the dockworkers' union or I make a stink about how the Barksdale probe was handled. Burrell agrees.

Back at prison, Tilghman delivers his package of hot shots and inmates begin to die of overdoses. But not D'Angelo Barksdale, forewarned by his doting uncle.

episode
seventeen

HARD CASES
"If I hear the music, I'm gonna dance." — GREGGS
Directed by Elodie Keene
Story by David Simon & Joy Lusco Kecken; teleplay by Joy Lusco Kecken

Frank Sobotka makes nephew Nick meet him early one morning along a stretch of the Patapsco River and reprimands him for stealing the digital cameras. He wants the cameras returned, arguing that work is so hard to come by these days in Baltimore that they can't risk losing more through stupidity.

Too late, says Nick, already fenced. When Nick says that being honest ain't helping him make ends meet – "I'm on my ass, Uncle Frank" – he makes reference to the off-the-books cash Sobotka always has at hand, pissing off the older man.

"You think it's for me?" bellows Sobotka. Cooling down, he tells Nick not to flash the hot money around the docks.

At the prison, there's a media circus and administrative clusterfuck over the strychnine-laced dope that got inside and killed five inmates.

D'Angelo Barksdale is ungrateful. Could have been me the other night, D'Angelo tells his uncle, except that just before the bad dope started going around, it was "Avon to the rescue."

We need to use what happened to our advantage, Avon tells him. But D'Angelo won't budge from his newfound moral center: he wants to know if Avon had the poisoned dope brought in.

"We got it all covered," says Avon.

"Leave me the fuck outta that," says D.

Soon, Barksdale house counsel Maurice Levy is trading horses with prison officials, telling them his client, Mr. Barksdale, is willing to provide information on the bad dope in exchange for having some years shaved off his incarceration as Bell sets up Tilghman for the fall.

At police HQ, McNulty sweeps into the homicide unit like the prodigal son. He's hot to identify his Jane Doe floater, while Bunk reminds him yet again that they need Omar to put Bird away for the Gant murder.

In the bag, lies McNulty, who is soon on the street, desperately pulling loose threads to find the man.

Though Valchek asked for him by name to run his union investigation, Daniels tells Burrell that he's turned in his resignation papers and will sit for the bar in a month.

Burrell says he's willing to clean the slate and start fresh, promising Daniels a major's position and an independent investigative unit if he accepts the new detail and placates Valchek.

Daniels agrees, as long as he can pick his own people for the detail. Fine, says Burrell, subject to Rawls's approval.

On the docks, Ziggy can't help flashing all kinds of money from the camera heist while being resented by his co-workers.

Nick brings his cash home to his girlfriend, Aimee. Lying about having come into some back pay, he talks about moving out of his parents' rowhouse basement.

[Soon they will find out that the traditional South Baltimore rowhouses are now high-priced townhomes.]

Stuck with all the unsolved Jane Doe murders, Bunk and Freamon, accompanied by Russell, learn as much as they can about the movement of containers through the port, bemoaning that Russell has no helpful informants.

Rawls tells Daniels he can have everyone he's asked for to work the Valchek detail – a pissing match between two Polacks that Rawls sees as a waste of time.

Herc, no problem; Prez, fine. Carver and Greggs and Freamon, sure thing.

Everyone except McNulty.

"He quits or he drowns," says Rawls. "That's the only two things getting him off the fuckin' boat, so help me God."

Across town, Stringer Bell is left to run a drug ring that can't get good product and so begins diluting dope that's already weak.

The Greek's people want to talk to Nick and Ziggy about stealing tons of legal and uncontrolled chemicals, which are used for thinner if you're a housepainter, and cocaine processing if you're a drug trafficker.

McNulty decides to play nice guy with his wife, Elena, signing the separation papers her attorney drew up as a way of getting back into her good graces and, hopefully, the house and bedroom.

And he uses Bubbles to locate the elusive Omar in time for Bird's trial date.

At HQ, Detective Greggs, killing time at her desk in the property forfeiture unit, is visited by Daniels, who asks if she wants in on the new detail.

Both of them are having trouble at home with spouses who want them out of police work. Greggs: "I'll tell your wife if you tell mine."

Bunk, Freamon, and Russell visit the Clement Street Bar, pressing Frank Sobotka and letting him know that the girls in the can were murdered. Sobotka, suddenly nauseous, excuses himself and retreats into the bathroom, where he leans over the sink and looks to his right.

There, a print of a famous Aubrey Bodine photograph from the pages of the *Baltimore Sun* in its glory days stares back at him.

Stevedores – black, white and plentiful – work a crowded Baltimore pier in the first half of the last century. Steeled again to fight for the greater good, Sobotka walks out.

episode
eighteen

UNDERTOW
"They used to make steel there, no?" — SPIROS VONDAS
Directed by Steve Shill
Story by David Simon & Ed Burns; teleplay by Ed Burns

Ziggy, playing drug dealer in his organically incompetent way, gets burned on a package by a white corner boy named Frog. Before Zig makes it to the end of the block, he's stopped by a hard-ass dealer named Cheese and his crew of thugs, who drag him out of his car.

Cheese has fronted Ziggy the package of dope lost to Frog and he is unsympathetic to excuses, of which Ziggy has many. Cheese takes Ziggy's car and what cash the stevedore has on him, threatening to kill him if the debt is not repaid by the end of the week.

Downtown, Lieutenant Daniels tells newly minted sergeant Ellis Carver that he wants him on the detail investigating possible corruption on the waterfront.

"Why me?" asks Carver, who was Burrell's snitch in the detail from the year before.

Daniels explains that having caught Carver once, he expects it will be a long time before he is disloyal again. Carver gives his word and Daniels tells him that his stripes carry no weight in the detail and he will report to Greggs.

With his team assembled – Herc, Carver, Greggs, and Prez – Daniels orders a review of the International Brotherhood of Stevedores' union finances and approves undercover drug buys in areas where dockworkers are likely to cop dope.

When Freamon walks into the detail – another shithole of an office, but at least above ground – he looks at the photo of the target on the wall and says: "Frank Sobotka."

The detective has already met Sobotka through the stalled investigation into the dead stowaways.

In a prison visitors' room, Donette brings D'Angelo's son to him. She tries to warm D'Angelo to Avon's attempts to help and return him to the fold. He is unmoved.

"When they got no more use for you, that family shit disappears," he says. "It's just about business."

Back at the Pit, where D'Angelo once did family business, the Barksdale dope is so weak that junkies are walking blocks out of their way for something better.

Banged and bruised, Ziggy tells his cousin Nick that black dealers on the Eastside beat him and took his car, and Nick, knowing Ziggy, tells him it must be his own fault.

Ziggy explains that he needs $2,700 by Friday or he's dead, and Nick, who gave his cash to his girl for an apartment, cannot help him.

On the docks, Bunk shows up to serve grand jury warrants to Horseface, Johnny 50 and other stevedores who worked the *Atlantic Light*.

Livid, Sobotka tells Bunk to take his best shot and equates the Baltimore cop with past generations of notable union busters. Under oath before the grand jury, the dock boys don't know nothing. And without info from the inside, Bunk tells Beadie, all they've got is nothing.

On a street in the southeast part of town, where white boys work drug packages for the locals, Herc buys dope from Frog and his crew.

Not far away, at Little Johnny's diner, Nicky Sobotka tells Vondas about the grand jury subpoenas and that his Uncle Frank wants to stop doing business for a while.

Also, he says, Frank wants a meeting with The Greek.

Frustrated by her ineffectiveness, Beadie Russell pays a visit to Maui, a stevedore she once dated, using him to gain information that might help the murder investigation.

Flattered (with nothing to show for it afterward) Maui points her in the right direction: the port computers.

Later, in the shipping tower at the marine terminal, a compliant Sobotka gives Bunk and Russell a walk-through of how cargo is moved and how easily it can get lost with the best of intentions.

"They're playing us," says Bunk when the lesson is over, and together with Russell, they argue to Daniels and Landsman that the only hope for the murder probe is to clone the port administration's computers and begin collecting data.

Eventually, they will monitor the on- and off-loading of ships in real time.

Desperate to help Ziggy, Nick and a black longshoreman named La-La pay a visit to Cheese, trying to buy Ziggy some time and get back his car, which they say will be sold to pay off the debt.

Nice offer, says Cheese, directing Nick's attention around the corner, where the vehicle is already aflame, the camera holding for a moment on the rear license plate holder as it melts: "Happiness is Being Ziggy."

At the prison, Stringer tells Avon Barksdale that each package they're getting from Atlanta – the substitute connection now that the Dominicans have cut them off – is weaker than the last. Yet other dealers in town have excellent product.

Trying to placate Sobotka, The Greek sends word that he will double the fee for the smuggling of containers but refuses to meet with him. Sobotka says he's out.

By episode's end, The Greek has tripled the fee for hot containers and Sobotka agrees, rationalizing that he's got no choice if the waterfront is to be saved.

ZIGGY SOBOTKA: ANGRY PRINCE OF GOOFS

"There's an innate frustration in Baltimore with just trying to get by. People will try anything."
- JAMES "P. J." RANSONE, LOCAL BOY

Growing up in one of Baltimore's tonier villages north of the city – an area of colonial-era quarries and horse farms called Phoenix – P.J. Ransone was never quite sure where he fit in.

He was too creative not to be bored hanging out and drinking with the kids "doing donuts" on the school parking lot.

And a little too rough and crude for the "show-tune lunatics" who took classes with him at the Carver School for the Arts in suburban Towson.

"I was the white-trash kid at art school," said Ransone, who turned 30 on June 2, 2009. "Just because you grew up with a little more money than some people doesn't mean you were any more highbrow than what people think of as white trash."

Ransone says he drew on that conflict – neither this and not quite that, yet wanting to be accepted anyway – to find the soul of the waterfront jester Ziggy Sobotka.

"Ziggy wasn't as stupid as people wanted to make him out to be. He didn't just want to be in a gang. There was a lot more to it than that," he said.

"To me it was about how hard it is to live in Baltimore. It's a town of incredibly talented and eccentric people who wind up doing nothing."

Born James Finley Ransone III, the grandson of a man who owned a string of liquor stores, "P.J." grew up along Dulaney Valley Road, far enough away from downtown that he felt like a tourist on grade-school trips to the National Aquarium at Baltimore's Inner Harbor downtown.

In elementary school, he took part in plays and won roles in theater projects at Towson State University. During this time he auditioned a part in Barry Levinon's 1990 Baltimore immigrant story *Avalon*, a role given to a young Elijah Wood.

While at Cockeysville Middle School, his mother, Joyce Ransone, heard that the county was opening a magnet school for the arts and took him for an audition.

"I knew he didn't fit in with the jocks and the preps," said Mrs. Ransone.

On his own or with friends, the teenaged P.J. would head down Interstate-83 into Baltimore City and notice the stuff that wasn't in Phoenix or on exhibit at the Inner Harbor.

Baltimore is "a bizarre, conflicted place – a racist Southern town stuck in the Northeast," said Ransone. "Just look at the incredible shit they put on the benches. The whole time I was growing up, it was 'The City That Reads,' and now it says 'The Greatest City in America.'

"Are they kidding? It ought to say 'The Most Insane City in the Universe.'"

How insane?

"Once," he said, "my friend saw two humongous black lesbians dressed up in baseball uniforms beat the fuck out of a homeless guy with their bats."

Combined with that white trash business is an acknowledgement that his father was the model for some of Ziggy's less appealing social attitudes.

"P.J.'s father grew up in a working-class family and had quite a reputation for being wild," said Mrs. Ransone, an assistant to the president of a financial company. "And his dad has more of the Baltimore accent."

Ah, the Bawlmer accent, the song of sirens who pronounce all of their *o*'s as though they'd just seen a dog run down in the street.

"Oh, no!"

A singular mixture of Tidewater drawl, Appalachian twang, immigrant pidgin, and leftover Cockney, the tone and cadence of the Baltimore accent is typically a white, ethnic parlance that long ago followed many of its practitioners to the suburbs.

It has only one sibling that resembles it: South Philadelphia.

And while the degree of a resident's Bawlmerese varies according to education and social status, there are surprising anomalies. Funniest of all, says Ransone, are those people – unaware that their own tongues are lathered with it – who ridicule others for "talkin' 'at way."

Al Brown, who played Major Stan Valchek, a careerist who angles his way to acting police commissioner by series end, is a Philly native and comes by the accent honestly, especially when barking things like "If you don't want my finger in your eye . . ." or calling a roomful of cops and prosecutors "ratfuckers."

But the accent hangs badly on New Yorkers who think they can find the way in through Brooklyn or Jersey. Folks from the South or the Midwest have to be gifted mimics to nail it, although Brits seem to do fine.

But it was programmed into P.J. at birth. All he had to do when the director called "Action" was let go.

"It really comes out," he said, "when I get angry."

Throughout the second season of *The Wire* – when people were tossing Ziggy atop shipping containers, setting his car on fire, or laughing themselves sick when his diamond-studded pet duck drank itself to death – there was much for the Prince of Goofs to be angry about.

•

After graduating from Carver in 1997, Ransone landed in New York, where he enrolled in film school. He dropped out, explained his mother

– as only a mother can – because "he didn't apply himself."

Drag queens gave him a tour of Manhattan; he managed to land an agent, got a few commercials, and then a handful of television and independent film roles. He has been known to play bass in metal bands.

In his role as Ziggy, a doomed son of a son of a stevedore, raised for a world that is slowly dying out, Ransone says he was pushed to some of his best work as an actor by Chris Bauer – who played his father, the union boss Frank Sobotka.

"To me the most brilliant moment [of Season Two] was when Frank goes to see Ziggy in prison and sees his son through the glass," said Bauer.

"Zig is in a tank of sharks and all he is is food. Frank Sobotka's legacy is not dredging the harbor for more work, it's sitting right there in prison."

The scene was the hardest for Joyce Ransone to watch or forget.

"The night Ziggy shot the Greek guy and the young boy, I had one of those nights where I couldn't sleep," she said.

Did Ziggy survive lock-up?

"Probably," said P.J.

Less difficult, said Mrs. Ransone, was one of the first scenes of the season when Ziggy jumps atop a saloon table and exposes himself. For this, she said, P.J. had gone to some effort to prepare her.

"He said, 'Mom, you're not going to believe this, but HBO has designed a prosthetic penis for me and I have to whip this thing out,'" Mrs. Ransone recalled.

"I give these young actors a lot of credit. It takes a lot of bravery to play a part like that."

Bravery, perhaps, is not the right word.

"*The Wire* tested every ability I have as an actor," said Ransone. "You couldn't be on that show and be one-dimensional.

"I went in with the Johnny Depp approach: just show up and lie your ass off. With Chris, I was able to bleed into a universe where you cut away everyone around you except the person in the scene you're talking to."

•

As the second season of *The Wire* was wrapping up, Ransone got a part in *A Dirty Shame*, the 2004 film by fellow Baltimorean John Waters. He played a dirt worshiper named Dingy Dave.

"He's really into dirt," says Ransone, who became friends with the director during the shoot and now considers him a confidant.

From there, he went on to play US Marine Corporal Josh Ray Person in David Simon's HBO miniseries *Generation Kill*, a young warrior with the wit of Ziggy Sobotka and the balls of Omar Little.

Intimates have suggested to Ransone that the divide between Ziggy and Person was negligible, but he doesn't buy it, noting that while he embraced the "lovable fuck-up" in his youth, the P.J. who played Ray Person had moved on from there.

Asked how a place as burdened as Baltimore could remain charming, Ransone once quipped, "Look at me. I'm broke and I'm still charming."

And then allowed how, given all he believes to be true about a place romanticized in 1960s beer commercials as "The Land of Pleasant Living," he expects to come home for good one day.

"I still dream of buying a house there, in a really nice neighborhood near Loch Raven," he said. "I'll probably die in Baltimore, but I can't tell you why. Maybe because, as dysfunctional as everybody is down there, it's still a family town."

episode
nineteen

ALL PROLOGUE
"It don't matter that some fool say he
different . . ." – D'ANGELO

Directed by Steve Shill
Story by David Simon & Ed Burns; teleplay by David Simon

Omar the Terror is ready to take the stage in a Baltimore City courtroom
to testify against Marquis "Bird" Hilton for last season's murder of the
maintenance man Gant. He tells the court that his occupation for the last
eight years or so has been robbing drug dealers.

And thus he is comfortable with the world of people like Bird, whom
Omar knows from both prison and the streets. From the stand, he identifies
Bird as the triggerman as well as putting the murder weapon on him.

At the detail, early reports on Frank Sobotka peg him as a workingman with a modest house outside the city, a paid-off truck, and a little bit of savings. Nothing dramatic. The union – with fewer than a hundred dues-paying members – is somewhat threadbare, according to available records.

All of which makes the hiring of high-roller lobbyist Bruce DiBiago, and the payment of some $70,000 to various political organizations in past months, more than a little suspicious.

Russell, Freamon, and Bunk show Daniels a computer graphic of how ships are worked by the longshoremen, specifically the *Atlantic Light* on the day the can with the women was off-loaded.

The container with the dead girls was not immediately entered into the computer, only to be logged some four hours later. All cans they are able to identify as being logged in this fashion come from the same shipping line – Talco – and one checker is always on the job: Thomas "Horseface" Pakusa.

At Little Johnny's, Vondas introduces Nick to an Israeli named Eton to discuss delivery of the chemicals. Nick can get as much as they want. There's just one thing holding up the delivery: Ziggy's in trouble with an Eastside dope dealer named Cheese.

Vondas agrees to intercede on Ziggy's behalf. The intercession is successful, notably because Cheese works for Eastside drug kingpin Proposition Joe, whose product is supplied by The Greek's organization.

Later, when Vondas offers to pay Nick for the stolen chemicals in heroin instead of money, Ziggy urges him to take the dope to turn a better profit. Nick takes half in cash, half in heroin, telling his cousin that this time, he'll handle the dope.

McNulty has given up trying to identify his Jane Doe floater and gives Doc Frazier the okay to ship her body to the anatomy board for use by medical students. He tells Bunk that he is done waging war with the department and turns his attention to what remains of his marriage.

He cajoles Elena into accepting a date and at dinner claims to be effectively retired from the ways of the old Jimmy. The leopard, he declares, has changed his spots. When McNulty asks his wife for another chance, Elena dryly offers him, instead, a "fuck for the road."

Cut to: great sex.

Cut to: the morning after, when McNulty, ready to move back home, is reminded that it was just sex. And please leave before the boys come home today.

Stringer reaches out to a Washington connection for an important job, something he can't do with Baltimore labor. About which the DC boy surmises, "If Stringer Bell reachin' all the way past Baltimore with this kind of work, then we got a real mystery going on."

Greggs visits the stripper Shardene, now retired from the pole, living happily with Lester Freamon and going to nursing school. The detective wants info on immigrant girls, mostly Eastern Europeans, working the club circuit.

Shardene tells her to try a joint off of Holabird Avenue near the docks and ask for a friend of hers. Greggs and Prez pursue that angle and attempt to follow the trail of sex workers that snakes through Baltimore strip clubs and bordellos.

At a union meeting, Sobotka gives his men an update on the effort to lobby the General Assembly for a new grain pier and dredging of the main shipping channel, if not the canal.

A stevedore asks where the money is coming from to do it all. Help from the national office, says Sobotka, and some friends coming through in a pinch.

After the meeting, fellow labor official Nat Coxson calls Sobotka on his lies about the money and cautions, "Watch your ass, Frank."

At the Clement Street Bar, Ziggy gets $2,400 from Nick for the burned Camaro, and buys the bar a round while lighting a cigarette with a $100 bill.

Frank Sobotka waits outside the bar for Ziggy to leave and drags the wayward kid down memory lane along the rotting grain pier. When Frank begins to suggest that he made mistakes as a father, Ziggy gently tells him not to go there and then brings up all the good things he remembers about growing up in a waterfront family.

"What else do you remember?" asks Sobotka.

"Everything," says Ziggy.

In prison, D'Angelo dumps the rest of his dope down the toilet, tells his mother to tell Avon, Stringer, and Donette to leave him alone and participates in a discussion of The Great Gatsby in a book group.

From his take on Fitzgerald, it is clear that D'Angelo sees his own tragedy clearly.

"It don't matter that some fool say he different 'cause the only thing that make you different is what you really do or what you really go through. . . . [Gatsby] got all them books and he ain't read near one of 'em. . . . He was who he was and he did what he did . . . [and] that shit caught up to him."

At episode's end, D'Angelo is jumped by a fellow inmate and hanged with a belt hooked around a library doorknob.

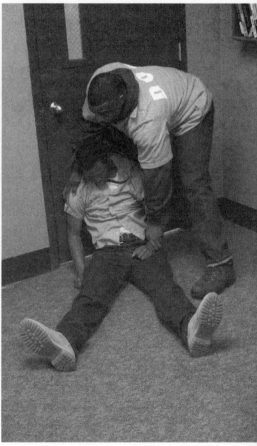

INEVITABLE FATES:
D'ANGELO, WALLACE, AND DUKIE

"The Wire was an epiphany to me ... I was so unaware of the real-life Dukies ..."
— JERMAINE CRAWFORD, ACTOR

Wallace got it in Season One: shot dead by his homeboys Bodie and Poot, as disbelieving of the betrayal as he was afraid. His plea is simple, as though a shared childhood counted for something. "This is me, yo ..."

D'Angelo went down in Season Two, choked to death by a fellow inmate in a murder secretly contracted by his uncle's most trusted lieutenant, Stringer Bell.

And Dukie?

Man, I just seen that dusty bitch the other day, headed down the alley with the dope fiends.

"Broke my heart," said Sean Lindsay, an elementary school teacher in Long Beach, California, who has used *The Wire* in his graduate studies in education.

Broke Jermaine Crawford's heart too.

"If you're not 'muscle' or 'street' you get the short end of the stick," said Crawford, who played the impoverished middle school student Duquan "Dukie" Weems. "There's nowhere to go."

Unlike Wallace, no final plea was afforded D'Angelo, who is killed as he begins to assert his dignity separate from the "corporation" of his uncle's drug empire.

Stringer Bell makes sure that doesn't happen. Just keeping the boy "close" wasn't close enough anymore.

While Bell and Barksdale house counsel Maurice Levy try to keep D'Angelo in bounds after his drug arrest on the New Jersey Turnpike, D doesn't play ball. All he wants to know is what happened to the naïve younger boy he tried to protect as best he could.

"Where Wallace?"

No answer.

This time with contempt: "Where Wallace?"

D'Angelo is assaulted in the prison library, a belt tightened around his neck and made to look as though he'd hanged himself from a doorknob.

His last words came in a soliloquy delivered a few moments earlier while discussing *The Great Gatsby* in a prison literature class taught by Richard Price, the novelist and screenwriter making a cameo.

Fitzgerald, said D'Angelo, "is saying that the past is always with us. Where we come from, what we go through, how we go through it, all of this shit matters.

". . . you can say you somebody new, you can give yourself a whole new story, but what came first is who you really are. It don't matter that some fool say he different 'cause the only thing that make you different is what you really do . . ."

Solid insight, enough for a B or better at any high school in the country. In D'Angelo's universe, it earned an F for foreboding.

•

The core audience of *The Wire* – a cult within a cult – is made up of gangsters and cops, both real and wannabes; egghead intellectuals, and – in the wake of all five seasons being released on DVD – virtually every hipster in the United Kingdom where *Wire*-mania picked up speed in 2008 and was in full swing in 2009 with midnight broadcasts on the BBC.

"The most operatic TV I've ever seen . . . so much of it was heart-wrenching. The death of Wallace was tragic, but beautifully wrought," said Anna Hall, a 40-year-old writer from Yorkshire, UK, living in New York City.

Like the copy of *Gravity's Rainbow* or *Ulysses* kept by the bed in hopes that one day the portal to their riches will reveal itself, *The Wire* did not easily open for Hall.

"I tried three times to watch the first episode and couldn't get into it," said Hall. "But so many people I trust told me it was great that I persevered. Once my husband and I were hooked, we were watching three episodes a night."

While making references in online posts to *Hamlet* and Dickens, fans chatting online have fun with their favorite characters while holding their breath that their darlings won't be gunned down each time a shadow emerges from a dark street.

They are the "Wireheads", who have carried on since the show left the air and been joined by those who found the show online, in reruns and through DVDS.

Though a "Wirehead" Internet search also leads to instructions on converting your petrol burner to an electric car, female fans of Idris Elba (and more than a few men) are known as "Stringabellas".

The followers of Omar were known as "Cheeseheads" before Method Man took the role of Prop Joe's nephew "Cheese" – and there's one guy who signs all his posts, "In the Bunk We Trust."

David Simon has said that the undercurrent of humor in *The Wire* – the ironic observations of Sergeant Jay Landsman, Herc and Carver's shenanigans, the slapstick of Ziggy Sobotka and the perfect timing of a Bunk comeback – made "the horror bearable."

But not easier to stomach the slaughter of Wallace and D'Angelo.

"I was absolutely shocked when they killed D'Angelo, did not see it coming," said Hall. "I thought he'd become the new [drug] kingpin."

Larry Gilliard Jr., the Baltimore-born actor who played D'Angelo can sympathize, saying he "felt bad" for the audience when his storyline met an abrupt end.

Gilliard grew up in public housing, graduating from the Baltimore School for the Arts in 1985.

"I knew a lot of guys growing up who got in the game and got out, and I was really hoping that D'Angelo would be one of the ones who did," said Gilliard. "People connect to characters with a lot of heart, they attach themselves to a character who might possibly find a way out.

"Unfortunately, we don't have many stories like that."

The actor, who had a small part in Martin Scorsese's *Gangs of New York*, and played "Ray" on the 2009 Patrick Swayze series *The Beast*, said he tried to layer the character of D'Angelo.

He had ". . . more dimensions than just a scared punk selling drugs . . . I was hoping for a better ending for him because of it."

The truth about Wallace was shown early in Season One when he is found playing with an action toy instead of paying attention as a corner lookout, prompting Bodie to toss a bottle at him.

And his enthusiasm for things beyond the gangster life is affirmed when D'Angelo chastises him and Bodie for playing checkers with chess pieces. Hard-ass Bodie doesn't give a shit.

But Wallace wants to learn and D'Angelo is happy to teach.

As in Season Four, when Michael tries to teach his hapless friend Dukie how to survive. They go for shooting lessons and Michael gives him a small-time job on the corner, but Dukie, who'd have made a great science nerd in any halfway supportive environment, couldn't hang.

Soon, Michael was paying him just to babysit his little brother.

D'Angelo and Michael both tried to protect their weaker friends. Wallace was doubly haunted: by the tortured corpse of Omar's lover displayed atop a burned-out car for all the world to see and the profit he made by spotting the boy in a video arcade.

"The demise of a scared little boy who escaped by using the drugs he was selling," said Marlene Allen, a Los Angeles social worker and fan of the show.

In her many years of trying to help whoever might be helped (actually saving them is another, sadder story), Allen found that most kids like those on the streets of *The Wire* end up "in jail or dead . . . . D'Angelo ended in both places."

The deaths of D and Wallace, said Drew Johnson, an Annapolis native living in North Carolina, was punishment for "the characters each exhibiting some amount of humanity."

Jermaine Crawford used the exposure afforded him by *The Wire* to lend humanity to homeless teenagers living in conditions both similar to and worse than Dukie's.

His project is a documentary called *Teenager Homelessness in America: A Change is Gonna Come.* Crawford directs and is the on-screen narrator as the film follows five homeless young people in cities across the United States.

"It was hard for me to separate from Dukie, hard to leave him behind when I walked off set," said Crawford, born in 1992, raised in the Washington suburb of Mitchellville and home-schooled by his parents.

"It was rough playing Dukie, he was very intelligent but weak. He smelled bad. Michael took care of him, but he wasn't respected," said Crawford. "As [Season Four] unraveled there was the realization that he was far more complicated than I thought."

The child of addicts who sell everything their son acquires for booze or dope, Dukie may even have been unknowable even to himself.

Accepted wisdom in the field of recovery is the notion that the emotional maturity of an addict stops upon taking their first drink or hit of dope. If that person is like Dukie – not only young but emotionally immature for their age – the problem is near hopeless.

Fran Boyd, a recovering addict who worked with *The Wire* sound editors throughout the show's run, knew Dukie was headed down Bubbles Boulevard when the kid started borrowing money from his math teacher, Prez.

"Oh my goodness, that hurt me so bad," said Boyd. "But that's how it happens."

episode
twenty

BACKWASH
"Don't worry, kid. You're still on the clock."
— HORSEFACE

Directed by Thomas J. Wright

Story by David Simon & Rafael Alvarez; teleplay by Rafael Alvarez

The episode opens with Bodie going to buy flowers for D'Angelo's funeral. He settles on an arrangement made up to look like the high-rise project tower once under D's control.

Bunk and Beadie Russell tell Sergeant Landsman that they've cloned a port computer, which they've been using at Daniels's off-site location, trying to connect dirt on the docks to the dead girls in the container.

Landsman blows a gasket: Rawls ain't playing and you two better not be either.

But they are in earnest. Lester Freamon is getting good at watching the ships load and unload on the cloned computer and can tell when the checkers are losing a can on purpose.

Bunk tells Russell that the next move is to have the dock boys persuaded that the investigation has dried up. Back in uniform, Russell cruises the docks in her patrol car just like the good old days, telling Sobotka she is off the investigation.

Daniels tries to explain to Rawls why Bunk is ensconced in the detail office on a murder investigation, and Rawls, seizing the opportunity, pushes Daniels to take responsibility for clearing all the Jane Doe cases. Daniels balks.

Later, at home with his wife, Marla, Daniels tries to convince her that he's been keeping the detail narrow and focused. He won't taint his work with a bunch of unsolved murders, telling Marla that he's back on a career track.

Mrs. Daniels doesn't buy it and walks away disgusted.

Nick begins moving the dope he got from The Greek through the corner boy, Frog. When an elderly resident looks at him from inside her screen door, Nicky is suddenly made aware that he is no longer a longshoreman, but a drug dealer.

His conscience is comforted when he's able to go home and tell Aimee to start looking for a two-bedroom apartment, that things have taken an upswing on the docks and he's making some money on the side working as a foreman at a warehouse.

Yet right outside their door, Herc and Carver, having followed Nicky home from Frog's corner, are checking his truck tag, noting that his last name is the same name as the detail's target: Sobotka.

At prison, Wee-Bey tries to make a devastated Avon Barksdale feel less guilt over his nephew's apparent suicide while Bell pays a D.C. gangster for the hit on D.

Stringer then arrives at the wake to console Brianna, holed up with her grief in the bedroom. Next day at the graveside, Proposition Joe tells Stringer he can provide good dope, straight off the boat.

You got the real estate, Joe reasons, I got the product.

Stringer brings the proposition to Avon on his next prison visit, asking just enough questions to assure himself that Barksdale believes D'Angelo's death a suicide.

As for Prop Joe's offer, Avon flatly refuses. We'll get through on our own, he says.

At the port, Sobotka glimpses the future of the waterfront during a presentation of how the state-of-the-art Rotterdam port handles cargo using robotics. The writing on the wall is clear and ominous.

Technology also allows Freamon to ascertain that Horseface will soon be working a Talco ship called the *Esmeralda*.

The detail sets up surveillance to follow whatever container might go missing. One soon does and is followed from the docks to an industrial area warehouse in Southeast Baltimore: Pyramid Incorporated on Newkirk Street.

Whereupon the detail goes to Assistant State's Attorney Rhonda Pearlman – McNulty's booty buddy from Season One – to okay a wiretap.

They show that every time Sobotka calls Horseface Pakusa from his cell phone, Pakusa is working a Talco ship the next day. They argue for conspiracy, suggesting that the hot containers may contain more stowaway women.

Pearlman says they've got to do better than that, as prostitution doesn't meet the standards for a wire under the law.

Freamon goes to Daniels and works his conscience about the women who died in the shipping container: "This case needs to be worked."

The episode moves toward a close with an all-too-familiar alarm going off at the Clement Street Bar: stevedore down, berth five. It's New Charles with a crushed leg.

And it ends with Daniels finally telling Rawls he'll take the open murders. "But what I need from you I get," Daniels says. "No bullshit, no arguments."

episode
twenty-one

DUCK AND COVER
"How come they don't fly away?" – ZIGGY
Directed by Daniel Attias
Story by David Simon & George Pelecanos; teleplay by George Pelecanos

Daniels lets the detail know that he is now officially on the hook with Rawls for solving the Jane Doe plus 13.

Freamon tells prosecutor Pearlman they've now got the drug connection needed for a wiretap: the phone at the warehouse where the hot container was trucked has been used to call at least three known dealers, including Proposition Joe Stewart. Convinced, Pearlman goes to a judge for authorization.

McNulty calls Elena drunk from a bar payphone – please, baby; please, baby – but gets the answering machine. He responds by wrecking his car – twice.

With his hand still bleeding, he picks up a waitress from an all-night diner, later confessing to Bunk that if Elena won't take him back, ain't nothing worth living for but police work.

Bunk and Freamon plead McNulty's case to Daniels, who goes to bat for him with Rawls, reminding the colonel that he took the open murders with a promise that he would get whatever he needed. Rawls reluctantly agrees.

On the docks, Horseface and the boys egg on Ziggy to take his best shot at Maui, the much larger longshoreman who'd played a practical joke on Sobotka the Younger by sending him fake paternity papers.

"His ass is candy," Horse assures him. "You? You're a legend, a legend of the docks."

Ziggy ends up atop a container stack – "You motherfuckers gave me bad advice!" he screams at his baiters.

Down from the mountain of stacked containers, Ziggy goes to see Mr. Diz, an old man in the neighborhood who raced pigeons with his grandfather in the old days.

He buys a live duck and asks the old man why they don't fly away. Because, says Diz, their wings are clipped.

Nick now rolls in a new truck. He hands Ziggy his share of the dope profits but Ziggy, still bitter about being marginalized, responds by throwing the fat wad of cash out the window.

Soon, he's drinking down at Clement Street with his pet duck, for whom he has bought a diamond choker necklace. Every time Zig orders a round, the bird gets one, too.

Monitoring calls to and from the warehouse and the cell phone of one of The Greek's men – Serge Malatov – Prez notes that this crew isn't "as careful as Barksdale's people were."

"This ain't West Baltimore," says Greggs. "They're on their phones because they don't expect us to be on 'em."

There are slip-ups on the police side of things as well; the next time Frank Sobotka goes to pay his overdue cell phone bill, he finds that his account has been flagged: do not disconnect for nonpayment.

Prosecutor Rhonda Pearlman and the detectives make plans to raid the brothel discovered by Greggs and Prez. Newly arrived in the detail, McNulty is tapped for a role he was born to play: It Takes A Whore to Catch a Whore.

In the projects, Barksdale's business is "slower than a white man in slippers," but across the street, where independent dealers have set up shop, business is booming.

By now, Sobotka is good and spooked: first by the flag on his cell phone and again when he learns that Beadie Russell lied about being taken off the homicide investigation.

On a day when The Greek has two cans to be smuggled off the docks, Sobotka tells Horseface to process one of the dirty cans as legit cargo and hide it in the stacks.

He then "smuggles" a clean can off the cargo terminal to see if the police follow it. They do, and Sobotka calls Spiros Vondas with his fears, demanding a meeting with The Greek.

Serge delivers the can to an appliance store only to find it is not filled with Russian vodka but curtain rods, baby dolls, and dollar-store crap. The angry phone call that results is clocked by the detail's wiretap.

Sobotka and Nick meet The Greek at Johnny's diner, and Nick realizes that the real chief is the old man who was at the diner counter during so many other meetings with Vondas.

The Greek tells Sobotka to lose more clean cans and deliver them to the warehouse, to see if the cops are really onto them, and if so, that they've got nothing to hide.

When Nick says they need to be paid no matter what they're moving off the docks, The Greek balks. And when Sobotka insists, saying he needs money for the union's lobbying effort, the old man has a change of heart, saying, "I want you should be happy."

THE LEGEND OF THE ORANGE SOFA AND THE UNLIKELY HOLLYWOOD CAREERS OF VINCE PERANIO AND PAT MORAN

"If Simon has the nerve to write this stuff, we have the obligation to put the story together."

– PAT MORAN

The drama of *The Wire* generally takes place at the center of your TV screen.

It is there that the ideas of the writers and producers – be it Jimmy McNulty feeling up a mannequin to charm his estranged wife, Stringer Bell sipping tea while plotting to import drugs into Baltimore or the millionaire drug lord Marlo Stanfield shoplifting 50 cents worth of lollipops – are animated.

Even on a sprawling show as finely woven as *The Wire*, the story is almost always front and center.

"The most intricately plotted drama on television," said the *Miami Herald*.

That leaves a lot of space to be filled in the margins. Which is where Vince Peranio and Pat Moran, who worked respectively as the show's art director and the on-location casting director, do some of their best work.

"Vince," said Moran of her old friend in the spring of 2009, "can make anything look like anything."

But they love Baltimore best, having devoted their careers – from the films of John Waters and Barry Levinson, through *Homicide: Life on the Street*, *The Corner* and *The Wire* – to the marginal metropolis they love.

"*The Wire* was harder than any of them, hardest show I ever worked on," said Moran. "It had more characters than a Chinese novel and it was accurate."

And accuracy is paramount when portraying the Queen City of the Patapsco River drainage basin, royalty that never takes time to put on make-up and is often found walking down the street in hair curlers and bedroom slippers.

"If you just concentrate on the people in the center, the film falls apart," said Moran from her office in an old broom factory on the Canton waterfront. "All the people you see in the background, the ones who don't speak, that's very much a Baltimore reality."

Said Peranio, a historian of all things Crabtown: "All of us who worked on *The Wire* can safely say that [viewers] are seeing 'the real.'"

Moran handed out business cards to people hanging around the set in neighborhoods where the show is filmed, asking folks to call if they're interested in being extras.

"Talent detectives," she said. "When it comes down to the corner, nobody can fill that space but people from the corner. These kids know what goes on down there and it makes the show better.

"We're not there to exploit them, but to tell their story . . . what we portrayed was not racially ambiguous kids who could have played a sitcom. We cast Baltimore."

One of Moran's great finds was Washington actor S. Robert Morgan, the blind actor who portrays the barkeep Butchie, both bank and mentor to Omar.

"Here we are doing Greek tragedy and Pat Moran brings us the physical manifestation of an ancient seer," said David Simon, who said he was thrilled with Morgan's work.

Heavy-set drug supplier Proposition Joe Stewart – the Eastside's logical and understated answer to Avon Barksdale – is played by a true son of the Eastside, Patterson High School: Robert F. Chew from the class of 1978.

Chew, whose great-great-grandfather was Korean, teaches and performs at the Arena Players theater group. A fan of sitcoms from TV's golden age, Chew appeared as "Prop Joe" in all five seasons of *The Wire*.

"And he was spectacular," said Moran. "I've known him a long time."

The Baltimore School for the Arts has been a strong resource, sending both students and teachers.

"Stinkum [Brandon Price] went there," said Moran.

Maria Broom, who plays Marla Daniels, estranged wife of Lieutenant Cedric Daniels, teaches at the downtown high school.

Built into the city's old Aleazar Hotel, the arts school is also where Moran found Corey Parker Robinson – Detective Leander Sydnor – when he was still a teenager and she was casting *Homicide*.

Others, like Butchie, have come from that town about a 40-minute drive south of Baltimore that Moran calls Dullsville, better known as the nation's capital.

More than a few walk-ons would seem to stop by the casting office after visting their probation officer.

"On any of David Simon's pet projects, we've hired many felons, certainly drug dealers or people with drug dealing somewhere in their life," said Moran. "A few murderers, too, but they're all really nice to me."

A cream puff typecast as a tough cookie because of her gruff, blunt demeanor, a bit of a bark and fire-engine-red hair, Moran has cowed more than a few acknowledged killers during auditions.

Her rasp of "state your name" and demand that all actors "stay on book" in each audition and callback are an essential rite of passage for local actors.

"When they sit in that [casting] chair, I'm not interested in their past," she said. "If you get the part, follow the rules. If you can't, we'll find someone else."

Asked if giving a little work to kids from neighborhoods as rough as anything Dickens wrote about might have saved a few lives, Moran eats the question in one bite: "I'm not Mother Teresa."

More than once, especially when civic leaders are riding him for broadcasting the city's ills over every hill and dale in the world with a DVD player, Simon has argued that the tragedies shown in *The Wire* could be filmed in any number of American cities.

Yet the show rings especially true in its cradle of Baltimore, where many of the people who make the show happen, including Peranio and Moran, were born and raised.

"Baltimore is notorious for breeding odd ducks. Mencken was the biggest odd duck of them all," said Moran, a graduate of Mount de Sales, a Catholic high school for girls.

"Put them together with the transplant goofs that are drawn here – maniacs like Poe and the Duchess of Windsor, come *on* now – and you've got a whole region of offbeat people.

"It's a cheap, comfortable place to live," said Moran. "There's no bullshit."

Odd ducks swimming along ponds bereft of bullshit: that is the charmed and tragic city that drives *The Wire*.

A character bleak and unvanquished.

A star.

"Ugly can be very interesting." said Peranio, whose initials, V.E., for Vincent Eugene, commemorate his 1945 birthday of May 8, when the Allied "Victory in Europe" was declared.

"I'm intensely interested in the vacant houses and the peeling paint and how the flat, repetitive rhythm of the city is [ruined] when an abandoned house goes down. It makes a huge statement when something is missing from repetition – like having a tooth pulled – and it lends visual excitement to the city."

Peranio grew up playing in the alleys around Cross Street Market, not far from Frank Sobotka's old waterfront neighborhood in Locust Point.

"I think every Baltimorean is born with two things built into their personality," he said. "Nostalgia and apathy."

His nostalgia is often for the back alleys he played in as a kid, passageways gone to hell by the time he worked on *The Wire*.

"Baltimore has some of the best ghetto alleys in the country," he said. "Especially in the summer when they're like jungles overgrown with weeds and debris and trash that's literally been tossed out of the back windows."

To Peranio's keen eye, the city has become a more desperate place in the last 20 years, while Moran would argue that things have improved a bit.

More times than not, it's an up and down tempo responding – usually late – to job opportunities, how afraid the middle class is to return to the city to restore old housing and whatever administration – be it Democrats who legislate from the bottom up or Republicans who do the opposite – control the White House and Congress.

Peranio, who watches little or no television, particularly cop shows, takes particular pride in designing crack houses and police stations.

And, it would seem, what passes for patio furniture in the hood.

Many projects and paychecks down the road from the days when he made the 15-foot long lobster that raped Divine in John Waters's 1971 film, *Multiple Maniacs*, Peranio now buys most of what he needs or directs someone else to build it.

"But I still love finding that one little thing in the alley . . . the orange couch that played such a big role in the first year is a good example."

Scouting locations for *The Wire* pilot, Peranio found the orange, crushed-velvet sofa, a larger-than-life relic of the 1970s not unlike a Chrysler Newport, propped against a dumpster.

The supernova beauty of it dominated the pilot, which went on to become the show's first episode, as alfresco HQ for D'Angelo Barksdale's ragtag crew of drug slingers in The Pit.

[The sofa wound up adorning the back cover of a CD of *The Wire* music called . . . *and all the pieces matter*, released by Nonesuch Records in 2008.]

"It's rare for a pilot to get picked up and become a show, so after we wrapped, we didn't think about the orange sofa," he said. "A month later, *The Wire* gets picked up and I told my staff to go get the couch."

Nobody moved, and Peranio became immediately aware, and more than a little angry, that the couch had been tossed.

They had three weeks to find a perfect match for an item out of style since Gerald Ford was handing out pardons, and soon enough it became clear it wasn't going to happen.

"Our carpenters built a new one from scratch, but we still had to upholster it," said Peranio.

"We searched everywhere between here and New York and couldn't find orange crushed velvet. It was from that gold and avocado period of the 1970s and was long out of style. The only place that had something that matched was a homemade-wallpaper shop in England."

By the time they had cloned the rained-on, spit-on, and torn-down couch – "After we built it, we had to rip it apart and make it filthy," said Peranio – it had cost the art department $3,000.

"We didn't tell the producers, we just put it out there and no one knew any different," said Peranio.

No one except for producer Nina Noble, who had signed the expense order for the orange velvet.

In the fall of 2003, an orange couch and retro-hipsters were featured on the cover of an issue of the *New York Times Sunday Magazine*.

Someone should have told Mott the Hoople: the 1970s were back.

Several weeks before filming started in May 2004 on Season Three, the orange couch from The Pit was set to be auctioned on eBay for charity, raising money for a fund that honors the lifework of Ella Thompson, heroine of *The Corner*.

"In the old days, back when I was an anti-art director, we'd take stuff to the dump and come back with more than we took," mused Peranio. "Now they're in a hurry to bulldoze everything.

"But when I started in this business, you could go to the dump and see a mountain of refrigerators on fire with rats running through them. That was good pickings."

For Season Three, Moran had more than two dozen principal roles to cast, and Peranio was given the challenge of building a 1950s-era police precinct inside *The Wire*'s soundstage, an old Sam's Club a few miles east over the city line near Essex.

[By Season Four, the sound stage would be moved to the quintessentially suburban city of Columbia in Howard County, to the west of Baltimore.]

"I've got 29 principal roles to be cast and that's just the first episode," said Moran of Season Three. "That's not counting extras for atmosphere and crime scenes."

New characters include a heavy-set policewoman named Caroline with ears so fine she can hear dust settle on the wiretap; an ill-tempered drug slinger named Fruit, and a string of district-level plainclothesmen, sergeants, and lieutenants.

The show's New York casting director, Alexa Fogle, who sent Michael Kenneth Williams to the producers for the role of Omar – saw more experienced actors for such parts as Baltimore's incumbent Mayor Royce, the new drug king Marlo and the old street muscle Cutty.

"I know I've cast at least a thousand people [for the first two seasons] and from the look of this first new episode, add another thousand," said Moran. "It's like *Ben-Hur* goes to The Bottom."

A note for out-of-towners: The Bottom was once a rough-and-tumble area of West Baltimore so named because it encompassed the bottom of black Baltimore's famed grand concourse, Pennsylvania Avenue.

What was once The Bottom is now divided into thirds: a small strip of rehabbed row homes, a stretch of the Martin Luther King Boulevard, and a part of the University of Maryland's medical and law campus.

It is a sign of Moran's Crabtown pedigree that she even remembers the term.

Peranio built the inside of the Western District for Season Three with the facade of St. Brigid's Catholic School on Hudson Street in Canton used for the outside. The school's fenced-in playground, devoid of swing sets and monkey bars, served as the district's back lot.

"St. Brigid's and the Western District came out of that same period of Baltimore architecture in the late 1940s and 1950s, modern but not contemporary – that brutal, fascist look just before the crazy 1960s hit.

"The Western was always the roughest, always overcrowded, and we're reproducing it in layers of history and chaos and piles of furniture in the hallways and lobby."

The Peranio version was, he said, "without charm because nobody cares . . . they built grand entrances back then, but they're never used. They didn't anticipate people parking around back and coming in a side door."

Moran and Peranio have worked on virtually every film made by their old friend and fellow traveler John Waters, from the crazy kid stuff [1969's 16mm *The Diane Linkletter Story*] on through what now passes for mainstream in the Waters canon [2004's *A Dirty Shame*].

Like Waters, and a recent protégé, the young writer/director Matthew Porterfield, whom he calls the best filmmaker to come out of Baltimore in years, they are devoted to their hometown.

So, yeah, the weather is great in L.A.

The big shots are in New York.

And there's more money in both of those places than any string of ten Baltimores put together.

So what?

When Hollywood crossed the continent to find Moran and Peranio in their own backyard, they were ready.

"You better be," says Moran, "because it moves like a freight train."

episode
twenty-two

STRAY ROUNDS
"The world is a smaller place now." — THE GREEK
Directed by Tim Van Patten
Story by David Simon & Ed Burns; teleplay by David Simon

Bang!

A street shoot-out between Bodie's gang and the independent crew stealing business from The Pit. Bullets everywhere, hitting nary a dealer or anyone else in the game but finding a kid getting ready for school inside a shitty rowhouse bedroom.

The battle brings an army of cops to throw slingers and junkies against the walls and to the ground. On the scene, Major Howard Colvin of the

Detective Jimmy McNulty at a crime scene amid the all-too-familiar yellow police tape.

Stringer Bell discusses business in the low-rise projects – "The Pit"– with D'Angelo Barksdale, nephew of kingpin Avon Barksdale.

The target: Avon Barksdale. What McNulty and his crew wouldn't have given for this photo in the early going of Season One.

▲ The low-rise crew at the office (left to right): the manchild Wallace; Poot, the follower; D'Angelo, the reluctant thug; and Bodie in the role he was born for.

▼ Lester Freamon, recently sprung from the pawn unit, with his true calling: dollhouse miniatures.

▲ Lieutenant Cedric Daniels face-to-face with the personification of bureaucratic ruthlessness: the statistics-obsessed Colonel William A. Rawls.

▼ Detectives Pryzbylewski, Hauk, and Carver are sheepish after the mini-riot they sparked in the Westside high-rises.

Omar the Terror: "I ain't never put my gun on no citizen." ▶

▲ Union boss Frank Sobotka on the waterfront he loves as much as or more than his own family.

◀ Nick Sobotka of the stevedores' local – smarter than Ziggy and too smart for his own good.

▲ Stringer Bell and Proposition Joe after D'Angelo's funeral: "I got a proposition for you," says Joe, living up to his moniker.

▼ Frank Sobotka is arrested by the FBI and his nemesis, Major Stan Valchek, in a well-orchestrated media circus.

Ziggy Sobotka: "I'm tired of being the punch line to every joke . . ." ▶▶

Western District – soon to be a key protagonist in Season Three – says wearily: "Fucking pointless . . . chasing this shit from one corner to the next like it's a plan."

The detectives assigned to solve the nine-year-old's murder – a "red ball" priority straight from City Hall – work the case while Bodie explains his logic to a disgusted Stringer Bell.

Bell orders Bodie to dispose of all the weapons used in the shootout, and Bodie tosses them off a bridge in the Curtis Bay neighborhood and right on the deck of a passing barge.

Prop Joe's offer of better drugs for better territory is sounding better and better to Bell. Though he does not have Avon's approval, Stringer gives up three of his six high-rise towers to Eastsiders in exchange for Joe's steady package of "the real."

Stringer then tries to get Brianna to sell the deal to her brother, but Avon is insistent on keeping his territory. Not only is he looking for a new connection, he has contracted the fabled Brother Mouzone to keep the towers in Barksdale control.

On the wire, when customers call the warehouse for narcotics – asking for La-Z-Boy recliners when they want heroin, davinas for coke – they're told that those models are "no longer carried."

On the eyeball surveillance, nothing has gone into the warehouse or come out, and McNulty worries that they might have tipped their hand. But Freamon points out that if they were sure the police were on them, the smugglers would've closed shop entirely.

Nick, waiting on a re-up from The Greek, is told by Vondas that the meager size of his purchases make him a small potato and passes him off to a corner boy named "White Mike" McArdle.

Hell-bent on proving himself a player in some kind of game, Ziggy hooks up with Johnny 50 on a fresh caper. He goes to George "Double-G" Glekas – the guy who moves hot goods from The Greek through his East Baltimore appliance store – and offers stolen Mercedes cars as if from a catalogue.

Another can disappears from a Talco ship with Horseface on the job, and the detail lets it go: they know where it'll end up. They also get a new number from a call made by Serge and go for a second wiretap.

Agent Fitzhugh, McNulty's friend from the FBI, does Jimmy a favor by running names through a federal crime computer and comes up with an old hit on Glekas.

Fitzhugh puts a call in to the agent who handled the case, and the minute the agent, a Greek named Koutris, gets off the phone, he makes a personal call on his cell phone saying hello in his native tongue, then adding in English, "We need to talk."

Soon, Glekas is at the Ikaros restaurant on Eastern Avenue with The Greek and Vondas, along with Eton and the madam of their whores – a conclave of bosses and lieutenants.

"Our friend in Washington does not know why" the cops are interested in Glekas, says The Greek. "Only that they are asking."

To repay the favor to their "friend," The Greek meets Kourtis on a public bench and blows the whistle on dope coming into Baltimore from South America. It is both a favor to a friend and a payback to the Colombians who have reneged on the agreed price for the chemicals stolen by Nick and Ziggy used to process coke.

McNulty gets inside the brothel, and shows little self-control. The detail raids the location, further establishing a conspiracy case against the Greeks, although there is the embarrassment of noting that McNulty,

left alone in a room with two whores, followed through on what comes naturally.

From a cell phone, the detail hears Serge say to White Mike about a body found in the street: "Did he have hands? Did he have a face? Yes? Then it wasn't us."

And Ziggy's duck?

Couldn't hold its liquor and drops dead.

episode
twenty-three

STORM WARNINGS

"It pays to go with the union card every time."
— ZIGGY

Directed by Rob Bailey

Story by David Simon & Ed Burns; teleplay by Ed Burns

Open on Roland Pryzbylewski alone in the detail office, quietly arranging photos and names of various targets on a corkboard as a tape plays of Johnny Cash singing "I Walk the Line."

Very comfortable with puzzles, Prez enjoys the slow, thoughtful process of connecting the dots: from the original target Sobotka and the dock boys on through The Greek's organization and Prop Joe's Eastside drug ring.

All the way to an index card that simply says "Boss Man."

"Fuckin'-A," says Prez.

On the street, the new Barksdale dope, courtesy of Stringer's deal with Prop Joe, is fabulous, so good that Bodie can't remember when a package sold so well.

When Stringer tells Bodie to accommodate the presence of Cheese and the Eastsiders — who have been given three high-rise towers in which to "grind," Bodie can hardly stomach it.

The detail team has put global-positioning trackers on the cars of The Greek's crew, including Eton, Glekas, and the brothel madam.

This takes them to a pair of regular meeting places: Little Johnny's diner and the seawall along the old Fort Howard Veterans Administration hospital in North Point.

Having started the detail as his own personal vendetta, Major Valchek rages over the fact that the target has become more than Frank Sobotka.

Valchek calls in the FBI, who are interested in the idea of union corruption but little else with regard to inner-city drug trafficking or prostitution.

When the FBI starts keyboarding local suspects into their database — Eton, Glekas, the madam, and Serge as targets along with Sobotka and Horseface — the info once again pops up on the screen of FBI agent Koutris.

Koutris meets The Greek at a Washington art gallery (the paintings on the wall are the work of former *Wire* staffer Amelia Cleary) and warns him: "They're on you with wiretaps. Several phones, several addresses."

Ziggy and Johnny 50 cut through the chain-link that fences in a field of new cars and begin driving them away, making it look like an outside job, though in fact the luxury sedans are going back into containers to be shipped abroad.

In the high-rise towers, Brother Mouzone arrives from New York and immediately makes his presence known, wounding Cheese with a slug of ratshot and rousting the Eastsiders from the projects. All of it is witnessed from the sidelines by Bubbles.

Cheese goes to Proposition Joe seeking vengeance. Joe balks: Mouzone is too tough and Stringer can't cross Avon. But there is one man who might take the job, but for pride, not money, says Joe, picking up the phone.

With the stolen cars headed overseas, Ziggy shows up at Double-G's appliance store to collect his money, only to be chumped when Glekas says he'll only pay ten percent instead of the agreed-upon 20.

It is the last insult for Ziggy, who goes back to his car, a stolen Mercedes, and grabs a handgun he bought with pawn money from his duck's diamond necklace.

Ziggy wounds a clerk and puts several slugs in Glekas's back as the man tries to run away. When Glekas begs for his life, Ziggy utters the word that so many of The Greek's crew have used to ridicule him – *malaka* – firing a final bullet next to Glekas's eye.

Tossing the money at the wounded clerk, Ziggy goes outside to wait for the police, later signing a full confession.

McNulty and Bunk, on the trail of the GPS trackers, use the police boat to anchor off the banks of Fort Howard, taking pictures of Vondas and Eton talking on the seawall. The suspects then throw their cell phones into the bay while Vondas sends a text message on a separate device.

Later, McNulty will use the GPS coordinates of the seawall where Vondas stood to isolate the text message through its cell provider. Soon they are looking at subpoenaed text messages in Greek.

Butchie, Omar's bank and mentor, receives a visit from Proposition Joe, who says Stringer is hot for a meeting with Omar, but won't say why.

Don't feel right, says Butchie: the Barksdale people can't be trusted. But Butchie agrees to the meet provided he is able to provide the security.

At the detail office, Valchek enters to find his worst fears confirmed, the detectives are working with the FBI and the investigation continues to sprawl well beyond Sobotka.

Furious, Valchek tries to pull his son-in-law, Prez, from the detail, and Prez sucker-punches him.

Nicky tells Frank Sobotka that his son has just been charged with murder.

As the episode draws to a close, the detail decodes a text message that indicates the Greeks are shutting down. They race the clock for search-and-seizure and arrest warrants while The Greek's crew works to rid the appliance store and the warehouse of every scrap of paper and every speck of dope.

episode
twenty-four

BAD DREAMS

"I need to get clean." — FRANK SOBOTKA

Directed by Ernest Dickerson

Story by David Simon & George Pelecanos; teleplay by George Pelecanos

As Nick sleeps in the bed of a neighborhood girl, hungover from a night of drinking away Ziggy's tragedy, the police raid his parents' rowhouse in Locust Point, finding drugs and money and shaming the family.

Detectives and FBI agents hit the warehouse and appliance shop, finding nothing but a bloodstain on the floor of the Eastern Avenue store.

White Mike is picked up in South Baltimore, and Serge is handcuffed at home. Vondas is left on the street, if only so that he might again try to contact whoever it was that sent him the text message, ordering him to clean up.

Sobotka visits Ziggy in prison, where he has already been smacked around by the other inmates. He asks what happened and Zig says he got tired of being the punchline to every joke.

Sobotka tells his son that if things were that bad, he should have come to him for help, and Ziggy suggests that the union was his father's one love.

Meanwhile, Daniels blows a gasket and confronts Landsman when he finds out that the son of one target, Ziggy, murdered another target, Glekas, and no one from homicide thought to give the detail a call before the crime scene was swept clean.

The Feds pass up a chance to grab Sobotka at his house in Glen Burnie because nabbing him at the union hall makes for better TV. When they do, Valchek is there to deliver a payback over a stained glass church window that now seems like a beef from a long, long time ago.

The Feds take a shot at flipping Frank Sobotka, but do so hoping that he will detail union racketeering and corruption rather than give them chapter and verse on The Greek.

You can help yourself and your union, they assure him.

Sobotka tells the agents that he and his people have been dying a slow death for decades: "Now you want to help us?"

White Mike immediately rolls for detectives and fingers Eton for dope and Serge as muscle. The Greek's lieutenants are more disciplined.

Bunk and McNulty sit on Vondas's upper-middle-class house in suburbia, watch him drive away, and follow the car to a downtown parking garage. Using Russell, they follow him into a waterfront hotel and get the number of the room that he enters.

Eventually, Vondas is seen leaving the hotel with a man in a dignified blue suit. Rather than go back to his car in the garage, Vondas and the man in the suit leave in a separate vehicle, telling a subordinate his own car is hot. The detectives lose Vondas, but go to work trying to ID the man in the suit.

Pearlman offers White Mike probation and witness protection if he turns in his suppliers, and Russell, hearing this, wants to know why Frank Sobotka can't get a deal as good as or better than a two-bit street dealer.

See what you can do, Pearlman tells her, but don't offer him anything specific.

Russell and Sobotka genuinely like each other. When Beadie goes to help him, Sobotka says he knew it was wrong, "but in my head I thought I was wrong for the right reasons."

Sobotka learns that the publicity surrounding his federal charges have state legislators running for cover; there is no way his lobbyist, Bruce DiBiago, can muster votes for dredging or pier repairs.

Come with me, says Russell. Tell your story in earnest. You're a better man, she says, than the guys you got in bed with.

Sobotka agrees, deciding to give up everything he has on the Greeks in exchange for moving his son to a safer lockup and leniency for the drug charges against his nephew Nick.

But he will not give up any union members. Sobotka is urged to come back with his own attorney to formalize the deal.

Stringer meets with Omar amid tight security and compliments him on the burdens he has heaped upon the Barksdale organization: Bird in jail; Wee-Bey there, too, for the rest of his life and a day; and Stinkum dead, all to settle the death of Omar's lover Brandon.

Stringer denies any personal role in Brandon's torture and lays the responsibility for that excess on a contract killer from New York: Brother Mouzone. If it will clear the feud, Bell will point Omar in Mouzone's direction.

Omar takes the information and ambushes Mouzone at a run-down motel. But before finishing off the wounded hitman, Omar insists on explaining his motivation. In Mouzone's response, Omar realizes that Stringer has played him.

Instead of firing a last shot into Mouzone's head, Omar dials 911, reports a shooting, and leaves.

Still on the street, days after the raids, Nick Sobotka hasn't turned up yet, and Herc and Carver sit on his parents' rowhouse in Locust Point. Inside, Nick's father, Louis, is scolding his younger brother, Frank Sobotka, for cutting moral corners with their children.

Chastened, Sobotka heads down to the docks for a hard day's labor, loading and unloading ships as men have done for centuries in Crabtown.

He needs to sweat, he says, "to get clean."

At Ikaros restaurant, The Greek and Vondas dine alone. Vondas has lost his appetite, but not The Greek, who decides to systematically eliminate anyone who might turn on them.

Vondas asks: If I could make sure that Sobotka and his nephew wouldn't talk, might we spare their lives?

He tells The Greek that if they shape the evidence against Ziggy toward self-defense, it will be enough for Frank and Nicky Sobotka to keep their secrets.

Soon, Vondas is on a park bench with Nicky in South Baltimore to make his deal. We can do many things, he says, and we only ask loyalty in return.

Before Sobotka can finalize his deal with the cops, Nick calls and urges him not to talk to the police. He tells his uncle The Greek has a better deal, one that will spring Ziggy.

And so, Sobotka takes a long walk beneath the Francis Scott Key Bridge to meet The Greek and Vondas and hear them out. Frank goes alone, having forbidden Nick to accompany him.

As Sobotka approaches, The Greek takes a phone call from Agent Koutris, who has been informed of Sobotka's pending cooperation.

Hanging up, The Greek turns to Vondas as Sobotka approaches and says: "Your way . . . it won't work."

episode
twenty-five

PORT IN A STORM
"Business. Always business." — THE GREEK

Directed by Robert F. Colesberry
Story by David Simon & Ed Burns; teleplay by David Simon

The final episode of Season Two opens as the first episode did: with a police boat plucking a body out of Baltimore harbor.

It's Frank Sobotka, the Polish Don Quixote of a shrinking waterfront, staring into space with his throat cut.

As the medical examiner's staff rolls Sobotka into the back of their wagon, Beadie Russell wipes tears from her eyes.

Still sitting on Vondas's suburban home to no avail, the detail fears they have lost him and learn that Stephen Rados – to whom the Inner Harbor hotel room was rented – is not The Greek but a big-shot Washington defense attorney.

Bell visits Brother Mouzone at the hospital, and the contract killer curtly dismisses him, telling him the arrangement with Avon is voided and he'll handle his own problems.

When Bell tells Avon this in prison, Barksdale is furious, and we witness the first true falling out between the childhood friends. His attempt to shore

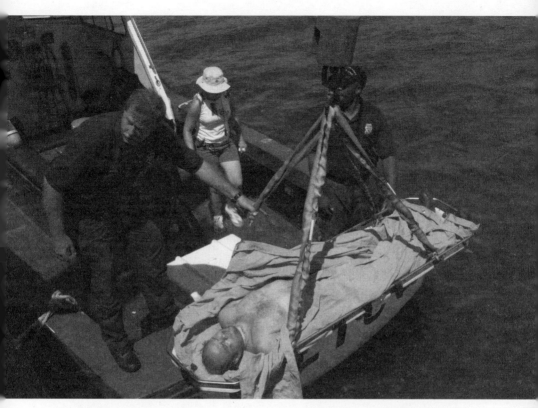

up his operation with new muscle now thwarted, Barksdale reluctantly allows Bell to take the deal with Proposition Joe, though he makes it clear that things will change once he is out of jail.

Enraged by his uncle's death, Nick vows to kill The Greek and every one of his people, but La-La and the other stevedores hold him back, saying he'll only end up like Ziggy.

Nick's father enters and tells him simply that it's time to go, and father and son show up at the Southeastern District, where Nick turns himself in.

Lester Freamon, who is receiving police data on headless torsos, a response to Serge's uttered line on the wiretap, happens to be at the Southeast duty desk and takes charge of Nick Sobotka.

Soon, Nick is seated before Pearlman, who offers him the same deal she had put on the table for Sobotka the day before. Nobody could help your cousin, says Bunk, because we've got the gun and he signed a confession.

Nick cops to the smuggling, but says no one in the union knew they were bringing girls into port on the containers. He then offers what he knows about The Greek and his people and makes a game play to get Horseface out of the soup.

"Horse don't know shit . . . I'll testify to that."

Shown the picture of Vondas leaving the hotel, he can't identify the man in the suit accompanying Vondas. But he points to an older man leaving in the background: "That's The Greek right there."

When Daniels tells Valchek of Frank Sobotka's fate, the major says, "I almost feel sorry for the son of a bitch."

And then Daniels tries to salvage Prez, as Valchek lays out the penance that his son-in-law will perform, including a formal letter of apology to everyone who witnessed the punch, an in-person apology to Valchek, and two months of midnight shift on the Southeastern desk.

After that, says Valchek, washing his hands of the mess, I don't give a shit.

Bubbles calls Greggs after getting locked up for an attempt to boost drugs from a city medic wagon. He tells her and McNulty about the dispute between Brother Mouzone and Cheese that led to Cheese getting shot.

It's as though Stringer Bell and the Eastside boys are now "sharing" territory, says Bubbles. And the dope is good again. The apparent absurdity of this interests McNulty, and the info is good enough to get Bubbles and his sidekick Johnny out of handcuffs.

Still pressing The Greek's lieutenants to cooperate, Bunk and Russell go to Philadelphia and retrieve a security-camera videotape taken the night the engineer from the *Atlantic Light* was murdered.

The tape – along with Serge's famous words on the wiretap – "Did he have hands? Did he have a face?" – are used against the Russian. Serge pins the murder of the engineer on Vondas and the murder of the girls in the can on the engineer.

Though no one will be charged, Daniels has just cleared the 14 murders for Rawls.

On the docks, the FBI threatens to decertify the union if honest elections aren't held soon. Which is all the prompting the dock boys need to re-elect Frank Sobotka posthumously.

The union hall will soon enough be padlocked by federal marshals.

Daniels and Fitzhugh inspect a container of dope abandoned on the docks by The Greek, and – as it was with Barksdale the year before – Daniels sighs, "This might have been a hell of a case."

Nick and his girlfriend and their daughter are ushered into a low-budget motel by the Feds until witness protection can move them to something better. With no other future in sight for him, Nick goes back to the docks where the grain pier that Frankie Sobotka so badly wanted to see up and running again to get more ships into Baltimore is being developed into condominiums.

Leaving a hotel room, Vondas and The Greek prepare to reinvent themselves in another part of the world and share a laugh.

"My name is not my name," says Vondas.

"And of course," says The Greek, "I'm not even Greek."

THE RULES OF THE GAME

Given the general customs of American filmed entertainment utilizing crime and criminals as its subject matter – gripping narratives that resolve in satisfying endings that reaffirm the audience's sense of the fundamental justice of the world – there is no reason for anyone to watch *The Wire*. We, the audience, are warned from the first that there will likely be no grand victories, no vanquished enemies, no heroes riding off into the sunset in police-issue SUVs. There are rules to this "game" of the TV crime drama, and *The Wire* flouts all of them, bringing us into a world where those charged to serve and protect are often more concerned with career advancement and bureaucratic number-crunching than with any conventional notion of justice. Our ragtag band of hero cops are flawed far beyond the threshold of easy sympathy. The bad-guy criminals they haphazardly pursue are portrayed as being so deeply, at times poignantly, circumscribed by the mean streets to which they themselves contribute meanness that easy hatred of them is likewise difficult. *The Wire* is playing its own game.

I confess to a secret life as a dedicated consumer of crime drama. From a childhood ordered by *Streets of San Francisco, Hawaii Five-O*, and *Rockford Files*, through a young adulthood of *Miami Vice, Hill Street Blues*, and *Homicide*, to a maturity of *CSI, NYPD Blue*, and *Law and Order*, I have consciously, deeply, and cheerfully imbibed the rules of the genre. Throughout *The Wire*'s Season One I kept stubbornly waiting for drug kingpin Avon Barksdale to die: to be killed in a gruesome fashion commensurate with the sum total of the lives his criminal activities had destroyed. I actively wanted it. Barring this, I wanted him sentenced to life without parole in the Hole at Marion. Week by week, *The Wire* kept alive these expectations; in fact, deliberately manipulated and toyed with them; but ultimately, in the end – meaning the end of Season One – betrayed them.

If Avon Barksdale was the villain in *The Wire*'s first season, then it would follow that Jimmy McNulty was the hero, the knight-errant whose self-appointed task was to set the corrupt city of Baltimore to rights. Such was my expectation: McNulty was the Percival who, however bumbling, would ultimately attain his goal, be granted a sight of the grail of perfection and heal the unhealed wound of the land. He failed spectacularly in his role as triumphant hero just as Avon failed in the role of vanquished villain. Judged by the rules of TV crime drama, the show was a monumental failure. "Monumental" being the operative term. *The Wire* was only masquerading at the form, deliberately turning its conventions inside out in the service of a different end.

Drama was first defined in Aristotle's *Poetics* as the "imitation of action in the form of action." "Action" (praxis), as Aristotle meant it, referred to human life as it is actually lived and experienced: reason, emotion, desire, suffering. This is where *The Wire*, I think, begins to expand and redefine its genre. As literary critic Francis Fergusson wrote of great drama in *The Idea of a Theater*, "the realm of experience it takes for its own is the contingent, fallible, changing one which is this side of final truth, and in constant touch with common sense." Its elements of composition are not qualities of feeling or abstract concepts, "but beings, real people in a real world, related to each other in a vast and intricate web of analogies." *The Wire* was not interested in McNulty's ultimately futile quest so much as it was in probing the unhealed wound itself: in fingering the jagged grain of Baltimore; beyond that, of the human suffering in America's urban core.

TV crime drama has its origins in the western, in America's mythic Wild West and the novels and movies that engendered and sustained this myth. The traditional western rests on a belief in a world that is in essence innocent, albeit eternally menaced by evil: the hero plays a role in purging a specific threat. *The Wire* by contrast assumes a fallen world. There is no specific threat. Corruption is the state of things. Or rather, *innocence*, not evil, is the threat to the status quo, because when you set off a chain of events in *innocence*, a nice word for "ignorance," you have no way of knowing, or even suspecting, how much damage you might cause.

Jimmy McNulty and D'Angelo Barksdale occupy roughly the same positions in their respective chains of command; both rage in various ways, both suffer, against the strictures of the hierarchies in which they find themselves, but both lack any real power to effect change. They are the catalysts of the chain of events in Season One – D'Angelo, through the crime that sets the scene for the opening trial, Jimmy, through his outrage at the result of this trial and "mouthing off" to the judge (who has his own motives for setting the hunt for Avon in motion) – but both are ultimately horrified by the changes they do effect, the trail of wreckage and bodies they leave in their wake. D'Angelo is unable to look at crime-scene photos when finally in custody; Jimmy, looking back toward the end, says, "What the fuck did I do?"

What Jimmy *did* (and stubbornly did again in Season Two) was simply to shake one thread of the "vast and intricate web" of relationships by which the city generally, seamlessly, runs itself; and in so doing, to make the invisible visible, before it inevitably settles back into place. No one is above or below this web, no one is immune. *The Wire* casts its unblinking eye on the upper and lower echelons of cops and criminals: each of them suffers, in various ways, from the malady of the city; even Avon Barksdale is perpetually menaced by competitors and by his own crew.

In the beauty and fullness of the show, Wallace, a lovely boy stranded at the bottom rung of the drug trade, is granted his challenges and trials of soul; the addict and informant Bubbles, motivated by love and a sense of responsibility, has moments of dignity; even Omar, the pitiless stalker of the pitiless, is shown to have human qualities and impulses. Every character is granted his reasons; *The Wire*, again to quote Fergusson, "catch[es] the creature in the very act of creating those partial rationalizations which make the whole substance of lesser dramas." There is no abstract principle of justice operating in this world, only real people; there is no good and evil, but there is right and wrong; actions do have consequences: lives are broken, shattered, lost, or saved, in a game that has no end.

I am, along with being a lover of crime drama, also a student of true crime: corporate malfeasance, from John D. Rockefeller and Andrew Carnegie to Enron and Worldcom; political corruption, with a special fascination for the morass of greed, brutality, and inhumanity that went into the making of my home city, Chicago; police corruption, from Boston to New York City to Los Angeles; and drug crime, having lost relatives and childhood friends to what might be termed "the game." In none of these various permutations of crime is there ever an end to the human cost involved; in none, given the vast interwoven chain of cause and effect, and the ultimate mystery of context or fate versus individual free will, can the journey of one individual, one Percival, stand for or redeem the whole.

This is the real – the fallen – world, an under-acknowledged aspect of our country, the United States, that *The Wire* so thoroughly, brutally, and compassionately portrays.

This brings me to what I would argue is the true achievement of *The Wire*: its subtle awareness and understated indictment of the larger game that occurs off-screen. As much as I enjoy crime drama, I am always on some level wary of shows that use urban suffering as a forum for entertainment. I am constantly searching for the escape, the "letting off the hook," that these shows give the predominantly middle-and upper-middle-class audience; the ritual purgation that allows the audience – myself included – to go on with their lives while the predominantly poor and African-American body count continues to accrue in real projects, in Bridgeport, Camden, St. Louis, Dallas, Denver, Oakland. In *The Wire*, there is no grand public outrage or outcry for the murders to be solved; these deaths have become so commonplace, as they have in our world, as to seem unremarkable. Even Jimmy McNulty comes to realize that the motivations behind his various quests have more to do with ambition and arrogance than they do with outrage at injustice.

I admired *The Wire*'s matter-of-fact awareness that the lives of inner-city blacks – to the cops, the community, and the larger public – are not worth a dime. But the show goes a step beyond this: it is aware that these lives are also, paradoxically, worth quite a bit. The profits of the drug and sex trades travel out from the projects to banks, corporations, politicians, developers, while the unutterable suffering through which that money is made remains geographically contained. For me, the most plangent of the show's many great lines was spoken in Season One, by the sacrificial lamb, 16-year-old Wallace: "If it ain't West Baltimore, I don't know it."

As articulated by D'Angelo in his classic set piece on the rules of chess, the pawns suffering on the game board don't see the larger game; to them, it *is* all in the game. The forces that profit from the game, that allow the carnage to occur – without outrage, without fear, without shame or guilt – include us, the audience and wider public off-screen, with our own comfortable notions of justice, our own necessities, our own reasons and partial rationalizations for doing nothing to demand that it stop. *The Wire*'s true greatness is its chilling awareness of this fact, that the wire that links society, that ties us all together – in this case symbolized by the pen register following the trail of money and ultimate responsibility – will be allowed to trace and implicate only so far. Beyond its scope, as the old maps of the flat and undiscovered world used to caution, there be monsters.

Anthony Walton

SEASON THREE

SEASON THREE OVERVIEW

YOU CAN'T GET THERE FROM HERE

Kurt Schmoke voiced his concerns about the war on drugs in 1988 ... he is a prophet without honor in this country ... but a prophet nonetheless ...

DAVID SIMON ON THE FORMER MAYOR OF BALTIMORE

Kurt Schmoke, one of Baltimore's brighter native lights, seriously harmed his political career when, as mayor of a city plagued by narcotics and its attendant violence, he suggested that America rethink the problem as a decriminalized health issue.

Schmoke, now dean of the Howard University School of Law in Washington, was mayor of Baltimore from 1987 through to 1999.

He embodied the role of a progressive Baltimore health commissioner with the same name in a pair of episodes – "Middle Ground" and "Mission Accomplished" – in Season Three of *The Wire*, which dramatized some of what Schmoke was trying to say decades earlier.

As for Hamsterdam, the idea preceded the name.

"It was the result of the reporting Ed [Burns] and I did for *The Corner* in 1993," said David Simon. "We would debate what might be done if the country walked away from its dysfunctional drug prohibition.

"I think the idea of a free zone was more my argument . . . Ed saw problems in the approach, which we depicted as well."

Simon said he and Burns agree that a societal – if not legal – acceptance of the drug problem as a health issue and not a problem for law enforcement is the only way to begin.

And that big fat war on drugs budget?

They suggest, Simon said, ". . . using the resources of the drug war to economically reintegrate one America with the other . . . [although] the strategy of Hamsterdam may or may not be practical for a variety of tactical reasons."

In sketching out ways to dramatize radical reform in the American inner city, "we began calling [Bunny] Colvin's program the Amsterdam experiment.

"And then someone – I believe it might have been Ed, but I could be wrong – said the kids would mishear it and say *Hamster*-dam.

"And that just killed us."

As swiftly as it put a serious dent into Kurt Schmoke's career and killed Bunny Colvin's.

•

Looking for new dramatic flashpoints after Season One on the streets and Season Two on the waterfront, *Wire* fans welcomed the insanity of Hamsterdam while looking for resolution of the established power struggles as the Neville Brothers announced Season Three with their interpretation of "Way Down in the Hole".

Will Bubbles – "that's me, born fucked up . . ." – beat junk?

When will Valchek get more than a punch in the face for being a world-class, rat-fucking prick?

How long before Omar gets Stringer got?

Season Three would see Avon return home from prison as puzzled by Hamsterdam as the runners and touts who work for Barksdale without ever having met him.

"The Greek" set sail but not Vondas, whose cold, businessman's ass would warm that Patterson Park bench above the streets of East Baltimore until the final credits rolled.

Omar?

What do *you* think?

"One thing that distinguishes Omar is his absolute patience," said David Simon. "He's willing to endure even longer surveillance than the police do. He's absolutely determined."

Finally, asked Simon, unaware when Season Three opened if there would be a Season Four: "How do we entertain the masses while at the same time laying bare the political processes through which an increasingly disenfranchised people are to seek redress?"

City Hall was to the third season what the Port of Baltimore was to the second and the West Baltimore housing projects were to the first:

the wall against which the core drama of the investigation will be thrown.

On staff to make it ring true is William F. Zorzi Jr., a veteran Baltimore newspaperman who specialized in backroom politics and hadn't a clue that before it was all over, TV viewers around the world would come to know his comely mug as though he were their cranky "Uncle Bill".

In the past, politics along the Chesapeake Bay (where early 17th-century refugees from Britain established the first Roman Catholic English colony in the New World) has nearly rivaled Louisiana as a haven for corrupt government.

"You're presuming dysfunction," chuckled Zorzi, whose long tenure at the *Baltimore Sun* included several years covering the General Assembly in Annapolis and a stint as assistant city editor from 2000 to 2002 before leaving the paper soon after.

"I see my job to make it as accurate a portrayal of city and state politics as possible," he said. "Not just the machinations of what makes the city move, but the very real things that happen in the course of a citywide election."

And this: "I'd like to get into things that people just don't talk about much – like the reality of race in politics."

As Carcetti mused: "Every day I wake up white in a city that ain't."

"We're going to see the world of City Hall and how it dovetails with the police department and the 'hood," said Zorzi. "It's a safe assumption that crime will be an issue."

Dead center in Season Three's take on crime is Robert Wisdom, reprising his Season Two cameo as Major Howard "Bunny" Colvin, the war-weary commander of the Western District.

"I grew up in Washington [in 1953], and when I look at Baltimore and see the boarded-up houses, there's a sadness," said Wisdom, who in 2007 appeared in the Hilary Swank movie *Freedom Writers*.

"As [a black man] I can speak the language of that foreign country – the invisible America – but I don't know the spiritual devastation."

To play Colvin, Wisdom said, he flipped "those feelings," demanding the character ask himself hard questions about a job that on the surface is about helping people but became a tool for career advancement and financial security.

"That is what feeds Colvin," he said. "This role is asking me to find my greatness. I'm at the point in my life where I can handle this much storytelling."

MAYOR O'MALLEY TO THE WIRE: DROP DEAD

"Violence and addiction were the sad facts of our past . . ."
— WISHFUL THINKING FROM MARTIN O'MALLEY, MAYOR OF BALTIMORE (2000-2006)

It's not exactly the boxed set of DVDs the Chamber of Commerce would use to lure entrepreneurs, tourists and new residents to their fair city.

First *Homicide*, followed by *The Corner* and then five brutal seasons of *The Wire*; each set in Baltimore, one darker and more desperate than the last, all from David Simon, that troublemaker with a notebook and an agenda.

The Wire is a thinly fictionalized, meticulously researched drama in which the city of Baltimore looms larger than any actor in the ensemble cast.

It's no secret that Martin O'Malley, who became governor of Maryland in 2006, was an inspiration, at least in part, for Mayor Tommy Carcetti, a white councilman who splits the black vote to become mayor and, by Season Five, governor of Maryland.

["One of several inspirations," said David Simon publicly about the O'Malley/Carcetti similarities, with characteristics of other local pols "whose names you wouldn't even know."]

In 2004, while still mayor, O'Malley said: "Along with *The Corner*, [*The Wire*] has branded us in the national and metropolitan eye in a way that is very counterproductive to growth, hope, violent-crime reduction and recovery."

Echoing Omar's taunting of Barksdale-organization defense attorney Maurice Levy, O'Malley continued, "The producers and the drug dealers are the only people who benefit from the perpetuation" of what the mayor termed "the city's past record of drugs and violence."

O'Malley's successor upon his election to the State House – former Baltimore City Council president Sheila Dixon – was not quite as aggressive in criticizing *The Wire*, but no more pleased.

"Some people have the perception from outside of the city that this is what the entire city looks like and it doesn't," said Dixon on a January 2008 edition of the Jim Lehrer *NewsHour* on PBS. "It's a small fraction of an environment here in the city."

Almost a year to the day after Dixon appeared on the Lehrer show, she was indicted on 12 counts of felony, theft, perjury, fraud and misconduct in office (in connection to gifts received from a former boyfriend and developer). On May 28, perjury charges were dismissed; seven other criminal charges – including theft – were left standing. Dixon's trial begins in September 2009.

In April of 2009, one of the hundreds of local actors sent to the set of *The Wire* by casting director Pat Moran – a 63-year-old self-described hustler named Harold Lee Able, Sr. – was shot in the head and killed.

Able was murdered in East Baltimore while working as an unlicensed cab driver, known as a "hack." A former laborer at the Bethlehem Steel shipyard in Sparrows Point east of the city, Able worked on Season Two of *The Wire* as a stevedore named "Moonshot."

[He has a scene at the Clement Street Bar with the other veteran stevedores talking with pride and bravado about the good old days of unloading ships with muscle and not technology.]

At the time of his death, Able had just completed a role as a gas station owner on a movie called *The Sins of the Fathers*.

In 1988, there were a mere 234 murders in Crabtown. That's right, only 234 – 191 of them by gunfire – the lowest number of homicides since just before the 1980s crack epidemic hit American cities. In 2007, there were 282 murders, closer to typical in a city where homicides have hovered near or above 300 a year for decades.

Just before the 2004 Memorial Day holiday, the news was filled with reports of one dead and eight wounded in four unrelated city shootings in a five-hour span.

Less than 48 hours later, three children under the age of ten were found decapitated in a Northwest Baltimore apartment.

These are the kind of headlines – "Nine People Shot in Five Hours" said the *Baltimore Sun* – that obliterate a closer parsing of statistics championed by politicians.

"Baltimore is reducing crime and overdose deaths faster than any major city in America this decade," said O'Malley, not long before running for governor.

Noting that he had nothing against *The Wire* as "art or entertainment," he argued that the show "has done nothing to help us in that important fight."

By the end of 2002, according to O'Malley, Baltimore led all large American cities in reducing crime, ahead of both Chicago and New York. Yet inside the police department, district commanders were being pressured to reduce crime statistics by any means necessary, resulting in the wholesale manipulation of those statistics. Some of those commanders would tell of their plight in private conversation with Simon and Burns, and the O'Malley administration's massaging of its crime stats became, in turn, a new theme of *The Wire*'s last season.

During his tenure, the annual average of homicides went down from about 320 before he took office to 260 in his first term.

One resident tried to help clean up her drug-plagued East Baltimore neighborhood by repeatedly calling police, testifying in court and going nose-to-nose with corners boys entrenched outside her home.

For these acts of citizenship, she paid dearly. Her fate was the sort of atrocity that was startling even by Baltimore standards, making national headlines that trumped anything *The Wire* had portrayed.

O'Malley called it his most difficult moment as mayor.

In October 2002, Angela Dawson, her husband Carnell Dawson Sr., and five of their children died in an arson fire – gasoline was spread on the front room of their home and set ablaze – as payback for the family's anti-crime efforts.

Just a week and a half before, the house at 1401 East Preston Street had been firebombed for the same reason. O'Malley called the attack "barbaric."

"The hardest moment of this administration was going to March Funeral Home and filing by five tiny caskets," O'Malley told the *Baltimore Sun*. "But the Dawson loss just strengthened my resolve.

"The tragedy was our Alamo, it was not our Waterloo."

Almost immediately, police arrested 21-year-old Darrell L. Brooks and charged him with multiple counts of homicide. Brooks pleaded guilty in federal court in 2003 and was sentenced to life without parole.

"These children will not have died in vain," the mayor promised. "This is not the future of our city. This has to become part of our past."

State Senator Nathaniel J. McFadden, a lifelong resident of the Eastside, likened the attacks on the Dawson family to Al Qaeda: "We have terrorist cells of juvenile drug dealers. And it's all over the city."

David Simon acknowledged that from the perspective of an elected official or the police commissioner, there isn't much reason to be a fan of *The Wire*.

"Our purpose and intention in presenting this material cannot and should not be the same as that of Baltimore's civic leaders," said Simon. "We are not merely trying to entertain viewers, but to speak to existing problems in a meaningful way – problems that are not confined to Baltimore, but are universal."

After the show's first season, the city held up routine film production permits, and reluctant city agencies referred all filming issues to the mayor's office.

Similarly, a Baltimore City Council subcommittee passed a resolution critical of the show while urging new efforts to promote a more positive municipal image.

Testifying before that committee, Simon said that he had no objection to any effort to enhance the city's image, but that government should not be involved in either the support or criticism of any given film, book, or other narrative.

After the second season, new leadership in Baltimore's Film Office made getting the show made in the city less difficult, a change for which Simon credits O'Malley.

He also contended that the department inherited by ex-commissioner Ed Norris, a New Yorker handpicked by O'Malley, was so dysfunctional and crime so overwhelming that any improvements were likely to have a good effect.

[While superintendent of the Maryland State Police in 2003, Norris was indicted on charges of spending money from an auxiliary fund of private donations assigned to the Police Commission on a variety of personal expenses. A year later, he pled guilty to federal corruption and tax charges included in the indictment.]

Norris was cast and appeared in *The Wire* before the trouble. He had a recurring role as homicide detective Edward Norris. Not the most natural of actors, he was, apart from the misallocation of the auxiliary fund – which amounted to little more than $200 – a good police administrator, said Simon.

Norris "had been a working policeman and more than any commissioner in decades, he understood actual police work," said Simon.

" . . . after successive administrations in which police work had been de-emphasized in Baltimore, any effort at reform was comparable to a

350-pound man on a diet," said Simon. "The first 20 pounds were easy."

In 2007, Mayor Sheila Dixon named Baltimore native and 26-year department veteran Frederick Bealefeld III as police commissioner.

Two years later, in May of 2009, Bealefeld went on local radio to decry light sentences for the sort of inane yet common atrocity that might easily have befallen Wallace or Dukie on *The Wire*.

Two schoolkids were abducted and tortured over a beef about a stolen PlayStation video game and the men convicted of the crime were given two years each.

"Those guys got fairly nominal sentences for some heinous stuff that they did to these kids," said Bealefeld on the talk show.

"If it happened in a white neighborhood in any other community in this state, we'd still be talking about it . . . people would be talking about life sentences."

SEASON THREE EPISODE GUIDE

"The city is worse than when I first came on. So what does that say about me? About my life?"

MAJOR HOWARD "BUNNY" COLVIN

The drug war is back, center stage: enter Marlo Stanfield.

Ambition takes the podium disguised as a promise of change in the form of Baltimore City Councilman Tommy Carcetti, "a venal pol with an idealistic streak," according to the *New Yorker*, who – with his face scrubbed and hair combed nice – looks like a Catholic boy in his First Communion suit.

And real reform arrives sans hype and unannounced when the boundaries of a new neighborhood are drawn along an especially fucked-up stretch of inner city Baltimore.

"Hamsterdam," with his grace Bunny Colvin as its benevolent dictator.

Within the strict boundaries of Hamsterdam, one may sling drugs with impunity. Try to do the same just one toke over the line and the cops will grind your teeth into paste.

And therein, literally, lies the drama.

"Would *The Wire* have been possible without [drug] prohibition?" asks Charles Allen, a Baton Rouge transplant to Los Angeles, one-time problem drug user and close student of the show.

"No corner boys, no Omar to rob them, no bodies in abandoned rowhouses, no Avon or Marlo or Stringer Bell. And no wire to eavesdrop on them."

episode
twenty-six

TIME AFTER TIME
"Don't matter how many times you get burnt,
you just keep doin' the same." — BODIE
Directed by Ed Bianchi
Story by Robert F. Colesberry & David Simon; teleplay by David Simon

KA-BOOM!

Season Three opens with a bang as the Franklin Terrace housing project – the "towers" and the "pit" from which the Barksdale gang has built its drug empire – are imploded to much fanfare.

"I'm kinda sad. Them towers be home to me," says Poot to Bodie, who mocks him.

"You gonna cry over a housing project?" he asks.

Good times there, says Poot, popped my first nut in Chantay in the seventh grade. And she gave you VD more than once, laughs Bodie.

Doing the rah-rah at the countdown-to-a-new-era ceremonies in view of the demolition is Mayor Royce, promising new, moderately priced housing to replace the nightmare.

In the immediate sights of Lieutenant Daniels's detail this year is the eastside drug organization headed by Proposition Joe Stewart, a reasonable man, as far as it goes, who lives by the dictum: Buy for one and sell for two.

Prop Joe has Cheese (played by Method Man), on the corner.

["There's always been this crowd of rappers who wanted to be on *The Wire*," David Simon told Alan Sepinwall of the Newark, N.J. *Star-Ledger*. "And (Cheese) was the only guy who walked into a casting office and read and said, 'Okay, tell me about the part.' We didn't take him because he was Method, we took him because he was the best read for Cheese."]

On the wire, Detectives Lester Freamon and Roland Pryzbylewski – backed up by Officer Caroline Massey, she of the most discerning ears in Crabtown, listen as one of Cheese's deputies yakety-yaks on his cell.

"Three months and we've yet to hear his [Cheese's] voice on a phone," notes Freamon with resignation.

With no real case to make, Daniels suggests – to the consternation bordering on contempt of Detective Jimmy McNulty – that they let the wire expire in two weeks.

With Avon in jail, Stringer Bell has moved the Barksdale organization's headquarters into a funeral home, where he gathers the rank-and-file to announce a new day has dawned in West Baltimore.

"Game ain't about territory no more," says Bell. "It' s about product."

At City Hall, where the bulk of the season's off-the-street drama takes place, it's about the product of that product: crime.

East Baltimore City Councilman Thomas J. Carcetti is taking new Police Commissioner Burrell and Deputy Commissioner William A. Rawls to task over the soaring rate of violence.

Out of sight of reporters, Carcetti tries to cut a deal with Burrell to get info on what the cops really need to take a bite out of crime, promising to take care of him in the long run. Burrell, who believes he owes his career to Mayor Clarence Royce [played by Glynn Turman], declines.

Royce will soon encourage Burrell to get the murder and felony rates down, to deflate Carcetti's crusade.

Avon, a short-timer in prison, is introduced by Wee-Bey to Dennis "Cutty" Wise, a former veteran of the game about to be released after serving 14 years.

Avon tries to recruit Cutty and, facing nothing better, the ex-con considers it, though his ambivalence leads Barksdale to surmise, "The joint mighta broke him."

Daniels's promised quid-pro-quo promotion hits a serious snag at City Hall due to the political ambitions of his estranged wife Marla, though their separation is a secret.

"The Mayor," Burrell tells Daniels, "is going to want to know who his friends are before he makes a new commander."

At Camden Yards – where McNulty and Moreland take in a ballgame – Jimmy sulks in the upper deck while staring down at his kids in good seats next to his ex-wife and her new boyfriend. Bunk takes a call on his cell phone: fresh murders on the board.

Rawls and Burrell, charged by Royce to reduce crime, take all of their district commanders to task. Felonies, barks Rawls, *must* drop by five percent and murders must be kept below 275 bodies.

"I don't care how you do it," growls Rawls, "just fucking do it."

episode twenty-seven

ALL DUE RESPECT
"There's never been a paper bag."
— BUNNY COLVIN

Directed by Steve Shill
Story by David Simon & Richard Price; teleplay by Richard Price

Omar, pretending to be an old man in a wheelchair, cons his way into a Barksdale stash house with new lieutenant, Kimmy. The heist is flawless and they get away with drugs and cash.

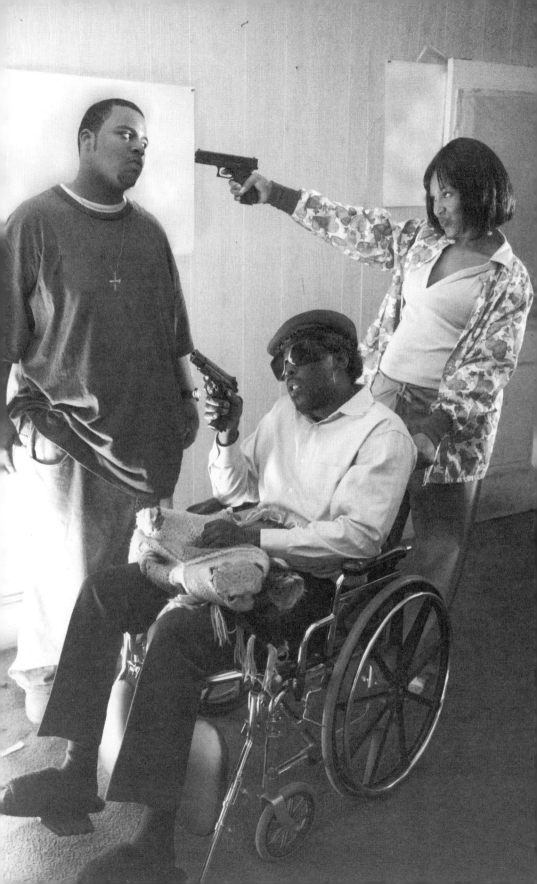

Visiting Avon in prison, Stringer Bell tells his partner that the towers are gone.

"All that battlin' we did to take them towers and now we out in the street with the rest of 'em we beat," says Avon before Bell sends their corner boys to new intersections across the westside.

There, Bodie encounters Marlo, offering him good product at a good price, only to be told – with a coldness out of Avon's go-fuck-yourself playbook – to roll out.

Without making eye contact, Marlo says, "I'm being a gentleman about it for the moment."

[Jamie Hector, who plays Marlo, is known to be a gentleman. Playing Marlo, Hector has said, allows him to "explore that side of the coin."]

At the Medical Examiner's office, McNulty stirs the pot on D'Angelo Barksdale's prison "suicide" from the year before. Looking at autopsy photos, he suspects that D was murdered and remains fixated on locking up Stringer Bell and making it stick.

Carcetti leans on Major Valchek, who plays department politics like a saloon poker champ, to broker a second meeting with Burrell in the hope that the commissioner will see his future no longer lies in protecting Mayor Royce.

"I should tell him what?" asks Valchek of the impertinent councilman. "Make nice or invest heavily in petroleum jelly?"

Burrell sees the wisdom in making nice and tells Carcetti that he's having trouble getting police cruisers repaired and back on the street, thus leaving holes in patrols on every shift.

Carcetti makes good on his promise and 20 squad cars are soon back in service. And he lets Burrell know that the mayor, who cancelled an incoming class of police academy cadets claiming budget restraints, "fucked you . . . I know that money was in the budget."

And again: I can be a better friend to you than Royce.

When Cheese's pit bull loses to another dog in a stakes fight, Cheese shoots the animal. When it appears that the other side cheated, a dope dealer named Triage kills a soldier named Jelly who works for the winning dog's owner, Dazz.

News of which soon crackles over the wire and into the ears of Greggs, Freamon, Prez, and Caroline.

Assuming Cheese is talking openly of murder, Greggs says: "[He's] only a level below Proposition Joe. All of a sudden, this case has legs."

The pressure from Rawls to get stats down does not relent and Daniels uses some wiretap info to make arrests. McNulty argues that the arrests will force them to reveal themselves and pushes his boss to bide his time.

Nonetheless, Cheese is arrested and brought in by Bunk and McNulty. It soon becomes clear that the case is, literally, a dog.

"We're charging his ass," says Bunk with more bravado than conviction.

"Improper disposal of an animal. Discharging a firearm in city limits," adds McNulty.

"Animal cruelty, if we wanna run wild with it," adds Bunk.

And the wire goes silent over the execution of a dog.

At the bar later, McNulty hits on Pearlman, who, having had enough bites out of that apple, goes home with Cedric Daniels.

At Greggs's home, Cheryl is the resentful spouse and mother: Kima is never around and when she is, doesn't take much interest in their new baby. Before long, Greggs is doing "the McNulty" – making excuses and stepping out.

When a Western District drug bust set up by Sergeant Carver in the Western goes to shit, Officer Dozerman – who'd been sent out alone – is shot.

"Fucking solo cars," says Carver, further distressed that Dozerman's gun is missing. "I shoulda teamed him. I fucked up."

Leaving the scene of Dozerman's shooting, Colvin visits "The Deacon" (played by Melvin Williams), and confides: "Tonight is a good night. Why? Because my shot cop didn't die. And it hit me . . . This is what makes a good night on my watch: absence of a negative."

Addressing his officers the next day, Bunny Colvin hints at an idea he's been percolating since the my-way-or-the-highway, deliver-the-stats speech by Rawls.

He explains that "the corner is, was and always will be the poor man's lounge" and that back in the day, drinking in public became a crime and cops spent a lot of time locking up folks for getting half-a-load on in public.

And then some forgotten wino put his shorty in a paper bag and the boys were able to drink in peace while the cops went about their sworn duties.

"Dozerman got shot last night trying to buy three vials," Colvin says. "There's never been a paper bag for drugs. Until now."

And no one is quite sure what he's saying.

episode
twenty-eight

DEAD SOLDIERS
"The gods will not save you."
— BURRELL

Directed by Rob Bailey

Story by David Simon & Dennis Lehane; teleplay by Dennis Lehane

Crime keeps rising, and Rawls and Burrell publicly humiliate their commanders for the failure. Eastern District commander Marvin Taylor is fired by Burrell on the spot and immediately replaced by his second-in-command.

Omar – "the one guy who stood up against the institutions," according to Ed Burns – cases another Barksdale stash house with his crew of Dante, Tosha and Kimmy.

When they pull the job, however, they are met with gunfire, some of it friendly, as Tosha – played by Edwina Findley – takes a bullet in the head from Dante. A Barksdale soldier also goes down.

The thug who shot Dozerman is found and thoroughly beaten by the cops, prompting a full confession, saying he sold the wounded cop's gun to Peanut, a kid on the street.

On principle, Sergeant Landsman orders Bunk to recover the gun, prompting McNulty to quip: "In one of the most heavily armed cities in the known, gun-loving world, what do these ignorant motherfuckers care about one goddamn semi-auto, more or less?"

Carcetti leaks it to a *Baltimore Sun* reporter that Mayor Royce – penny-wise and dollar-foolish – is not going to pay for a police academy class this year.

Royce tells Burrell to fudge the bad news, tell the media whatever you need to tell them, just take your lumps and keep it away from me.

The mayor then publicly comes to the rescue of the nearly aborted class of cadets.

With the wire silenced, Daniels sends the detail on the trail of a drug dealer named Kintel "Prince K" Williamson, a Jamaican from Northwest Baltimore believed to have recently killed three people.

McNulty does not hear Daniels's directive; he is inspecting the prison doorknob from which D'Angelo Barksdale allegedly hung himself.

Acting out the scene, McNulty puts the belt used by D'Angelo around his neck, discovering that it will not constrict tight enough to kill someone. Once suspicious, he is now convinced: D was murdered.

The following day, homicide detective Ray Cole dies while working out at the gym, the plot line needed to cover the unexpected passing of Robert F. Colesberry, the *Wire* producer who portrayed Cole with quiet humility.

While his fellow commanders are cooking down the stats with administrative sleight-of-hand, Bunny Colvin tells his people not to do the same.

At the next meeting of commanders called by Burrell and Rawls, Colvin is the only one not reporting a drop in crime and explains: "Sometimes the gods are uncooperative."

To which Burrell replies: "If the gods are fucking you, you find a way to fuck them back. It's Baltimore, gentlemen, the gods will not save you."

Colvin's numbers aren't down but the revenue from Stanfield dealer Fruit is, and when Marlo demands to know why, he's told that the Barksdale boys have set up shop around the way and are stealing customers.

When Marlo suggests that Fruit and the "young guns" give the Barksdale crew "a workout," they directly do so, with baseball bats and a vengeance.

And then, in a meeting with trusted lieutenants back at the Western, Bunny Colvin unveils Hamsterdam: We are going to let the drug trade operate in one of three specifically outlined areas – spots that are especially bleak even by standards of the Baltimore 'hood – and nowhere else.

"You need to take the long view here," Colvin tells his outraged staff. "Look at it this way, gentlemen: would you rather shoot at fish in the ocean? Or gather 'em all up in a few small barrels and start emptying your clips then?"

At Kavanaugh's pub, friends and fellow cops have a final drink with the late Ray Cole, who lies in state upon the pool table.

"We're police," says Landsman, "so no lies between us: He wasn't the greatest detective and he wasn't the worst. He put down some good cases and he dogged a few bad ones. But the motherfucker had his moments. Yes, he fucking did."

On another side of town, they are laying Tosha to rest; the funeral home is busy with Barksdale people looking to cap a grieving Omar.

Omar, however, mourns solo from across the street, smoking a cigarette in the shadows.

episode
twenty-nine

HAMSTERDAM
"Why you got to go and fuck with the program?"
– FRUIT

Directed by Ernest Dickerson
Story by David Simon & George Pelecanos; teleplay by George Pelecanos

At a westside community meeting, angry residents will not be mollified when cops and politicians try to say that they are in control of the drug war being waged on their streets.

"My cousin Billy Gant cooperated," says one resident of the ill-fated maintenance man from Season One. "Went downtown and testified. He deader than Tupac today."

Colvin addresses the crowd and says: "Truth is, I can't promise you it's gonna get better. We can't lock up the thousands that are out on those corners. There's no place to put them if we could.

"This here is the world we've got, and it's time that all of us had the good sense to at least admit that much."

And then he admits that he isn't sure what the answer is, but whatever it may be, it can't be a lie.

Greggs and McNulty learn from Bubbles that some of the best narcotics real estate is now owned by "a young boy named Marlo."

Along with that intel he provides the tag number of Marlo's ride. Marlo, the cops learn, had been a suspect in a murder until the prime witness turned up dead.

Cutty, the recently released convict whom Avon sensed might have had his soldier's heart cut out of him after years in prison, gives an honest day's work a try with a gang of landscapers, most of them Hispanics.

When a fellow ex-con shows him that a fickle lawn mower needs to be primed before it will run, the foreman tells Cutty, "You wanna stay on the straight, ain't gonna be no big reward to it. This is it right here."

It is then that Cutty approaches the Barksdale group, via Slim Charles, saying he's ready to go back to his chosen profession.

"Game's the same," Slim Charles tells him. "Just got more fierce."

And Bunk keeps looking under every rock for Dozerman's gun.

In the detail office, Freamon continues to harangue McNulty over his insubordination of Daniels, especially noting that Jimmy's obsession with Stringer Bell is flagrant disrespect of a boss trying to do right by his people.

"Fuck loyalty," says McNulty. "And fuck you, Lester. I never thought I'd hear that chain-of-command horseshit outta your mouth."

As Colvin lunches with Johns Hopkins University officials to talk about his post-retirement career as the school's No. 2 security man – a nice $80k a year gig – his troops begin spreading the word on the street that there will be a "free zone."

It is as if the cops have begun speaking Chinese.

Says Carver: "This corner's indicted. We're coming back tomorrow and when we do, everybody wears bracelets – unless you people move your shit down to Vincent Street, down where the houses are all vacant. You do that and we don't give a shit."

Explains another cop: "Vincent Street is like Switzerland. Or Amsterdam."

For Fruit, it don't compute: "Look: we grind, and y'all try to stop it. That's how we do. Why you got to go and fuck with the program?"

At a local community college, McNulty follows a hunch, gets Stringer Bell's cell phone number from the registrar and wanders the halls until he glimpses Bell in an economics class.

Goddamn!

He will later follow Stringer to a meeting with an architect, a real estate developer and State Senator Clayton Davis.

Double goddamn.

Later, Freamon will bring McNulty down a peg by telling him that he not only already had Bell's cell number, but that Stringer only uses the line for legal business.

"Stringer Bell's worse than a drug dealer," says Freamon.

"He's a developer," says Prez.

In a bar in Little Italy, the eastside neighborhood that launched the legendary and real-life Baltimore mayor Thomas J. D'Alesandro (1903–1987) – father

of current United States Speaker of the House, Nancy Pelosi – Tommy Carcetti tells confidants he will run for mayor.

In walks a classy, good-looking woman and Carcetti bets the table he can talk her into letting him buy her a drink. He does, but it's because he already knows her: Theresa D'Agostino, a local girl made good down the parkway in DC, a fixer of campaigns.

While pretending to sweet-talk her for his friends, Carcetti is asking D'Agostino to manage his campaign.

Impatient with the lack of progress in getting the street dealers to buy into his brainstorm, Colvin has all the dealers rounded up and brought to a high school auditorium so they can hear the gospel of a new day loud and clear.

At the meeting are Bodie and Poot, a few others from the Barksdale team, as well as Fruit, Jamal and Boo from Marlo's crews. Colvin can't do a thing to get them to listen until a small black woman – the vice principal who knows the boys and their families – walks in and tells them to shut up.

The second she leaves, however: bedlam.

Across town, Cutty goes to a Barksdale house party that a man in prison might dream about for years upon end: drugs, music, booze, and a plenitude of pulchritude.

If Cutty doubted it before, he knows it now: he's back.

THE WRITER'S AMBITION

A few years ago, a network newsmagazine show produced a piece on me as part of their ongoing series of profiles on crime novelists. The crew came to Washington, D.C. to film the segment. On the second night of the shoot we filmed at Thirteenth and Clifton in Shaw, alongside the once notorious Clifton Terrace apartments, subsidized housing known not only as a breeding ground for poverty and crime but also for its location on the edge of the Piedmont Plateau, offering one of the most glorious views in the city.

As the cameraman shot me curbside, standing beside my car, wearing a black leather jacket with a turtleneck beneath it (a consciously cool but improbable pose, as I would ordinarily not stand outside in this part of the city at night), a group of local kids approached me and made their way into the shot.

One of them, who said his name was Peanut Butter and Jelly ("'cause that's what I like to eat, most time"), asked me why I was being filmed – his way of saying, I suppose, that I didn't look particularly special.

"I'm a book writer," I said, not using the word "novelist," or simply "writer," knowing that this description would be the one he would most succinctly understand.

"You gonna put me in one of your books?" he said in the bold way of the street kid with nothing to lose.

"Okay," I said, adding, "and that's a promise, too."

I was thinking that he had probably already been on the bad end of many broken promises in his short life, and I did not intend to add my name to the list of those who had let him down.

I did write a minor character, a kid named Peanut Butter and Jelly, into my next book. I am fairly certain that the real Peanut Butter and Jelly does not know this. The editor of the program left him in the piece as well, which was nationally broadcast on a Sunday morning several months later. I am equally certain that the boy has not seen it.

So what was the point of our efforts?

To honor the bargain would be the easy, noble answer. But the real answer, more about us than it is about him, is more complicated.

The night I met Peanut Butter and Jelly, I drove uptown in my high-performance BMW to a nice neighborhood where my wife and children slept safely and comfortably in a house I'd built with the proceeds of my career as a novelist, screenwriter, and film and television producer.

I cannot say with certainty what kind of environment Peanut Butter and Jelly returned to that evening, but it is safe to assume that it was nothing like the one I share with my family.

If he is like most of the kids I meet in the inner city, he lives in a spare dwelling with a single parent, if he lives with a parent at all. He walks through drug-infested streets to get to a dilapidated school that will undereducate him and ultimately leave him unskilled and unprepared to face a world of productivity in which he does not belong.

And what did I do for him that night? I learned his name, and I put it in a book. A small thing, really. Not nearly enough to bring anything of import to his life.

I make my living writing about people who, because of an accident of birth and circumstance, are less fortunate than me. In interviews I often say that my mission is to illuminate and dignify their lives to a public that rarely reads about them or recognizes their humanity in film, television, and fiction.

This is true, but it is only a partial truth. What goes unsaid is the gnawing feeling that I am also exploiting them for my personal gain. It is the same feeling I sometimes get while working on *The Wire*, which takes our shoot to some of the most impoverished sections of Baltimore.

On set we often meet kids who greet us as if the circus has come to town. Many of us indulge them by bringing them into the video village, letting them watch the monitors, wear the headphones, and eat candy and junk food from the craft service tables. This makes them happy for a little while and, undeniably, allows us to feel good about ourselves.

But at the end of the day we go back to our lives and they go back to theirs. For them, nothing has changed.

In a recent interview with a national newspaper, I was repeatedly asked if I felt that I was doing some sort of public service by writing novels that expose social ills or by working on *The Wire*, a television series that attempts to present a complete, accurate world populated by fully fleshed-out characters, the types most folks routinely look away from on the street.

I refused to answer in the affirmative because I do not for one moment harbor such illusions. My ambition is to do good, honest work. At best, a viewer might watch our show and be inspired to become the kind of extraordinary person – teacher, coach, foster-parent, mentor – that I can only conjure up as a fictional character in my head. The kind of person, that is to say, who is far better than me.

As for Peanut Butter and Jelly, I think of him less frequently as time goes on. Occasionally I wonder what became of him, but then the moment passes. I have my own family to dream about and worry over, and they occupy most of my thoughts.

Them, and the books I have yet to write.

George Pelecanos

episode
thirty

STRAIGHT AND TRUE
"I had such fuckin' hopes for us."
– MCNULTY

Directed by Dan Attias

Story by David Simon & Ed Burns; teleplay by Ed Burns

Johnny tries to get Bubbles to stop snitching, arguing that they are doing pretty well for themselves without it.

"Oh yeah," says Bubs. "We getting by. Out here every damn day, rippin' and runnin' and ain't got shit to show for it."

When they do get something to show for it early in the episode – $10 given to Johnny for "rescuing" a man on a ladder from Bubbles – Johnny disappears with the cash.

Awaking with a hatchet-in-the-head hangover after the party, Cutty is told by his grandmother that his ex-girlfriend called again to remind him of a commitment he made to visit her church.

"She say there's a job in it, if you still lookin'," says the grandmother.

McNulty, on a deathly dull surveillance of the photocopy shop Bell runs, decides to just go in and say hello.

"Ain't seen you round the way," he tells Bell, who replies that he doesn't go around the way anymore; that he is now into real estate.

Even though McNulty is the only one who seems to care, Freamon believes Bell is now truly out of the reach of handcuffs.

"He won't go near the street," Freamon tells Jimmy. "He is insulated from the day-to-day operations on the corners.

"The money that comes back is laundered through enough straight business investments that there's no way to trace it back. A player gets to that point, there's no way for working police to tie a can to his tail."

Somehow, this gets through to McNulty, who decides to channel his efforts into catching the dealer Kintel Williamson, who is still close to the streets where the cops have a chance.

Omar and his attrition-depleted crew prepare to take off another job, with the boss having to make an uneasy peace between Dante and Kimmy, who argue over the roles they will play.

Says Omar: "This time we have to do it right."

With his own men as skeptical of his sling-with-impunity scheme as the dealers, Colvin drops in on Daniels to get the names of mid-level dealers, reckoning that he will need their help in getting the corner boys to play ball.

When Carver and Herc try to bring in Marlo for a meet with Colvin, it appears a fight will erupt until Carver tells Herc to back off.

They do, however, have better luck with others who – incredulous – are introduced to their new stomping grounds along Vincent Street. Now the problem strikes at the foundation of capitalism: no customers.

Says Colvin to a still-reluctant Bodie: "I swear to God, I have over 200 sworn personnel and I will free them all up to brutalize every one of you they can.

"If you're on a corner in my district, it will not be just a humble or a loitering charge. It will be some Biblical shit that happens to you on the way into that jail wagon. You understand? We will not be playing by any rules that you recognize."

Emerging to glimpse this Baltimore Moses with new tablets of "thou shalts" from on high is an aged woman still living in one of the all-but-falling-down houses, a resident overlooked.

"We musta missed her," says Lieutenant Dennis Mello, played by the real-life retired Baltimore homicide sergeant Jay Landsman.

"One more thing to do, then," answers Colvin.

Scanning the morning paper, Carcetti, seeing that another witness in an important drug case has been murdered, is livid.

"You let a witness get killed in a high-profile case like this, it says the city's broke and can't be fixed," he tells fellow councilman, Anthony Gray, played by Christopher Mann.

"You want your cape and the little red underpants?" needles Gray. "Or do you stash that shit in the phone booth?"

Carcetti tells Mayor Royce he will take the case to the media if he doesn't make the witness homicide a priority. He most definitely has Royce's attention.

Taking time out from his new Barksdale duties, Cutty finds out that his old girlfriend, Grace, has no romantic interest in him and that the church to which she sent him has no job to offer.

But he also finds that the job he does have, working for Avon, sickens him in a way it didn't before he went to prison. "An elevation in [Cutty's] growth," said Chad Coleman, the actor who portrayed him, in an online interview with Marcus Vanderberg.

Bunk does double-duty trying to find Dozerman's gun while working Tosha's murder and concludes, via an eyewitness, that Omar was present when she was killed. Before he can get the witness downtown, however, Landsman shows up and orders him back on the Glock-in-a-haystack search.

Bell, not as far removed from the game as McNulty may believe, convenes a meeting of major, citywide players in the drug trade – Marlo being conspicuous by his absence – and preaches to them the benefits of working together.

"All in favor of goin' in together so as to pull the best discount on a New York package, raise up," he says, a show of hands passing the motion.

Observes Prop Joe: "For a cold-ass crew of gangsters, y'all carried it like Republicans an' shit."

Afterward, Bell tries to enlighten Marlo on the wisdom of joining the co-op. Greggs, on info from Bubbles, follows Marlo to the meeting, flabbergasted when Bell shows up. Summoning McNulty, the pair almost wet their pants with glee: Stringer is still in the game.

Like rats scrambling for cheese, van loads of junkies are set loose by Colvin's troops in the drug free zone, which is almost immediately christened "Hamsterdam."

Stunned and spooked – their disease bigger than whatever their misgivings may be – dope fiends buy their medicine out in the open, as amazed as the dealers when the cops simply stand by.

At a Catholic grade school parent/teacher meeting, McNulty – in the company of his ex – meets Carcetti's kingmaker, Theresa D'Agostino, goes home with her and beds her.

And Avon Barksdale comes home from prison. After lavish welcome-home celebrations, Stringer takes his old friend to a waterfront condo he's bought, a new Lincoln Navigator parked below.

"We makin' so much straight money," says Bell. "We can carry shit like this out in the open now, in our own names."

episode
thirty-one

HOMECOMING

"Just a gangster, I suppose."
— AVON BARKSDALE

Directed by Leslie Libman

Story by David Simon & Rafael Alvarez; teleplay by Rafael Alvarez

When Sergeant Carver tells Bunny Colvin that some dealers remain resistant to the free zones, Colvin tells the cops to "bang them senseless.

"Anything you need to do, you do. Up to a body that can't walk itself out of an emergency room, I will back you and your men."

They do worse than bust heads: expensive sneakers are thrown into sewers, fine cars are towed to who-knows-where and many of the dealers themselves are driven far outside the city boundaries and left to fend for themselves.

Stringer and Avon find out that the legit world has its own share of headaches; the price of steel has doubled and there is this thing that goes against a gangster's nature: city permits, as in asking for and then paying for the permission to do as one pleases.

Stringer tries to bribe a consultant to the contractor doing work for his own "B&B" development firm.

"He goes downtown and does for us what we can't do for ourselves," the contractor explains. "Democracy in action, Mr. Bell."

Keen to do business and do it quickly, Bell pays a visit to the consultant: State Senator Clay Davis, who sets the price to speed up the permit process at $25,000.

Says Davis: "Twenty gets you the permits. Five is to me for bribin' these downtown motherfuckers. I mean, I'm the one got to risk walkin' up to these thievin' bitches with cash in hand, right?"

McNulty and Greggs argue to Daniels that if they don't get a green light to dog Bell and Barksdale, they will soon be so insulated from the drug trade as to be untouchable.

Daniels will not be moved. "Stringer Bell is quiet," he says. "And if he's

quiet, I don't give a fuck if we come back a year from now and find out he's on the Greater Baltimore Committee. This unit is about the bodies."

Avon, unaware that Stringer has extended the olive branch to Marlo, is far more disturbed by the up-and-comers' drug corner real estate than he is pleased with the legit property coming into his control through Stringer's entrepreneurship.

Bunk lets Tosha's family know that she was not an innocent bystander in the incident that caused her death. In fact, he says, she was likely killed unintentionally by a member of Omar's gang.

Hoping the family will lead him to Omar, Bunk says: "Y'all need to get word to the right people."

They do and Omar sends word back to his fellow alumnus of Edmondson High School: ". . . tell 'em she caught one from the boys she tried to take off. Tell 'em there ain't no need to involve no police in any of it."

Working to tie up every loose end that keeps him awake at night, McNulty – backed-up by Greggs – tries to get the state to change D'Angelo Barksdale's cause of death from suicide to murder.

The State's Attorney prosecutor tells them: "I don't know how you city guys do it. But down here in Annapolis, we try to duck a punch or two. Not lean into every last one."

Barksdale and Bell have a serious conversation about the future of their partnership. Barksdale, upset that Marlo has gone unchallenged on his prime street corners, is not consoled by Bell's argument that they're

making so much money they don't need any more turf wars.

"How many corners do we need?" asks Bell.

"More than a nigger can spend," says Avon.

"And we ain't gonna be around to spend what we don't got," reasons Bell, telling Barksdale they can invest the cash they now have into more real estate: "We in a money game where nary a motherfucker goes to jail. We could be past the run-and-gun, Avon. We could finance the packages and never touch nothing but cash.

"No corners, no territory, nothing but making like a goddamn bank. We let the young 'uns worry about how to wholesale, where to retail. I mean, who give a fuck who standing on what corner, when we pulling our cut off the top and putting that money to good use?"

Avon gives a fuck, saying that he "ain't no shirt-wearin' suit like you. Just a gangster, I suppose. And I want my corners."

Told about Hamsterdam by Bodie, Bell drops by to see the experiment in action, though he remains skeptical.

"Put some of our people down here," he tells Bodie. "Not too many. Just some of the young 'uns. Keep the package real small, in case this is a trap."

Avon orders his crew to "put a hurt to this Marlo. I want my corners," and the strategy falls to Cutty. It begins to go awry, however, when a Barksdale soldier named Chipper ignores Cutty's orders and rushes into action to his death.

Armed, Cutty corners Fruit but as he stares into his rival's eyes, he finds he is no longer a man who can pull the trigger and Fruit gets away.

Bubbles tips Greggs that Marlo and Barksdale are at war. At first Greggs isn't too excited – the detail has orders to pursue other targets and bring the crime rate down – and then she learns that two Barksdale boys have been killed.

"Westside gonna be all Baghdad an' shit," says Bubbles.

But even bodies falling in West Baltimore aren't enough to persuade Lieutenant Daniels to set Greggs and McNulty loose on the drug war and he throws them out of his office.

Says Greggs to McNulty: "If your old friend Bunny Colvin's up to his ass in bodies, I'd bet he'd take all the help he can get. Not that you'd ever go behind anyone's back or anything like that, right?"

Right.

Avon and Bell respond like a hawk and dove respectively to the beating they took in the offensive against Marlo.

"Ain't got no more motherfuckin' time now," said Barksdale. "When word of this get out that the boy, Marlo, punked me, what am I gonna look like?"

Bell warns Avon that if he's anywhere close to a violent crime, he's going back to jail. Avon tells Cutty and Slim Charles to take care of Marlo themselves.

Donette tells Brianna that McNulty stopped by, suggesting that D'Angelo may have been murdered. It's something Brianna has never considered in regard to her son's death. But she's thinking hard on it now.

Omar pays a visit to Bunk, just to clear things up. No one will talk and the eyewitness the detective found has "had a change of heart."

Enraged, Bunk reminds Omar that they grew up together, that once they lived in a place where people cared.

"Rough as that neighborhood could be, we had us a community. Wasn't nobody, no victim, who didn't matter. Now all we got is bodies, and predatory motherfuckers like you."

Carcetti continues his campaign to get Theresa D'Agostino to run his campaign for mayor. "Crime is outta fucking control," he argues. "Black, white, green – people are pissed off."

Upset that he let Fruit get away, Cutty has a heart-to-heart with Avon and admits he couldn't pull the trigger, explaining: "Whatever it is in you that lets you flow like you flow, it ain't in me no more."

episode
thirty-two

BACK BURNERS
"Conscience do cost."
— BUTCHIE

Directed by Tim Van Patten
Story by David Simon & Joy Lusco Kecken; teleplay by Joy Lusco Kecken

On a tour of the old neighborhood, Avon is told by Slim Charles that Marlo has closed up shop on the street and is working strictly as a behind-the-scenes wholesaler.

"And I was just beginning to respect the motherfucker for showin' heart," says Avon.

Herc, on duty in Hamsterdam, is stunned to see Avon cruise by in a SUV and Cutty is back with the yard work crew.

"You walked through them old doors, didn't you?" his foreman asks.

"Tried to," says Cutty, confiding that things have not gone very well lately.

Earlier, Daniels had his ass handed to him by Burrell and Rawls over the body count in the Marlo/Avon struggle for the Westside.

Now, back in the detail office, Daniels tells his crew that Kintel is no longer in focus, the new targets are the well-known Stringer Bell and the newcomer Marlo Stanfield.

Daniels then calls McNulty into his office and asks him point blank if he went to Colvin behind his back. Not one to lie to authority, McNulty admits that he did.

"When the cuffs go on Stringer," says a furious Daniels, "you need to find a new home. You're done in this unit."

Omar, on advice from Butchie, makes plans to buy Officer Dozerman's missing gun, which appears almost as soon as Omar puts out word that he wants it. Of course it has to be the right one.

"Tell him I'll pay when it proves itself," says Omar to Butchie.

"Told him that already," says the blind man. "He say you can make it $1,500 for his trouble . . . conscience do cost."

In this way, Bunk gets his gun and Landsman off his back.

A Barksdale soldier named Bernard brings in a new delivery of "burners," cell phones to use and throw away once the minutes are used up.

Shamrock tells him to bring 60 more in a few days and as Bernard goes about his business, buying a few at a time here and there, his girlfriend nags him to just buy them as fast as he can so they can go to the movies.

The news out of greater metropolitan Hamsterdam: shootings and aggravated assaults are down five percent in nearly every neighborhood across the Western District.

Info from a Fruit "burner" phone – salvaged by Bubbles and turned over to Greggs – shows calls made to a network of numbers no longer in use.

"It's all historical," says Freamon. "We can find the network no problem, but when we do it's a week old and they've dumped their phones. How we get a wire up, that part I haven't figured out yet."

Over dinner, Donette infuriates Stringer Bell by telling him not only that the cops are suspicious of D'Angelo's death but she passed the info along to Brianna.

"It's her son," she says. "Ain't she got a right to know?"

Bubbles, selling classic white T-shirts from a supermarket cart on the street, makes a visit to Hamsterdam, witnessing if not the Netherlands, a netherworld of drug use with abandon: fiends firing, others smoking crack, prostitutes selling their ass, all sorts of fighting and all-around chaos.

More importantly, he sees out-of-work corner boys standing around, no longer needed as runners or look-outs.

Carver will later tell dealers who have put the kids out of work to pay them a sort of unemployment insurance, that if they want to do business in Hamsterdam they will have to pay a tax.

"If I find anyone holding out, he's . . . back on the street getting his head busted," says Carver. To which Herc comments: "What are you, a fucking Communist?"

At home, Cheryl tells Greggs to move out.

"I miss us," Greggs says, noting that she only agreed to have a baby to keep the relationship.

Finding out that the mayor has lied to him about strengthening the witness protection program, Carcetti goes to City Hall to lean on Royce.

The mayor – mentioning meat and potatoes necessities like snow removal and trash pick-up – says the city is in such weak shape financially that it's the best he can do.

When Bodie and a crew are pulled over with a large amount of narcotics in their car, they protest that they are "untouchable" because they are headed to "the free zone."

McNulty and Greggs have no idea what Bodie is talking about and the shit gets weird and tense until Bunny Colvin shows up.

Colvin asks McNulty to let it ride and not spill the beans on the free zone at HQ: ". . . before you decide to lose your minds over this, you might take a moment and ride past some of my drug corners. Empty. All of them . . . district-wide, my crime is down five percent."

They concede, as McNulty owes Colvin a favor for getting Daniels to put them back on Stringer Bell. And from the car they recover a live cell phone with minutes left on it, a prize for Lester Freamon.

[Indeed, it won't take long for Freamon to build a case with the phone – he instructs the detail to gather up as many Barksdale "burners" as they can – even though by the time a wiretap goes up, the dealers will have discarded other important phones.]

Cutty makes a return visit to his friend Grace's church and has a heart-to-heart with the Deacon about beginning a new life.

He confesses he " . . . had this feelin' for a long time now like I'm outside of myself, watching me do things I don't wanna do, you know?"

Herc stuns McNulty and Greggs by telling them that Avon Barksdale is running free, that he just saw him cruising the 'hood.

"Jesus, Herc. He's at Jessup, down for four or five at least," says Greggs. "What, we all look alike to you?"

Avon Barksdale has walked and sure enough will be running.

WAY DOWN IN THE HOLE
The Music of The Wire

Steve Earle is not the kind of man who asks for much. But when the last shot to perform *The Wire* theme song rolled around, "I begged," he said.

"Way Down in the Hole" had passed through many capable hands since the show's 2002 debut: The Blind Boys of Alabama recorded it first; the original version – majestically croaked by the song's composer, Tom Waits, launched Season Two; the Neville Brothers were up next.

In the fourth year, a heartbreaking story about middle-school kids, the song was handled by a group of Baltimore teenagers calling themselves DoMaJe.

Earle played the recovering drug addict Walon, the clean and sober hillbilly who worked as Bubbles's on-again, off-again Narcotics Anonymous sponsor, and knew *The Wire* would bow out after Season Five.

"He said he had an idea for it and described a kind of broke-down street sound," recalled Simon. "It sounded right for the homeless/false serial killer motif."

Earle's notion for the song came together with Los Angeles producer John King, half of the Dust Brothers duo who produced Beck's 1996 album *Odelay*.

"I did my vocal with a resonator guitar, posted a [computer] file and sent it to John," said Earle in June of 2009, speaking before a concert with John Prine in Vienna, Virginia.

"[King] sent it back to me, flute and bass went in last and later I re-recorded the voice and guitar."

Simon, who'd considered Earle for one of the longshoremen in Season Two until schedules conflicted, liked the result, using the rendition for the concluding season.

The experience of recording "Way Down in the Hole" together convinced King and Earle to work on songs that became 2007's *Washington Square Serenade*, winner of a Grammy for Best Contemporary Folk/Americana album and one for King as producer.

"*The Wire*," said Earle of the collaboration, "was the deciding factor on both sides."

.

John Lennon described the blues as "a chair . . . not a design for a chair, but the first chair."

So sturdy is that chair that countless musicians – from its first builders in the Mississippi Delta to the White Stripes – have been able to sit in it comfortably.

In some ways, said Earle, "Way Down in the Hole" – though constructed from weathered planks of gospel – served that purpose for the various performers who settled into it over the *The Wire*'s five-season arc.

"The show," said Earle, is ". . . a story following people on both sides of the drug war with as many good guys as bad guys on both sides. That makes the choice of 'Way Down in the Hole' very interesting" as a theme.

He noted, however, "you're treading on thin ice if you try to figure out if it's a gospel song" in message. "In form it is, but in terms of how much it has to do with Christianity, that's dangerous and probably more dangerous to talk about with Waits."

The 60-year-old Waits – whose unauthorized biography, *Low Side of the Road*, was published by British author Barney Hoskyns in 2009 – is a hero to any songwriter of "my generation," said Earle. Not just for his staggering repertoire of American music, but "the way he carries himself as an artist."

"The Blind Boys obviously approached it as a gospel song," said Earle. "It's hard to say with the Nevilles, they have a long history of approaching gospel music secularly."

Earle said that DoMaJe – with vocals by Ivan Ashford, Markel Steele, Cameron Brown, Tariq Al-Sabir, and Avery Bargasse – took the most unique approach.

"They fucked with it more than anybody to make it work with the beat," he said. "They proved the universality of the song."

•

On the soundtrack to David Simon's life, the money song never shows up on time.

"My song never plays on the radio at my moment," he said. "It's always somebody else's song."

The music found in *The Wire* echoes that.

"What you don't want is to script a song that speaks to the moment, which is something a lot of people in TV don't get," he said. "If the lyrics are dead-on with [the story] . . . it's redundant.

"In real life you don't get to punch the button on the song that you want to be playing when you get into the bar fight, when you're in a car chase."

After waiting years for a soundtrack to *The Wire*, fans can hit the button on two separate discs of songs from the show.

Released by Nonesuch Records, *The Wire: . . . and all the pieces matter*, intersperses dialogue from the show with 23 songs – from "What You Know About Baltimore" by Ogun featuring Phathead to "The Body of An American" by the Pogues.

It also includes the first four versions of "Way Down in the Hole," but not Earle's, which appears on *Washington Square Serenade*.

The companion disc is *Beyond Hamsterdam: Baltimore Tracks From The Wire*.

The final track on . . . *and all the pieces matter*, is the oddly soothing, atmospheric instrumental that meanders toward silence as the final credits roll. Titled "The Fall," it was composed by *Wire* music director, Blake Leyh, who has followed Simon to the New Orleans *Treme* project.

Decidedly not on either soundtrack are these gems: "Brandy (You're a Fine Girl)," the 1972 hit by Looking Glass, played on a beat-up radio in the stevedores' pier-side shack as Frank Sobotka worries about a can of contraband languishing on the docks. The Tokens singing "The Lion Sleeps Tonight" (the "whimaway" song) as Jimmy McNulty and his two boys follow Stringer Bell through a city market.

Nor sadly, is Gram Parsons' "Streets of Baltimore," which Bunk Moreland suffered through on a night of drinking with McNulty. Or the plaintive work of Lucinda Williams, which plays quietly as city prosecutor Rhonda Pearlman is stuck at home with paperwork.

But there is "Sixteen Tons," the Merle Travis song sent to No. 1 in 1955 by Tennessee Ernie Ford and barrel-housed in Season Two by the Nighthawks of Washington, D.C.

Said former 'hawks guitarist Pete Kanaras of the day the band was filmed live at the Clement Street Bar: "My favorite moments occurred during a break . . . George Pelecanos came over and said, 'You must be the Greek!'

"And a crew member came over to take pictures of my shoes – cordovan red Fluevog Buicks. She said they were badass!"

•

While making *The Wire* pilot, David Simon and Bob Colesberry deliberated for weeks about which song – and, just as importantly, by whom – would best serve the show as its theme.

"Songs can be on point, but only up to a point," said Simon. "A lot of different things I listen to are like that, but all of Tom Waits is like that . . . never on point but they lend themselves cinematically.

"He's painting pictures in those songs and they're never linear. At least they haven't been for a long time."

With Tom as the early favorite, Simon began playing the Waits catalog for Colesberry in search of "the mood of a broken world."

"Way Down in the Hole," off the 1987 album *Frank's Wild Years*, emerged as an early contender.

"We kept listening to it over and over again, and at some point somebody handed me a copy of a CD by the Blind Boys of Alabama doing a lot of gospel stuff with rock-and-roll origins," said Simon. "At this point I was arguing for John Hammond's version of 'Get Behind the Mule.'"

The lyrics to "Mule" – from the 2001 *Wicked Grin* album of Waits covers by Hammond – speak to getting up every morning, getting behind the mule, and going out to plow, a primitive take on the rat race.

But the Blind Boys ultimately carried the day with "Way Down in the Hole," Simon swayed by "the African-American voices" charting Waits's sensibility.

In seeking permission to use the song, Simon did not have the honor of speaking with one of his heroes.

"He wanted to see some episodes first to know how it was going to be used," said Simon. "We sent him a bunch of tapes and didn't hear anything for weeks."

Finally, post-production chief Karen Thorson got in touch and Waits explained that he hadn't gotten around to watching the show because he didn't know how to operate the family VCR.

He assured Thorson that "my wife will be home soon and she knows how to work it."

"The next day," said Simon. "He approved it."

episode
thirty-three

"MORAL MIDGETRY"
"Pretty don't even come close to the problem."
— THE DEACON

Directed by Agnieszka Holland
Story by David Simon & Richard Price; teleplay by Richard Price

This episode, said screenwriter Price, "was about how quickly utopian visions can create dystopic hells."

Hamsterdam is thriving – from college kids to fiends with no veins left to puncture scoring dope; flourishing so well, in fact, that all manner of criminals are drawn to it for easy scores.

Believing the cops have betrayed their word to keep the free zone safe – a veritable "Valley of Eden" – the dealers are extremely angry.

Bunny Colvin shows the Deacon a cleaned-up street corner and the preacher wants to know how this miracle was accomplished. Colvin then takes him to Hamsterdam.

In the zone, Bunny hears about the robbery and says the dealers are right to believe they will be protected.

"We tell 'em they have to come down here without the guns, then we fall down on providing protection," he tells Carver, who points out the upwards of 60 kids just hanging out because they lost their corner jobs.

Colvin suggests that Carver hire them as patrolmen, to use their keen eyes and ears to look out for predators. To which the Deacon exclaims – both appalled and intrigued – "What in God's name did you do here?"

He then damns the zone as "a great village of pain" and insists Colvin make arrangements for needle exchanges, condom distribution and drug treatment for those who want it.

At the detail, Prez has traced Bodie's cell phone from manufacturer to a suburban Washington convenience store where Bernard bought it.

Speed-dial numbers have been traced to Bodie's grandmother and a half-dozen other burner cells. All of the Barksdale disposable cells were bought along Interstate-95.

"They're driving 200 miles every couple weeks out of sheer caution," marvels Freamon. "They're dumping phones every two weeks or so and still they're worried about catching a wiretap."

At the funeral of Rico, the Barksdale boy gunned down by Marlo, Avon says: "This motherfucker Marlo? Time to go deep on this nigger."

When Stringer complains to State Senator Davis – he of the "sheee-it" tagline – that there has been no movement on the promised and paid-for permits, the pol tells him it won't be more than a few more days.

Not only that, he promises to bring Stringer into the land of flowing milk and honey known as government procurement. And chides that impatience – "buggin'" – is a sign of the old life on the street.

With Theresa D'Agostino in the gallery, Carcetti chairs a meeting of the Public Safety subcommittee and asks Rawls and Burrell why a crime reduction in the Western accounts for half of the reduced stats citywide.

"Statistical aberration," says Burrell before Carcetti unloads once again on the cops for not providing adequate protection to state witnesses.

Later, D'Agostino will tell him he needs to work on being more likable if he wants to get elected to anything higher than the First District of Baltimore City.

Greggs and McNulty acquire convenience-store surveillance tape south of Baltimore, hoping it has caught a Barksdale worker buying cell phones.

Later, they meet FBI Special Agent Terrance Fitzhugh (played by former Golden Gloves boxer Doug Olear) at the Detail Office and, thanks to a computer program he's brought along, bingo: they zoom in on the Barksdale soldier who buys the burners and manage to extract a license number.

[For Olear, sharking with friend and party buddy Dominic West was always a treat – "We'd be joking right up to someone said 'Action!'," he said – but being directed by and working with Agnieszka Holland was an honor. Holland is a legend in Poland and her work spans 1970s *Jesus Christ's Sin* to David Simon's 2009 HBO pilot *Treme*.]

At a meeting of police commanders, Bunny Colvin labors to explain the Western District's crime drop without spilling the beans on Hamsterdam.

Rawls is skeptical: "Seriously, Bunny, I already got the City Council asking questions about the eight percent. We want to please the mayor, not go to jail behind this shit."

"Sometimes," answers Colvin, "the gods listen, sir."

Brianna Barksdale leans on McNulty for details of D'Angelo's death and Jimmy tells her that however her son may have died, it wasn't with the belt found around his neck.

"I'm sorry I brought you into the whole mess-up to begin with," says McNulty, "because frankly nobody's gonna do shit about it anyhow."

Asked why he went to Donette and not to her, McNulty says: "I was looking for someone who cared about the kid. I mean, like I said, you told him to take the years."

Avon sets out to track down Omar, using info from a social worker, while Clay Davis introduces Stringer to a suit who can toss him some minority contract money from the Board of Education contract to procure lightbulbs.

Having set up Marlo in a honey trap – a woman who shares her charms and then makes a date with him at a carry-out called the Lake Trout – the planned hit goes bad when Marlo's scouts notice the Barksdale crew and light up Avon's car, hitting him.

While having his shoulder cleaned and stitched by a veterinarian, Avon unloads on Stringer, who looks on.

"You know the difference between me and you," rues Avon bitterly. "I'm bleedin' red and you bleedin' green. I look at you these days, String, you know what I see? I see a man without a country.

"Not hard enough for this right here and maybe, just maybe, not smart enough for them out there."

In response, Stringer tells Avon that he was the one who had D'Angelo killed in prison. Enraged, Avon jumps Stringer, who subdues his friend after a short struggle.

"I took that shit off you and put it on me, because that motherfucker was out of pocket, with 20 years above his fucking head," says Stringer. "He flips, they have you, me, Brianna. No fucking way."

episode
thirty-four

SLAPSTICK
"... while you're waiting for moments that never come ..."
— FREAMON

Directed by Alex Zakrzewski
Story by David Simon & George Pelecanos; teleplay by David Simon

Cutty is now going by his given name of Dennis, the street life behind him. As Dennis clears out a space he hopes to turn into a gym to teach kids to box, the Deacon stops by.

"All you gonna need is the permits," says the Deacon. Dennis has no idea what he's talking about.

Gerard and Sapper, a pair of Barksdale soldiers, see Omar leave a cab in front of his grandmother's house and go inside. They try to get their immediate boss, Slim Charles, on the line to see if they should violate the ghetto custom of Sunday ceasefire to hit Omar.

Slim Charles doesn't answer. Next they try Shamrock, who is with Stringer Bell, who gives the green light: "Do it."

As Omar, in his Sunday best, escorts his grandmother to church, the boys open fire in the middle of the street, glass shattering as the cab drives away with the startled old woman, who is cut when the back windshield is blown out.

"Barksdale gotta be got," Omar says later. "Stringer, too. This thing gotta end."

Kimmy wants no part of it, Dante says he's with his lover to the end, but Omar turns away from both of them, saying: "This one about me. Ain't about no one else."

Daniels tells the detail that a new wire on the Barksdale burner phones will be up soon. Bernard, the soldier with the disposable phone assignment, next runs west along Interstate-70 for a bag of cells. Detective Sydnor tracks his every move.

And Bubbles wears a police wire into the Sodom that is Hamsterdam, hoping to get Bodie to make a call on a burner phone for a re-up. It works like a charm and Bodie puts in an order for a new package of heroin.

On a run for Chinese food with McNulty, Prez (who in Season One was reprimanded for shooting up his police vehicle) responds to a call, shooting and killing a decorated, undercover black cop – Derrick Waggoner – he had mistaken for a criminal.

Later, at HQ, Prez is beside himself with grief. When Daniels urges him to get a lawyer, Prez answers: "No, sir, I'm done." Quietly, Daniels puts him on suicide watch.

Avon Barksdale continues to live in the past, his differences with Bell smoothed but far from gone: "We gonna be back where we was, String. I can smell it, man. Just gotta get this boy Marlo and then spread out like we do."

Avon then asks Stringer straight-up if he gave the okay to take Omar on the Sabbath.

"Sunday truce been there as long as the game itself," Barksdale says. "I mean, you can do some shit and say what the fuck, but, hey, never on no Sunday."

Prop Joe offers to broker a peace between Marlo and Avon. When told by Marlo's rep that Barksdale is weak at the moment, Joe answers: "You ever know Avon Barksdale to back down from anything?"

When Carcetti's friend and City Council colleague Anthony Gray unveils his "Gray for Mayor" bumper stickers, all Tommy can say is "nice colors."

Gray, completely in the dark about Carcetti's plans, invites him to run on his ticket for City Council president.

When a black teenager turns up dead in Hamsterdam, Bunny Colvin's social experiment is more threatened than ever.

Carver asks Herc to help him move the body a few blocks away from the free zone and Herc angrily refuses. He is so mad, in fact, he makes a call to the City Desk of the *Baltimore Sun*.

To the Hamsterdam dealers, Bunny says: "... come tomorrow, if I don't have a shooter in bracelets, the Hamsterdam thing is over, finished. It's back to the corners for all of us and fuck y'all any way we can ... it was good while it lasted."

Stringer Bell will make sure that someone cops to the murder.

Brianna meets Avon and Stringer but they won't give up the party line on D'Angelo's death, noting that McNulty is a liar.

Losing his temper, Avon tells his sister: "The fuck you even thinking? That I had something to do with it? That I could do that to my own kin? Is that what you think? The fuck is in your head, Brie? I ain't do nothing to D. I ain't have shit to do with it."

Asks Brianna: "To do with what?"

episode
thirty-five

REFORMATION
"Call it a crisis of leadership."
– PROPOSITION JOE
Directed by Christine Moore
Story by David Simon & Ed Burns; teleplay by Ed Burns

Brother Mouzone and his somewhat hapless right-hand-man Lamar – show up at the site where the Franklin Terrace high-rise projects once stood.

"Reform, Lamar. Reform," says Mouzone, who has more important things on his mind, like avenging himself with the man who shot him on his last trip to Baltimore, whose name he does not know.

And Marlo and Avon continue to drop bodies on one another in their ongoing war.

At the detail, Freamon connects a disposable phone to Bodie when he uses it to call his grandmother while Daniels and Pearlman visit Judge Phelan to get the wiretap approved as soon as possible.

Ever flirtatious with Rhonda, Phelan tells her: ". . . give me a boiler-plate affidavit with the [probable cause] from the court report. And as you get fresh numbers for new disposables, you call me any time, day or night . . ."

At the Western, a reporter has called and Mello relays the info to Bunny: the *Baltimore Sun* has been to all three free zones and is chasing quotes before going to press.

Colvin meets the reporter at Hamsterdam and lies, saying that the command staff is well aware of the project. Prosecution of the dealers will begin shortly, he says, almost begging for the reporter to hold his story for a few weeks.

Cutty goes to Hamsterdam to recruit young boxers, where Carver urges the kids to check out the gym.

Brother Mouzone discovers that he was shot by a stickup artist named Omar, an independent who is not part of any crew and happens to be gay.

D'Agostino, now on board with the Carcetti campaign, advises Tommy that he needs more black faces on his team. And she says that it is in his best interest if Tony Gray has a strong run at the job, taking votes away from the incumbent Royce.

Avon has put three new bodyguards on Stringer, their job to spy on him as much as protect him. He makes the muscle stay in the car when he meets Prop Joe in a Westside liquor store where Joe says that if the bodies don't stop falling in the Marlo/Avon war, Stringer will be cut off from the supply of good dope.

Says Joe: "The feeling is it ain't right for you to be at the head of our [co-op] table, when you can't call off your dog. Call it a crisis of leadership."

Taking the message back to Avon, Stringer says: "Prop Joe and them niggers, they took a vote . . . we ain't gonna have the product to put it on the fucking corners."

When Avon refuses to listen – despite the news that Marlo has just killed the woman they sent to seduce him before the Lake Trout assignation – Stringer makes a call to a police source.

Desperate to get a wire up on cell phones used by the Barksdale gang – who are throwing them away almost as soon as they're purchased – the detail tries to convince Phelan of a new approach.

Asks the judge: "You want to sell drug traffickers a series of cell phones that are pre-approved for telephonic intercepts. And you want me to sign off on court-ordered taps on a bunch of phones that . . . have not been used for any illegal activity?"

In a word, yes. Phelan agrees.

Through Bubbles, the detail gets a line on Squeak, girlfriend of Bernard the burner boy. Bubbles's pitch on cell phones is straight up "why pay more?"

Posing as a hustler, Freamon – in an act worthy of the British stage – sells a cautious Bernard on the deal.

And at the weekly HQ ass-rape known as the Comstat meeting, Bunny Colvin comes clean on how he reduced crime in his district, laying out Hamsterdam step-by-step from concept to that very morning.

"Don't you see what he' s done?" says Rawls. "He legalized drugs!"

"What I did, I did knowingly and on my own," says Colvin. "My men had nothin' to do with it. They thought it was all part of an elaborate trap. So if you need me to fall on that sword, I'm good with that."

"I got to give it to you, a brilliant idea," says Rawls. "Insane and illegal, but stone fuckin' brilliant nonetheless. After all my puttin' my foot up people's asses to get the numbers down, he comes along and in one stroke, gets a 14 fuckin' percent decrease. Fuckin' shame it's gonna end our careers, but still."

episode
thirty-six

MIDDLE GROUND
"We don't need to dream no more."
— STRINGER BELL

Directed by Joe Chappelle
Story by David Simon & George Pelecanos; teleplay by George Pelecanos

Tracking Omar to a darkened street, Brother Mouzone gets to the point: how best to get an angle on Stringer Bell?

At the detail, the Bubbles burners are paying off as the wire crackles with info, but not enough to reach Stringer, who is not using the disposables. McNulty finds technology that will help grab calls from cell towers in his own backyard: there are three devices, unopened, in HQ storage.

Burrell and Rawls debate the best way to play and spin the Hamsterdam fiasco, though the mayor – also scrambling to get ahead of the curve – will make the final call.

Says Royce to his advisors: "A 14 percent decline in felonies citywide and I might be untouchable on this. We need to see if there's some way to keep this thing going without calling it what it is."

Upset that his raggedy-ass gym equipment might cause one of his boxing students to be hurt, Cutty asks Avon for help and is thrilled when Barksdale lays $15k on him, half-a-large more than he requested.

Burrell, puzzled that Royce has not shut down Hamsterdam and fearing he will be the fall guy when the shit inevitably hits the fan, tells Carcetti about it.

Bell, having been played by Clay Davis, shows up drunk and pissed-off at Barksdale's safe house. While waiting, he tells Slim Charles to kill the state senator Clay Davis.

Says Charles: "Murder ain't no thing, but this here is some assassination shit."

Freamon grabs Bell's private cell number from the tower and is startled to see that Stringer has been on the line to Bunny Colvin.

At a meeting in a graveyard, Bell betrays his childhood friend and longtime partner in crime to Colvin, giving him the address of Barksdale's safe house where a veritable ordnance of munitions is amassed.

When Colvin suggests that Barksdale must have crossed Bell, Stringer says: "It's only business."

Mouzone finds Avon getting a haircut and tells him he knows that Stringer set up the hit on him via Omar.

"What you got here is your word and your reputation," says Mouzone. "With that alone, you've still got an open line to New York. Without it, you're done."

As is the friendship between Barksdale and Bell, whose life of crime together goes back to stealing a badminton set from a toy store.

Colvin takes Carcetti on a tour of his all but crime-free district and brings him to a community meeting where residents are pleased to have their neighborhoods back. As impressed as he is with the good side of the experiment, the flip side – the reality of Hamsterdam – appalls the councilman.

At the construction site where he bitches to the contractor about the lack of progress, Stringer Bell meets his maker at the end of Omar's shotgun and Mouzone's sidearm.

"I thought for sure we'd be cancelled after that," said Andre Royo, who played Bubbles. "Once you kill Stringer Bell, the party over. But the story was bigger than Stringer."

RUSSELL "STRINGER" BELL (1969-2004)

American Businessman

"Naw, man. We're done worrying about territory, man, what corner we got, what projects. Game ain't about that no more. It's about product."

- STRINGER BELL, TALKING TO THE WALL THAT IS AVON BARKSDALE

The day the folks in charge of *The Wire* killed off Stringer Bell, said Michael Kenneth Williams, "was a rough day at the office."

As Omar the stickup artist, Williams chased Bell for many weeks and months across the first three seasons of the show, catching him in "Middle Ground," the sixth episode of Season Three.

Omar and his sawed-off, accompanied by the professional assassin Brother Mouzone, corner Bell in a building Stringer was hoping to renovate in his foray into a world he craved: legitimate, high-rolling capitalism.

"Killing Stringer was a high-profile scene and it weighed on me," said Williams, who said when at the moment of letting loose a blast Bell shouts, "Well, get on with it," it took him to a very dark place.

"I battled with the whole black-on-black violence thing. Was I perpetuating something or just telling a story?"

Chief intelligence officer and second-in-command to his childhood friend and drug lord Barksdale, Bell's story was key to one of *The Wire*'s primary arguments: If you deny an entire segment of society access to the big game, they will create a shadow game mirroring the establishment in every way but societal legitimacy.

A gangster who used half-lens reading glasses, a murderer fond of parliamentary procedure and hot cups of tea, Stringer Bell was played exquisitely by Idris Elba, who called his character "a bad guy with a brain and power."

Of the show, and Bell specifically, the *New York Times* editorial page had this to say: "A good villain is hard to find. To create a truly wicked character, one dastardly enough to be loathsome but complex enough to fascinate, is among the most challenging tasks a writer faces.

"To slowly twist readers or viewers around until they sympathize with the very same character is a feat only for the foolhardy or the brilliant. This is the genius of the character Stringer Bell . . ."

Even those on the inside, the folks who contributed the stitching with which the amazing, muted-color flak-jacket of *The Wire* was made, marveled at Bell's high-wire act.

"I was fascinated by Stringer for what I'm sure are the same reasons that made him such an icon" to viewers, said Joe Incaprera, a native Baltimorean who got his start as a PA on NBC's *Homicide*, and on *The Wire* rose from an assistant director to unit production manager.

All about business (the books upon his shelf include a copy of Adam Smith's *The Wealth of Nations*), Bell is ruthless in protecting the small empire he and Barksdale – "us" – built with blood and guts.

"Stringer just gets in there, orders the deed and bam – that's it, it's done," Elba has said. "He doesn't think twice about it."

And is perplexed beyond words when his enduring beef with Omar cannot be fixed with money.

"Here's this guy who clearly wants to belong to one world and has the skills to be successful, but grew up on the streets of Baltimore in the middle of 'the game,'" said Incaprera.

"He navigated this world of gangsters and police as a businessman playing every angle despite a daily threat of a catching a bullet or going to jail.

"There was no room for error in Stringer Bell's world."

Yet as we live, we will surely err. And, oh shit, here come Omar.

"The day we filmed [Stringer's death] was surreal," said Williams, whose character, time and again, declared the torture of his lover Brandon – orchestrated by Stringer as a payback for an Omar stickup – as beyond the pale.*

"On a personal level, no one was happy with it because we had become family. I was friends with Idris. No one wanted him to leave the show."

Once he did, however, Idris Elba became, if not a fully-fledged movie star, a much brighter Hollywood light thanks to his work on *The Wire*.

He starred in the 2009 romantic thriller *Obsessed* with Beyoncé Knowles, and the same year had a six-episode role as the boss of Michael Scott (Steve Carrell) in the American version of *The Office*.

The only child of a Sierra Leonean father and a mother from Ghana, the DJ turned actor was born Idrissa Akuna Elba in 1972 and grew up in Hackney, East London.

Divorced from the Liberian actress and dancer Dormowa Sherman, the pair became parents in 2002 when their daughter Isan was born.

The year before he became a father, Elba played Achilles in a New York production of Shakespeare's *Troilus and Cressida*, directed by Sir Peter Hall.

---

* In an early draft of "Middle Ground," Omar urinates on Stringer Bell after he and Brother Mouzone gun down the Barksdale lieutenant.

"Idris was unhappy at the idea; it bothered him," said David Simon, noting, of course, that the stunt would have required the actor to be actually present for the filming of such. "I was prepared to go ahead with it on the basis that it spoke to something ugly at the heart of Omar and his Ronin-like quest.

"But then George [Pelecanos], author of the episode, soured on the idea after his initial draft and argued against it."

Said theater critic Bruce Weber of the performance: ". . . with an ever-present wine goblet in his hand and a controlling arm often around his doting companion, Patroclus, [Elba has] the swagger to convey both his physical prowess and his graceless egomania."

Elba's first credited role came in 1995 as a gigolo on Britain's *Absolutely Fabulous*. By the end of the decade he was playing a forensic scientist on *Dangerfield*.

Soon afterward, he moved to New York City and there – between spinning records in the East Village – came to the attention of the people casting a new HBO series set in Baltimore.

One of the actor's first goals was to get his mouth around the way in which black folks talk in Crabtown. To that end, he worked briefly with a Maryland dialect coach, BettyAnn Leeseberg-Lange.

In a 2003 interview with longtime *Baltimore Sun* reporter Carl Schoettler, Leeseberg-Lange said Elba came to her "speaking a London accent which is very close to Cockney . . . [but] he wanted to sound like an African-American from this area.

"He went and talked to black cops and really got a sense of what the neighborhood speech was like . . . he has a wonderful ear.

"He and I [ultimately] agreed that we weren't going to work [together] because he needed to hear the other musicality . . . mine is a white musicality."

Though Elba has appeared in many mainstream productions, from a Tyler Perry comedy to the HBO movie *Sometimes in April* about the Rwandan genocide, Stringer Bell remains his most enduring role.

Said Elba: "I fell in love with what [Bell] accomplished."

And many viewers, no matter the conflicts Bell's character presented, fell for him.

"Just a magnetically attractive man," said Katherine Porterfield, a 44-year-old psychologist born and raised in Baltimore, now living in New York.

"But what really got me were the scenes of him sitting in business class at [community] college with his little reading glasses on. That just nailed it for me."

It wasn't so much Stringer's quest for success in the real world that seduced Porterfield beyond his looks, "it was seeing him show that ambitious, brainy part of himself," regardless of the arena.

She did, however, "have to fight the creepiness factor when Stringer started sleeping with D'Angelo's girlfriend after having had him killed.

"Even when he faced death after realizing there was no way out and said, 'Get on with it,' that just made him more mythic – R.I.P."

episode
thirty-seven

MISSION ACCOMPLISHED
"... we fight on the lie."
— SLIM CHARLES
Directed by Ernest Dickerson
Story by David Simon & Ed Burns; teleplay by David Simon

Ding-dong, Stringer Bell is dead, Bunk gets the case and McNulty is robbed of an obsession that has driven him for two solid years.

Avon Barksdale accomplished what the great Jimmy McNulty could not: he brought down Stringer Bell.

His partner's death, and his role in it, has an effect on Avon that the cold-ass gangster didn't anticipate. It is powerful enough for him to see that perhaps Stringer was right about the game all along.

"Fuck Marlo," says Avon when Slim Charles says they will go hard on the enemy. "And fuck this fucking war. All this beefin' over a couple of fuckin' corners."

In the eye-for-an-eye argument that makes everybody blind, Charles says: ". . . don't matter who did what to whom. Fact is, we went to war an' now there ain't no goin' back . . . If it's a lie, then we fight on the lie."

On Hamsterdam, which Carcetti is reluctant to exploit, D'Agostino says: "C'mon, Tommy. They dealt you a winning hand and you're acting like you forgot how to play."

The detail suspects Marlo to be Stringer's killer and Colvin passes Avon's safe house address to McNulty, a bit of tit-for-tat from the grave.

Daniels tells the detail to sit on the safe house until Avon appears.

Przybylewski and Freamon talk about what charges Prez may face – the case is being referred to the grand jury – for killing a cop.

When Royce orders Burrell to take the fall for Hamsterdam, the commissioner responds that he also has a story – "[you] brought your liberal-ass do-gooders in here to seriously consider this horseshit" – and is prepared to tell it.

Burrell then angles for a full, five-year term as police commissioner in exchange for putting Bunny Colvin in the public's crosshairs while taking whatever flack deflects the shit from City Hall.

When the cops roust everyone from Hamsterdam, Johnny the junkie's body is found in an abandoned rowhouse. Marlo is found at his favorite rim shop and Avon shows up at the safe house to prepare to settle the score. Before he can come back out, the cops descend.

McNulty says Avon will finish out his previous sentence on a parole violation and then hands Barksdale the warrant showing that it was Stringer Bell who betrayed him.

Later, without complicated gangsters to chase or a new skirt under which to stick his head, a lonely McNulty stops by to see Beadie Russell, the cute port cop from Season Two.

Jimmy is looking for a new way, perhaps as a Western District beat cop who finds it in him to be faithful to a good woman.

For his audacious and arguably successful social experiment, Colvin not only loses his big security job at Hopkins but is busted to lieutenant, robbing him of his major's pension.

Hamsterdam is razed and Marlo's boys return to the corners. With the old game back in swing, Cutty's boys, who suddenly have something more lucrative on offer than the discipline it takes to perfect the sweet science, desert his gym.

At City Hall hearings on the Hamsterdam fiasco, Carcetti listens to Rawls's explanation that Bunny Colvin was a solitary cowboy and says: "We can forgive Major Colvin, who in his frustration and despair found himself condoning something which can't possibly be condoned.

"But, gentlemen, what we can't forgive – what I can't forgive, ever – is how, we – you, me, this administration, all of us, have turned away from those streets in West Baltimore . . . that we surrendered to the horrors of the drug trade."

THE POLITICS OF BALTIMORE

Sheee-it.

Yup. That's it. Of all the words written for all the characters in *The Wire*'s political realm, that's the one best remembered.

And, I'm chagrined to admit, the writers had little to nothing to do with it.

The wit and nuance of that utterance was all Isiah Whitlock Jr., the actor portraying R. Clayton Davis, the shamelessly larcenous state senator who popped up time and again in and around the edges of the Baltimore drug game. He just trotted it out one day on set, and it was an instant hit.

Ironically, Isiah's rendition of that old favorite was exactly the reaction of most of the writers when the notion of a political storyline in *The Wire* was floated for Season Three.

Nonstarter.

In fact, if it had been up to the majority of writers on *The Wire*, the political storyline would have been immediately dispatched, never to be heard of again. It was a hard sell, close to being lost in a not-even-close vote, victim to a chorus of "Not our show" and "Not *The Wire*."

Okay. Politics is difficult. It can be boring to some folks. Inside-baseball stuff. Besides, in film terms, there's no action. It's all sitting behind desks and talking. Not necessarily compelling TV. They almost convinced *me* – and I didn't even have a vote on that committee.

Thankfully, for me and my then-future employment possibilities, balder heads prevailed, and David Simon convinced the others that this was the way to go. With that, the fictional universe of *The Wire*'s Baltimore expanded yet again, this time swallowing City Hall.

At first, it seemed a tough fit for a white city councilman named Thomas J. "Tommy" Carcetti, a guy with skyrocket-high political aspirations, to find a raison d'être in *The Wire* World. It was not exactly a seamless match with the established storylines on a show best known for its real-life insight into the urban drug culture.

Sure, state Senator Clay Davis made the first of his recurring appearances early in the series – back in Season One, before I started – but he seemed to meld perfectly. He was a politician who understood his West Baltimore constituents, the street, the life and especially the draw of the long con. He played it so well.

On the surface, the politics practiced by Carcetti and others in the Establishment didn't seem to lend itself to the life-and-death questions that the street world and police work often deal with.

Yet, it is exactly that machinery that pulls the strings, causing the chain reactions down the line, from City Hall to police headquarters, on out to the corner.

It wasn't so far-fetched. It was a natural. Politics has everything to do with the war on drugs. After all, it was invented by politicians.

It seemed a natural for me, as well. I grew up with the politics of the city and state all around me. My father was a newspaperman and covered politics. It was always talked about at the dinner table. It was in the blood. And then I spent nearly 20 years covering government and politics for the *Baltimore Sun*.

So, I had street cred to do this. All I needed to do was carve out a little space for Carcetti in *The Wire* and populate it.

I stole shamelessly from the stories I knew – some true, some thought to be true, some too good to be true. I spent hours upon hours in the writers'

room with Ed Burns – an initially reluctant, but ultimately very good sport (as he is wont to be) – running out the threads of potential storylines, many of which fell by the wayside for want of airtime.

While some of the characters who inhabit the political realm are rooted in reality, they are composites, drawn from any number of politicians we've known over the years.

Viewers are always asking if such and such a character is so and so. (And usually make the pronouncement that a particular character is absolutely based on a single, real-life person.)

I always hate to disappoint them, though they can rarely be persuaded otherwise, but story was always paramount, and that meant that no storyline was ever twisted or bent in order to squeeze in a "real" character. If anything, it was the other way around. Some characters were just pure fiction, created solely for the purpose of story.

Which is not to say there wasn't room for a little hometown homage. The political piece of *The Wire* did present an opportunity for a tip of the hat to some of the pols we'd known – the power-brokering "b'hoys" and the solid party-line-voting muldoons alike – who inhabit the world of Maryland politics.

Among those folks I wanted to salute in some way were Thomas J. D'Alesandro, Jr., aka "Big Tommy," a three-time Baltimore mayor, and his son, Thomas J. D'Alesandro III, "Young Tommy," who was elected mayor eight years after his father was finally defeated, but called it quits after just one term.

In Season Four, Carcetti has lunch with a former mayor very much modeled on Young Tommy – we called the character "Tony" – who advises the councilman and mayoral aspirant on the daily pain and difficulties of holding that office.

He recounts one of my all-time favorite stories, first told by Tommy in his waning days as mayor in the early 1970s, though I'd heard it many years later. The shorthand for it would be "the bowl-of-shit story." It involves the mayor sitting in City Hall on his first day in office, only to be served, and forced to eat, silver bowl after silver bowl of shit, each sent by another constituency.

"And you know what?" an aide tells the young mayor. "That's what it is: you sit there eating shit, all day long, day after day, year after year."

Then there's the story of D'Alesandro's father, Big Tommy, sometimes known as "Old Tommy," and what could best be called "the conversation between desks."

I first heard the tale from my father, a political reporter for the old *News-Post* and Sunday *American* who had covered D'Alesandro's City Hall. But the conversation apparently had occurred with more than one reporter and been repeated countless times over.

David Simon had heard it and saw that it was included in my Episode 52 script in Season Five. In the version he'd heard, Frank P.L. Somerville was the reporter. Somerville, now long retired, was the *Sun*'s religion editor (earning the nickname "Father Frank"), one-time night editor and all-round desk hand who'd been a young reporter in Big Tommy's last years as mayor.

As the story goes, the reporter tells the mayor that his "desk" – a common reference to a newspaper's editors, particularly when a reporter's looking for cover – wanted to know some sort of information that the mayor didn't want to give up.

At that point, Big Tommy, seated at his desk, puts his ear down to the blotter, nods a couple times, mutters a few words, looks up at the bewildered reporter and says: "My desk tells your desk to go fuck itself."

THOMAS J. "TOMMY"

Very funny stuff. All the more so because it's true.

There are other familiar touches, as well. About a minute into the opening title sequence of Season Three flashes a quick shot of a little shrine designed and assembled by the art department, mainly production designer and Baltimore boy Vince Peranio, behind a bar that was supposed to be in Carcetti's political clubhouse.

The tavern never made it as a permanent set, but the display is captured on film for good. It includes mock campaign literature for Rep. Nancy Pelosi – the California Democrat who is Big Tommy's daughter and Young Tommy's sister, and now speaker of the US House of Representatives – and a poster based on a real flyer from nearly 60 years ago.

The poster is designed around a piece of campaign literature from the 1955 Democratic primary that I found among my late father's political memorabilia, a pamphlet promoting at the top of the ticket the elder D'Alesandro for mayor and Leon Abramson for City Council president.

Also being pushed are four candidates for City Council from Northeast Baltimore's Third District, including the father of the former Maryland Attorney General, J. Joseph Curran, Jr., who also happens to be the father-in-law of Martin O'Malley, once Baltimore's mayor and currently Maryland's governor.

Viewers always seem to invoke O'Malley's name when talking about Carcetti, though they are different animals.

True, Carcetti's rise to mayor from city councilman has elements of O'Malley's own ascension. O'Malley's election as mayor is a fascinating study on many levels, but particularly because it happened in a city that's 65-plus percent black.

So surprising was O'Malley's 1999 win that the *Washington Post* recorded the event with this politically incorrect headline on its front page: "White Man Gets Mayoral Nomination In Baltimore." It was big news that this white man won. And how it happened was a good story.

I had always seen the political storyline on *The Wire* as an opportunity to examine politics and race, a subject that seems almost dated, but not quite, now that we've elected an African-American president of the United States.

We never explored it completely, but we touched on it, and Carcetti's mayoral bid was one of the ways.

O'Malley made no secret of his disdain for *The Wire* and publicly attacked it on more than one occasion. Nevertheless, we asked him to appear in a cameo, as we had other politicians. The question was barely raised before it was shot down.

One former mayor who had no qualms about appearing was Kurt L. Schmoke, now dean of Howard University School of Law. Schmoke turns up in Season Three as the city's health commissioner, advising fictional Mayor Clarence V. Royce when Hamsterdam and its *de facto* legalization of drugs come to light.

The irony is that early in his own mayoral tenure, Schmoke, also once the city's top prosecutor, had recommended a national debate about "decriminalizing" drugs, suggesting that perhaps it should be treated as a public health issue, rather than a criminal one. Needless to say, his suggestion hit the fan and some believe derailed an otherwise bright political future.

Reacting to his comments in a rather hyperbolic diatribe, US Rep. Charles B. Rangel, the New York Democrat, went so far as to call Schmoke "the most dangerous man in America."

So, it is with a barely concealed grin that Royce's health commissioner, played by Schmoke, warns the mayor, "Better watch out, Clarence, or they'll be calling you the most dangerous man in America."

There were more than a few inside jokes like that.

In Season Four, then-Governor Robert L. Ehrlich, Jr., a Republican, portrays a Maryland state trooper who intercepts Mayor Carcetti and aide-de-camp Norman Wilson at the door of the State House after the two tire of waiting to see the fictional governor about school funding.

This was not unlike what really happened once when Mayor O'Malley was forced to go see Ehrlich, hat in hand, about a city schools budget shortfall.

Ehrlich had asked to appear in the show, and a brief exchange with Carcetti was his commercial cable debut.

In Season Five, there's Carcetti's mention of having dinner with "the P.G. County boys" specifically referring to "Steny, Miller and Maloney."

The reference is to three very real Democrats from Prince George's County – US House Majority Leader Steny H. Hoyer, Maryland Senate President Thomas V. Mike Miller, and Timothy F. Maloney, a one-time

power in the Maryland House of Delegates who still carries some political sway in the Washington suburbs.

And lest we forget, in the final season, Clay Davis appears on a radio talk show program with one Larry Young.

Who is Larry Young?

He's an actual radio talk show host in Baltimore. But he's also a Democratic former state senator from West Baltimore who was ousted from the Maryland Senate in 1998 for ethical breaches and later tried, and acquitted, on political corruption charges.

Why the hell not? Politics is, after all, an insider's game.

Sheee-it.

William F. Zorzi

VICTORY UNDECLARED

"After Season Three, I said to Simon:'Let's declare victory,' and he said, 'No, there's more to tell . . .'"
- CHRIS ALBRECHT, THE MAN WHO PUT THE WIRE ON THE AIR

You didn't have to follow *The Wire* extraordinarily closely to sense a disconnect between the end of Season Three just before Christmas 2004 and the debut of Season Four nearly two years later.

"The show was never going to be a hit and it wasn't a failure," said David Simon in New Orleans in February 2009 at the start of filming *Treme*, his new HBO pilot. "So we wrote for closure in case we weren't renewed."

Closure as the curtain falls on Hamsterdam, the failed, off-the-grid social experiment in legalizing drugs along a small corridor of town.

Blood brother gangsters Stringer Bell and Avon Barksdale – "us" their vow since adolescence – betray one another over the best way to run an illegal drug business.

On a tip from Avon, Omar and Brother Mouzone track down Stringer – " . . . seem like I can't say nothin' to change ya'll minds" – and execute him.

Avon returns to prison, along with the bulk of his crew, after police raid his weapons warehouse on info from Stringer.

With Barksdale's life's work in pieces, young buck Marlo Stansfield takes over the corners – meet the new boss, twice the sociopath as the old boss – and the West Baltimore drug trade percolates as before.

And Jimmy McNulty is back in uniform, walking a beat in West Baltimore where he got his start as a Bawlmer po-lice; smiling for the good people on the stoops, as content as a malcontent can be.

"I think that when McNulty is back on the street at the end of Season Three it showed how heroically unambitious he really is," said Dominic West.

"Part of what makes him likeable and heroic was his indifference to self-advancement, which he believed was all that his superiors were interested in," said West. "He was happy to be back on the beat that gave substance to real police work."

All wrapped up neatly enough for a reluctant swan song.

"A lot less explanations needed at the end of Season Three of *The Wire* than David Chase had to make for [the finale] of the Sopranos," said Albrecht, HBO chief from 2002 to 2007, a year before the show's final season.

"There was a giant pivot between [Season] Three and Four," he said. "It was a big maneuver for the show, even though it lived in the same world."

The pivot was greased by an idea that executive producer Ed Burns – former cop, former middle school teacher – had for a novel; the story of a kid who witnessed a murder and wanted to trade that chip to get out of some other trouble he'd waded into.

"Ed desperately wanted to do [a season] on education," said Simon, "so I asked him, 'Are you going to write that novel, because I think I can sell it as Season Four?'"

And he did, along with the fifth and final season about the media and its complicity in all American ills portrayed in the previous seasons.

By this time, the show was about to enter its second life; a word-of-mouth, "you've got to see this show" phenomenon via DVD and the Internet – a run that still continues and has become bigger than the original broadcasts on HBO.

"Chris ordered Season Five on the Tuesday after the premiere of Season Four, a day after [mediocre] ratings came out," said Simon. "He reached back for what HBO was famous for."

"If we didn't put it on, who would?" concluded Albrecht. "I said, 'Fuck it. Let's do it.'"

SEASON FOUR

SEASON FOUR OVERVIEW

UP IN THE MORNING AND OFF TO SCHOOL

"In America, before we notice things, things have to become bad . . ."

— ED BURNS, TO THE NEW YORK TIMES

It is known as the season "about the kids."

And the kids – four boys navigating their way to manhood while making obligatory appearances in school – were every bit as compelling as gangsters selling dope, cops chasing gangsters, and a waterfront full of hard-drinking stevedores.

"I got real caught up in the story of those boys," said Susan "Tootsie" Duvall who played assistant principal Marcia Donnelly at Edward J. Tilghman Middle School.

The boys were played by Tristan Wilds (Michael), Jermaine Crawford (Dukie), Julito McCullum as Namond, and, portraying Randy Wagstaff, Maestro Harrell.

The quartet was coached by Robert Chew, the Baltimore-born veteran of local theater who played Prop Joe.

Key casting input came from Ed Burns, who taught middle school geography in Baltimore after retiring from the police department and was keen on finding actors who, he told the *Baltimore Sun*, "still had the stamp of childhood on their faces."

As Marcia Donnelly, it was Duvall who made sure those childhoods were served, against all odds, with a minimum of what public education in America promises.

It is Donnelly, if anyone, whom the kids obey. She who manages to get enough of them to show up – viz. the scene of paying Cutty Wise and others as freelance truant officers rounding up enough kids for a single day

of class to protect state funding – and Donnelly who sends clothes home to Dukie.

Known for her textbook (white) Baltimore accent, the 1971 graduate of Catonsville High School taught the trick of exaggerating O's while swallowing gerunds to Tracey Ullman for John Waters's 2004 film *A Dirty Shame*.

"Marcia Donnelly struck a nerve with a lot of teachers," said Duvall. "So many of them told me how glad they were to see the real bureaucracy of education exposed for what it is . . . some people who approached me didn't realize that we were actors."

A stage protégé of Jean "Edith Bunker" Stapleton, Duvall began working with David Simon during the filming of *The Corner*, the 2000 HBO miniseries based on the book by Simon and Burns.

Researching *The Corner*, Simon has said, led him to oppose the war on drugs as a war against the poor. On the show, Duvall played Mary, owner of the Sea Pride crab house where the fictional De'Andre McCullough (based on the young man who played "Lamar" on *The Wire*) worked with his addict father.

Seeing herself on screen as "Miss Mary" was not pleasant, nor, she said, "very pretty" – "I was 200 pounds in a hair net and lost a lot of weight after watching."

Watching herself on *The Wire* was just as difficult, and, though less personal, more heart-wrenching.

"The kids you really rooted for fell to the street," she said. "Somehow Namond doesn't."

Of Duvall's role, David Simon said: "We knew the assistant principal would be the institutional representative of whatever order and discipline existed at the middle school.

"We didn't want to make her a bitch or a bleeding heart [and] we knew whatever we gave Toots, she would handle deftly."

Duvall, 60, beat breast cancer after Season Four of *The Wire* wrapped. That, combined with a dearth of films shooting in Maryland since the entrenchment of the recession, persuaded her to step away from acting for an office job in a suburban high school.

At Reservoir High School in Howard County, Duvall is in charge of attendance and truancy records for some 1,500 kids, a job not unlike the duties Marcia Donnelly tackled with less support but no less moxie.

The high school lies about halfway between Baltimore and Washington, some 20 miles from the desperate stretch of asphalt where Michael, Namond, Dukie, and Randy hung out, scrawling "Fayette Mafia Crew 4-evah" to mark their turf.

Daily walks through Reservoir High – where the economic spectrum runs from wealthy to very poor – afford more than a few glimpses of what the world saw of Baltimore on *The Wire*, said Duvall.

[Including mothers pulling each other's hair in the school office and otherwise personable kids forced to act tough when Mom is around because Mom expects it.]

"The suburbs don't seem to influence the city," said Duvall. "The city influences the suburbs.

"We have kids who know that if they're absent 15 consecutive days we can un-enroll them so they miss ten days, show up for one, miss ten, show up for one."

Reservoir High is graced with a real-life Bunny Colvin in the person of Gorham L. Black III, a retired army colonel (and the son of a Tuskegee airman) who fills in as a substitute teacher and conducts a once-a-week "advisory" class for 25 African-American freshmen.

"I try to tell them it's okay to be smart, to be respectful of yourself and others, to pull up your pants. I tell them that in prison, if your pants are around your knees it means your ass belongs to somebody else," said Black, who is 66.

On the American news program *Nightline*, Ed Burns explained the lure of the drug dealer for kids in neighborhoods beyond mere poverty.

"He's the man in the neighborhood that has what nobody else in the neighborhood has, which is standing, which is money, which is power," said Burns. "Kids naturally want to go in that direction."

Gorham Black hopes the boys he works with – one of whom needed to talk because his mother had been arrested – will see something worth emulating in the example, set by himself, of what a black man can and should be.

"When they come into class they have to shake my hand and say, 'Good afternoon, Mr. Black.' I watch their grades, talk to their teachers. A lot of them don't have parents to do it."

Black said an especially poignant scene for him during Season Four came when Bunny took the winning engineering team from his "project" class to a downtown steakhouse. The outing soon implodes along the fault lines of culture and etiquette separating the kids' world from the one beyond the 'hood.

In a second "advisory" class, this one for all male students in their junior and senior year called "What It Is To Be A Man," Black works to prepare the boys for whatever even remotely formal events may await them.

The boys learn how to tie a necktie, write thank-you notes, and shake hands and look someone in the eye, among other courtesies, in a sort of finishing school for kids off to a rocky start.

At the end of the school year, Black hosts a reception out of his own pocket, hiring a caterer to serve finger sandwiches with cake and punch.

"They have to wear a pair of khakis with a white dress shirt, something useful they can wear for anything from church to dinner," said Black.

"I have other teachers drop in on the reception as guests and teach the boys that if someone comes up to you and you have a piece of cake in one hand and a glass of punch in the other, you put one of them down, shake hands and say hello."

The victories are small, some would say symbolic, but Black has seen grades improve among half of his kids, along with self-esteem.

The old soldier is reminded that one of the searing points of Season Four, one voiced through Bunny Colvin, is that most of these kids are smart enough to know that traditional learning isn't worth much in a society that has already decided it has no use for them.

To accept this, said Black, would be the same as giving up.

"I'm convinced that what we do here will transform itself when they leave," said Black. "Be polite, be respectful at home and outside. Be kind. I have to believe those things will make a difference or I'm dead."

•

One of the most memorable acts of kindness in any season of *The Wire* came early in Season Four after a girl named Chiquan in Mr. Prezbo's class refuses to sit next to Dukie because of his body odor.

Like an ornery wasp going from pistil to pistil, Chiquan agitates other students – using jewelry to reflect the sun in another girl's eyes – until one of them slashes her across the face with a razor.

Prez, who just a year ago accidentally killed a man while working as a cop, is momentarily paralyzed. Blood gushes from Chiquan's face, pandemonium reigns and an ambulance is called.

In the chaos, the slasher slumps to the floor, alone except for the attention of Dukie, who uses a cheap, battery-powered mini-fan he found and repaired to blow air across the face of a dazed girl who just inflicted a wound that will need 200 stitches to close.

All season long, said Duvall, Jermaine Crawford played scenes like that "with an intuition you can't teach . . . he made you care."

High praise from someone who spent close to 40 years in the theater and for a decade taught the craft at Towson State University, alma mater of *Corner* director Roc Dutton.

As long as there have been neighborhoods, said Duvall, there have been neighborhood tough guys, becoming more violent with each era until 14-year-olds like Michael Lee are calculated, cold-blooded killers.

"Every generation has their rebels without a cause," she said. "But Dukie embodied the sad side of it that rarely gets shown."

When that sad, gentle soul embraces his all but assured end at the tip of a hypodermic needle, Duvall took it hard.

"My last scene is with Dukie, he comes to school to borrow money again from Prez and I won't let him in," said Duvall. "And then he goes down the alley to shoot heroin. I was home, watching by myself and I wept."

OMAR'S WHISTLE

Jen Ralston and the Sound of The Wire

When Michael Kenneth Williams appeared on the set as a World War II soldier named Tucker in Spike Lee's 2008 movie *Miracle at St. Anna*, the director called out: "Here come Omar, here come Omar!"

It is, said Williams, something he has learned to live with. On *The Wire*, Omar the stickup artist often announced his presence by whistling the "The Farmer in the Dell" nursery rhyme.

What none but a few know, however, is that the ominous whistle belongs not to the man who made the shotgun-toting assassin one of the most feared villains in television history, but a 57-year-old Maryland woman named Susan Allenback.

Michael K. Williams, for all of his many talents, cannot whistle.

"My claim to fame," said Allenback, a founder of Women in Film and Video of Maryland who had bit parts in the films *Syriana* and John Waters's *A Dirty Shame*.

"At one of the first looping sessions, someone asked if I could whistle. I said yes and they showed me footage of Omar walking through a deserted street at night, carrying a sawed-off shotgun . . . whistling to let people know they should clear the way because someone was going down."

Allenback whistled in sync with William's feeble attempt and sound editor Jen Ralston lined it up flawlessly.

Said Allenback: "I always loved the fact that my white middle-aged woman alter ego was a badass black homosexual criminal!"

.

The Baltimore "loop group" that Allenback was part of – some dozen or so people, both pros and lay folk providing voices for footage that needed fixing – was helmed by Jen Ralston, supervising sound editor for all five seasons of *The Wire*.

A New York University graduate and native of Bloomsburg, PA, the 38-year-old Ralston got her start as a radio station intern, noting that sound editing is not something you dream about when you first become enamored of filmmaking.

Now a 15-year veteran of sound editing, she is only half-kidding when she tells young people, "Don't get good at things you don't really want to do . . . it's soul-sucking to spend all your time helping someone else achieve *their* vision."

But good she is, having succeeded in delivering to David Simon the sound of a feature film and not a television show.

"The sound aesthetic of *The Wire* was closer to documentary than straight-ahead narrative," said Ralston, who also edited Simon's 2009 HBO pilot, *Treme*.

"Verisimilitude was the watchword. Whatever sounds got used the most were a reflection strictly of what the show was about."

["Jen never traveled without her little digital recorder," said Allenback. "At a moment's notice she would capture the sound of ice cream trucks and city traffic, kids playing in the park . . . Baltimore was her palette for the landscape of *The Wire*."]

In Season One when the wire detail is in the courthouse basement, "extras kept walking by on the sidewalk above the windows," said Ralston.

"We had to look at those shoes, determine if they were sneakers, heels, loafers, boots, etc. and then sync up the appropriate type of footsteps to the action . . . that's not a cut-and-paste job."

Season Two, of course, enlarged an already vast canvas to include the port of Baltimore, the centuries-old economic engine for the state of Maryland.

Aural field work was assigned to sound effects editor Ben Cheah.

▲ Omar in consult with his confidant, Butchie the barkeep.

▼ Lester schools the troops.

▲ Brianna Barksdale, mother of D'Angelo, at the funeral home headquarters of Stringer Bell, who orchestrated her son's prison death.

◀ The actors Michael Kenneth Williams (Omar) and Michael Potts (Brother Mouzone) pose at Baltimore's North Avenue Motel between scenes of the episode where Omar shoots Mouzone.

▲ Avon Barksdale and Stringer Bell discuss business during Bell's prison visit to his partner.

◄ Dennis "Cutty" Wise, drug executioner turned convict turned boxing coach of young boys with bleak futures.

▲ Thomas "Herc" Hauk at one of his
least favorite spots – his desk.

▼ Jimmy McNulty and the woman he only wanted once she
was gone: ex-wife Elena McNulty, the mother of his boys.

▲ The small world of a junkie: Johnny
and Bubbles between blasts.

▼ The well-tailored criminals Stringer Bell and
would-be mentor, State Senator Clay Davis.

▲ Stringer Bell, running for his life; Omar moseying behind; Brother Mouzone in wait.

▼ City councilmen Carcetti and Gray, not long before Carcetti throws his friend aside in a run for mayor.

▲ "Under My Wheels": car thief extraordinaire Donut (left), out of sight of the cops who can never quite catch him.

▼ Commissioner Burrell and his deputy – Col. Rawls – try to put a positive spin on crime in Baltimore before the City Council.

▲ Homeboys Michael, Randy and Namond in the 'hood.

▼ Prop Joe and his lieutenant Slim Charles on the eastside.

"Cold, winter 2003 . . . after September 11 port security was very intense and you could sense how locked down those parts of the country had become," said Cheah, an editor on the 2000 film *Joe Gould's Secret*, based on the book by the great Joseph Mitchell.

"The area [covered] was enormous," said Cheah, ". . . and Bob [Colesberry] was very clear about wanting to hear heavy machinery . . . the cranes and container movers along with the seagulls."

Courtroom or container, the question always to be answered, said Ralston, was "What would the characters hear where they are right now [and] what of that do *we* want to hear without getting in the way of the dialogue?"

The Wire loop group included Tootsie Duvall, who played assistant school principal Marcia Donnelly in Season Four; and Fran Boyd, mother of De'Andre McCullough, who played Lamar, Brother Mouzone's go-fer.

Screen Actors Guild members in "loop" included Tim McAdams, Bill Thomas and Matt Ryb working "behind the glass" along with Fran's brother "Scoogie" Boyd, who appears on screen telling Stringer he's not sure how much more dilution an already weak batch of dope can take.

"Scoogie and Blue (George Epps) bantering in a bar about a drug deal, talking off the top of their heads, that made the hair on your neck stand up for its reality," said Allenback.

A second Boyd son – De'Rodd, along with his girlfriend Denita – and Tyreeka, mother of De'Andre's young son, also worked the show.

"Anyone they needed, I would bring," said Fran Boyd, whose own journey from addict to productive citizen (she is a counselor at West Baltimore's Bon Secours Hospital, established in 1919) was detailed in the David Simon HBO miniseries, *The Corner*.

In 2007, Boyd married Donnie Andrews, a convicted murderer and Baltimore stickup artist whose life was a partial inspiration for Omar, with whom Donnie shares a scene in Season Five.

The Boyd/Andrews love affair, begun while Donnie was in federal prison, was detailed in a *New York Times* society page wedding announcement that listed David Simon as the couple's best man.

"We did so doggone many of those looping scenes," said Fran. "If there was a shooting on the streets we go [into the booth] and scream things like, 'OH MY GOD!'"

With her troops gathered at Producers Video on Malden Avenue in a Baltimore neighborhood known as "Television Hill," Ralston would lay out that day's work.

Workers in a voting precinct; a telephone operator; almost always a police dispatcher; couples having intimate restaurant conversations; TV news reporters – once a televised dog show – a screaming woman; all manner of squad room bullshitting; cops singing at an Irish wake for Detective Ray Cole . . . on and on and on.

What is called "rhubarb" in Great Britain is known as "walla" in the States – sound effects imitating the murmur of a crowd behind or to the sides of the main action.

Before the walla could be layered, "sweetened", and dropped precisely where it needed to be, it was often scripted by whatever writer was assigned to the loop group that day.

Other times Ralston, whose first major sound job was working as a foley editor on *The Big Lebowski*, would give her rowdy loopers a free pass to what became known as "ad-lib-ville", culling what she needed from the resulting soundscape.

[Isn't this how Beatle John and Sir George Martin did it on "I Am the Walrus"?]

"TV is so sonically flat because it's almost all exposition: we're here, this is what we see, this is what we say about it, next scene," said Ralston. "That's the pacing and language of television."

"Movies," she said, "try to immerse you in a deeper world with a pace that isn't dictated by commercial breaks. The screen is bigger, the sound is surround . . . there's more emotional involvement with the characters as they run the bases.

"On *The Wire* we had to build something that sounded like a movie – all those schoolkids in Season Four and the touts in Hamsterdam were created in looping – but with the budget and schedule of a television show.

"Pick any scene from *The Wire*," said Ralston, "remove all of the principal dialogue and you are left with "an entire world of off-camera conversations.

"And we made sure they all made sense, they all belonged there – right terminology, right accents. That's a scale of detail that many movies don't even bother with these days."

In addition to detail worthy of a Maysles Brothers documentary, much of the background sounds supported overall themes and character arcs in ways the actors were rarely aware of.

["Loop group was always separate from the rest of production, it was easy for us to feel like stepchildren," said Allenback. "There was never any mention of Jen at the wrap parties or the gag reels. But we knew we were there and what we did."]

"Do I think they achieved the goal of having a TV show sound like a feature film?" asked Ralston. "Well, they didn't fire me . . ."

An especially poignant example of subtle support for the storyline involves Detective Jimmy McNulty and neighborhood dogs.

Said Ralston: "If Jimmy showed up at Ronnie [Pearlman's] in the middle of the night for a drunken booty call, he would set the local dogs to barking.

"It was a judgment on him," she said. "Whenever he was being a dog, dogs barked at him."

To which Dominic West – who inhabited the McNulty role for more than five years without connecting dogs to Jimmy's liberal definition of sexual fidelity – said: "Brilliant!"

"I never realized it . . . one of the myriad hidden details laid to please the [most] astute viewer."

SEASON FOUR EPISODE GUIDE

"Everything changes ... one minute the ice cream truck be the only thing you wanna hear ... next thing, them touts callin' out the her-ron be the only thing you can hear ..."
BUBBLES

In which we witness the making of a corner kid, the transformation of another youngster – born with more or less the same moral tuning fork as anyone else – who isn't necessarily seduced or jerked into the drug trade.

Often, they simply wade into it, like the high-school sophomore who walks into a hamburger joint and asks for a job.

This season, said Tristan Wilds, who played the middle schooler turned drug dealer Michael Lee, "you get to see why."

Asked how the show chose to set the drama in a middle school instead of high school, *The Wire* producer and former Baltimore cop and public school teacher Ed Burns said that by high school, most of the important choices in the life of an inner city kid have already been made.

"What drugs have not destroyed," David Simon has said, "the war on them has ..."

episode
thirty-eight

BOYS OF SUMMER
"Lambs to the slaughter here."
— MARCIA DONNELLY
Directed by Joe Chappelle
Story by David Simon & Ed Burns; teleplay by David Simon

Snoop pores over nail guns at a suburban home improvement superstore, and is quickly educated by a middle-aged sales assistant as to the finer points of new-generation power tools.

"You're looking at two people, again, from two different cultures," explained Ed Burns to public radio "Fresh Air" host Terry Gross in September, 2006. "They've crossed the chasm."

As Omar might say, they have crossed indeed.

"We could kill a couple motherfuckers with this right here," says Snoop to her assassin boss Chris Partlow as she gets in the car with the nail gun.

Meanwhile, in the Clinton Street offsite detail office, detectives Lester Freamon and Kima Greggs meet with Assistant State's Attorney Rhonda Pearlman to review the members of the Marlo Stanfield organization who've been caught on the wire.

To get the proper signatures to keep the wire up and running for at least another month, Greggs gets her supervising lieutenant to sign the necessary subpoenas by burying the paperwork under a requisition for an office fan.

Again, the Barksdale money trail – the breadcrumbs through the 'hood that keep getting swept away by official corruption and incompetence – is uppermost in Freamon's mind.

Bodie works a corner with a lethally jealous young man named Lex, who complains that the mother of his child is now dating Marlo's boy Fruit. Working for Bodie is a wise-ass middle-school kid named Namond Brice, played by Julito McCullum.

To Bodie's complaints that Marlo's crew has the good corners, Slim Charles says: "Nary a Barksdale left, so you on your own out here."

He does have the son of a Barksdale soldier, however, in Namond, the middle-schooler with the pony-tail, and progeny of Wee-Bey and a woman named De'Londa, a half-assed student and half-assed corner boy whom Bodie claims to employ simply out of respect for the kid's father.

Carecetti, calling for two debates with Mayor Royce, is dismissed by the incumbent as "a lost-ball-in-high-grass-motherfucker."

Snoop and Chris shoot and kill a man in a gutted rowhouse, with Snoop pouring quicklime on the body. The man had begged for his life only to be shot and wrapped in an old shower curtain. The killers leave with tools in hand like a couple of guys working off a Mr. Handyman home repair truck.

They are building a mausoleum of sorts: the Tomb of the Unknown Homeboy.

Tilghman Middle School assistant principal Marcia Donnelly and principal Claudell Withers look up to find their new math teacher: Roland Pryzbylewski, a cop without a teaching certificate who not long ago killed another cop in an accidental shooting.

Teachers are hard to come by and Prez is in.

Over at the Western District, the house that Bunny Colvin built, Cedric Daniels is now in charge as major. When a uniformed patrolman with a winning smile – Officer James McNulty – comes knocking, Daniels tells him to leave the beat and help them solve cases. Jimmy declines.

On Bodie's corner, plainclothes DEU Sergeant Ellis Carver and Officer Anthony Colicchio pull up. McNulty arrives, ordering Bodie to shut it down in an hour. Meanwhile Carver waits for a proper farewell.

"A good evening to you, Sergeant Carver," says Bodie.

To a puzzled Colicchio, Carver explains: "You bust every head, who you gonna talk to when the shit happens?"

At "Carcetti for Mayor" HQ, Tommy is admonished for being behind schedule and reluctantly begins making cold calls looking for campaign donations.

Lex murders Fruit in front of his baby's mama, Patrice, says hello to the horrified woman, and walks away. It doesn't start a gang war, but it does put Lex on Marlo's radar.

In the detail office, Bunk allows that it's odd that someone controlling as much of the West Baltimore drug trade as Marlo hasn't generated more homicides.

Dukie keeps getting beat up and his homeys decide to retaliate by luring the Terrace Boys into a trap where they will be pelted with balloons filled with urine. The plan, alas, has some holes in it.

In the race for mayor, Royce buys $300,000 of TV ads. Carcetti is left to get his message out via the radio. The first poll will place him running third.

And Prez is assigned his homeroom, a shitty nook in a shitty cranny of a shithole school system.

episode
thirty-nine

SOFT EYES
"I still wake up white in a city that ain't."
- CARCETTI

Directed by Christine Moore

Story by Ed Burns & David Mills; teleplay by David Mills

The arc of the next two years of Herc's life is established when he walks in on Mayor Royce while hizzoner is getting a down-on-her-knees blow job from his secretary.

The wise-ass Namond and his mother visit the boy's father – Barksdale soldier Wee-Bey – in prison. At the meeting, the boy's mother admonishes him for missing work and spending his money on dumb shit.

Of his son's pony tail, Wee-Bey says, "Even the white police lookin' out from three blocks away gonna be able to spot you from every nigga out there."

A Marlo lieutenant hands out cash to kids going back to school – seed money for the labor pool – and Cutty turns down a job in the 'burbs running his own gardening crew.

On the corner, Namond persuades Bodie to let Michael Lee (played by Tristan Wilds) be his surrogate as Bunk and Carver ask about the murder of Lex, done in for taking out Stanfield soldier Fruit.

With his rolling, "we bring the product to you" T-shirt business in a

shopping cart, Bubbles realizes that Sherrod – this year's Johnny on the Spot – cannot do simple math and demands he return to school.

Carcetti fails to win the Fraternal Order of Police endorsement and, preparing for the first debate, is all but assured that he has lost the race.

When Michael refuses Marlo's walk-around money, the big man steps up to the schoolkid, taken with the boy's sense of self and says: "Ain't no thing, shorty. We cool."

[Michael will also turn down Cutty's offer to teach him to box, though he is intrigued by the idea.]

Randy Wagstaff, one of the four best friends highlighted this year – along with Michael, Namond and Dukie – is cornered in an alley by a Western District patrolman, who takes $200 off the boy.

[Wagstaff is played by Maestro Harrell, who portrayed the young Cassius Clay in the 2001 Michael Mann film *Ali*.]

With info gleaned from the wire, developer Andrew Krawczyk and state senator Clay Davis are served subpoenas.

Herc goes to Major Valchek, who has known a cocksucker or two in his long police career, for advice on the long-and-short of what he saw in the mayor's office.

Says Valcheck: "Kid, careers have been launched on a helluva lot less. Just shut up and play dumb."

Doing what he can to launch Carcetti into City Hall, Valcheck feeds the candidate info about another witness in a drug case turning up dead. Buoyed by this, Carcetti uses the dead witness to broadside Royce in the debate, admonishing him for not spending money procured from the federal government on witness protection.

Back in the detail, the wiretap crew marvels at Marlo's voice showing up on a cell.

When Namond gets home, his mother has a spread of new schools for him. When he turns on the TV in his room, the Carcetti-Royce debate drones on about the failure of public education.

The boy switches over to his Xbox and begins killing bad guys.

episode forty

"HOME ROOMS"
"Love the first day, man. Everybody all friendly an' shit."
— NAMOND

Directed by Seith Mann
Story by Ed Burns & Richard Price; teleplay by Richard Price

Omar Little, with a new lover and protégé – Renaldo – wakes up to the sound of a garbage truck and walks to the corner store for cereal in his pajamas.

Just the sight of him is enough for a bag of ready-to-sell vials of cocaine to drop at his feet. This, he tells Renaldo later, is no fun.

"It ain't what you takin', it's who you takin' it from," he explains. "How you expect to run with the wolves come night when you spend all day sportin' with puppies?"

The Deacon tells former police major Howard "Bunny" Colvin that he has greased a job for him at the University of Maryland – where the academics are enamored of the cop who tried to legalize drugs – working with repeat violent offenders.

Colvin, now working security at a downtown hotel, passes. He changes his mind when he is prevented from arresting a hotel guest who has beaten up a prostitute because the guest brings a lot of business to the Inner Harbor.

Marlo and his assassins Chris and Snoop roll up on Bodie, Little Kevin and Michael on a corner from which Bodie has worked hard to make a modest profit. Bodie tenses but the visitors are just there, they say, to talk.

"Two choices," says Marlo, who continues to see a valuable employee in Michael, "you start takin' our package or you can step off."

Bodie, who is making a go of it because the New Day Co-op dope is superior to what Marlo has on the street, also admires Michael's mettle and tries to get him to work the afternoon rush hour shift. But Michael, having paid back the money he needed to get back-to-school supplies for himself and his little brother – Aaron "Bug" Manigault – says he's finished.

After the debate with Carcetti – in which the brash white boy beat the seasoned pol over the head with his inability to protect witnesses in drug and murder cases – Royce finds the challenger up eight points in the polls. Time, the mayor tells his team, to start kicking back and kicking hard.

Greggs makes "Old Face Andre's" store for a stash house while Omar and new boy Renaldo watch the detective come and go from the building. The store had recently shown up on the wire with a call from Andre to Stanfield lieutenant Monk.

The New Day Co-op leaders – Prop Joe, Slim Charles and Fat-face Rick – wonder how to push back against an encroachment of dealers from New York. And they are certain that Marlo, whom they could use in fighting the out-of-towners, is hiding the bodies that his crew are killing around the Westside.

Bunk and Freamon are more than intrigued: victims are disappearing without giving the detectives the courtesy of leaving their bodies behind. Even Leakin Park, a legendary West Baltimore dumping ground, is empty. After checking the city sewers, Bunk tells Freamon to give it a rest.

At HQ, Rawls tells a toady by the name of Lieutenant Marimow that he's now in charge of the Major Crimes Unit. And as such, he will chase real criminals and stay away from the lives of well-intentioned public servants. At least until after the election.

At the same time, Lieutenant Jimmy Asher (played by Gene Terinoni) – the guy who signed the subpoenas that caused so much indigestion in powerful parlors across the city – is transferred to a Siberian outpost known as the Telephone Reporting Unit.

Bunk is able to get McNulty out of the house at Beadie Russell's – as close to a Norman Rockwell existence as Jimmy has ever known – for a beer by the railroad tracks. For old times' sake lasts but a beer before McNulty packs it in for home.

En route to the first day of school, good friends Randy, Michael – shepherding his little brother "Bug" – and Dukie walk over to Namond's house. Randy gives his lunch to Dukie on the way, but Namond's mother lets everyone inside but Dukie – he's dressed like the rag man and he smells.

First day of teaching school – the hardest job Ed Burns ever had, according to the former cop and Vietnam veteran – is a struggle for Prez.

The ex-cop needs back-up – the help of colleague Grace Sampson (played by Dravon James) to establish a minimum of order.

Herc's reward for keeping his mouth shut, more or less, about the mayor's at-the-desk blow job? He's promoted to sergeant and gets a better assignment as detective than City Hall bodyguard.

Marimow, dancing to whatever tune Rawls whistles, shuts down everything that doesn't result in pat-on-the-back statistics: no more meandering wire taps, no more subpoenas, and once and for all, the Barksdale investigation is closed.

And the exodus from major crimes is on.

Omar and Renaldo hit Andre's store in an especially clever manner – after the robbery Omar buys a pack of Newports and demands the proper change – and when they've finished business the master tells the greenhorn: "That's why we get up in the morning."

Colvin, now in the warrens of academia, is asked to find at-risk young people for University of Maryland research and immediately schools the professors on the reality that by age 18, most of these folks are on an unalterable path. He suggests sixth and eighth graders instead.

Called to the carpet by Rawls for the sneaky subpoena caper, Freamon is praised for being one hell of an investigator and reminded that his career has suffered in the past for being good at what he does.

"You have a gift for martyrdom," says Rawls to Freamon. "But I wonder, are your disciples as keen for the cross?"

Freamon falls on his sword to protect his friends and Rawls rewards him with a transfer back to the homicide unit, telling him that one day he will see it as a blessing.

Finally, how many times do you have to write "I Will Not Slice My Classmate's Face with a Razor" on the blackboard before the teacher lets you out of the doghouse?

Chiquan, the girl who refused to sit next to Dukie because of his body odor, has felt a need to cause a ruckus all through the episode.

She then uses a piece of jewelry to reflect bright sunshine into the eyes of a student named Laetitia. When the pestering continues, Laetitia jumps up and, with a blade, gives Chiquan a wound that will take 200 stitches to close.

Nothing has prepared Prez for this; he stands flat-footed, and it is Grace who calls for an ambulance. In the chaos, Dukie gently approaches the girl who attacked, taking a mini-fan out of his pocket – a piece of junk that he found on the street and repaired – and blowing it on the face of the kid with blood on her hands.

OMAR

"Omar is who he is ..."
— MICHAEL KENNETH WILLIAMS

Here it comes.

A nursery rhyme whistled through narrow streets of boarded-up rowhouses and trashed alleys, a child's tune offered with the cool confidence of a killer so serene he can announce himself and his shotgun to the melody of "The Farmer in the Dell."

"Hi-ho, the derry-o . . ."

The mouse takes the cheese, baby.

•

"Omar was my breakout character as an actor but he also let me know how deep I can go on a personal level – I went real deep with Omar," said Michael Kenneth Williams, speaking by phone from South Africa in May of 2009, while filming a network pilot with Neve Campbell.

"*The Wire* is here," said Williams, noting that he was recognized as Omar in South Africa. And Campbell, who played a coming-of-age secretary to a doomed F. Scott Fitzgerald in the Henry Bromell film *Last Call*, told Williams "eight out of every ten conversations" among London hipsters were about *The Wire*.

And near or at the top of everyone's list of favorite *The Wire* characters was Omar, the stickup man with a sawed-off shotgun beneath his Wild West duster; the last of the independents, a loner with a strict code of morals that need only make sense to himself.

"I [tried to] make him believable by playing him from a sensitive perspective, not as an alpha male. I played him very vulnerable. When you hurt Omar's feelings, he acts a certain way," said Williams.

"In Season One he was happy and in love with Brandon. Then he went into a dark depression when they killed Brandon. He fell in love again in Season Four but went down the rabbit hole after they killed [his confidant] Butchie.

"I did a lot of research for that role," the actor continued. "I got into levels of street life in Baltimore that the average actor would never see. I went in looking for a character and I came out with family and friends."

In a world where alcoholic cops consider diving down a flight of stairs for a disability pension and apprentice gangsters devour their childhood homeys for profit and promotion, Omar is a man of abiding consistencies for whom we can cheer.

He doesn't use drugs or brutalize addicts; he's even been known to give away a taste to a sister up against withdrawal. He doesn't wear flashy clothes or jewelry. Never curses and does not turn his weapon or his wiles against "citizens" not part of the street game.

"Being on *The Wire* was a lot bigger for me than just playing Omar," said Williams. "Baltimore is not a Hollywood set – the show was always about the city, about the story. We rolled up our sleeves, got to work and got to know each other.

"It set the bar for me on the stories I want to tell."

•

Born in 1966, the son of a woman from the Bahamas who owned a Brooklyn, NY, daycare business, Williams was raised in East Flatbush.

"Mom worked hard," he said of Paula Williams, now in her eighties, was "sharp as a tack," and relocated to Pennsylvania. "I didn't know we were poor until I left the projects."

[*The Wire*, said Williams, is not "Mom's cup of tea" and she has seen little of it. She did, however, love her son's role in the R. Kelly 'Trapped in the Closet' video.]

Williams broke into show business as a street dancer and then a choreographer. Fashion photographers David LaChapelle and Steven Klein pushed him into a modeling career.

"I'm a big fucking kid – a late bloomer," said Williams, who was cast as a lead in the Todd Solondz film *Forgiveness* and had a part in director John Hillcoat's 2009 adaptation of Cormac McCarthy's novel, *The Road*.

No matter the role, it's difficult to keep your eyes off of him and that tantalizing, yes-it's-real scar snaking down his dark mug like the famous thunderbolt across the face of David Bowie on the cover of *Aladdin Sane*.

Williams's fashion work caught the attention of Baltimore-educated rapper Tupac Shakur, who cast Williams to play his brother in the 1996 film *Bullet*, which also starred Mickey Rourke. A small part as a drug dealer in Martin Scorsese's 1999 paramedic drama *Bringing Out the Dead* followed.

Not long after that, Manhattan casting agent Alexa Fogel called with an audition for a new HBO cop show set in Baltimore.

"I put myself on tape in [Fogel's] office," said Williams. "And then I got a call telling me to report to Baltimore."

"You can smell the 'hood in Baltimore before you get there," said Williams of the warren of manifold poverties in which he immediately felt at home. "The garbage baking in the sun a mile away, the piss in the [project] elevators.

"I've been traveling a lot lately and I go to the 'hood to meet the people and eat the food. Detroit, Chicago, DC – from Brooklyn to Compton – you've got variations of *The Wire*, the same thing, happening all over. I saw it in South Africa.

"In Baltimore, I made it my business to learn the dialect. I didn't want to sound or dress like a New York dude. Baltimore has its own swagger and style – just a white T and a do-rag. They keep it simple and clean."

Mild-mannered, exceedingly polite and heterosexual, Williams is distinct from the character he portrays, although he said that Omar became his alter ego after years of inhabiting the role.

To the amusement of Ed Burns, who went to the set the first day that Omar worked in front of the cameras, Williams didn't know how to hold a shotgun much less draw it from under a desperado's duster and stick it in some fool's face.

"The stickup guys are mavericks," said Ed Burns. "They're a totally different breed" from other criminals.

Burns was a cop in his native Baltimore for some 20 years before retiring in 1992. He worked for five years in the escape-and-apprehension unit and a dozen more in homicide, specializing in violent drug gangs.

Along the way, he met stickup boys with names like Apex and Ferdinand, Cadillac and Anthony. Some – like the legend Shorty Boyd – are still out there, alive and well after decades, though most are no longer in the game. Others are long dead.

"Man, if I had a dime for every time someone in Baltimore came up to me and said he knew who my character was based on: this dude and that dude," said Williams.

Omar, however, was created out of a little bit from each of them.

"These are guys that can't function in an organization, who don't like taking orders from anybody," said Burns. "The great ones – the Anthonys and the Ferdinands – were lone wolves who had their own vast or semi-vast network of snitches working for them.

"After they'd take off a dealer, they'd parcel out some of the product to their snitch."

Before the onslaught of cheap cocaine and crack turned the drug trade upside down in the 1980s, a relative order was imposed by organizations with a sense of discipline that's been lost since the game trickled down to kids as young as nine and ten years old.

In the 1970s, said Burns, a drug gang called the New Day Co-op hired assassins to kill the stickup artists disrupting business. The smarter stickup boys had "good runs" in the game, according to Burns, because they knew whom not to prey on.

Others did not have the reps to keep the wolves away.

"I once watched Ferdinand walk up into a [project] courtyard and come up to a guy with his Jesse James duster coat on," Burns remembered. "He apparently thought the guy wasn't giving up everything he had, so then you see the shotgun slide out and shoot the guy in the leg."

Ferdinand leaned down to take whatever else his victim had in his pockets, much as Omar would do. And then he walked out of the courtyard and into the arms of the waiting Burns and his partner.

Another thing about the men who rob drug dealers: they can often be caught on a weapons charge and, once caught, they can make excellent informants, knowing as much as they do about the city drug trade.

Williams said that over five seasons, he never had to go to Simon or Burns for direction beyond what was on the page.

"The first time I met Simon he said he was going to make [the *Wire* gangsters] the show's Wild Bunch," said Williams, referencing the 1969 Peckinpah film, one of Simon's favorites.

Williams was not familiar with the movie – nor John Ford's 1962 western, *The Man Who Shot Liberty Valance* – which Simon also recommended.

"He told me to watch those two movies," said Williams. "That was my research. They were thinking of killing off Omar in the first season but didn't. And they made sure that none of the directors ever tried to tweak Omar . . . all I had to do was commit to the character."

Openly gay, Omar is indifferent to societal or institutional sanction of his sexuality, just as he is without apology for his line of work.

"The character we've created uses everything he sees in this world, and whatever he sees, he's going to take advantage of," said Burns. "By now, he's mythological."

Most crucial to his survival, Omar sees the street as his natural habitat. Near the end of the show's five-season run, just before his beef with new drug king Marlo reaches its climax, Omar stands on a fucked-up, deserted street corner and yells for all the world to hear.

"I'm out here in these streets every day, me and my lonesome. Where he at? Huh? Yo, you put it in his ear: 'Marlo Stanfield is NOT A MAN FOR THIS TOWN!'"

The most focused peek into Omar's soul was provided midway through Season Two by Omar himself.

In the harsh light of a courtroom, Omar willingly testifies against a Barksdale-employed sociopath named Marquis "Bird" Hilton.

For the court, Omar identifies Bird as the man who murdered a man named Gant, a state witness whose death launched the arc of Season One. Bird was, in fact, the shooter of Gant, but whether Omar was there to witness the murder is in question.

Armed with enough accurate information about the slaying to make the accusation stick, Omar is on the stand not on behalf of Gant but to avenge the death of his lover.

With customary arrogance, the Barksdale organization's house lawyer Maurice Levy tries to chip away at the credibility and nerve of Omar, who has just given his job description to the court.

"I robs drug dealers."

At last Levy thinks he's making a dent, reiterating, "So you rob drug dealers."

"Yes, sir."

"You walk the streets of Baltimore with a gun, taking what you want, when you want it ... willing to use violence when your demands aren't met?"

Omar nods yes, and Levy describes him as someone who would, if he was in the mood, "shoot a man down on a housing project parking lot and then lie to the police about it."

Omar takes offense: "I ain't never put my gun on no citizen."

"You are feeding off the violence and the despair of the drug trade . . . stealing from those who themselves are stealing the lifeblood from our city . . . a parasite . . ."

"Just like you, man."

"Excuse me?" sputters Levy.

"I got the shotgun, you got the briefcase."

Neither shotgun nor briefcase could protect Omar near the end of the final season when, limping into a convenience store while on the hunt for Marlo, the legend's final words are spoken through bullet-proof glass to an Asian cashier.

"Gimme a pack of Newports . . . soft pack."

Silence and a pause.

"Let me get one of them too . . ."

BANG!

Blood and brain splatter against the thick plastic. The Korean grocer screams and the knees of an assassin no more than 12 years old knock as young David shakes before the fallen Goliath.

"I'm glad Omar went the way he did," said Williams. "I've met kids in Baltimore who were straight-up assassins."

episode
forty-one

REFUGEES
"No one wins. One side just loses more slowly."
— PREZ

Directed by Jim McKay
Story by Ed Burns & Dennis Lehane; teleplay by Dennis Lehane

Leaving an all-night poker game, where he plays cool, close to the vest and now and again is taken by the older and the wiser, Marlo steps out into the early morning sunlight.

At a corner grocery, he buys a bottle of water while brazenly stealing a couple of lollipops in front of a chumped and angry rent-a-cop.

You "act like you don't even know I'm there," the guard says.

"I don't," answers Marlo.

It was a move, said Malcolm Azania, a Canadian novelist who publishes under the pseudonym Minister Faust, "simply to prove his untouchability . . . his urban catacombs containing scores of victims who disappeared as completely as if they were in Pinochet's Chile."

At Cutty's gym, all the talk among the boys is about the cutting in Prez's class. Randy gives them a credible bio of the girl with the blade who lives in a group home: enough to make anyone want to attack someone.

On her first day in homicide, Greggs bumps into fellow refugee Lester Freamon, and new boss Sergeant Jay Landsman assures Kima she'll learn the ropes in no time. And then she is initiated into the family of "murder police" in a series of pranks involving "methane probes," a corpse holding a note identifying his assailant – "Tater killed me" – and a call from the zoo from a "Mr. Lyon."

The funny stuff comes to an end when Rawls and Burrell decide to give the investigation of the dead state witness that Carcetti is making such a stink about to Greggs – "the rookie" – as a way of keeping it out of public view.

At the rim shop, Old Face Andre does the alibi shuffle trying to explain to Marlo how he lost the package to Omar. The boss man doesn't want to hear it, takes an expensive ring from Andre and tells him to make good on what he lost.

"Omar ain't no terrorist," says Marlo, ". . . just another nigger with a gun."

When Andre leaves, Marlo tells Partlow he needs $150,000 cash for the next card game, determined to beat the "old heads" at the poker table.

Prez tries to engage his class in a discussion of the assault, but they are more interested in the rumor that he used to be a cop and whether he ever shot anyone. When he tells them that he was a cop but being a police officer "was about working with the community", they laugh in his face.

At the Univeristy of Maryland sociology department, Bunny Colvin helps a professor named Parenti put together a pitch to the school system about studying just the kind of kids that Prez is trying to reach and teach.

One of the school superintendents cautiously allows the program to proceed with one, ill-defined prohibition: They can do "nothing that gets anyone upset . . . there's an election going on and we don't want to put our schools in the middle of that mess."

Sydnor and Officer Massey shut down the wire room and head back to the street with Marimow pleased as punch. Already on the street, Bunk visits Lex's mother, finding a small shrine and a frightened woman: "I don't know where my son is," she says.

Prop Joe pitches Marlo on the New Day Co-op: good dope at quality prices and if you've got a phone, you've got a lawyer and a bail bondsman.

Perhaps best of all, "No one fucks with you," says Joe.

"No one fucks with me now," replies Marlo.

A room full of black ministers, however, give Carcetti the eye-fuck when he comes calling for their support.

"Wherever I go, people want the same things . . . but they're just not getting them. I'm going to change that," he says. "My door is open to you, regardless of who you endorse."

The ministers thank him, somewhat coldly, and Carcetti reasons that if nothing else, they'll respect him for meeting them on the up-and-up.

Drinking with Bunk when the shift is over, Freamon tries to figure out where the corpses are that the Stanfield group is dropping and muses about the possibility of a dumping ground.

Snoop and Chris work to recruit Michael, scoping out the derelict rowhouse he lives in with his little brother, watching the pair walk to school together and surmising that Michael only attends class to get out of the hell that is home.

Says Snoop: "Make a good run at that boy, he'll be on a corner, no problem."

At a parley with Omar at Blind Butchie's gin mill, Prop Joe insists he had nothing to do with the Stringer Bell/Brother Mouzone attempt on his life. To clear the air, he gives Omar a tip on a high-stakes card game on the Westside, lots of cash on the table.

After making sure that Bug has a snack and is doing his homework, Michael makes his way to Cutty's gym about the same time that the badge of the security guard who confronted Marlo over the lollipops is tossed inside Snoop and Partlow's boarded-up boneyard.

In an attempt to school Sherrod in basic math – both to keep the younger man in his T-shirt business and maybe help him in general – Bubbles has managed to enroll his friend in school.

Watching Sherrod study one night in the shithole they are squatting in, Bubbles notices that the student is using a dictionary to reference algebra homework.

"It ain't no thing," says Sherrod, weakly playing the lie.

"I see that," says Bubbles.

What viewers saw on Andre Royo's face in that scene, the actor said, is the look of being fed a plate of bullshit, something he remembers on his parents' faces when, as a kid in the Bronx, he'd try to dance around the fact that his room wasn't clean, he was late getting home and why his grades were not what they should have been.

"Everybody," said Royo, "knows that look."

When Omar and Renaldo stickup the card game, Marlo says: "That's my money."

To which Omar replies, in an echo of Jason Compson IV, an unlikely predecessor from *The Sound and the Fury*: "Money ain't got no owners, only spenders."

Omar takes the ring that Marlo took from Andre and the stone-faced Stanfield tells him to "Wear it in health."

DENNIS LEHANE & THE STOLEN LOLLIPOPS

On the October, 2006 night that his Season Four teleplay of "Refugees" debuted on HBO, the Boston-born crime novelist Dennis Lehane was quoted in the *St. Petersburg Times* of Florida about *The Wire* and television in general.

"*The Wire* is the most anti-TV show out there," said Lehane. "The vision is almost completely uncompromising, makes almost no concessions to the audience.

"There's zero wish fulfillment in it . . . a very scabrous, uncompromising vision."

Scabrous: rough to the touch; having scales, small raised dots or points. A word you don't hear everyday.

Lehane helped *The Wire* realize its prickly vision over the last three seasons with the scripts "Dead Soldiers" (2004); "Refugees" (2006); and in 2008, the final year, "Clarifications."

Season Four, he said – the one about public education – was particularly special.

"The story of those four kids trying to navigate middle school while the street is sucking at their heels, that hit a nerve like no other," said Lehane, who in Season Three had a cameo as a police officer named Sullivan in charge of special equipment.

Ed Burns, who worked as a Baltimore police detective and middle school teacher before working on *The Wire*, has said the lure of the drug dealer is the most potent force in poor neighborhoods where few others have much to show for their lives.

Though Lehane has given life to many a bad man in novels that include *Gone, Baby, Gone, Mystic River*, and most recently, *The Given Day* (in which the Baltimore-born Babe Ruth is a recurring character) few villains have struck him as stone cold as Marlo Stanfield.

"Marlo is very *de*-human," said Lehane. "That's different than sub-human which suggests an evolutionary disconnect or an insult in regard to intelligence.

"Marlo is exceptionally intelligent and in an evolutionary sense he's Machiavelli's ideal . . . he's been dehumanized to the point where he's incapable of understanding why he should care about anyone or anything that doesn't enrich his bottom line.

"Where other characters on the show had a lot of flash – I'm talking about everyone from Omar to Bunk to McNulty, even Bodie – Marlo is practically Stalinist in his lack of it. That makes him all the more terrifying.

"It's hard to expect mercy from someone you can't imagine telling a joke or having a mother."

And mercy is certainly not what the rankled security guard at the grocery store received when he had the temerity to approach Marlo – "he talked back," was the offense, according to Chris Partlow – when Marlo stole a few early morning lollipops after an all-night poker game.

"The death of the security guard was where we started," said Lehane. "How to get there became the issue . . . the lollipops came to us at some point. It just seemed like something Marlo would do and something [to] exemplify how cheap life can be out there.

"One place where David [Simon] and I have always been particularly simpatico is in making people die over stupid shit. We both get really geeked up over that," said Lehane, who also wrote the scene of Omar's death at the hands of a 12-year-old while buying a pack of cigarettes.

"There's zero nobility in it," he said. "That's the street."

episode
forty-two

ALLIANCES
"If you with us, you with us . . ."
— CHRIS PARTLOW
Directed by David Platt
Story by David Simon & Ed Burns; teleplay by Ed Burns

The youngsters at the heart of the story – Namond, Randy, Michael, and Dukie, joined by a young boy named Donut who is obsessed with cars and stealing them for fun – sit near an abandoned factory late at night telling ghost stories.

Real-life ghost stories from around the way – dead people in rowhouses – stories to scare the shit out of a kid the way Boy Scouts might put a spin on Mary Shelley while sitting around a campfire.

Says Namond: "They *zombies*. [Partlow] got the power. He say come and they got to come – like the devil do with the damned."

"There's dead, then there's special dead," says Donut, adding that Marlo is so powerful the undead work for him as spies.

Dukie – the kid always getting punked, the one supposedly dumber than the rest – doesn't believe any of it and later tells Randy that he saw Chris Partlow walk a boy into a vacant rowhouse.

Valchek lets Carcetti know that the department brass have given the case of Braddock – the dead witness – to a rookie detective and Norm Wilson feeds the info to Tony Gray, accomplishing their mission while staying away from the fallout.

Says Wilson with a grin: "I'm a devious motherfucker once I get going."

Gray doesn't fall for it and Wilson draws the picture for him: You're going to lose but if you use the leak about the Braddock case to boost your poll number, you'll have some credibility in a year or so for the state legislature, maybe Congress.

Gray doesn't like it, but he sees it and accepts it, and is soon sharing the Braddock info at a televised press conference. Concluding that Burrell can only hurt him – whether the mistakes are honest or not, he's not sure – Mayor Royce turns to Rawls and says: "I need you to make this go away . . . I won't forget."

Marimow's marching orders for the major crimes unit remain unchanged: catch Marlo and as many of his players with dope on the table. He's not interested in anything else.

Raids on Stanfield corners and other addresses are ordered by Marimow based on the low-level info gleaned from the now-defunct wire.

The cops have very low hopes for the endeavor, meager expectations that are soon fulfilled. Pearlman is both disillusioned and worn out enough by the never-ending drug war to tell Daniels she's ready for a career change.

As Pearlman has had it trying to make a real difference in the face of political and bureaucratic idiocy, so state Delegate Odell Watkins (played by Frederick Strother), whose support is all but necessary for a successful campaign, has had it with the callous arrogance of Mayor Royce.

When Prez tries to help the ever-mistrustful Michael in class, the boy just stares at a blank notebook page and is given detention. Namond is a bit harder to control, much less teach, screaming: "Get your police stick out the desk and beat me. You know you fuckin' want to."

Leaving the class, Namond bumps into Grace Sampson, Colvin, and Professor Parenti, there to begin selecting students for their project, which will study "good" kids versus "corner" kids.

Colvin says that Namond is the kind of kid they are seeking for the corner study.

Prez soon begins to empathize with his errant students, realizing that if he teaches them anything it most likely will not be math. He gives Dukie a fresh set of clothes and Donut swiftly pops the teacher's car open when Prez locks his keys inside.

Later, when Prez confidentially asks a student why Dukie doesn't wear any of the clothes he bought him, he's told that the boy's family sells his clothes for drugs.

Marlo puts a price on Omar's head but Partlow suggests they find a better way to skin the cat, noting that "[Avon] Barksdale turned this town upside down huntin' him and all he ended up lookin' was weak."

Hanging out again at the abandoned factory, the quartet of middle-schoolers are surprised and a bit frightened to see Partlow and Snoop show up. Telling everyone but Michael to beat it, the Stanfield assassins tell him they've heard good things about him and there's work if he wants it.

Michael begs off, claiming family responsibilities, and is told: "We be around if you need something."

Marlo gets word that Prop Joe was behind the card game stickup. Old Face Andre is summoned and told they're going to fake a robbery at his store and blame it on Omar. Andre doesn't like it, but there's not much a beleaguered employee can do.

Indeed, Andre is pistol-whipped by Partlow – who also kills a delivery woman – in the staged robbery as Snoop stands by. A bloodied Old Face will soon name Omar as the killer in the homicide interrogation room.

[Later, a very skeptical McNulty will say to a fellow officer: "You ever know Omar to do a citizen?"]

Visiting his father in prison, Namond is told by Wee-Bey that Bodie did the right thing in working Marlo's package. The game, he tells his son, has changed.

As Carcetti knocks on doors for votes along a rough stretch of East Baltimore, Rawls surprises them with the news that Odell Watkins has broken with Mayor Royce and that he, for one, would be happy to wake up to a new morning at City Hall.

The moment he leaves, Carcetti and his right-hand, Norm Wilson, make a beeline for Watkins.

In the event, reasons Carcetti to Watkins, that he becomes "a white mayor in a majority black city . . . you will have a voice within my administration simply because I'm gonna need it."

When Watkins says Royce is ahead by seven points in the polls, Carcetti responds that it's only four.

In his meeting with Marlo in a Christian Science Reading Room, Prop Joe says he knew about the robbery of the card game but not that there was a police camera scoping Marlo's lair, the motivation it takes for Stanfield to join the narcotics co-op.

The episode ends with Dukie taking Michael and Randy to the vacant house to which he saw Chris Partlow walk someone who never walked out. The boys pry the plywood off the door and, creeping toward the back, find the decaying bodies left there by Snoop and Chris.

His point proven, Dukie declares: "There ain't no special dead . . . there's just dead."

episode
forty-three

MARGIN OF ERROR
"Don't try this shit at home."
— NORMAN WILSON

Directed by Dan Attias
Story by Ed Burns & Eric Overmyer; teleplay by Eric Overmyer

It's the day before the election, a Sunday, and the candidates attend worship services with their respective families and supporters.

Ever the opportunist, Carcetti attends the church where a politically influential black minister controls the pulpit: the Rev. Reid Franklin preaching the divine word about "men of truth who fear God and hate covetousness."

Afterward, Carcetti seeks Franklin's support – has not Watkins already broken with the incumbent? – and the reverend promises to keep an open mind.

Herc, working surveillance on Marlo's lair via the hidden (but not undetected) camera, sees nothing of note while Marlo plays up to the spying cops.

Taking a call, Marlo asks what time he should pick up "the skinny girl from New York," saying it's a job he has to do himself. Reading Marlo's lips with the help of an interpreter, Herc and Sydnor surmise that "skinny girl" is cocaine.

The stunt will later make Herc look very foolish – to Marlo's delight – with the Amtrak police.

Brianna Barksdale tells Namond's mother – De'Londa – that the gravy train of cash, sort of a pension based on Wee-Bey's loyalty to the organization, has stopped running. When De'Londa says that if Wee-Bey talks, Avon will be facing more time in prison, the mother of the murdered D'Angelo replies "I don't give a shit what happens to Avon."

Namond, who wouldn't be much better off than his neighborhood friends without the drug money, is later told by his mama that it's time for him to step up and get in the family business for real.

[In interviews, the actor McCullum said that Namond (rhymes with Raymond) "had to do what he had to do."]

And Prez does what he doesn't have to do, presenting Dukie with a safe home away from an unbearable one: clean clothes, soap, and a laundry bag in the gym, where he can shower if he gets to school early enough. The teacher says he will take care of making sure the clothes are laundered and returned.

When the ten students for the University of Maryland study are selected – their teachers happy to see them exit class – Namond is on the list.

Though Randy Wagstaff is not part of the study, he is called into assistant principal Donnelly's office about the rape of a classmate named Tiffany. Worried that the school will call his foster home, the boy allows that he has a card to play: "I know about a murder."

When she takes the info to Prez, he convinces her to let him pass the info along to someone he trusts in the police department so Randy doesn't "get chewed up by the system."

Clay Davis knows that the momentum in the mayor's race is steadily moving toward Carcetti and asks for a meeting with the councilman.

He can't endorse Tommy this close to the election (indeed, Davis will stand shoulder-to-shoulder with Royce on election day) but – for a fee – he can see that people in key precincts pull the right lever.

On election day morning, Randy gets a job handing out a box of flyers for $50 and recruits Dukie, Donut, and Kenard (Thuliso Dingwald) to help. Michael decides to go to Cutty's gym, working a bag.

Namond, now with his own package of dope to sell (which his mother forced Bodie to give him) comes to the gym to ask Michael if he wants to work it with him. Michael passes (unfortunate for Namond, who has no idea what he's doing) and remains cool to Cutty, whom he doesn't trust.

Spotting a squad car outside a grocery, Omar hides his weapon behind a rack of beer and, once arrested on the say-so of Old Face Andre for the murder of the delivery woman, calls Butchie to let him know he's going downtown. Once at Central Booking, among many bad men he has robbed, we see something rare cross Omar's face: a look of fear.

He relaxes, though not at first, when a pair of muscular inmates are put in the holding cell. One of them ominously pulls a shank before telling Omar: "Butchie sent us."

When Carcetti gets the news that he has won – that Royce has conceded – he is walking along the Inner Harbor tourist promenade with his wife, Jennifer.

"Are we happy about that?" asks Jennifer.

Her husband, the presumptive mayor-elect, thinks so.

DAVID SIMON ON
JAMIE HECTOR AS
MARLO STANFIELD

"Jamie Hector's performance as Marlo Stanfield was so understated and restrained that there were many viewers who initially mistook the minimalist choices for a lack of range."

"This was amusing to the writers, who had seen enough of Jamie's work to know how good he is and how disciplined and self-denying a performance he was offering. At the end of [Marlo's] arc, when his emotion finally breaks — not over any threat to his money, or even to his power, but to the authority of his name and reputation — he made everything perfectly and wonderfully certain."

"That was the key to Marlo Stanfield. He represented the ultimate totalitarian impulse — beyond money, beyond power or the exercise of power for its own sake, but instead that strange combination of self-love and self-loathing that rarely dares speak its name openly."

"Marlo wanted money and power not for their own sake, but so the world would know they were his and his alone. He defined, for the purposes of The Wire, the emotional end-game for any and every power pyramid depicted."

"Jamie nailed that. A great, great actor."

episode
forty-four

UNTO OTHERS
"Aw Yeah. That Golden Rule."
- BUNK

Directed by Anthony Hemingway

Story by Ed Burns & William F. Zorzi; teleplay by William F. Zorzi

In his cell at Central Booking, Omar is helped by Donnie (real-life stickup artist, Donnie Andrews, now reformed), and a second convict known as "Big Guy."

For a protective vest, the pair strap books around Omar's torso. When someone tries to stab Omar in the food line, he turns the tables, literally shoving the shank up his assailant's ass.

A battle won, a message sent, but the price on Omar's head is up to five figures, to be happily paid by Marlo Stanfield. Omar makes a call to a cop who owes him a solid, his fellow Edmondson High School classmate, Bunk Moreland.

Bunk, however, tells Omar that helping him find a policeman's missing service revolver isn't enough currency to get cut loose on a first-degree murder charge with an eyewitness.

Omar realizes not only that he's surely been set up, but he isn't sure how long he might survive lock-up.

"If I knew I'd be sharin' quarters with all these boys," says Omar. "I might not robbed so many of 'em."

Bunk calls in a favor and gets Omar moved to protective custody.

Finding Spider on the corner, Cutty asks the kid – one of his best fighters now working the drug trade – where he's been; only to be told, "You ain't my fucking father."

In Prez's homeroom, now empty of Namond, the former cop uses lunchtime poker games to teach math skills. When he goes looking for a set of dice to teach them probability, he is amazed at what he finds: a cache of textbooks, video equipment, and a computer, all new and untouched.

With the election over, the cops have a green light to work the case of the dead witness – Braddock – the way it should be worked. The first thing Greggs and Norris do is bring in an inmate named Anthony Wardell for questioning.

As Namond works a corner, some boys down the block let him know they're taking over his territory, showing a 9mm handgun to back up the threat.

One of the runners on the rival crew is Sherrod, Bubbles's homeless, illiterate, and doomed surrogate son played by Rashad Orange. Sherrod, armed and all coked up, pushes and punches Namond near Cutty's gym, demanding he give up the corner.

Though Namond will say it "ain't no thing," both Cutty and Michael – who claims it's none of their business – know better.

In his own wanderings – trying to sell DVDs on the street – Bubbles is again hassled by "the Fiend" for dope or money, whatever he's got.

Downtown, a nervous Pearlman meets her new boss, Rupert Bond, the freshly elected State's Attorney for the City of Baltimore. He puts Rhonda in charge of prosecuting all homicides, saying with a nod to the subpoena caper: "I admire your courage, if not your loyalty."

In his first meeting with the big shots at police HQ, Carcetti gets some hard truths from Daniels, who speaks freely in front of Burrell: murders are down but all other violent crime is up. The problem, Daniels says, is a policy of reducing statistics instead of doing fundamental police work.

Herc is desperate to get his spy camera back from Marlo, who has installed it at his pigeon coops. When Herc questions Randy about the murder he claims to know about, Randy does some big-league snitching: Little Kevin told him that Chris and Snoop killed Lex. With this, Herc makes a beeline for the pigeons.

Greggs goes to the scene of Braddock's murder to re-enact the crime, theorizing over various trajectories, broken bottles on a dresser suggesting there may have been some target practice going on.

With some of the troublemakers like Namond gone from the class – and "Mr. Prezbo" earning their trust by being fair and consisistent – the kids begin working out number problems by shooting dice for pots of Monopoly money.

"You trick 'em into thinking they aren't learning," says Prez, "and they do."

As fate somehow conspires to trick the City of Baltimore into electing Thomas J. Carcetti their new mayor.

It seems that the dead state witness whose corpse Carcetti was able to use to derail the Royce express wasn't murdered at all: he was the accidental victim of someone shooting target practice indoors.

When Greggs brings Norris a .38 slug from the crime scene that matches one found during Braddock's autopsy, the veteran detective says: "Our guy's dead from a stray? And this fuck Carcetti gets to be the mayor behind the stupidity. I fucking love this town."

episode
forty-five

"CORNER BOYS"

"We got our thing, but it's just part of the big thing."
— ZENOBIA

Directed by Agnieszka Holland
Story by Ed Burns & Richard Price; teleplay by Richard Price

As Prez moves on from number problems to word problems in math class – he will later be told to "teach the test" so the schools aren't taken over by the state – Jay Landsman tells the homicide unit that Carcetti will be coming around on a "fact-finding" mission.

Landsman also eulogizes recent cancer victim and colleague Raymond Foerster.

"The man served 39 years, obtaining the rank of colonel without leaving a trail of bitterness or betrayal. In this department, that's not a career – it's a miracle."

Like the death of Detective Ray Cole the season before, Foerster's on-screen passing reflected off-screen reality. Richard De Angelis, a former stand-up comic under the name "Richy Roach," played Colonel Foerster with a pragmatic sense of resignation. He died on December 28, 2005 after a battle with prostate cancer.

In Bunny Colvin and Professor Parenti's project class, the students finally settle down: they now understand they can throw as many tantrums as they wish, it won't get them thrown out of school.

Colvin has come to see the school as the jail, and the teachers as the police: dress rehearsal for the corner. When he gets the kids talking about what makes a good corner boy, the discussion becomes lively.

When Herc pulls Marlo over and asks for his camera back, Marlo tells him: "You do me one, I'll do you."

The way things are with Marimow, Herc would rather trade horses with a ruthless killer than tell his boss he lost a piece of equipment that really doesn't cost all that much.

Across town in East Baltimore, Chris and Snoop put the bodies of New York boys they've removed from Monument Street corners – as Marlo promised Prop Joe he would – in another boarded-up rowhouse.

Marlo then gives Herc's business card, which he got in the little parley about the missing camera, to Prop Joe, who is grateful but points out to Marlo that if they "disappear" all of the bodies of the New York boys, what will be the message to others willing to take their place?

Enlisting Detective Vernon Holley to give him a hand, Bunk visits Old Face Andre's store to go over the robbery-murder now pinned on Omar. Bunk again clocks all the signs of a stash house and Holley is now on board in thinking that Andre is full of shit. They will later return with summonses for the Grand Jury.

Namond, ever the braggart, tells Michael and Randy about a class in which they talk about what it's like on the corner and then passes up going to the gym to put his dope in vials, sell it with his crew on Fayette Street and re-up.

Later, his mother – the worst kind of stage mother for a corner boy – tells him not to bring the dope into the house: "That's what you have a lieutenant for."

Carcetti, having gone on a drug bust ride-along after his visit to homicide, complains to Rawls about all the manpower going into busting people for $20 worth of dope.

To show that arrests are up, Rawls answers, they have to make arrests, even bullshit arrests. He lays this policy at the feet of Burrell, saying he would be very interested in the chance to do things a new way.

The opinion of Major Cedric Daniels will also be sought by Carcetti, and Pearlman tells her lover – one who has treated her so much better than that dog McNulty ever did – to unload on Rawls and Burrell; to tell all he knows about the manifold dysfunctions of the Baltimore Police Department. When Daniels gets his meeting, Carcetti offers him Foerster's job as CID commander under Rawls.

"How for real are you?" asks Daniels, to which Carcetti replies that they'll figure that out as they go along.

At home, Michael's mother has sold all of the food in the house – "out of our mouths," the kid says – to buy dope. It only gets worse for Michael when his stepfather – Bug's biological dad – is released early from prison. Mom promises that they won't be on social services anymore because her man is "gonna take care of all that for us."

Back in "special" class after being chastised by De'Londa for making the mistakes of a rookie drug dealer, Namond is told, along with the others, to make a list of laws one must follow to be a corner boy. Colvin makes it a group project.

Herc, Dozerman and plainclothes drug cops Colicchio and Carrick show up at Marlo's open-air hangout and search everywhere for the missing camera, with Herc promising they will do it "every day" until the camera is returned.

Herc's obsession extends to Partlow and Snoop, whom he pulls over for a car search. All the cops see is lime and a nail gun, overlooking a trap door in the dashboard where they stow their firearms.

Next stop on this merry-go-round: Little Kevin.

Making the suspects sit on the curb, Herc fires a nail from the gun into the street near Snoop's leg, saying: "I want my fucking camera," before giving the nail gun back.

Following Prop Joe's suggestion to Marlo that he leave calling cards while clearing corners, Partlow and Snoop shoot a New York boy in the head and leave him where he falls.

When Michael shows up at an after-school rec center to pick up Bug, he's told that the boy's father already collected him. It is heavily suggested, though never said outright, that Michael, was molested by the man. The fact that Bug is alone with him sends Michael into a panic and when he finds Bug doing homework with his father, he orders the kid to come with him immediately.

And it seems that Bunk and Holley did their homework too well, handing in a report on the dead delivery woman murder for which Omar is already in custody. Landsman chews them out for "unsolving" a murder.

THE FOUNDATION OF A FREE
SOCIETY

Early in Season Four, a school secretary sums up *The Wire*'s views about
the Baltimore school system.

"Not a goddamn thing up in here works like it should," she says about a
malfunctioning door. Indeed, precious little works at fictionalized Edward
Tilghman Middle School.

Classrooms and hallways are chaotic. Girls pull razors on each other.
And students shout, "Fuck you!" at teachers with impunity.

Jaded administrators roam the neighborhood each fall to round up
students for a single day of school – just enough to ensure state funding
is preserved. Teachers worry more about "teaching to the test" than about

actually *teaching* the students anything. And multi-million-dollar budget screw-ups cause momentary heartburn among the politicians though nobody pays a real price.

Along the way, the schools again and again short-change young people at perhaps the most vulnerable junctures of their lives. The season paints an unforgiving portrait of educational dysfunction.

And yet, many Baltimoreans – teachers, administrators, students, and parents alike – can only nod in recognition, no longer shocked by bad news coming out of the schools. They know that the system can and does lose countless good kids like Randy and Dukie.

Those of us who are involved in the system take heart in the occasional success stories it manages to produce. But overall, it remains a failure, with shockingly low scores on standardized tests and graduation rates.

There's plenty of blame to go around, as *The Wire* made clear. Burned-out teachers lack the spark to meet the intense demands of the job. And administrators avoid risk-taking, choosing instead to persevere long enough to retire with a comfortable pension.

But the bigger problem – one that is beyond the control of educators – is that many thousands of Baltimore children are sent to school poorly prepared to learn.

Poverty, crime, and drug abuse define many of their lives, and financial instability forces many families to move through the school year, disrupting kids' educations. Students arrive from homes without books or a sense of reading, much less a love for it. In many cases, the parents themselves struggled in school and don't appreciate the value of education.

Can an urban American system like Baltimore's find a way to educate the real Dukies and Randys of Baltimore?

Only with a revolutionary infusion of money and commitment.

•

Brian White saw something of himself in *The Wire*'s Roland Pryzbylewski – Mr. Prezbo, based on the experiences of *Wire* producer Ed Burns when he became a middle-school teacher after retiring from the police department.

White decided to become a teacher in the early 2000s after losing a job in banking. He received a mere three weeks' training and was thrown into the toughest of assignments – middle-school math in an aging school in a neighborhood surrounded by public housing.

With little mentoring, he learned on the job. Breaking up fights, he was kicked in the leg and bitten in the arm. Students cursed him, mainly, he figured, to get a rise out of him. Many students simply failed to show up for dozens of days a year; others wandered in a couple of hours late without consequence.

Even some of his fellow teachers often missed school, their students foisted on the teachers who did show up, making already crowded classrooms all but un-teachable.

Although the school required uniforms, gang-bangers in training sported gang colors – shoelaces, undershirts, bracelets, and earrings – red for the Bloods and blue for the Crips.

Students often couldn't stay after school for activities or required detention sessions because they had to pick up younger siblings and watch over them. Like *The Wire*'s Michael Lee, they were already parents themselves.

Over time, Brian White came to understand the poverty and family trauma many of his students endured. Students confided in him about a mother strung out on drugs; in other cases, the dirty clothes or lack of hygiene made clear that kids were not being cared for.

"It's so rough at home that a lot of these kids are raising themselves. They were 12 going on 20," White says. "They've got other things to worry about than a teacher saying, 'Where's your homework?'

For some of these kids, school is not the No. 1 priority. Survival is the No. 1 priority."

His students had often already failed a grade and were too old to be in middle school. Social promotion was inevitable and the kids knew it.

"They didn't want to do anything. They knew they were going to pass because they were too old. It was a very tough situation. What could you do? The kids were right."

.

The Baltimore schools, like those in many other large American cities, have been buffeted by profound racial change in the last half-century.

Through the 1950s and into the 1960s, the system was predominantly white and generally well-regarded. As the Baltimore schools integrated to comply with court rulings, a wave of white families left the city for the suburbs. Between 1950 and 1990, the white population of Baltimore declined by 430,000.

In the mid-1970s, the city became officially majority-black; among the white families remaining, fewer and fewer chose to enroll their children in the schools.

More affluent families, in particular, sent their kids to private schools while the middle class often chose parochial education. Many middle-class black families also fled the city for the promise of suburbia.

The school system increasingly became home to lower-income, African-American students – in other words, the students with the greatest needs. Perversely, while the needs of the school system were mounting, resources were declining, and, not surprisingly, educational results fell.

The mayor at the time was an old-line white pol named William Donald Schaefer, a product of Baltimore public schools. Mayor from 1971 to 1987,

Schaefer had a devotion to neighborhoods while apparently recognizing that the floundering system was a lost cause.

Schaefer focused on high-profile downtown developments, including the touristy Inner Harbor, a convention center, and, eventually, a light rail project and new professional sports stadiums. Progress on these bricks-and-mortar projects was easy to observe and each was opened with high-profile festivities as the schools continued to decline.

The public grew accustomed to bad news – boxes of unopened books found in school warehouses as students went without; astonishingly poor scores on standardized tests; bureaucrats stubbornly refusing to try new approaches or innovative curriculums.

One memorable day at a North Baltimore high school, the beleaguered principal suspended 1,200 of the school's 1,800 students when they refused to obey a directive to return to their homerooms. The stories mounted and support for the system fell.

African-American educators cemented control of the system and black patronage replaced white patronage. Membership in the right African-American sororities or churches was helpful in boosting careers.

By the 1990s, the system was reaching rock bottom, hampered by inadequate funding and a series of leaders unable to blow up the status quo.

A turning point came in 1997, when the city's first elected black mayor, Kurt L. Schmoke, agreed to share control of its schools with the state of Maryland in exchange for hundreds of millions of dollars in new funding. Some black legislators from Baltimore decried the move to cede some control to the state as "racist paternalism."

Perhaps, but more than anything, the move was a profound admission of failure.

·

Over the years, I've tutored a couple of third-grade boys from a struggling West Baltimore school.

One boy – call him Isaac – was wiry and moved with tenacious energy. On tutoring days, we'd sit in our little cubby, with a map of

the world pinned to the bulletin board, and I'd coax him to read passages aloud.

Sometime Isaac managed to get through them, sometimes he would get distracted and fixate on something else – the chalk at the chalkboard, the map on the wall, the snacks.

A few weeks into our sessions, I pressed him one morning to focus and do the reading. He burst into tears. I watched dumbfounded as he crawled under the table and curled up. He stayed there for a while.

Over time, I pieced together details of his life: a mother on drugs, a father in a wheelchair – no doubt a victim of the city's violent crime – and out of Isaac's life. The tears came a few more times during our weekly lessons. I didn't help his reading all that much, but I gave him a safe place to let out some emotion.

Isaac today is likely in the kind of West Baltimore middle school portrayed on *The Wire*. I'm sure it is not the kind of place where boys are allowed to cry.

•

Season Four of *The Wire* focused on one extremely troubled middle school. It is far from atypical; many real-life Baltimore schools are failing.

But the show provides an incomplete picture. Thanks in part to state funding that increased in the 2000s and attention from local and national foundations, the system has made progress.

Test scores, particularly at the elementary level, have gone up significantly. School enrollment has actually crept up – a possible sign that the public is embracing the progress.

Meanwhile at a number of top schools, including the ones both of my sons attended, virtually every student graduates and students regularly earn places at some of the nation's most selective colleges.

By 2009, the Baltimore schools were under the leadership of an unlikely outsider, Andres Alonso, a soft-spoken, Cuban-born immigrant who once taught special education in the troubled schools of Newark, New Jersey.

Alonso has purged hundreds of bureaucrats from the central administrative office, known as "North Avenue," and reallocated spending to the schools.

Publicly, he insists that the system must expect *all* students to do well in school. It is an admirably idealistic goal, maybe even the right one for a public system determined to foster equal opportunity.

Be sure, however, that not all of Baltimore's young people will conquer basic reading, writing and math skills or, perhaps, learn a trade; much less master algebra or interpret Shakespeare.

The reality is that the hardships that cripple so many of the city's families, particularly drug abuse and poverty, and the lure of the streets, are far too powerful for many young people to overcome.

Many thousands of Baltimore children will continue to fail to graduate or, if they do, be inadequately prepared for a productive working career – except, perhaps, a quick and likely fatal run at Baltimore's drug trade.

Things will change only if the people, and then the politicians, decide that things *must* change.

The only question is just how many young people we will lose while the public settles for a failed system. *The Wire*'s dark portrayal of Baltimore suggests that it will be a long wait.

I'm afraid they're right.

Tom Waldron

episode
forty-six

"KNOW YOUR PLACE"
"Might as well dump 'em, get another."
— PROPOSITION JOE

Directed by Alex Zakrzewski

Story by Ed Burns & Kia Corthron; teleplay by Kia Corthron

Poot is back after serving 15 months of his four-year sentence, back with Bodie and joined by Little Kevin when Herc and Dozerman hit their corner. The cops leave with nothing.

"These police out here knew how to flip it even just a little, my shit'd be in handcuffs," says Kevin.

When Namond shows up, Bodie and Poot tell him where to station his lookouts and, to his shame, not to send his mother to the corner anymore.

Omar, released from a county detention center on Greggs's old-fashioned police work, is immediately met by Bunk, who barks: "No more fuckin' bodies from you. No comebacks or get-evens on this. No more killing."

The killer agrees but cannot leave a town where he grew up, a town where real-life cops have found suspects in heinous crimes hiding under their mothers' bed.

"Baltimore all I know," says Omar. "Man gotta live what he know."

New City Council President Nerese Campbell, chief Carcetti strategist Norm Wilson, newly elected State's Attorney Rupert Bond and other city officials meet with Carcetti about his plans.

It is soon apparent that the maverick's desire to fight crime with a new police commissioner will face major hurdles.

Later, when Campbell opposes him on the idea of a waterfront casino, it comes out that Royce had promised she'd be next in line for mayor.

Carcetti tells her she still can be – "without so much as a campaign speech" – for he already has eyes on the governor's mansion. But now, he needs her support in City Hall.

The days of good 'ole Erv Burrell, as political a police commissioner as there is, would seem to be numbered.

"If you want me to go," he will later tell Carcetti. "You gonna have to shitcan me."

Prop Joe tells Marlo and Chris that the cop on their business card – Herc – was part of the detail that managed to tap Stringer Bell's phone, even though the dead and legendary gangster changed his cell every day. Marlo gets the message.

While Greggs drives Bubbles through the 'hood in search of the guy who's been fucking with him, Partlow tells Marlo that Old Face Andre has not been seen and may be singing for the cops.

Marlo tells him to hold off on killing the carpetbagging boys from Gotham, that "this shit with Andre? Job one."

It's also at the top of Omar's to-do list, as he and Renaldo stake out the store. "That man got some explainin' to do," says Omar, reprising one of Ricky Ricardo's favorite lines for a new day in the 'hood.

When Marlo later shows up at the store, they recognize him as one of the guys Omar robbed at the poker game.

"No wonder he don't like me," chuckles Omar.

Randy, with Dukie along for the ride, buys his way into a dice game and leaves with a nice payday. When one of the losers asks where he learned his game, Randy proudly replies: "Edward Tilghman Middle."

Greggs turns Bubbles and his hard-on for the Fiend over to Herc and Dozerman, who tell him they'll take care of his nemesis if he can identify Little Kevin with the red hat trick, Bubbles's vaudeville version of the Judas kiss.

Michael's stepfather demands the Social Services ATM card, but the boy refuses, saying the money for the month is gone.

In Colvin's project class, the kids have to build a scale model using an erector set, the winners to go downtown for a meal in a nice restaurant. One catch: no instructions; pull it off on your wits.

Quips Namond: "It ain't like we follow the instructions anywhere else, right?" And then proceeds to lead his team in building something that looks enough like the Eiffel Tower to be recognizable.

With his girlfriend visited by Snoop and Partlow and a warning bullet, a scared-to-death Andre turns to Prop Joe for help, offering the deed to his store in exchange for cash to skip town. He reluctantly accepts $2,000 for the real estate and heads north.

Or so he thinks. Double-crossed by Prop Joe, he winds up in the company of Partlow and Snoop, who march him to his death.

In a pow-wow with Rawls, Carcetti says he wants Burrell to run the big-picture initiatives while the colonel handles the day-to-day. And then says that Valchek becomes deputy commissioner of administration as a political payback. He also wants to bump Daniels to colonel and give him "carte blanche to fix the investigative units."

Rawls agrees to all of it, while noting, with some resistance, Daniels's "independent streak."

When Michael asks Randy and Dukie whom he should talk to about getting his junkie mother some help, the boys suggest Cutty.

"He's too friendly," objects Michael. "Like he some type of faggot or something. Everybody just too motherfuckin' friendly."

And then takes his problem to someone not renowned for his friendliness: Marlo.

Colvin treats Namond's winning engineering team to a meal at Ruth's Chris, perhaps the finest steakhouse at the Inner Harbor. They are fish out of water – reminiscent of D'Angelo's date at a similarly swank joint in Season One – and the trip falls apart.

Later, Colvin will tell Parenti: "How do you get them to believe in themselves when they can't admit their feelings about who they are and what they're doing in this world?"

A nervous Bubbles holds the Fiend at bay for as long as he can while waiting for Herc to come to the rescue as promised. But Herc is busy listening to a raft of horseshit from Little Kevin, a fat man in a red hat. Defenseless, Bubbles is beaten by the Fiend with a metal pipe.

The night before his promotion to colonel, Daniels and Pearlman enjoy a quiet evening together and toast their good fortune over leftovers.

"Funny," says Daniels, noting all the years he tried to get ahead by "kissing ass, covering ass and doing what I'm told." And when he finally says what he really thinks, he gets promoted.

"Maybe," he says, "it's not going to be so unbelievably fucked-up anymore."

Carver shows up at Cutty's gym to lay down the law about the corner to Namond and his buddies Kenard and Donut: "I see you out there a second time and everyone takes a beating," and goes to juvenile lock-up.

When Cutty tells Carver who Namond's father is, he adds: "Same blood, but not the same heart."

episode forty-seven

"MISGIVINGS"

"The world goin' one way, people another."
— POOT

Directed by Ernest Dickerson
Story by Ed Burns & Eric Overmyer; teleplay by Eric Overmyer

Thomas J. Carcetti is mayor-elect of the City of Baltimore, having won the general election by 82 percent in the heavily Democratic city.

Immediately, a new dance of political jockeying commences. First comes Clay Davis, who intimates that he and Carcetti may be working together in the state capital before long; while behind the scenes Rawls and Burrell wrangle, interpreting policy and stats as best suits their desire to run the show.

Donut crashes a stolen SUV and when Officer Eddie Walker catches up with him, the cop breaks several of the boy's fingers in anger over the paperwork he now has to do.

At Tilghman Middle, Grace Sampson tells Prez the school keeps the heat on high so pupils are too drowsy to act up during the teaching of the mandatory state exam.

"From now 'til they're done," she says, "everything's about the tests." To Colvin's disgust, this philosophy extends to the project class he is running with Professor Parenti.

Omar and Renaldo stay vigilant on their surveillance of Marlo and his crew. When Renaldo asks his mentor if he'd have robbed Marlo if he'd known who he was, Omar replies: "Woulda enjoyed it that much more."

To make up for the "communication problem," that led to Bubbles getting worked over with a metal pipe, Herc brings a peace offering of chicken wings, a cell phone and news that the reward for the camera is $500.

Angry, the junkie replies: "Five hunnert for a camera and a chicken box for Bubs, huh?" and then explains he doesn't want money, he wants the peace of mind to go about his livelihood without being terrorized.

When Little Kevin goes to Marlo to explain why the cops have been talking to him, the fat man in the red hat is pushed into the back of an SUV and the word goes out that Randy Wagstaff is a snitch. It isn't long before it comes back on the boy.

What most intrigues Omar, however, is that a Barksdale lieutenant – Slim Charles – was present when the Stanfield crew drove Kevin away.

On Namond's corner, Carver finds drugs sloppily dropped to the ground and cuffs the boy. Back at the Western, the troops are told to focus on minor, quality-of-life violations to double the amount of arrests in the next month.

When Michael points out his stepfather to Chris Partlow and Snoop, he says: "I just want him gone."

Snoop asks: "What the fuck he do to you?" and when Michael can't bring himself to answer, a sympathetic Chris promises that they'll take care of it.

Herc and the spy camera remain worlds apart and the lovable knucklehead decides to come clean with Lieutenant Marimow about what happened. As he does – blaming sloppy paperwork – a call comes in from Bubbles.

Marimow forces Herc to ignore the call, reprimands him for the fuck-up at the train station involving Marlo and the "skinny girl," and in the midst of this, Herc changes his mind about telling the truth about the camera.

And again, Bubbles languishes, deciding to get even by telling Herc that a Westside preacher has dope on him from Marlo. When nothing turns up but a Bible, the minister gets Herc's name and badge number.

Bunny agrees to take his errant student home with him and when his wife remarks how well-behaved Namond is, the ex-cop smiles and says: "Don't be fooled. This is his Eddie Haskell act."

Later, when Colvin takes Namond back to his house, his mother De'Londa shouts at him to "leave my son the fuck alone."

Bodie and Poot get a visit from Slim Charles, who reports on the fate of Little Kevin, saying that Chris Partlow and Snoop "walked him down an alley. He in a vacant now."

While the area superintendent of schools shadows his class, Prez focuses on the sample exam questions. The moment the bureaucrat leaves, its back to West Baltimore Monte Carlo games for his students.

When another superintendent meets with Colvin and Professor Parenti – questioning the lack of prep for the state test – Colvin says: "They're not fools, these kids . . . Jesus, they see right through us."

The school system professionals aren't impressed, saying what they saw "wasn't education as I understand the term."

Discussing the fate of Little Kevin – who was not a snitch – Bodie tells Poot that Marlo is just a "cold motherfucker."

"It's a cold world, Bodie," says Poot. "The world goin' one way, people another."

And getting colder by the moment for Michael's stepfather, whom Partlow, while marching him to his death, keeps asking if he likes "fucking little boys."

Partlow, in the company of Snoop, pistol-whips the man to the point of being unrecognizable; an emotional execution following candid dialogue about what a man – some men anyway – has to do in prison if he wants sex. "Man gotta bust his nut, know what I'm sayin'?" says Michael's stepfather.

"I do," says Partlow and then administers a beating unlike anything we've seen from him before.

At home, Michael tells his agitated mother she best stop waiting around for her man to get back from the store because "he ain't coming back."

FELICIA "SNOOP" PEARSON

Baby girl never really knew her daddy and what she remembers of her mama she'd sooner forget: a crack fiend who didn't care enough about the baby she was carrying to give up the dope. Baby girl came into the world addicted, cross-eyed, and barely big enough to thrive. But she lived and she thrived because Felicia "Snoop" Pearson is a survivor.

There's little else to explain her journey. Crack baby. Foster child. Baby-faced gangsta. Teenaged murderer. Prison inmate. Drug dealer. Actor.

As the androgynous, nail gun assassin on *The Wire*, Pearson not only looked the part with her cap of braided hair, oversized T-shirts and baggy shorts, she lived it.

"My world was ruled by street smarts. If you have them, you survive; if you don't you die. That was an exciting idea." [1]

Pearson learned early on that no good would come from a mother who'd sell the Sunday dress off her daughter's back to cop another high. She saw the beautiful lady of her dreams for what she really was and would never be. As a child, she was smart enough to know that the elderly couple who had taken her into their East Baltimore home, Cora and Levi Pearson, were all the parents she would need.

Mama and Pop loved and cared for her and young FeFe loved them back.

From the time she was an infant, Pearson was raised by the couple with all sorts of family coming and going and staying. Their two-story, brick row house in the 2400 block of East Oliver Street was home for Pearson.

"She never gave my mother any trouble," says James Jackson, 68, of York, PA, one of Cora and Levi Pearson's four children.

On the streets of East Baltimore, Felicia was different, a girl who looked and acted like a boy and was proud of it. Book-smart and street-wise, she was enticed by the world beyond the front door of the Oliver Street row house.

Pearson's devotion to the foster parents who eventually adopted her wasn't enough to keep her in school or out of harm's way.

"Being outside Mama's house was always more interesting than being inside . . . The streets were screaming at me – that's for sure. But the streets were screaming at everyone. Some kids ignored those screams. I didn't.

"I had to see what the screaming was all about." [2]

The drug trade was lively at the corner of Oliver and Montford, a few feet from the Pearsons' front stoop. A boy could earn good money working as a lookout or guarding the stash of the local drug dealer. He could earn big money if he led a corner crew.

And FeFe was more boy than girl, despite her brown doe eyes and angelic face. She dressed like a boy 'cause that's who she was. She knew then she preferred girls to boys for sex, experimented at a tender age, and wasn't ashamed of it.

---

1. From Felicia "Snoop" Pearson and David Ritz, *Grace After Midnight: A Memoir* (Grand Central Publishing, 2007), p. 44
2. Pearson and Ritz, p. 26 & p. 24

A drug dealer who fondly nicknamed her Snoop – after comic-strip character Charlie Brown's pet beagle – befriended her and tried to keep her out of trouble and in school. He was as close to her as any uncle, but she wouldn't listen.

By the time she was ten, she had a 9mm gun stashed under her mama's back porch. At 13, she had left behind an all-girl crew to run with the boys, doing a nigga's business. Pistol-whip a bitch for stealing drugs. Trade shots with some Westside boys who don't belong here. Pop a few niggas in a mall parking lot.

No way to live. Only way to survive.

"Seemed like death rode down Oliver Street more often than the ice cream truck. Death was a regular. Even as a baby girl, death – up close and real as rain – was a part of my life." [3]

April 27, 1995, three weeks before her 15th birthday, Pearson was out in the neighborhood walking when she saw a street fight brewing. She couldn't ignore it, walked right into the middle of it, and when a baseball bat came swinging at her head, she ducked and then tried to stop it the only way she thought she could.

She pulled a gun and fired. The girl with the bat hit the ground. Death was at Snoop's door. She was 14 and a killer.

It took two years for the case to wend its way through the courts as she sat in Baltimore City Jail. After pleading guilty to second-degree murder and a gun charge, she received a 25-year sentence, all but eight years suspended, and a 20-year sentence with 12 years suspended, both to run concurrently.

Pearson arrived at the Maryland Correctional Institution for Women in December 1996. She was 16 years old.

"So you get in the Cut and you find your place. My place was to fly under the radar. I didn't want to be no star in Grandma's house. I'd rather not be noticed." [4]

Besides earning her General Equivalency Diploma and lying low, Snoop fell in love with a prison guard and found grace while locked up. The love

---

3. Pearson and Ritz, p. 12
4. Pearson and Ritz, p. 107

affair didn't last, but word of the death of her mentor, a drug dealer she called "Uncle," overwhelmed her with rage and grief and – miraculously – cracked open her heart to the power of redemption.

"I believed in the grace business. I knew I was blessed. And knowing that gave me patience. Gave me fortitude. Gave me the wherewithal to grind it out, hour after hour, day after day."[5]

That knowledge sustained her through the rest of her prison stay. Pearson was released July 7, 2000, determined to begin anew and do right. She got a $15-an-hour job making car bumpers, but when her employer discovered she had been in prison, she was fired.

Pearson then worked for a book store. That too didn't last once they learned of her past. But the streets were ready to take her back, and back she went, returning to the drug trade's easy money, no questions asked.

And that was her life until a man she didn't know or recognize noticed her in a club on Guilford Avenue in downtown Baltimore. The man had a nasty scar on his face.

"He was looking at me so I told my cousin, Man this guy right here looking at me. He say, Who? I say this guy right here. He say, Man's Omar. I say, You

5. Pearson and Ritz, p. 166

know him? Yeah, he play on The Wire *. . . Finally he came over and he say, I have a question for you, Is you a girl or a boy?"* [6]

The conversation with actor Michael Kenneth Williams led to an introduction to producer-writer Ed Burns who recognized her potential and authentic voice.

Pearson wasn't sure what would come of it, but when Burns and Simon cast her as the icy hit woman for drug kingpin Marlo Stanfield, she slipped into the role as though she was born to it. Packing the Lexus of nail guns, the character Snoop was a hip-hop executioner for our times.

Baby girl in a different game now and working it as hard. Signing with an agent, studying with an acting coach, lending her insights when a scene or script didn't feel right and working hard to do right. Pearson was determined to make good on this chance.

"At first she was just being herself. By the end of the show, she was hitting every mark," says Simon.

Added Burns: "She knows she had a big break. And she's one of the few people that I've met in my journey that took advantage of the break. She is giving it a hell of a shot. I think she has a lot more to offer to the camera."

Since *The Wire* ended, Pearson has pushed ahead with her new life. She bought a house on a street of neat bungalows and tidy lawns, miles away from the old neighborhood. She has landed parts in two movies, and like other actors identified with a particular role, struggled to keep from being typecast.

Pearson penned an autobiography, *Grace After Midnight*, with writer David Ritz and it's a gritty, provocative portrait of her life on the streets. She's also recorded two songs, hoping to make her mark as a rap singer.

"I keep encouraging her not to step back, to keep going forward," says Mr. Jackson, her adoptive big brother. "I do worry about her. She is the only sister I got. I hate to see her not do good.

"I think everybody in life deserve a break and seeing as she is getting hers I want her to keep on doing good."

But can playing an iconic character on an acclaimed HBO series for a couple of seasons completely change the trajectory of a life?

---

6. Felicia "Snoop" Pearson Q&A with *The Wire* writer William F. Zorzi, Jr. Podcast of appearance at Enoch Pratt Free Library, November 14, 2008.

Last year, Pearson found herself back in court, in handcuffs and leg irons, a witness to a murder whom prosecutors claimed wasn't cooperating, a scene not unlike one the writers for *The Wire* might have scripted.

But Pearson's lawyer insisted that his client had not been an unwilling participant. And when the judge who issued the warrant for her arrest realized Pearson hadn't received notice of the court dates in the murder case, he apologized to her, noting that her past troubles "were a world away."

While promoting her book at the Enoch Pratt Free Library last year, Pearson talked about her past with a self-awareness of the responsibility she now bears.

"I just thank God every night that I'm here. You know just to tell my story. This is my chance. I could probably change a couple peoples' lives in this room. There are lot of trials and tribulations that I went through. Just hold your head up. Don't let nothing steer you wrong. Just keep positive people around you . . . People ask me all the time now that they read the book, if you could change one thing in your life what would you change. I said I go back to that day when I was running toward [a fight] and I shot and killed somebody."[7]

In Felicia Pearson's old neighborhood, vacant, boarded-up houses seem to outnumber those where families live. Shirley's Honey Hole bar is busy even at midday.

Trash is strewn in alleys and behind rundown houses. Pearson still comes round by East Oliver Street where Alicia Ford and Quantay Johnson are quick to distinguish the girl they grew up with from the terrifying character she played on television.

"She funny. She aggravating at the same time. She's a giver, a friendly soul," says Johnson, 33, a Pearson relative. "She real strong as a person . . . strong enough to grow up in a family she didn't know. But everybody loved her. My grandmother is real proud of her."

Says the 26-year-old Ford: "No matter what she does, she always going to be Felicia Pearson to us. We look at her no different. She's blood."

"We don't even call her Snoop," adds Johnson. "We call her FeFe."

Ann LoLordo

---

7. Pearson Q&A with Zorzi, November 14, 2008

episode
forty-eight

"A NEW DAY"
"You play in dirt, you get dirty."
— MCNULTY

Directed by Brad Anderson
Story by David Simon & Ed Burns; teleplay by Ed Burns

Randy is petrified upon learning the fate of Little Kevin, last seen headed for a row of vacant houses near the playground. Tired of being run off by Officer Walker, the cop who broke Donut's fingers, the boys think of ways to get back at him. Michael says that he's "got this one."

Carcetti gets a visit from the powerful minister Reid Franklin, who comes complaining about Herc's stop-and-search of a fellow man of the cloth.

Franklin wants a civilian review board of police behavior to ensure that complaints will be taken seriously. Carcetti is eating his first true bowl of damned-if-you-do-damned-if-you-don't shit. If he fires Herc, the department rebels. If he doesn't, the African-American political base is enraged.

At school, Prez soldiers on, teaching practical math, and Randy, now saddled with the snitch rep is shunned trying to sell his candy to kids who used to greet him happily.

Following Slim Charles in a commandeered taxi-cab, Omar and Renaldo trail him to Prop Joe's eastside appliance store, upon which Omar remarks: "... on this caper, the more we learn, the less we know."

In a talk with the homicide unit, Pearlman and Daniels – head of the courthouse Violent Crimes Unit and the police department's Criminal Investigation Division, respectively – claim that a new day has dawned.

Asking for suggestions about how to make things better, they are told everything from "better witness protection" to "more Scotch."

When Carcetti right-hand Norm Wilson tells Rawls that the mayor wants all police districts to steer away from wide-net arrests and concentrate on quality-of-life problems and big-picture investigations, Rawls asks straight up why Burrell hasn't been fired.

Apprised of the problem with Herc and the ruffled minister, Rawls says to dump the problem on Daniels's desk. When Daniels doesn't see much to the incident in terms of true misconduct, Rawls tells him that City Hall is looking for him to "do the right thing."

Putting the payback of Officer Walker into action, Dukie keys the cop's private car and, when chased, leads the man into an alley. There, a masked Michael points a gun at the off-duty, somewhat inebriated officer, saying: "You the police like to fuck with a nigga?" and fires a warning shot.

But then he sees a ring on Walker's finger, the ill-fated Old Face Andre ring that has made its way from pillar to post: from Andre to Marlo to Omar to Walker.

Michael tells Walker to hand it over and when he does, Namond tosses a bucket of yellow paint on the cop. When Walker claims in the station house that the attack on him was a gang declaration of war – "us against them" – McNulty cannot conceal his contempt, saying: "Yellow paint a declaration of war?"

A group of thugs step up to Randy outside of school and accuse him of talking to the police. Randy denies it and they turn on Michael, wanting to know what he's doing hanging with a snitch.

Michael responds with a punch and by the time Prez can break it up, Randy is on the ground, bloody and stunned. Michael and Dukie stand by as Prez helps Randy, who swears he only told the cops common knowledge: that Lex was killed on a playground and he heard about it from Little Kevin. Michael says the best policy is not to talk to cops no matter what and Prez agrees.

Talk of Michael standing up for a snitch, however, soon makes it back to Marlo.

Carcetti is determined to find a five percent pay raise for the police department while Rawls distributes the new mayor's order calling for quality police work over statistics. At the end of the meeting, Daniels asks permission to reorganize the Major Crimes Unit, the detail that did such good work over the years only to be stymied by political agendas. Rawls says okay.

Taking this good news to Lester Freamon, Daniels tells the savvy detective to pick the squad of his dreams, that it's "morning in Baltimore, Lester. Wake up and smell the coffee."

The Slim Charles trail leads Omar and Renaldo to a seminar room at the Holiday Inn with a "New Day Co-op" sign and a table around which sit Prop Joe, Fat Face Rick and others. When Marlo joins them, Omar's blood begins to sing.

"If it's what I think it is," he says, "our little clutch of chickens might be putting all their eggs up in one basket."

As Freamon packs up his desk in homicide to again begin working more complicated cases, Carver comes in looking for Bunk, wanting to know what happened with the promise to look after Randy Wagstaff, the kid from the Lex murder.

Bunk doesn't know what he's talking about and Carver, embarrassed, says Herc was supposed to bring the boy to Bunk for safekeeping.

Working the good cop/bad cop routine on Herc, Bunk and Freamon interrogate their colleague about the fate of Randy. Bunk takes the ogre role, storming out to leave Freamon to play the understanding shrink.

Herc lays it out for Lester, including info about the nail gun he found on Partlow and Snoop. Though the workingman's tool meant nothing to Herc, Lester makes note of it.

At the Western District roll call, Carcetti announces the five percent raise he's managed to put together, along with the new order of abandoning quotas in favor of quality police work.

"If the old dogs can't handle the job, I'll find new ones who can," he vows.

With reluctance, Carcetti meets with Burrell, who concedes that while the big picture of policing is not what he does best, the slap on the wrist that Daniels gave Herc for jacking up a black minister will not sit well in the community. His solution: look for dirt in the six years that Herc worked narcotics, a beat in which "there are no virgins."

Carcetti fully understands now that while Burrell may not be much of a cop, he's a hell of a politician. He will later realize that he promised the cops a meager pay raise without knowing that he inherited a $54 million school system deficit from the Royce Administration.

"How the fuck," he asks, "do we deal with that?"

Reconciled and reunited with Sherrod (no match for the streets as a solo act) Bubbles is doing a bang-up business with his mobile "Bubbles Depot."

Finding a toppled aluminum utility pole – easily worth a cool hundred as scrap – makes for good feelings all around. Until the Fiend shows up: same old story, same old song and beatdown.

Omar and Renaldo raid Prop Joe's appliance store, holding heavy weapons on Joe and his lieutenants, Cheese and Slim Charles. Prop Joe promises to lead Omar to Marlo's package. If you don't, says Omar, I'll tell the boy you set him up for the poker heist.

When Bunk and Freamon complain to Prez that Randy's "math teacher" won't let him talk to cops, Prez backs it up: "I'm siding with my kids."

Lester understands but Bunk presses for something, anything. Prez gives up the address of the playground where Randy told Lex to meet a girl. "That's all he did," Prez insists.

When Dukie is one of five eighth graders told they will be promoted to high school, he is crestfallen: he will be leaving his friends behind, a smaller fish in a more dangerous pond.

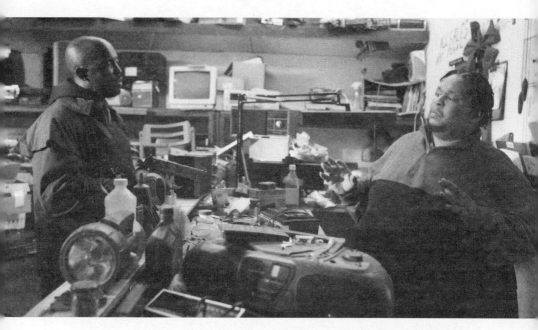

Colvin and Professor Parenti also get bad news from Marcia Donnelly: "They pulled the pin on your program."

Bunny and the academic plead for the class to the school superintendent, arguing that attendance has been near-perfect, there were no suspensions for behavior problems and regular classes have improved with the troublemakers removed.

In short, they would like to expand the project to the entire eighth grade. The superintendent doesn't disagree that progress has been made, but hasn't the courage to do the right thing in the face of the deficit.

"If City Hall were to sign off on this, we could go forward . . . but now is not the time to rock any boats."

At the abandoned playground, Bunk and Freamon take in the big picture, the little picture, the whole picture. Freamon notices that it is surrounded on three sides by vacant rowhouses and heads up to the back of one for a closer look.

The plywood on the rear door is so weathered that it comes loose with a little bit of hand pressure. Lester keeps moving down the row, checking the plywood until he comes to one secured with machine-drive nails.

"This a tomb," he says. "Lex is in there."

episode
forty-nine

"THAT'S GOT HIS OWN"
"That all there is to it?"
— BUBBLES

Directed by Joe Chappelle

Story by Ed Burns & George Pelecanos; teleplay by George Pelecanos

Call it paint-ball for apprentice assassins.

Chris Partlow and Snoop put Michael through a training program in a vacant warehouse. When the boy moves toward Chris – sweating and bleeding after being chased by Michael – he is asked by his panting victim what the next move is.

"One to the head, I keep it quick," says Michael.

"Not yet, motherfucker," says Snoop, pleased with their protégé. "You shoot live rounds like paint, boy, you gonna be the shit."

The results of such attention to detail – the badly decomposed body of Lex – is examined by crime lab techs as Lester Freamon looks on.

However his supervisor, Sergeant Landsman, still rolls with the stats and says: "Do you see a tool belt on me?

"Three weeks left in the year, our unit clearance rate is under 50 percent. We do not go looking for bodies, especially moldering John Does."

He then issues an order not to "pull down any more fucking wood."

A launched-into-orbit Carcetti bitches at a city budget meeting over the $54 million school deficit.

"I just ran a clean-up-the-streets campaign," he says when the only suggestions call for scaling back services in an already cash-strapped municipality ". . . and I just got done promising the world to every cop in the city."

Nerese Campbell says the only answer is to go to Annapolis, see the governor, and "beg his Republican ass."

Omar and Renaldo follow Cheese to a meet with Marlo's people, where a runner hands Prop Joe's nephew a book bag of cash: 25 large for what they were short before and $150k to re-up.

When Cheese says he's not sure if there will be enough coming off the boat for all that Marlo wants, he's told: "Short someone else."

Co-op, indeed.

In the Major Crimes Unit, Freamon and his new crew – which includes Herc, Sydnor, and Dozerman – watch as Marimow, the department hack, packs up.

They are silent and somewhat smug about it: live by the petty political sword, die by the petty political sword. As soon as Marimow is gone, they laugh their asses off.

And then Freamon calls the shot: Marlo is still the target. Landsman won't let him chase the murders – if a body falls in West Baltimore does anyone hear it? – but they can follow the dope.

When Colvin tells the Deacon the research project has been killed by the school system, the preacher tells him to tell Delegate Watkins about it, a play Colvin was hoping to make.

At the "a-rabber" stables – the spot where men who sell fruit and vegetables from horse-drawn carts meet – Bubbles consults with the elders of the street for advice on how to rid himself of the Fiend.

The answer: lace a shot of dope with sodium cyanide.

Says one of the sages, "Ain't no thing to kill a nigger if he's already 'bout the business of killin' hisself."

In the Missing Persons Unit, where budget cuts have kept the sole detective off the street and buried under paperwork, Freamon finds photos and paperwork on Lex and Little Kevin.

When Namond tells Michael that Kenard reported his stash stolen, Michael soon concludes that he's being played and Kenard kept the dope.

"And now," says Michael, "you gotta step to him, put somethin' real behind them words." Later, Namond's mother will concur, saying he should have made Kenard "feel pain," that he is no chip off the old block.

When Namond reminds her that his father is in prison – thus making it difficult for him to measure up – his mother gives him a whack.

In the midst of telling Butchie that he's rounding up a crew to go after Marlo, but he's going to "go subtle," Omar gets a call from Kimmy. She's looking for work.

At the State House in Annapolis, where he arrives hat in hand for his broken school system, Carcetti is made to wait more than an hour for a governor who, sensing Tommy will go after his job in two years, has publicly questioned "local oversight of the system."

Tired of waiting when one hour starts eating into two, Carcetti is about to walk out of the State House when he is finally summoned for his meeting.

When the kids in Colvin's special class are told they need to study for the statewide test to keep moving ahead, Darnell Tyson retorts: "I ain't movin' nowhere but out this motherfucker."

Namond adds that now they aren't any different than the kids learning worthless shit in the other classrooms. Colvin cannot disagree.

Going around Landsman the way he is wont to go around whatever stands in the way of a good investigation, Freamon explains the vacant house burial grounds to Daniels and Pearlman: he can link Lex to at least two other murders by Marlo via the wire that was prematurely shut down.

Prez sits with a depressed Dukie, trying to persuade the boy that high school is the next right thing. He is less than convincing; the argument that anything is worth doing is further voided when Dukie comes home to see an eviction notice and all of his family's belongings on the street.

Once more, the rent went to the dope man.

Michael invites Dukie to live with him and Bug in the very nice accommodations provided by his new employer, Marlo Stanfield.

Daniels shares Freamon's idea that there is a connection between the missing persons and the bodies found in the vacant houses and adds that it would be prudent if it came out now so the murders would be attributed to the last year of the Royce administration.

When Rawls comments that Daniels is now thinking like a political animal, Daniels replies: "I'm learning as I go."

"I bet you fucking are," says Rawls, ordering Daniels to keep the conversation between the two of them.

As they speak, Freamon is betting Bunk that they'll find bodies in any vacant house with matching nails in the plywood. It's a bet that Freamon wins easily.

Namond asks Michael to go with him to confront Kenard about the missing dope. When questioned, he tells Namond, "Package up my ass, Gump."

When Namond hesitates, Michael beats the shit out of the kid with a fury new to Namond. When Michael then tells Namond to grab the package and go, the wanna-be corner boy runs away.

Back in the vacant houses, Freamon declines to call the crime lab on the new corpses: until the bosses say there are bodies, there will be no bodies.

Carcetti gives the green light to begin hauling them out. Adamant that the department no longer play fast and loose with statistics, he is pleased that the murders will fall at the end of Royce's watch and not in January when he takes office.

The work of opening up all the vacants sealed with airtight plywood, will take some extra manpower and Daniels tells Freamon to pick two people he wants from CID.

Carver stops by Randy's house but the boy's guardian – "Miss Anna" Jeffries, his foster mother (played by Denise Hart), says they want to wait a while longer before he goes back to school.

Carver, invited to stay for breakfast, assures her that the snitching brouhaha will blow over in a week or two.

When Bubbles awakes in the derelict rowhouse he and Sherrod call home, he finds his young friend deathly still alongside a littering of empty vials that were supposed to avenge him with the Fiend.

"No, no, no . . . what you do? What you do?" cries Bubbles, weeping upon the dead boy's chest.

At the appliance store, Slim Charles enters to tell Prop Joe the money from Marlo is on its way and the dope is too. Omar puts his crew into action.

Namond, a coward and a bully, begins picking on Dukie at Cutty's gym – calling him a "dogshit smellin' nigga" – when Michael won't talk to him. Michael turns on Namond, throwing him against a wall and beating him until he cries.

When the gym clears, Carver shows up and Namond is honest with Cutty and the cop: he can't go home. His mother expects him to be a fierce gangster like his father but it's not in him.

While Carver tries to figure out what to do with Namond, Cutty goes to Michael's house where no one is home but his drug addict mother.

As Cutty leaves, she says: "You find that boy, you let him know I need some help around here."

When Cutty does find Michael, he's hanging with Marlo's boys, including top Stanfield lieutenant Monk Metcalf (Kwame Patterson).

When Cutty tries to talk to Michael – "This here ain't you" – the boy ignores him. Michael tells Cutty to back off and when Cutty dismisses him, Monk shoots the coach in the thigh.

When he aims the barrel at Cutty's head, Michael gently pushes it away – not unlike Brando pushing away Rod Steiger's revolver in the back of a car in *On the Waterfront* – and waits with the wounded man for the ambulance.

Realizing that the boy is lost, that indeed Michael is not unlike the Cutty that it took 17 years in prison to soften, the coach tells him to "go with your people." And he does, leaving Cutty bleeding in the street.

Omar and Renaldo suit up for combat while Kimmy wears a torn housedress and fake fur coat, posing as a hooker to distract security guards at the industrial site where the narcotics are to be delivered.

Initially interested in only taking what was headed to Marlo (on a promise from Prop Joe he would tip him off to that spot), Omar now has his heart set on the whole kit-and-caboodle of the "right off the boat" shipment of dope.

When Renaldo's crew – a couple of Hispanic men posing as painters – shows up in a van, they block the tractor and trailer delivering the narcotics to Cheese, and Omar springs the heist. Cheese reports the commando-style raid to Joe, declaring: "I say we go find this faggot . . . first thing [the Co-op] gonna wonder about is us."

A block away from Miss Anna's house, a Tilghman school punk calls 911 to say that a cop has been shot on the other side of West Baltimore. As the plainclothes car in front of the house where Randy lives roars off, gasoline bottle bombs are tossed inside. In moments, the house is aflame.

At the hospital, Carver finds Miss Anna with second- and third-degree burns and Randy crying in a counseling room.

"I'm sorry, son," Carver says, ". . . we'll get you some help."

At first refusing to look at the cop, Randy screams after Carver as he leaves: "You gonna help, huh? You gonna look out for me?"

Miss Anna, the best thing that ever happened to the kid, dies of her wounds. Randy is shipped back to a group home.

episode
fifty

"FINAL GRADES"
"If animal trapped call 410-844-6286"
BALTIMORE, TRADITIONAL
Directed by Ernest Dickerson
Story by David Simon & Ed Burns; teleplay by David Simon

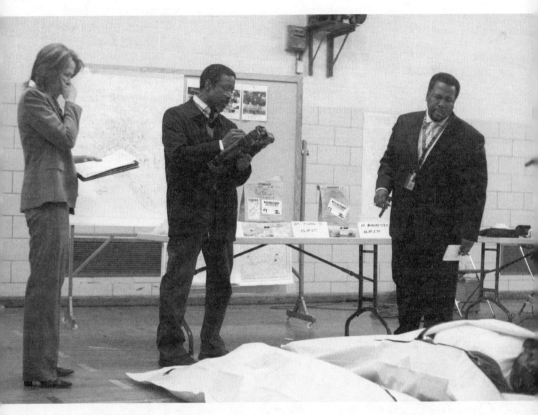

Merry Christmas.

Homicide supervisor Jay Landsman's holiday spirit is quickly dampened by red names on the board – Freamon is emptying the vacant houses – and vomit on his shoes.

After turning himself in for the inadvertent death of Sherrod, Bubbles begins puking from withdrawal in the interrogation room. When Landsman and Norris return from cleaning themselves up, they find Baltimore's best snitch hanging from the ceiling by his belt.

The attempt fails and instead of charging him in the death, Landsman elects to ship Bubbles off to rehab, "something with soft walls."

As forensic teams go house-to-house recovering bullet casings, hair and fibers as well as laser images of footprints, the jockeying at police headquarters over who is going to get out ahead of the curve is in full swing.

Daniels returns from the multiple crime scenes and tells Commissioner Burrell that the Stanfield organization, on whom they had wiretaps until Lieutenant Marimow pulled them three months ago, is the likely cause of the bodies.

Burrell tells Daniels he has the department at his disposal and Daniels leaves to begin a citywide search of other vacant houses, with patrol shifts across the city mobilized and the body count rising.

Rawls tells Burrell that if Daniels is credited with solving this one, he will move closer to the commissioner's job.

Not only is Daniels nowhere near his "throne," says Burrell – warning Rawls never to cross him again – but you don't have a prayer either.

As Marlo and Chris Partlow look on, the New Day Co-op lords confront Prop Joe and Slim Charles over the stolen delivery. It is on Joe, they say, to make it right.

"Share in the good, share in the bad," reasons Joe, rejecting the idea but feeling the need – to protect his livelihood and his life – to give Marlo the direct number of the supplier present when Omar took the delivery.

After dividing up that delivery among his crew, Omar still has "26 raw," which Butchie suggests selling back to Prop Joe. The straight-up "fuck you" of the idea tickles Omar.

Greggs hits the streets to look for the suspended-without-pay Herc and find the nail he shot into the road.

In the hospital with his leg wound – watching HBO's *Deadwood* in his room – Cutty gets a hard time from a nurse who takes him for a gangster. Colvin visits, seeking advice about how best to handle Namond, whom Bunny has come to care for.

On the way out, Colvin lets the nurse know that Cutty isn't a criminal. He got shot trying to help a kid escape the corner.

It is to Wee-Bey, an aging corner boy serving multiple life sentences for murder, that Colvin makes a pitch for Namond, asking Wee-Bey to sign the boy over to him as legal guardian.

Wee-Bey: "You askin' too much."

"Yeah," says Colvin, "but I'm asking."

Back at the vacant houses – as the story makes national news – a crowd has gathered as Little Kevin's body comes out and Bodie loses it, yelling about Marlo the murderer and throwing a true fit, punching in windows on a parked squad car.

McNulty watches and tells the other cops "that's his friend in the bag," but they lock Bodie up anyway.

Watching on television, Carcetti knows his administration will have to clean up the mess. More complicated, says Wilson, is the lingering school mess and how taking state money to fix city schools is sure to be a political liability one way or the other.

He advises Tommy to "go back to Annapolis, eat his shit," but Carcetti's pride gets the better of him and, after another visit to the State House, he turns the bailout down.

Back at the store after doing their best to pacify the other Co-op leaders, Prop Joe and Slim Charles go over their handling of Marlo. Cheese thinks the supply is now at risk with Marlo in direct contact with the overseas shipment. Joe says he had no choice, when . . .

Knock-knock.

Who's there?

Omar.

Omar who?

Omar here to sell back the dope I just stole from you at popular prices – 20 cents on the dollar. And don't you know that ole Joe knows a worthy proposition when he sees one.

In a gymnasium, the bodies mount to 17. Wandering in looking for Pearlman – he wants her signature to get charges against

Bodie dropped – McNulty can't quite keep the born detective inside of him quiet.

He peppers Bunk and Freamon with questions and they tease him about what it must be like to be a "police" who can't work such a tasty case.

Bunk and Greggs have identified the model of the nail gun but found no trace of the nail Herc fired. They've called for a metal detector and will sweep the street. Other than that, some luck with the hair, fibers and blood would be welcome.

The next move is to issue search warrants and hope Partlow and Snoop are still in possession of the nail gun, whose purchase – both comical and ominous – launched the entire season.

When Pearlman points out that it's no crime to own power tools, Bunk says they also have a witness linking Partlow and Snoop to the bodies, referencing Randy. Freamon, in fidelity to Prez, corrects Bunk by saying they only have a source, not a witness.

Frustrated, Bunk says he needs an hour to clear something up. Greggs follows him out.

Dukie shows up for his first day at Frederick Douglass High School, named for the African-American author and abolitionist (1818–1895), born a slave on the Eastern Shore of Maryland.

When he is pushed by a group of bigger kids, Dukie packs it in and leaves. Back at Tilghman, Prez's class is taking the system's all-important statewide performance test. Some try, some are frustrated and some don't care.

When the scores come back, Prez almost swoons at the results: improvement across the board with a goodly number of the kids shown to be "proficient."

His seltzer water goes flat, however, when Grace Sampson points out that the state defines proficient as two grades below their level and "advanced" at or a grade below their level.

The most improved?

"Mr. Prezbo."

A rather lousy cop, Roland "Prez" Pryzbylewski has become a teacher.

At Lex's house, Bunk and Greggs are told by the dead man's mother that his body was in such bad shape they wouldn't let her see it. When Bunk points out that she could have cooperated a lot sooner, she says she heard that Snoop and Chris killed her son.

Trying to do right by Randy, Carver tells the Department of Social Services that he will sign up to be the boy's foster parent if it will keep him out of a group home. No dice.

Using the info from Lex's mother for a warrant, Greggs and Bunk jack up Partlow and Snoop and have them cuffed and sitting on the curb while they search their car.

No nail gun and not a trace of lime but Greggs knows the deadly duo would not be "riding tame" and feels around under the dash. She finds a wire, connects it to the ignition wire and voila!

A drop box pops open, revealing a pistol.

"Ain't even our car," says Snoop.

A buffer between Marlo and Prop Joe, the Greek's man in Baltimore – Spiros "Vondas" Vondopoulos – assures Stanfield that the stickup of the delivery was not a fraud.

Marlo takes Vondas at his word (later telling Monk to put a tail on their supplier), assures Joe he's good for $90k – his share in the stolen dope – and promises to hunt down Omar.

When Monk shows up at Central Booking with a bail bondsman to spring Chris and Snoop on the gun charge, he sees Bodie leaving with McNulty (who has sprung him and offered lunch).

Before they are released, Partlow and Snoop are forced to give blood and hair samples.

Enjoying sandwiches and each other's company in an arboretum – they are hardly strangers – Bodie tells McNulty that he's no snitch but he's fed up with his life as one of "them little bitches on the chessboard" – the pawns explained to him by D'Angelo in Season One.

He is both frustrated and angry enough to be willing to do away with "Marlo and his kind."

"You're a soldier," says McNulty, back in the game. Once news of their pleasant afternoon gets back to Marlo, Bodie's head is on the block.

The last words of Preston "Bodie" Broadus before a Stanfield rookie named O-Dog puts a bullet in his skull: "This is my corner, I ain't runnin' nowhere."

Marlo visits Michael to tell him he's been given Bodie's corner – and another, unspecified assignment – and notices the fabled Old Face Andre's ring around the boy's neck.

Asked where he got it, Michael replies – to Marlo's obvious amusement and wonder – "Took it from a nigga."

Trying to salvage the University of Maryland pilot project at City Hall, Colvin – self-conscious about his rep as the cop who tried to legalize drugs – and Professor Parenti lay out their accomplishments.

Told they must teach the curriculum or be responsible for leaving some students behind while others move on, Colvin snaps: "We leave 'em all behind, we just don't admit it."

The meeting is abruptly adjourned and Colvin blames himself, telling Parenti: "Seems like every time I open my mouth in this town, I'm telling people what they don't wanna know . . . when do the shit change?"

When Wee-Bey tells De'Londa during a prison visit that he wants her to turn Namond over to Colvin, she balks until he reminds her that one word from him and she will wish she had done otherwise.

Of Colvin, Wee-Bey says with pride: "Man came down here to say my son can be anything he damn please."

"Except a soldier," says De'Londa, only to be told by Wee-Bey to take a good look around the visiting room.

"Who the fuck would wanna be that if they could be anything else?"

After Omar pays Butchie a share for "his pains" in helping out with the big heist, the blind man warns that when you steal as much as he did, "It ain't over."

When a grieving McNulty catches up with Poot on the corner, he makes sure no one is watching and demands to know who killed Bodie.

"Ya'll did," said Poot, referencing the lunch and – not wanting to be the next suspected snitch to take one in the head – tells McNulty to throw him off the corner like a proper police.

Needing to work off his guilt and anger – not unlike Carver's when Ellis delivered Randy to the group home – McNulty pleads his way back to the Major Crimes Unit.

The golden rule?

"Chain of command, Colonel," he tells Daniels.

In the gymnasium, the death count is up to 22. However, nothing connects any of the bodies to Partlow and Snoop, and, says Freamon, they're in for the long haul.

At detox, Bubbles is visited by Walon (Steve Earle) and falls into his recovery sponsor's arms, hurting, ashamed and in tears.

His first day on the job as the boss of his own corner, Michael puts a bullet in the head of an anonymous dope slinger and hops in Partlow's SUV.

As they pull away, Partlow tells him: "You can look 'em in the eye now."

And then comes the season-ending montage, set to a version of "Walk on Gilded Splinters" by Paul Weller of The Jam fame as the arc of the coming days and months plays out.

Namond, the would-be corner boy without the heart for the game, goes with Colvin – we last see him eating a wholesome breakfast before school in a quiet neighborhood.

McNulty looks at a photo of Marlo like he hasn't since Stringer Bell died; while Marlo and Partlow begin educating themselves about Vondas, Prop Joe and how the best dope in Baltimore gets from there to here.

Burdened with 22 unsolved murders, Bunk and Detective Crutchfield go over the evidence while Pearlman and Daniels lunch with Carcetti.

Prez watches Dukie work a corner with Poot while boss man Michael drives away in an SUV. The snitch label and its attendant violence has followed Randy to the group home.

On crutches, Cutty is back at his gym as Carver lectures an even younger gang of kids – the next wave of Michaels and Dukies – outside the abandoned factory.

In the apartment he shares with Bug, Michael helps the kid with his homework, an idyllic scene broken by one of him dumping his murder weapon down a storm drain.

And Season Four is washed away . . .

AN INTERVIEW WITH DAVID SIMON, BY NICK HORNBY

"My standard for verisimilitude is simple and I came to it when I started to write prose narrative: fuck the average reader."

Some things television is good for:
Catharsis
Depicting the "other" America
Pissing off the mayor

Three or four years ago, I got an email from a friend in which he described The Wire *as the best thing he'd ever seen on TV, "apart from* Abigail's Party." *Here was a recommendation designed to get anybody's attention. No mention of* The West Wing, *or* The Sopranos, *or* Curb Your Enthusiasm, *or any of the other shibboleths of contemporary TV criticism; just a smart-aleck nod to Mike Leigh's classic 1977 BBC play. It reeled me in, anyway, and I went out and bought a box set of the first series.*

I'd never heard of the show. It wasn't widely known or shown here in the UK, although whenever a new season starts, you can always find a piece in a broadsheet paper calling it "the best programme you've never heard of," and I didn't know what to expect. What I got was something that bore no resemblance to Abigail's Party, *predictably, and very little resemblance to any other cop show. At one stage I was simultaneously hooked on* The Wire *and the BBC's brilliant adaptation of* Bleak House, *and it struck me that Dickens serves as a useful point of comparison; David Simon and his team of writers (including George Pelecanos, Richard Price, Dennis Lehane) swoop from high to low, from the mayor's office to the street corner – and the street-corner dealers are shown more empathy and compassion than anyone has mustered before. The hapless Bubbles, forever dragging behind him his shopping trolley full of stolen goods, is Baltimore's answer to Joe the Crossing Sweeper.*

We talked via email. A couple of weeks later, we met in London – David Simon is making a show about the war in Iraq with my next-door neighbor.

(Really. He's really making a show about the war in Iraq, and the producer literally lives next door.) We talked a lot about sports and music.
– Nick Hornby

NICK HORNBY: Can I start by asking you something about the writing? How did you kick it off? All the seasons have had very unconventional shapes and paces to them, I think. Did you have something different in mind before you started, or did that happen during the creation of the series?

DAVID SIMON: I think what you sense in *The Wire* is that it is violating a good many of the conventions and tropes of episodic television. It isn't really structured as episodic television and it instead pursues the form of the modern, multi-POV novel. Why? Primarily because the creators and contributors are not by training or inclination television writers. In fact, it is a little bit remarkable that we ended up with a television drama on HBO or anywhere else. I am a newspaper reporter by training who wrote a couple of long, multi-POV nonfiction narratives, *Homicide* and *The Corner*. The first became the basis for the NBC drama of the same name; the second I was able to produce as a miniseries for HBO, airing in 2000. Both works are the result of a journalistic impulse, the first recounting a year I spent with the Baltimore Police Department's Homicide Unit, and the second book detailing a year spent in a drug-saturated West Baltimore neighborhood, following an extended, drug-involved family. Ed Burns, my co-author on *The Corner* and co-creator on *The Wire*, was a homicide detective who served in the BPD for 20 years and, following that for seven years, as a seventh-grade teacher at a Baltimore public school. The remaining writers – Richard Price [*Clockers*], Dennis Lehane [*Mystic River*], and George Pelecanos [*The Night Gardener*] – are novelists working at the highest level of the crime genre. Bill Zorzi covered state and municipal politics for the *Baltimore Sun* for 20 years; Rafael Alvarez, another *Sun* veteran, worked as a merchant seaman and comes from two generations of port workers. So we are all rooted in a different place than Hollywood.

We got the gig because as my newspaper was bought and butchered by an out-of-town newspaper chain, I was offered the chance to write scripts, and, ultimately, to learn to produce television by the fellows who were turning my first book into *Homicide: Life on the Street*. I took that gig and, ultimately, I was able to produce the second book for HBO on my own. Following that miniseries, HBO agreed to look at *The Wire* scripts. So I made an improbable and in many ways unplanned transition from journalist/author to TV producer. It was not a predictable transformation and I am vaguely amused that it actually happened. If I had a plan, it was to grow old on the *Baltimore Sun*'s copy desk, bumming cigarettes from young reporters and telling lies about what it was like working with H. L. Mencken and William Manchester.

Another reason the show may feel different than a lot of television: our model is not quite so Shakespearean as other high-end HBO fare. *The Sopranos* and *Deadwood* – two shows that I do admire – offer a good deal of *Macbeth* or *Richard III* or *Hamlet* in their focus on the angst and machinations of the central characters (Tony Soprano, Al Swearengen). Much of our modern theater seems rooted in the Shakespearean discovery of the modern mind. We're stealing instead from an earlier, less-traveled construct – the Greeks – lifting our thematic stance wholesale from Aeschylus, Sophocles, Euripides to create doomed and fated protagonists who confront a rigged game and their own mortality. The modern mind – particularly those of us in the West – finds such fatalism ancient and discomfiting, I think. We are a pretty self-actualized, self-worshipping crowd of postmoderns and the idea that for all of our wherewithal and discretionary income and leisure, we're still fated by indifferent gods, feels to us antiquated and superstitious. We don't accept our gods on such terms anymore; by and large, with the exception of the fundamentalists among us, we don't even grant Yahweh himself that kind of unbridled, interventionist authority.

But instead of the old gods, *The Wire* is a Greek tragedy in which the postmodern institutions are the Olympian forces. It's the police department, or the drug economy, or the political structures, or the school administration, or the macroeconomic forces that are throwing the lightning bolts and hitting people in the ass for no decent reason. In much of television, and in a good deal of our stage drama, individuals are often portrayed as rising above institutions to achieve catharsis. In this drama, the institutions always prove larger, and those characters with hubris enough to challenge the postmodern construct of American empire are invariably mocked, marginalized, or crushed. Greek tragedy for the new millennium, so to speak. Because so much of television is about providing catharsis and redemption and the triumph of character, a drama in which postmodern institutions trump individuality and morality and justice seems different in some ways, I think.

It also explains why we get good reviews but less of an audience than other storytelling. In this age of Enron, WorldCom, Iraq, and Katrina, many people want their television entertainments to distract them from the foibles of the society we actually inhabit. Which brings me to the last notion of why *The Wire* may feel different. The chumps making it live in Baltimore, or, in the case of guys like Price, Pelecanos, and Lehane, they are at least writing in their literary work about second-tier East Coast rust-belt places like Jersey City, northeast Washington, or Dorchester, rather than Manhattan, Georgetown, or Back Bay, Boston. We are of the other America or the America that has been left behind in the post-industrial age. We don't live in LA or go to their parties; we don't do what we do to try to triumph in the world of television entertainment by having a bona fide hit, and meeting the pretty people and getting the best table at the Ivy. Shit, the last time George and I went to the Ivy on a road trip, we waited 45 minutes for a table and then were announced as "the Pelican party." We don't belong there and we don't need the kind of money or the level of Zeitgeist required to belong there. We hang out in the Baltimores of the world, writing what we want to write about and never keeping one eye on whether or not it could sell as much as a drama that had, say, more white faces, more women with big tits, and more stuff that blows up or squirts blood real good.

Our impulses are all the natural reactions of writers who live in close proximity to a specific American experience – independent of Hollywood – and who are trying to capture that experience. And that too is an improbability, given how insulated the American entertainment industry normally is. I don't mean this to come off as some snotty declaration of classist, pseudo-proletarian pretension, but it is what it is. I live in Baltimore. How many yachts can I water-ski behind in Baltimore harbor? Fuck it, I'm happy to be getting paid what I'm paid to make a television show about what I would normally write magazine articles and newspaper series and narrative tomes about. And the other writers feel pretty much the same.

So we are misfits, and while we hope the show is entertaining enough, none of us think of ourselves as providing entertainment. The impulse is, again, either journalistic or literary. Hope this helps and doesn't sound as wrought and pompous as I think it does. Forgive us for actually thinking about this shit; we know it's television, but we can't help ourselves. But as you yourself probably know from your love of music, sometimes even three chords and the right guitar solo and a good chorus can be pretty much everything.

NH: How did you pitch it?

DS: I pitched *The Wire* to HBO as the anti-cop show, a rebellion of sorts against all the horseshit police procedurals afflicting American television. I am unalterably opposed to drug prohibition; what began as a war against illicit drugs generations ago has now mutated into a war on the American underclass, and what drugs have not destroyed in our inner cities, the war against them has. I suggested to HBO – which up to that point had produced groundbreaking drama by going where the broadcast networks couldn't (*The Sopranos*, *Sex and the City*, et al) – that they could further enhance their standing by embracing the ultimate network standard (cop show) and inverting the form. Instead of the usual good-guys-chasing-bad-guys framework, questions would be raised about the very labels of good and bad, and, indeed, whether such distinctly moral notions were really the point.

The show would instead be about untethered capitalism run amok, about how power and money actually root themselves in a postmodern American city, and, ultimately, about why we as an urban people are no longer able to solve our problems or heal our wounds. Early in the conception of the drama, Ed Burns and I – as well as the late Bob Colesberry, a consummate filmmaker who served as the directorial producer and created the visual template for *The Wire* – conceived of a show that would, with each season, slice off another piece of the American city, so that by the end of the run, a simulated Baltimore would stand in for urban America, and the fundamental problems of urbanity would be fully addressed.

First season: the dysfunction of the drug war and the general continuing theme of self-sustaining postmodern institutions devouring the individuals they are supposed to serve or who serve them. Second season: the death of work and the destruction of the American working class in the post-industrial era, for which we added the port of Baltimore. Third season: the political process and the possibility of reform, for which we added the City Hall component. Fourth season: equal opportunity, for which we added the public education system. The fifth and final season will be about the media and our capacity to recognize and address our own realities, for which we will add the city's daily newspaper and television components.

Did we mention these grandiose plans to HBO at the beginning? No, they would have laughed us out of the pitch meeting. Instead, we spoke only to the inversion of the cop show and a close examination of the drug war's dysfunction. But before shifting gears to the port in Season Two, I sat down with the HBO execs and laid out the argument to begin constructing an American city and examining the above themes through that construction. So here we are.

NH: Baltimore may have had more of an influence on me professionally than any other US city, now that I come to think about it. Certainly with *High Fidelity*, one of the things I was trying to do was cross Barry Levinson with Anne Tyler. Levinson, Tyler, *The Wire*, John Waters . . . None of these seem even to share an aesthetic, and yet there is an incredibly distinctive body of work that's come out of your city. I've never been there, although I'd like to visit. Can you explain how it might have produced this work?

DS: I'm somewhat at a loss to explain Baltimore's storytelling appeal. The interesting thing is that all of us are slicing off different pieces of the same city. My demi-monde is decidedly not the Baltimore of Barry Levinson or John Waters in terms of filmmaking, and none of us get close to the blue-blood districts of Anne Tyler's Roland Park. Laura Lippman moves all around the city, but her latest stand-alone novels are actually strongly referenced to Baltimore County, which is the suburban subdivision that actually encircles Baltimore city. She's been mining places like Towson and Padonia and Owings Mills, where a lot of the upper-middle-class wealth has migrated.

One thing that I do feel is that by getting out of the traditionally dominant locales of New York, Los Angeles, Washington, Chicago, writers stand a better chance of speaking to conditions that are reflective of a lot of less-than-unique or less-than-grandiose second-tier cities. New York, Los Angeles, Chicago, Washington – these are unique places, by dint of their size, their wealth, and unique aspects of their culture (New York as financial, fashion, and theater capital, and as cultural icon, or Washington as the government city, or Los Angeles as the film capital of the country). Baltimore is a post-industrial city, wedged between D.C. and Philadelphia, and struggling to find its future and reconcile its past. In that sense it's like St. Louis and Cleveland and Philly and a lot of other rust-belt American places, and so stories from here have a chance of being about more than Baltimore per se. The storytelling here might be quite detailed in referencing local geography and culture, but it translates easily to elsewhere and therefore acquires additional relevance easily.

I imagine, acknowledging my general ignorance, that a story set in London is de facto a London story, applicable nowhere else in the UK in terms of environment. But a story set in Manchester might more easily resonate in Leeds or Liverpool or Newcastle or wherever. We play ourselves as unique, and, in truth, we value that which is genuine to Baltimore, but on another level we come across as Everycity.

NH: There's a little bit in an Anne Tyler novel, I seem to remember, where characters are confused about whether Baltimore is a southern or a northern city – that must help a bit too, surely, that ambiguity, if you're trying to avoid the kind of big-city inflection you're talking about . . .

DS: Yes, that line about the most northern southern city or most southern northern city is one known to all Baltimoreans. Maryland (and Baltimore) was very divided at the outbreak of the Civil War and President Lincoln had to arrest the state legislature and hold them without charge at Fort McHenry to prevent the state from seceding and going with the Confederacy. Shades of Guantanamo. The Eastern Shore (on the other side of the Chesapeake Bay) was pro-slavery, as was southern Maryland and much of Baltimore. Western Maryland was pro-Union. And the first Civil War casualties occurred on Pratt Street in downtown Baltimore as citizens rioted and threw rocks at a Massachusetts regiment that was marching from one train station to the other to travel south and reinforce Washington at the start of the war. Oh, and John Wilkes Booth, who assassinated Lincoln, was a Baltimore native and his prominent family of actors, John Wilkes included, are buried downtown in Green Mount Cemetery.

To continue this useless history lesson, you may remember – from the point of view of king and country – that Fort McHenry was the place where our national anthem was penned by a fellow named Francis Scott Key, who was a prisoner on a British ship that was bombarding the fort during the War of 1812. You Brits had burned Washington and Philadelphia and you were set to torch Baltimore, having landed an army near the city. But unless the fleet could reduce the fort, the navy could not sail into the harbor and support the invasion. In the morning, the star-spangled banner still flew over McHenry and so we had something to sing at the beginning of sporting events, and the British army, having fought the Battle of North Point against Baltimore irregulars to a draw, re-embarked on His Majesty's ships and sailed away.

Which brings me to my ugliest moment as an American, one of which I am quite perversely proud. Years ago, I was touring the crypts of St. Paul's in London and we were shown all the generals who had the opportunity to be buried around Wellington. And this elfin little tour guide, who had as a young man stood on the cathedral roof during the Blitz and picked up incendiary sticks and hurled them away to save the edifice, got a twinkle in his eye and said, "You colonials might be interested to note the resting place of Major General Ross, who in 1812 burned your capital city." And so there he was. And his gravestone, as I recollect, declared: VICTOR OF THE BATTLES OF WASHINGTON AND PHILADELPHIA. ACTIVE AT THE BATTLE OF BALTIMORE.

If the ghetto dick-grab were known to me in 1985, I might've held on to mine when I uttered the following: "I'm from Baltimore. And I can tell you what 'active' means. It means we kicked his ass." An empty moment floated through the crypt, and the other Americans on the tour just about died. At that instant, I felt it was a good thing I didn't go on with what I knew, because Ross was actually mortally wounded at North Point by two Baltimoreans with squirrel rifles who crept through the brush and shot him off his horse, infuriating the British, who sent an entire detachment of Royal Marines to kill the sharpshooters, named Wells and McComas. (They are buried under a monument in the heart of the East Baltimore ghetto and have streets named after them near the fort.)

"Quite," said the tour guide, who mercifully smiled at me, vaguely amused. Or at least I like to imagine he was vaguely amused.

NH: I have to ask you about the casting, and whether the actors had any input into their characters. Because it seems to me that to delineate street-corner drug dealers as carefully as you have done, so that they're not just some faceless and indistinguishable army of violent no-hopers, must have required an extraordinary amount of patience and ingenuity. Was it all in the script? How involved were you in the casting? I've been watching *The Corner*, so I know that you've worked with some of those guys before (it's always very disconcerting, if you've watched *The Wire* first, to come across a crack-smoking cop/politician!). But what were you looking for? Are there many Baltimore kids in there? And how come you used so many English people?! I absolutely couldn't believe it when I found out that Idris Elba, who plays Stringer Bell, was actually English.

DS: We cast very carefully, and I'm involved – as are the other leading producers – in every decision on every continuing role. We try to avoid those moments in which well-known actors appear onscreen and throw viewers right out of their sense of *The Wire* as a documentarian exercise. We don't hire a lot of LA actors as a result; we lean more heavily on New York actors or even London stage actors, and wherever we can, utilizing actual Baltimoreans for small supporting roles. By having professional actors work off the real people, it makes the world we are depicting that much more improbable and idiosyncratic and, therefore, more credible.

In addition, the truth to the characterizations is that most, if not all, of the major characters are rooted in people that we know or knew in Baltimore – either through Ed Burns's having policed them as a detective or taught them as a schoolteacher, or Bill Zorzi or myself having written about them. This is not to say there is a one-to-one ratio between real people and the fictional characters. A drug dealer might have attributes of two or three real-life counterparts, and we will steal histories from one trafficker and apply them to another, or mix and match. But it is rooted

▲ Out for a stroll: Omar spreads fear even while walking
to buy cereal in his bathrobe.

Be careful what ▶
you hope for:
newly elected mayor
Tommy Carcetti.

◀◀ Cool Hand Marlo:
drug lord Stanfield
sharpens his aim.

▲ Chris Partlow, sans Snoop.

▼ Bubbles pulls the tried and true "red hat trick" – which IDs a suspect for cops watching the game – on Little Kevin.

▲ Gus Haynes tries to hold the line against executive editor
James Whiting and managing editor Tom Klebanow.

▼ Cedric Daniels with State Senator Clay Davis
as the heat rises in the political corruption case.

▲ Former homicide partners McNulty and Bunk, eye to eye after McNulty's manipulation of crime scenes becomes the one stunt that Bunk cannot abide.

▼ About as emotional as Marlo Stanfield gets: the young drug king surprised to be greeted by Avon Barksdale during a prison visit.

▲ City Council president Nerese Campbell on the morning that the city's sweetheart real estate deal with drug lord "Fat Rick" hits the front page of the *Baltimore Sun*.

▼ *Baltimore Sun* reporter Scott Templeton, trying to fathom the depths of homelessness with his business card.

▲ Jimmy McNulty monitors "the wire."

▼ Guess who's coming to lunch? McNulty and Bodie
share a sandwich and something close to real.

Extry! Extry! – Bubbles peddles the news. ▶▶

in the real, which I believe leads to unique and idiosyncratic portrayals. A lot of it is already in the script and we generally urge our actors to stay on book. But the actors are also pros and they are making each role their own. Sometimes they offer an ad-lib which is an improvement or enhancement to the story and we keep it. Sometimes we push them back on book. But there is a producer on set for every scene to make that decision and ensure that the scripts are honored, and our actors are very professional, and, at this point, trusting, about the material.

As to *The Corner*, or even *Homicide* – it's true that once we find a strong actor, we remember that we did. And since these actors are active on the East Coast, we tend to utilize them where we can. Clarke Peters, who plays Lester Freamon, has spent much of his career on the London stage (he's doing *Porgy and Bess* there now), and we saw him in the Kevin Spacey revival of *The Iceman Cometh* on Broadway. Aidan Gillen we also saw on the New York stage. Dominic West put himself on tape from London and gave a wonderful read on McNulty, so we called him back. And Idris, as Stringer? He came in and read in New York and just nailed it. We won't discriminate against a British actor who gives the best read, regardless of what you fucks did to our capital in 1812. And of course one benefit of an English actor is that unless they've been overexposed in American media, it adds to the credibility of our simulated Baltimore, provided they can master the accent. Their faces are unfamiliar and therefore less likely to pull viewers out of the moment.

We start filming in late March [2007] and go to mid-August. That will be our last season. It's funny. It took American audiences four seasons to find us, but this last season, something happened and find us they did. By the time we're off the air for a few years, we'll be a hit. In the last couple months, both the *New Yorker* and the *New York Times Magazine* have asked to have reporters follow filming to write curtain-raisers for the fifth season, which won't air until 2008. We in Baltimore are used to being ignored. We are moderately disturbed by the trend, but we will try to make do.

NH: I'm really interested in your relationship with Baltimore – I mean, on a practical level. You've accused just about every layer of officialdom of corruption, idleness, vindictiveness, and so on . . . What has been the official response? Do natives write? And what does your press make of it? I don't suppose any American city has ever had to deal with anything quite like you guys . . .

DS: The short answer is that those in the institutions depicted who represent labor or even middle management are by and large more likely to embrace the show than those people running things. The mayor – who is now our state's governor, having been recently elevated in last fall's election – pretty clearly hates the show. Initially, after the first season aired, he held up our permits and told city agencies not to cooperate with us, and in a subsequent conversation with me on the phone, said that Baltimore wanted to be "out of *The Wire* business." I reminded him that before turning the pilot script in to HBO, I had lunch with him and his chief of staff and I told them that the next drama, should it be picked up, would be a much darker, much more realistic vision of the city and its problems. I told him that I understood that Baltimore had already had two bites of the apple with *Homicide* and *The Corner*, and that if he wanted, I could certainly set and film the story in any number of other rust-belt cities. This is true of course; the problems we are depicting are not unique to Baltimore. "No," he said. "We're proud of the shows. Film it here."

On being reminded of this, the mayor asked whether it would be possible to move the show to some other city. I told him that I could not relocate for the second season (we had already built our second-season sets and the Maryland Port Authority was cooperating in giving us locations for the dockworkers' arc) but that I would pick up and move to Philadelphia immediately upon completion of filming.

"Will the show then be about Philadelphia?"

No, I explained. We'd already established that McNulty and Co. were Baltimore cops and that the city depicted was Baltimore. "I'm stuck and you're stuck. We had this conversation two years ago when I asked you that day at lunch, remember?"

"So Philadelphia would get the money for you filming there, but it would still be Baltimore."

"Exactly."

Long pause, followed by: "I'll reconsider your request for filming permits."

Then he hung up. To his credit, however, the mayor then became stoic and silent about the show, and the city agencies – which had turned uncooperative on us – suddenly did an about-face. And the Baltimore political and corporate infrastructure has been entirely professional for the ensuing three seasons of filming. I credit the mayor with a certain amount of maturation. We hear from beat cops, inner-city kids, drug dealers, longshoremen, lower-level political functionaries – those who follow it say they love it. That may not be everybody – after all, we're only hearing from the people with whom we have encounters and maybe those who don't enjoy or appreciate what we're doing are being polite with us. But when Omar or Stringer or Bodie came out of their trailers on an inner-city film set, they were greeted with absolute affection and allegiance by the people living in those neighborhoods. There is a sense in the "other" or neglected America that there is finally a televised drama that encompasses the world in which they live.

Tellingly, after the first season aired and when the mayor was angry, the city council sponsored a resolution urging a publicity campaign to improve Baltimore's image and citing the negative imagery of current television productions about Baltimore, of which there is only one. I had no problem with the city doing anything it wants to improve its image (including attending to its myriad social and economic problems, of course), and, privately, through the head of the state film commission, we urged the sponsors of the resolution to emphasize that positive action and divorce the measure from any reference, oblique or otherwise, to *The Wire*. Our argument being that government should not be in the business of commenting – as a governmental act, individuals can say what they like or dislike – on the value of any story told by anyone about anything. The sponsor ignored us and the resolution headed toward a committee vote.

I showed up at the hearing and introduced myself not as David Simon, executive producer of *The Wire*, or David Simon of HBO, or even David Simon, president of Blown Deadline Productions. I started out by saying that I lived on William Street in the First Councilmanic District and as a Baltimore resident, I objected to . . . Incredibly, I think they were surprised to see me at the hearing. I really think they believed I'd moved to Los Angeles or some shit. Anyway, I pissed them off even more with that performance, which likely led to the angry phone conversation with the mayor, as the sponsor of the resolution was a political ally. But I figure when they fire the first shot across your bow, you should, if you can, fire one back.

NH: Every time I think, Man, I'd love to write for *The Wire*, I quickly realize that I wouldn't know my "True dats" from my "narcos." Did you know all that before you started? Do you get input from those who might be more familiar with the idiom?

DS: My standard for verisimilitude is simple and I came to it when I started to write prose narrative: fuck the average reader. I was always told to write for the average reader in my newspaper life. The average reader, as they meant it, was some suburban white subscriber with two-point-whatever kids and three-point-whatever cars and a dog and a cat and lawn furniture. He knows nothing and he needs everything explained to him right away, so that exposition becomes this incredible, story-killing burden. Fuck him. Fuck him to hell.

Beginning with *Homicide*, the book, I decided to write for the people living the event, the people in that very world. I would reserve some of the exposition, assuming the reader/viewer knew more than he did, or could, with a sensible amount of effort, hang around long enough to figure it out. I also realized – and this was more important to me – that I would consider the book or film a failure if people in these worlds took in my story and felt that I did not get their existence, that I had not captured their world in any way that they would respect.

Make no mistake – with journalism, this doesn't mean I want the subjects to agree with every page. Sometimes the adversarial nature of what I am saying requires that I write what the subjects will not like, in terms of content. But in terms of dialogue, vernacular, description, tone – I want a homicide detective, or a drug slinger, or a longshoreman, or a politician anywhere in America to sit up and say, Whoa, that's how my day is. That's my goal. It derives not from pride or ambition or any writerly vanity, but from fear. Absolute fear. Like many writers, I live every day with the vague nightmare that at some point, someone more knowledgeable than myself is going to sit up and pen a massive screed indicating exactly where my work is shallow and fraudulent and rooted in lame, half-assed assumptions. I see myself labeled a writer, and I get good reviews, and I have the same doubts buried, latent, even after my successes. I suspect many, many writers feel this way. I think it is rooted in the absolute arrogance that comes with standing up at the community campfire and declaring, essentially, that we have the best story that ought to be told next and that people should fucking listen. Storytelling and storytellers are rooted in pay-attention-to-me onanism. Listen to this! I'm from Baltimore and I've got some shit you fucking need to see, people! Put down that CSI shit and pay some heed, motherfuckers! I'm gonna tell it best, and most authentic, and coolest, and . . . I mean, presenting yourself as the village griot is done, for me, with no more writerly credential than a dozen years as a police reporter in Baltimore and a C-average bachelor's degree in general studies from a large state university. On paper, why me? But I have a feeling every good writer, regardless of background, doubts his own voice just a little, and his own right to have that voice heard. It's the simple effrontery of the thing. Who died and made me Storyteller?

So yes, for the drug dealers and the cops, I spent years gathering string on who they are, how they think and talk. When we needed to add politicians, well, I covered some politics so I had the general tone, but we added Bill Zorzi, the *Baltimore Sun*'s best political reporter, to the writing staff. When it came to longshoremen, we added Rafael Alvarez, a former reporter and short-story writer who had quit to join the seamen's union and whose family was three generations in the maritime industry. And the rest of us, myself included, spent weeks getting to know longshoremen and the operations of the port and the port unions, just hanging around the shipping terminals for days on end, so as to credibly achieve those voices. Again, what I wanted was that longshoremen across America would watch *The Wire* and say, Cool, they know my world. I've never seen my world depicted on TV, and these guys got it. And I feared that one of them would stand up and say: No, that's complete bullshit. So that never changes for me.

Which brings us back to Average Reader. Because the truth is you can't write just for people living the event, if the market will not also follow. TV still being something of a mass medium, even with all the fractured cable universe now reducing audience size per channel. Well, here's a secret that I learned with *Homicide* and have held to: if you write something that is so credible that the insider will stay with you, then the outsider will follow as well. *Homicide, The Corner, The Wire, Generation Kill* – these are travelogues of a kind, allowing Average Reader/Viewer to go where he otherwise would not. He loves being immersed in a new, confusing, and possibly dangerous world that he will never see. He likes not knowing every bit of vernacular or idiom. He likes being trusted to acquire information on his terms, to make connections, to take the journey with only his intelligence to guide him. Most smart people cannot watch most TV, because it has generally been a condescending medium, explaining everything immediately, offering no ambiguities, and using dialogue that simplifies and mitigates against the idiosyncratic ways in which people in different worlds actually communicate. It eventually requires that characters from different places talk the same way as the viewer. This, of course, sucks.

There are two ways of traveling. One is with a tour guide, who takes you to the crap everyone sees. You take a snapshot and move on, experiencing nothing beyond a crude visual and the retention of a few facts. The other way to travel requires more time – hence the need for this kind of viewing to be a long-form series or miniseries, in this bad metaphor – but if you stay in one place, say, if you put up your bag and go down to the local pub or shebeen and you play the fool a bit and make some friends and open yourself up to a new place and new time and new people, soon you have a sense of another world entirely. We're after this: making television into that kind of travel, intellectually. Bringing those pieces of America that are obscured or ignored or otherwise segregated from the ordinary and effectively arguing their relevance and existence to ordinary Americans. Saying, in effect, this is part of the country you have made. This too is who we are and what we have built. Think again, motherfuckers.

And the only difference between what we're doing and a world traveler getting off the beaten path is that our viewers don't really have to play the fool. They don't even have to put their ass out of the sofa. They now have a sense of what is happening on a drug corner, or in a homicide unit, or inside a political campaign – and our content, if gently massaged to create drama, is nonetheless rooted in accurate reporting and experience.

And of course the last thing is that on some level, you have to love people. All different kinds. That seems to me a prerequisite for capturing dialogue well. Stand around and listen. A favorite story to finish: once Richard Price came to Baltimore to research part of *Freedomland*. We had a murder case similar to the one he was writing and he wanted a tour, so that he could acquire more of the tone of the thing, I guess. So down he comes and we go around and research his case, meet the witnesses and the detectives and whatever. And because he's Richard fucking Price and I've loved his ass ever since *The Wanderers*, I just gotta show my shit a little. I was researching and writing *The Corner*, the book, at the time. So we drive over to West Baltimore and I start to show him the 'hood where Ed and I are gathering our stuff. And at some point I run into Gary McCullough, one of my main characters. And Gary, who had just copped and was high as a kite, is talking with us and he laughs at something I say, and says, "Oh, man, you is an apple-scrapple." Apple-scrapple being a particular Baltimore phrase in the African-American idiom meaning, well, a special dessert or special treat. Gary says it and I see this look cross Price's face and I think, for just a second, Oh, shit. Now he's got apple-scrapple. I hope he doesn't publish before I do or he'll beat me to it. Sure enough, when Gary departs, Richard immediately turns to me and says, "Apple-scrapple. That's a keeper."

Fucking writers.

Nick Hornby

SEASON FIVE

SEASON FIVE OVERVIEW

WHO WANTS YESTERDAY'S PAPERS?

"In the back of my mind is a man looking upon the world as a newspaperman, even though I don't have a newspaper ..."
DAVID SIMON

For one year, Simon did have a newspaper, an alternate universe edition of the *Baltimore Sun* delivered to home subscribers via cable television. He did not write for this paper, he invented it.

At this paper, an ambitious reporter made things up to get ahead of his colleagues (and did so); top-level editors, chasing Pulitzer Prizes, chose not to investigate the fabrications in a way that an average reporter might; staff buyouts (to increase shareholder profits) and doing more with less impeded basic news-gathering; the one editor who cared enough to stand up for the news was dumped on the potter's field known as the copy desk . . .

And a fictional Bill Zorzi – channeling the real-life reporter of the same name, temperament and matinée-idol good looks – tells an editor who has already asked for the moon and the stars: "Why don't you just shove the broom up my ass and I'll sweep the floor while I'm at it?"

The make-believe Zorzi had been asked to cover two courthouses in the wake of the most recent buyout at the paper. The city court reporter headed for greener pastures and was not replaced.

This was the writing on the newsroom wall that would keep knowledge and foresight out of the paper: reporters who once embodied a single beat so thoroughly they were never at the mercy of "public information officers" were now too busy to meet sources for lunch, the paper too depleted to pay for that lunch.

"The trend we depicted is, I think, unmistakable," said Simon. "Profit-taking through cutbacks, an inability to confront and compete, [use of] the Internet, stunted coverage, small-time editorial ambitions, and a useless, self-absorbed prize culture.

"That," said Simon, "is what remains of the good grey lady of journalism."

•

When I left the *Baltimore Sun* in 2001, I'd had a desk in the newsroom for more than half my life; from the day I joined the sports department in 1978 to compile horse-race results (after a year in circulation) to the cold night in January when I walked out the back door onto Guilford Avenue for the last time.

Before I took a buyout (knowing my time was up, I'd best take my leave while there was still money was on the table), I'd been busted from general assignment reporting back to night rewriting, where 20 years earlier I'd learned the craft from the real Jay Spry for whom Donald Neal's *The Wire* character is named.

[For pure physical resemblance, Professor Irwin Corey – now in his 90s – would have been my choice to play Spry, never seen leaving the newsroom without an armload of unread papers.]

In the unraveling of my career as a newspaperman, there was no small measure of personality conflict, but the ultimate, unstated charge was that I cared more about personal ambition (a reduction of caring only for the stories I wanted to tell) than work deemed "good for the paper."

I found this a curious distinction, believing that what was good for readers – Baltimore natives, their offspring, and their neighbors, whom I knew better than my carpet-bagging bosses – was indisputably best for the paper. In the end, my preferred narratives were those with no newspeg and sometimes without reason, stories that have proved durable in a way that the scandal du jour does not.

I not only maintain that the mystical amidst the ordinary endures longer in the reader's imagination than mere news – illustrated in the story of Bubbles's rare triumph over heroin – but the daily record should be broad enough to leaven the hopelessness attendant to atrocities that no longer astonish.

The last editor to share a trench with me was the late and beloved Norm Wilson, a native New Yorker and the first African-American to cover City Hall for the Baltimore *Evening Sun*, the paper of Mencken, put to bed for the last time in September 1995.

[If he had it to do over again, Simon would have saved the homage of Norman's name for Season Five's city editor instead of using it for Mayor Tommy Carcetti's chief-of-staff.]

I worked rewrite and Norm ran the desk after the big shots had gone home. One night, most likely after an extended dinner hour wandering the city in search of something to please my constituency, Norman approached with intel about a boss indistinguishable from *The Wire*'s Tom Klebanow. Leaning down, Norm whispered a warning worthy of Blind Butchie: "They watching you."

And soon they would watch me walk from the rewrite desk to Guilford Avenue and out of daily journalism.

Guilford Avenue, where the boys from the composing room drank deep into the night after the final edition went to bed; parallel to the highway that connects Baltimore to Pennsylvania, below which a village of Bubbleses and Dukies have lived under tarps and cardboard since the Reagan Administration.

Guilford Avenue, where we first meet city editor Gus Haynes at the beginning of Season Five of *The Wire*, smoking with colleagues on the loading dock.

"Gus Haynes, the patron saint of journalism," said Clark Johnson, who played the role and directed the first and final episodes in *The Wire*'s five-season run. "That perfect editor." A good man fed into the cold maw of an institution – this time corporate journalism – too big to care about those who keep it going any more than those it was created to serve.

Just as Frank Sobotka and Bunny Colvin got theirs before him.

By turns, the five seasons of *The Wire* took near-documentary passes at the war on drugs; the death of labor in a post-industrial America; reform taken to the extreme of legalizing drugs; the failure of the urban school system; and, wrapping all of it up like haddock between the headlines, the media's failure to adequately report, much less explain and correct, all of the above.

"*The Wire* is about capital and labor and when capitalism triumphs, labor is diminished," said Simon. "Season Five is the same as what happens to labor and middle-management in every other [depicted] institution."

Before taking the role of city editor Gus Haynes, Clark Johnson's previous experience with newspaper work was delivering the *Toronto Star* (the paper for which the young Ernest Hemingway filed dispatches from Paris in the early 1920s) and writing a column for Ottawa's *Glebe Report*. "I did an exposé on old folks' homes," he said. Who hasn't?

As Haynes, Johnson relied on Simon and Zorzi for the finer points of a role "so well-written I didn't need to go too deep in my own research.

"That last season," he said, "showed what news-gathering really means, [and] how instincts play an important part in that." In many ways, said Johnson, *The Wire* served the social function that newspapers once did.

"If it was just a Robin Hood [adventure] show in a time far away," the end of the run wouldn't be much different from any other reasonably popular show going off the air.

"But Baltimore is still ticking away and we stopped talking about it," he said. "Shit is still going on but the 24-hour news cycle comes and goes and we move on.

"Are the problems solved? No. We have to talk about it."

But where?

In June of 1986, the *Baltimore Sun* was sold by the heirs of its founders to the Times Mirror Corporation for $600 million. The paper reportedly carried a $250 million price tag during 2008 negotiations between local investors and the Tribune Company of Chicago, which bought the Times Mirror media corporation in 2000 and declared bankruptcy in December of 2008.

By the following summer, a reasonable asking price for the *Baltimore Sun*, give or take, was said to be $23 million, including the entire city block on which it sits.

Variety called it the most on-target depiction of a newsroom in the history of film and television, a physical and atmospheric recreation leading former reporters with cameos to wonder if they'd taken a ride in Mr. Peabody's "wayback machine."

Beyond the usual variety of plots and intersecting arcs that make up the final season of *The Wire* – crowned with a villainous turn by Jimmy McNulty, who perpetuates a serial-killer hoax – the big drama was the slow, ugly death of the American newspaper.

"Season Five begins with a moment of first-rate journalism," said Simon, referencing the discovery by city editor Gus Haynes of a quid-pro-quo real estate scam between the city and Ricardo "Fat-Face Rick" Hendrix, a drug trafficker and strip club owner.

"And it ends on an act of first-rate journalism – the narrative account of a story that viewers know to be more than true, the salvation of Bubbles and his human worth, accurately depicted."

These tent-poles – pick-and-shovel investigative work on one end and the finely drawn portrait of a modern-day Lazarus on the other – provided a glimpse into the Big Top of big-city journalism as practiced for more than 170 years in Baltimore – which is barely practiced any longer.

"This was not the work of people angry at the *Sun* or trying to get even with this institution or that editor," said Simon, who took considerable heat for Season Five within the newspaper industry, particularly from those who saw it as a score-settling attack on top management in place when he left the *Sun* for a career in television.

"It was written by ex-journalists who love the craft and who fear for its future," he said. "When I left the *Sun* on the third buyout, I knew it was never going to be the paper I wanted it to be.

"When we wrote Season Five [in 2006-2007], after more buyouts, we knew the *Sun* was not going to be a paper anyone wanted it to be. That was the message of Season Five."

Set in the recent past, and bowing out in March of 2008, the final season of *The Wire* was set in the very recent past and pointed to a future that arrived sooner than expected.

In April of 2009, some 60 editorial employees, many of them longtime editors and veterans of positions from Jerusalem correspondent to chief of the copy desk – a full quarter of an already decimated staff – were laid off in a single day.

"As much as I expected [and foreshadowed] new layoffs at the *Sun*, my former home of 40 years, the extent of the slaughter was unimaginable," wrote David Michael Ettlin, a retired deskman who played himself in Season Five and keeps tabs on his old employer in a blog called The Real Muck (ettlin.blogspot.com).

The news was received throughout the state of Maryland as a bloodbath, and, like much of the violence in the real Baltimore channeled by *The Wire*, it trumped anything portrayed on the show.

"We did not envision layoffs [but] round after round of buyouts and attrition by hiring freeze until the paper was hollowed out and the last margin of profits taken," said Simon. "There is always some awe that reality provides."

•

Just before Omar dispatches Stringer Bell to the great shareholders' meeting in the sky, the stick-up artist blows away Bell's bodyguard. In the scene is the real estate developer Andy Krawczyk, teaching Stringer the cold truths of a new game.

When Bell's bodyguard falls, Krawczyk drops in fear, whimpering on his knees, hands over his head. The look of contempt Omar gives Krawczyk before striding away to bag Stringer is extraordinary.

Said Michael Kenneth Williams of Krawczyk: "That's your last word before you die? At least get on your feet. Say a prayer."

Without a prayer, newspapers are on their knees.

When death comes for Omar, the story of one of the most feared killers in the history of Baltimore doesn't make the paper because no reporter is familiar enough with life in the ghetto to know that the sun has set on a legend.

In the *Huffington Post*, David Simon wrote: "Any good journalist will – if he or she loves the business . . . wince at the stories systematically missed, the undiscovered and unreported tales of the city . . ."

But before you can wince, you have to be aware of what has slipped by: Carcetti, elected as a reformer, manipulates crime stats just as the mayor before him; the schools are teaching answers to a test that kids must pass for the system to look good; the execution of Prop Joe – the guy who floods the city with dope right off the boat – is taken at face value as the homicide of a used appliance store owner.

And the murder of Omar Little is missed because the paper doesn't have a source even once removed from the street – a cop, preacher, community activist, or the old busybody who knows everything – to tell them just who it is who has died.

"Someday," says Gus Haynes in those opening moments on Guilford Avenue, "I want to find out what it feels like to work for a real newspaper."

As you read this, Haynes' desire is all but moot and sure to be alien to a generation now being born, one that will only wonder what it must have been like to work for that thing called a newspaper.

"Something vibrant and essential to American life is passing," said Simon. "And unless a new economic model is created to accomplish what a healthy newspaper once did, we are all bereft."

The newsroom in-joke on Calvert Street these days?

That the obituary column will soon be renamed the "Subscriber Countdown" page.

COP REPORTERS AND THE WIRE

All George Morse ever wanted to do was to write for his hometown newspaper.

Morse, a 25-year-old J-school grad born and raised in East Providence, Rhode Island, is one of a dying breed: a young man fascinated by print journalism at a time when his classmates were seeking entry-level PR gigs.

Most of the cops in East Providence have grown to like the cub reporter, who knew about *The Wire* long before he filed his first police blotter.

"Before I was a newspaper reporter dealing with cops on a daily basis, I worked as an assistant manager for Blockbuster Video," said Morse. "Somewhere around 2005 I started seeing a spike in the number of kids coming in looking for this show called *The Wire*."

Despite being the kind of guy who scours the Internet for the ending to every new movie before he sees it, Morse knew nothing about the Baltimore cop show.

"I didn't give the people looking for this show much credit. Admittedly, it was my own prejudice, but a lot of the people asking for the show came in with baggy jeans speaking slang I don't understand."

He changed his mind when he began covering cops. He went from student to intern to full-time reporter in his senior year at the University of Rhode Island. As a local boy he already knew some of the officers.

Most cops will tell you that the popularity of *CSI: Crime Scene Investigation* has made their jobs harder. Juries don't want to hear witness testimonies anymore. They don't even need a murder weapon. They want fibers and DNA.

At the other end of the dial is *The Wire*.

"One day I asked one of the vice unit investigators about *The Wire*," Morse said. "I wanted to know if he was a fan . . . how the show chalked up with reality. He told me not only was he a fan of the show, but it's so accurate it has made his job tougher."

Said Sergeant Diego Mello: "They're teaching everyone our tricks."

Like "traps" – hidden compartments – the number of which have increased in East Providence, according to police, since *The Wire* gained in popularity.

Morse began watching not long after becoming a newspaper reporter.

"My editor recommended it to me, another reporter did the same," he said. "I fell in love with the show instantly and felt a twinge of guilt for the judgment I had cast on all those [video] customers I had written off as uneducated and immature."

Then he started to get to know some real cops. East Providence may not be Baltimore, but there are drugs and where there are drugs, there is violence.

The city's police department has a reputation for vigilance among traffickers. Mules are said to drive 20 miles out of their way to bypass the city on their way to markets in Fall River or Providence.

There are about 100 cops to police East Providence, a city of some 50,000 people, more than ten times smaller than Baltimore. But there are similarities.

Cops in East Providence are known to like a "taste" from time to time, as Bunk might say. And although there is no graveyard for beer cans on the department roof, Morse has, "on more than a few occasions . . . seen officers who have no business operating a vehicle stumble out of a bar and get behind the wheel."

Shades of Jimmy McNulty.

Plenty of pot rolls through East Providence, but what really stretches the cops thin is chasing shipments of cocaine and heroin that have given the city's section of Interstate-195 the nickname "Heroin Highway."

"Of all the cops I talk to, few interest me as much as the vice unit," said Morse. "Their office is filled with posters of drug paraphernalia and strange-looking bongs. There's also a dry erase board full of quotes from suspected drug dealers and users who were caught by the vice unit."

Quotes like this: "I get more of a high driving through East Providence than I do from heroin. Two-and-a-half-miles of pure adrenaline."

•

Kimberly M. Vetter, 34, has been a newspaper reporter for the past decade, covering a variety of beats. She worked as an editor and reporter at newspapers in Texas before the Baton Rouge *Advocate* hired her in 2006 to cover the police beat in Louisiana's capital.

Vetter says that much of what she saw on *The Wire* reflects her own experience covering cops in Baton Rouge, which, like virtually every American city and many of its towns, has its own corners and boys who work them.

The cops she covers have also said that the HBO drama is the only cop show they've seen that is "remotely accurate."

"It's surprising how little information [citizens] can get from police departments," said Vetter, often called by distressed residents of crime-plagued neighborhoods.

"I think there is a wide distrust for law enforcement out in the communities, especially in poor areas of town where a lot of the crime happens.

"They say that [the police] don't investigate crimes thoroughly. They just want to make arrests. A lot of murders [of young black men go] unsolved. People truly believe [the police] don't care."

Vetter heard about *The Wire* from a friend at work, a business reporter. She rented the DVDs and watched – from D'Angelo holding court on the orange couch to Dukie succumbing to dope – with her boyfriend.

"I literally flew through the five seasons," she said. "I spent a lot of late nights watching it," and was impressed by how closely what she saw on the screen mirrored her view as a crime reporter.

"You would go out for a murder or to cover a crime and the older people living in the neighborhood would say, 'If they could just get these boys off the corner.'

"They would describe them exactly like they were portrayed on the show . . . all young, they should be in school."

Vetter said Baton Rouge has a historically high murder rate, with violent crime rising since Hurricane Katrina drove tens of thousands of people west from New Orleans.

"It's always been high but since the hurricane, shootings happen daily," she said. "Last year, there were 82 or 83 murders in East Baton Rouge Parish." By early April of 2009, there were more than 20.

One notorious neighborhood a few miles south of Louisiana State University – the Gardere Lane area, with dozens of multi-unit apartments, some vacant and boarded up – has long been infested with drugs.

As a reporter accompanying sheriff's deputies, Vetter has gone into vacant houses, the plywood pulled away, to find squatters with crack pipes. Perhaps not as eloquent as Bubbles, but certainly as befuddled as his sidekick Johnny.

Asked if there were any Stringer Bells or Avon Barksdales behind the trade, Vetter said: "You do hear about some of the bigger fish . . . but the local cops aren't catching them."

It also rang true for her that the mayor's office, and not the chief of police, runs the police department. For political reasons, statistics are used to prove whatever best serves the administration at the moment.

Separating what is really going on from what the police say is going on is no small task. Among all fraternities, cops are among the most close-knit, complete with a "no snitching" code every bit as strong as the one on the street.

"There's not much you can do about it unless somebody on the inside is willing to stick their neck out and tell you what's going on."

Vetter said that the cops who have talked to her about the show were most impressed by the way it layered every side of an issue, how *The Wire* is not – like an old cop car – merely black and white.

"Crime isn't just because an individual is bad," she contended.

And, in the way that Bunny Colvin said that an aggravated assault can be redefined as a lesser crime but it's hard to hide a body, Vetter explained: "The main thing I focus on are murders. They can't mess with those."

Watching *The Wire*, she said, confirmed a certain loss of innocence: "You realize that everything you thought was true is being hidden from you."

•

Patrick O'Connell covers the police beat for the St. Louis *Post-Dispatch*. At 32 he, like Morse, has been a reporter since leaving college.

"The thing that is most interesting to me . . . is getting to go to places most people never see. I talk to a lot of friends and they've never been to areas I go into."

O'Connell isn't talking about fancy back rooms where deals are made or soirees at the country club, but "really crappy areas of St. Louis and in the county. Covering crimes takes you to these places."

Places photographed in all their fucked-up grandeur by cinem- atographers like Uta Briesewitz and Russell Fine on *The Wire*, a show O'Connell began watching, as so many did, after his friends told him that he *must*.

"Once you get in you're completely hooked by it. I liked it because it was real – more than any show I watched," the neighborhoods reminding him of the ones on his beat, ". . . kind of hauntingly beautiful in a way, burned out and boarded up."

O'Connell's appreciation of the show, however, didn't silence the reporter's instinct to call bullshit when he sees it, specifically in Season Five, his least favorite.

Unlike the spot-on portrayal of cops and drug dealers and their

respective bureaucracies, the final season – centered on a very real but fictional *Baltimore Sun* – didn't reflect journalism as O'Connell sees it practiced in the Gateway to the West.

"Everybody I know is hyper-protective about who they are talking to, checking sources, never changing quotes," he said.

Everybody he knows with a newspaper job steadily became a very select group as the 2009 recession accelerated the demise of an already beleaguered industry. That part of Season Five, admitted O'Connell, was right on the buy-out money.

"The lay-off stuff was almost painfully real," he said, having seen the ranks of the *Post-Dispatch* thinned in the autumn of 2008.

"The idea that we need to soldier on is very realistic."

Victor Paul Alvarez and Greg Garland

SEASON FIVE EPISODE GUIDE

"I thought, 'You gotta love Hollywood.' For 12 hours of work I got paid $60. When I went in later for 12 seconds, they gave me $500."
G. JEFFERSON PRICE III, FORMER MIDDLE EAST CORRESPONDENT FOR THE BALTIMORE SUN.

Jeff Price was just one of dozens of non-professionals given roles on *The Wire*, beginning with a few cameos early in the show's run and peaking in Season Five when David Simon cast many of his former colleagues at the *Baltimore Sun* as reporters.

Film editor Kate Sanford said it was always a challenge to "work around" performances that could be somewhat wooden, but the tension between authenticity and scripted drama usually served the stories well.

Such was the case with Price.

"I was one of several old timers from the *Sun* invited to [bc] extras in the scene where the buyouts and the closing of foreign bureaus are announced," he said.

"The editor steps down and I am approached to join him in his office, where, presumably, I am to be told my jig is up. In the first try at the scene, I became confused about what I was supposed to be doing when the editor approached. I said, 'Who? Me?'

"The production team came in and said, 'Hey, that was great, could you do it that way again?' I tried to explain that I was just reacting because I wasn't sure what to do but they said it looked natural and appropriate to the moment, so there developed what became known in Price family lore as Dad's 'Who Me?' scene.

"A woman who was another professional extra standing behind me hissed that I had wheedled myself into a 'speaking role'.

"This scene was shot over and over, so many times that we did not finish until about one a.m., having started at about one p.m. the previous day.

"I went home satisfied with having had my first experience watching a movie being made. The day's pay was $60 – which worked out to be less than minimum hourly wage, but the experience was interesting enough to make up for it.

"Afterward, I went off on an assignment in Central America and when I got back I got a call from the *Wire* people asking if I would mind coming in to do a voice over for my moment of glory.

"I said, 'Look, I spent 12 hours on that set for 60 bucks and it was interesting enough, but I don't want to do it again. I don't have the time.'

"They said, 'This'll only take a few minutes and we'll pay you $500!' I went over to their studio near Television Hill and true to their word it took exactly 12 seconds."

episode fifty-one

"MORE WITH LESS"

"The bigger the lie, the more they believe."
– BUNK

Directed by Joe Chappelle
Story by David Simon & Ed Burns; teleplay by David Simon

When someone lies on a polygraph test, the needle soars like a Geiger counter finding uranium in the desert and is said to "blow the box."

When a kid too dumb to know better submits to Bunk Moreland's photocopy lie machine, a piece of paper emerges emblazoned with the word: FALSE.

The machine, says Sergeant Landsman, is never wrong.

Police surveillance of Marlo's al fresco lair – including McNulty and Officer Dozerman – continues as Stanfield and Snoop tell a dealer that the new split on the package is 60/40 with the dealer on the short end.

Marlo and his people all know they are being watched.

At Western District roll call, Sergeant Ellis Carver can barely maintain order as the room of officers bitches and moans about lack of overtime – not to mention what's already due them – and shitty equipment.

Mayor Carcetti hears from Commissioner Burrell and his deputy Bill Rawls that with the current budget cuts, there's no way they'll be able to deliver a drop in crime. Carcetti is stymied; all the money is going to the schools.

Rawls says they could save some money by suspending the investigation into the bodies in the vacant houses, but Carcetti doesn't want the inevitable bad publicity that would surely follow. In private, Norman Wilson is pressed by the mayor to speak his mind: You should've swallowed your pride and taken the governor's money when it was on the table.

On the corner, Duquan "Dukie" Weems – having dropped out of school after being promoted to the ninth grade – is running Michael Lee's new corner, but none of the other boys respect him, particularly a kid named Spider.

Once Dukie is bounced – smarting from being demoted from a corner boy to a nanny for Bug – Spider falls in line.

The city budget crunch hits Lieutenant Cedric Daniels at work and at home: the investigation into the bodies in the vacant houses is on ice and he can no longer use a department vehicle in his off-hours.

On the loading dock behind the *Baltimore Sun* newspaper, city editor Gus Haynes discusses lay-off rumors with reporters Roger Twigg (named after a real-life *Sun* police reporter), and general assignment reporter Bill Zorzi (played by a former *Sun* reporter of the same name).

Back inside, Gus is dismayed to see Michael Olesker and Laura Lippman (two longtime journalists at the real *Sun* playing themselves) looking out a window at smoke rising across town, seasoned newshounds watching a fire like a couple of tourists.

"The *Sun* TV critic [David Zurawik, a fan of the show until Season Five] went out of his way to say how horrible we were playing ourselves," said Lippman, who left the paper to become one of the country's major mystery novelists.

"There have been dozens of 'stunt' cameos on *The Wire* over the years – the former governor, the former mayor, the former police commissioner – and I don't think we were any worse than the worst.

"But when the show went into the newsroom, it clearly struck a nerve, not just at the *Sun*, but at newspapers throughout the US. I guess some people got their feelings hurt, which is amusing to me.

"It turns out that a lot of reporters are much bigger babies than the public figures they cover," said Lippman.

Carcetti meets with City Council President Nerese Campbell and the US Attorney, hoping for federal resources to pursue the bodies in the vacant houses. In exchange, the prosecutor wants the city to turn the investigation into political corruption by state senator Clay Davis over to federal authorities.

Passing the buck, Carcetti insists it's the call of Maryland State's Attorney Rupert Bond (played by Dion Graham), who wants to handle it himself.

Greggs and Dozerman watch Marlo go into a Holiday Inn with a woman and assume it's a booty call. Inside, however, Marlo sends the woman to their room while he attends a meeting of the New Day Co-op drug cartel, of which Proposition Joe Stewart is the nominal head, already in progress.

Joe's pitch is for an Eastside dealer, put out of business when Johns Hopkins Hospital knocked down blocks of slum houses for expansion, to pick up territory along Route 40 and a black neighborhood near the old steel mill called Turners Station.

If Marlo has 99 problems, however, a Co-op ain't one of them and he ruffles feathers with an impolitic proposal, leading Slim Charles to tell Joe not to "sleep on Marlo."

Bubbles, hanging on to a fragile sobriety, is living in his sister's basement. Each day when she goes to work, however, he has to leave until she returns.

State's Attorney Bond, hot to nail Clay Davis, agrees to go to the mayor with Daniels when he learns that shutting down the case into the bodies in the vacant houses also impacts the Davis investigation.

As Pearlman, Daniels and Bond talk at the courthouse, Chris Partlow – played by native Marylander Gbenga Akinnagbe, a college wrestler at Bucknell – asks how to get to the clerk of the criminal court.

In the clerk's office, McNulty sees that Partlow has checked out the file on Sergei Malatov, the Russian member of The Greek's organization locked up during the dockworker case.

Bond and Daniels catch Carcetti leaving the building and the mayor gives them two minutes to plead their case. They say the same unit investigating the bodies in the vacants is the one collecting info on Clay Davis.

Two men to chase Davis, says the mayor, everything else stays down. As Carcetti leaves, Daniels says: "So one thieving politician trumps 22 dead bodies. Good to know."

At the newspaper's afternoon "budget meeting" – where it is decided which stories will get better play than others, which ones need more work, which ones won't run at all – mid-level editors are admonished by managing editor Tom Kelbanow for missing stories even though the staff has been reduced. Executive editor James C. Whiting III then kills a story about the University of Maryland failing to meet diversity goals and is suspected of doing so because of his personal ties to the school's dean of journalism.

All of which gives heartburn to Haynes, who sees an item buried in the City Council agenda about a vote to change zoning on a couple of parcels

in what amounts to a land swap between a known crime figure – Ricardo "Fat Face Rick" Hendrix, a strip club owner present at the New Day Co-op meeting at the Holiday Inn – and the city.

Haynes orders up reporting on all angles and eager beaver Scott Templeton can't hide his resentment when asked to play back-up to Alma Gutierrez, who takes the lead on the story.

Haynes fills in Klebanow on the fishy City Council land deal in which Fat Face Rick sells a building to the city for $1.2 million, and for a mere $200,000 they sell him a more choice address a few blocks away.

Greasing the deal is at least $40,000 in campaign contributions from Rick to City Council president Nerese Campbell, whom Haynes will trick into intimating that the contributions were considerably more. The story goes A1, cause for celebration by everyone but Templeton, who pouts that he didn't have a bigger role in it.

Daniels tells Freamon that the plug has been pulled on the investigation into Marlo Stanfield and the 22 bodies in vacant houses. Greggs and McNulty – who is back to his drunken alley cat ways in regard to the long-suffering Beadie Russell – are going back to homicide. Lester and Sydnor stay behind to chase Clay Davis.

Back in homicide, McNulty finds a greenhorn at his old desk and glares until the young man moves to another. As Jimmy falls into the chair, despondent, Landsman announces the return of "the prodigal son."

episode
fifty-two

"UNCONFIRMED REPORTS"
"This ain't Aruba, bitch." — BUNK

Directed by Ernest Dickerson

Story by David Simon & William F. Zorzi; teleplay by William F. Zorzi

Walon – played by the American singer Steve Earle ["When I walk down the street in Baltimore, it's 'Hey Walon!'"] leads a Narcotics Anonymous meeting in a church basement. When Walon urges Bubbles to speak, the newly sober junkie can't find anything worthwhile to say.

After the meeting, Walon tells Bubbles that if he doesn't come to terms with Sherrod's death, he may not stay clean for long.

Pulling the threads of Clay Davis's modus operandi, Sydnor and Freamon find that the senator is stealing from his own non-profit organizations. Lester says the bigger picture is cash that never appears anywhere: drug money for sure.

Back at Stanfield HQ, where the crew can feel that surveillance has backed off, Marlo gives orders: force Webster Franklin to buy his dope from them; kill June Bug for running his mouth, and find Omar.

When Partlow warns that Omar will come right back at them, Marlo – more interested in his prison meeting with Sergei – coolly brushes it off.

["A terrifying figure," said Malcolm "Minister Faust" Azania, a Canadian novelist who has interviewed Jamie Hector and many other *Wire* writers and actors. "From his scar to his widely-set eyes to his vocal and facial 'flat affect', Marlo is a shark on two legs – an indifferent predator, a super-consuming carnivore without the capacity to create anything but terror and pools of blood."]

Carcetti and his advisors settle upon a bump in reading scores for third-graders as a good prop for his gubernatorial run. He sure as hell can't run on his crime record. It is also noted that the real estate scandal which has snagged Nerese Campbell could trip him up as well.

Back on Calvert Street, the executive editor wants an education story that shows how the school system has betrayed the kids of Baltimore.

Reporter Scott Shane (played by *New York Times* reporter Scott Shane, a former Moscow bureau chief for the *Sun* and one of the most respected journalists in the paper's modern era) notes that the schools are just one of the many parties concerned – including parents – who have failed local children. Gus Haynes agrees.

Whiting presses on, brown-noser Templeton sides with him and gets the assignment. Scott is then tapped by managing editor Klebanow with writing the feature story on baseball's Opening Day at Oriole Park at Camden Yards the next day.

Haynes – the kind of scrupulous editor who wakes up in the middle of the night in a cold sweat thinking that he has transposed statistics in a story – tells Klebanow of the Templeton assignment: "You're the boss."

At his prison meeting to establish a new supply of product, Marlo – whose face rarely betrays any emotion – cracks a small smile when instead of Sergei sitting down to talk to him through the two-way glass, it's Avon Barksdale.

Avon says he can make the new connect happen – bypassing Prop Joe and the nettlesome Co-op – but it will cost a fee of $100,000 delivered to his sister. When Marlo agrees, he gets to talk to Sergei, whose connection is directly to Vondas and The Greek above him.

On the street, when Freamon tells McNulty that Stanfield's underlings are getting sloppy in their communications, the pair try to figure out what it would take – and where they might find the resources – to bring down the organization.

The partners take their problem to McNulty's old buddy from the FBI, Agent Terry Fitzhugh.

["McNulty and Fitzhugh became friends before 9/11 when the Feds still did a lot of drug cases in the city," said Doug Olear, who played the FBI agent. "After 9/11 it was all terrorism."]

Freamon and McNulty tell Fitz about the investigation into the vacant house case being shelved and tell him there's some good media play in cracking the case if he can help.

When Fitzhugh gets back to Jimmy, the news isn't good: forget about help from the Feds, the US Attorney is in a pissing match with Tommy Carcetti.

Returning to the newsroom from the ballgame, Templeton assures Gus he has "good stuff" and hypes a story about a 13-year-old kid crippled by a stray bullet who couldn't afford a ticket to the game.

As will become a pattern with Templeton stories, the kid is not identified and no photo was taken of him. For every question Haynes asks about the crippled kid, Templeton has a pat answer.

[Said Clark Johnson about the end of *The Wire*'s five-season run: "I would have loved to have gone one more season just to tell stories like the one about the kid in the wheelchair at the baseball game."]

As Haynes presses for verifiable facts about the paralyzed Oriole fan in order to run the story in good conscience, Whiting gives Templeton kudos for a job well done, effectively shutting down Haynes's reservations.

At a watering hole, Bunk, McNulty, and Lester drink and mourn their aborted investigation and a country in which the "misdemeanor homicides" of nearly two dozen young black men is less important than one missing white girl in Aruba – referencing the media frenzy over the 2005 disappearance of Alabama high school graduate Natalee Ann Holloway,

whose body has never been found.

As part of the June Bug execution team with Partlow and Snoop, Michael Lee is stationed at the back of the house and told to handle anyone who runs out. At his post, Michael hears gunfire and screams, taking aim with his 9mm when the rear door opens up. Escaping, however, is a young boy, not much older than Bug. Michael watches as the kid runs away.

Arriving at a possible homicide scene with a hatchet-in-the-head hangover – a pint in his pocket to take the edge off – McNulty finds the corpse of a homeless man most likely dispatched by drugs and alcohol.

And with his partner looking on, McNulty arrives at the most fateful crossroads of his life, playing God with the details in a way that nauseates Bunk. McNulty manipulates the evidence to make it look like the dead man has been strangled, inflicting wounds on the corpse's fingers to indicate a struggle.

As Bunk walks away in disgust, McNulty says: "There's a serial killer in Baltimore, Bunk. He preys on the weakest among us.

"He needs to be caught."

episode
fifty-three

"NOT FOR ATTRIBUTION"
"They're dead where it doesn't count."
– FLETCHER
Directed by Joy Kecken & Scott Kecken
Story by David Simon & Chris Collins; teleplay by Chris Collins

Fueled by Jameson's and genius, McNulty has spent all night in the homicide unit combing through unsolved cases to complement his invented murder of the homeless man: fuel for his campaign to get the funds necessary to keep the Stanfield investigation alive.

Arriving for work, Bunk says that Jimmy is going to land them both in jail and that Marlo isn't worth it. But McNulty is convinced he has found his ace and he's going to play it for all it's worth.

["The social and economic conditions of Baltimore worked well for the show – what *The Wire* said about Baltimore became 'true' for me," said Christopher Kubasik, a screenwriter in Los Angeles. "Budget issues bear down on all cities, but Baltimore's crisis – brought about by having no new economic growth to replace the dying economies – meant pressure could be brought to bear on all institutions and characters at the drop of a hat. And used as an excuse by the characters to justify their actions."]

McNulty is never able to justify his actions to Bunk, but he is able to persuade Moreland not to turn him in – as long as Bunk's name is kept out of the case file.

In his search for similar cases, Jimmy discovers a victim with a red ribbon tied around his wrist and an unsolved murder of a homeless man investigated by the late Detective Ray Cole.

[At Cole's barroom wake, the Pogues song "Body of an American" was played. A few years later, when the final episode of *The Wire* aired on March 9, 2008, David Simon passed up watching it – having seen it numerous times in post-production – to hear the Pogues live at the 9:30 Club in his native Washington, D.C.]

McNulty heads out to buy a spool of red ribbon, which he will soon attach to the wrists of homeless corpses at the morgue: let the games begin!

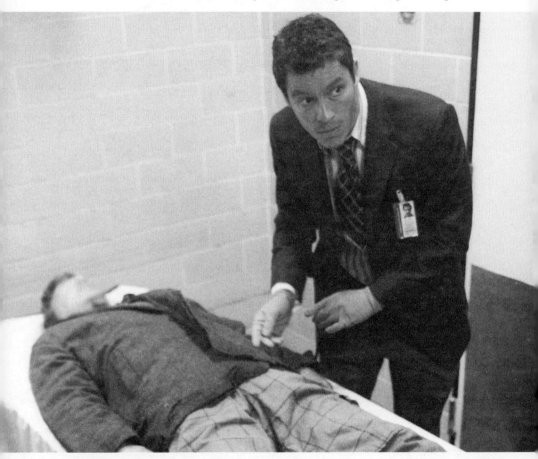

(It will take a few tries, but in time Jimmy's thinking-out-loud commentary about victims with red ribbons will jog the memory of Detective Frank Barlow, whose old, unsolved case involved a victim sporting a red ribbon.)

Noting a four percent increase in crime for two quarters running, the ever-prudent Stan Valcheck – now the police department's deputy commissioner for administration – tells Carcetti to fire Burrell and Rawls and make him commissioner until he retires, while grooming Cedric Daniels for the top cop job.

When Burrell comes in with statistics showing neither a drop nor spike in crime, Carcetti leans on him to provide authentic numbers. Burrell stands by his paperwork. When he leaves, Carcetti decides to leak info to the press that he is considering Daniels to replace Burrell.

Carcetti aide Norm Wilson meets Gus Haynes for drinks and tells him about Burrell being on thin ice with the mayor. The city editor assigns the story to Templeton, who, knowing nothing about Cedric Daniels, hands it off to old pro Roger Twigg, played by Bruce Fitzpatrick.

(The story will run on the front page, with another unattributed quote from Templeton, and drive a wedge between Burrell and Rawls.)

At the paper, which has amassed both fortune and renown since its founding in 1837, editors Whiting and Klebanow announce that corporate owners in Chicago have ordered the closing of bureaus in Beijing, Moscow, Jerusalem, Johannesburg, and London.

There will also be a new round of buy-outs to trim the staff, attrition that will claim Twigg, whose institutional memory – as evidenced by his knowledge of Daniels without having to consult clippings – is vast.

After his meeting with Sergei in prison – arranged on the good word of Avon Barksdale – Marlo and Snoop bring a briefcase of money to Little Johnny's Diner on South Clinton Street, the headquarters of The Greek's operation.

Handing the briefcase to the guy behind the counter, Marlo asks that it be passed along to Vondopoulos. The ability to simply hand over satchels of currency presents a problem of riches for Stanfield and he pays a visit to Prop Joe for advice on how to launder money.

With the help of an Eastside preacher, Joe explains that dirty comes clean through acts of goodwill: financing schools and hospitals in the Carribbean that never get built.

At home, Dukie can see that Michael is not himself, what with problems on the job involving split-second decisions about whether or not to shoot a little kid. Dukie suggests a day at the amusement park would do them all a world of good. Michael agrees and they have a jolly good time.

When Vondas tells Marlo he doesn't want money that is filthy from being out on the street – that if he is going to launder cash for him, the actual bills have to be cleaned up first – Marlo goes to Prop Joe with the problem.

Ever astute, Joe says he will freshen up the lucre gratis because they are part of the Co-op. Marlo then asks that the word be put on the street that he has a $50,000 reward for info leading to Omar.

Behind Joe's back, his nephew Cheese will tell Chris Partlow that Blind Butchie the barkeep may well know of Omar's whereabouts, pocketing the $50,000 reward.

When Landsman tells McNulty and Barlow he doesn't much care about a serial killer of vagrants, Jimmy drops a dime to Alma at the *Sun*.

[Asked why Jimmy the dog didn't try his charms on the young reporter when they meet at a diner, David Simon explained: "She had ethics. McNulty had no shot."]

The story will be buried on the inside of the metro section, warranting a little more interest than Landsman showed, but not much. The fat man does, however, give McNulty a few more days to work his "Ripper" hunch and then it's back to rotation, catching bodies as they surface.

In the Grand Jury room, Rhonda Pearlman presses Clay Davis's driver – "Day-Day" – about how he managed to simultaneously collect three salaries from three jobs, all the while driving the senator from meeting to meeting.

At Butchie's tavern, Snoop and Chris Partlow tie him up and torture him for info on Omar. When the blind man won't give anything up, they kill him and leave word for an employee of the saloon to make sure Omar gets word of what just went down.

Unbeknownst to one another, Omar and Marlo are both in the Carribbean: Omar in idyllic anonymity in Puerto Rico and Marlo on St. Martin, getting a look at his off-shore accounts.

Omar's respite, however, ends with the news that Butchie has been murdered.

When Clay Davis offers his help to Carcetti in exchange for the black ministers' support of replacing Burrell with Daniels, the mayor's chief of staff responds that the story about replacing the police commissioner has been out for a full day and no one has complained. Davis is sent away.

Watching as McNulty explains his serial killer scheme to Freamon, Bunk is relieved to hear Lester tell Jimmy that he "fucked up."

But Freamon takes the admonishment the other way, telling McNulty he didn't go far enough: it needs more juice, some sick fantasy angle.

And more dead people.

DIRECTING EPISODE NO. 53: "NOT FOR ATTRIBUTION"

A week before our first day of production, in the spring of 2007, a tech scout van was parked in front of the *Wire* offices on South Clinton Street along the Baltimore waterfront, waiting to take us on a tour for locations we would use in our episode.

The van held a skeleton crew of essential department heads who were prepping the upcoming shoot: Shelley Ziegler, first assistant director; Russell Lee Fine, director of photography; Vince Peranio, production designer; Charley Armstrong, location manager; and us, Scott and Joy Kecken, husband and wife directing team.

We were tasked with deciding not only which neighborhood we would have a small filmmaking army descend upon, but if that street or bar or apartment served the teleplay by Chris Collins.

Directing entailed many key creative decisions, but choosing a location was a top priority. This choice impacted every department.

Would the costumes clash against the color scheme in the house? Could all the camera equipment get up the stairs? It factored into our directing process – from where we would put the camera to whether we could shoot the scene on the Westside to make a 12-hour workday.

Over 30 locations had to be selected by us and then approved by the producers. For Omar's Caribbean island getaway, beaches in Ocean City, Maryland, and along the Florida coastline were in contention before deciding a separate unit would later pick up that scene in Puerto Rico. Scheduling was extremely important as we had a location-intensive shoot of 74 scenes.

Several sets that would be featured prominently throughout Season Five had already been built at the soundstage in Columbia, Maryland. We had been given blueprints of those interior sets, mainly for Police Headquarters, City Hall and the *Baltimore Sun*.

The challenge for this episode would be the penultimate scene where Executive Editor James Whiting delivers his monologue to a packed newsroom about the state of the newspaper industry. This set was so large it required over a hundred extras to fill it. We would get to that. Today was about scouting for *Sun* reporter Alma Guiterrez's apartment; the bar where City Editor Gus Haynes and Detective Lester Freamon would meet; and the *Baltimore Sun*'s Port Covington printing plant, in view of the docks so prominent in Season Two.

Usually the director rode shotgun next to the driver. Because there were two of us, we caused momentary discomfort in the pecking order.

In *Wire* parlance, a husband and wife directing team would be considered one of those things you don't see everyday. After five seasons on the air, it was the first time the show had hired a team. And it was the first time we had directed television.

Scott and I developed our directing chops together on two award-winning short films and a feature documentary that we had produced.

The first, *Louisville*, starred Andre Braugher from *Homicide: Life on the Street*, where I got my start right out of film school. The second was *Woman Hollering Creek*, with Larry Gilliard, Jr., who played D'Angelo Barksdale in *The Wire*. I had written for *The Wire* in the first three seasons.

My first *The Wire* script was "The Hunt," directed by Steve Shill, where the search was on for Greggs's shooter and D'Angelo had to drive Wee-Bey to Philly.

The second season as a staff writer was one of the most rewarding. Interviewing the longshoremen and researching the cargo terminals introduced me to a side of Baltimore that I had not seen before.

My episode "Hard Cases," directed by Elodie Keene, reflected the interconnectedness of two seemingly divergent worlds: one where Nick and Ziggy were pulled in deeper into the drug trade along the waterfront business, and one in which D'Angelo and his uncle Avon part ways while serving prison time together.

"Back Burners," directed by Tim Van Patten in Season Three, had Western District Major Howard "Bunny" Colvin come to terms with McNulty and his fellow detectives about the pros and cons of legalizing drugs in "Hamsterdam" while Avon returns to the streets to reclaim his crown from Marlo.

Three very talented, veteran directors delivered on my episodes. It was a dream come true for Scott and me to join them.

Picking a location is where we could put our stamp on the show, a collaborative process with the location team, the production designer, and the producers.

It allowed us to highlight our knowledge of the city (Scott is a Baltimore native), and visually add to the storytelling. At the *Sun* plant in Port

Covington, which would be operating as usual during filming, we were being given access to areas where safety was a consideration for cast and crew.

During the tech scout, we figured out exactly where Alma would cross the plant to capture the majesty of the huge printing presses and how raw newsprint would become a newspaper before rolling off the presses at ground level.

For Alma's apartment, the writers and producers had been very specific about the neighborhood where she should live – Charles Village, a somewhat upscale, hip area with grand rowhouses, a college vibe from Johns Hopkins University, and a local business strip that included Video Americain, Eddie's Market and Donna's Café.

An area like this was not seen very often on *The Wire*. Mostly white and solidly middle-class, it was a place where college kids could get high safely if they didn't get too out of hand.

Charley Armstrong had a number of apartments to show us, but we would select a less upscale one that would speak to the bank account of a young reporter just starting out. We walked from North Charles Street toward Hopkins and chose to shoot the exteriors on the business strip.

Eddie's Market would grant us permission to film inside the grocery store where McNulty would pick up red ribbon for his homeless "victims" that made up his fraudulent case about a serial killer.

The bar where Lester Freamon would meet Gus Haynes was a very specific place David Simon had in mind when Collins wrote the scene. The story behind the specific request came from the days when writer/producer Ed Burns was a cop. Simon and Burns would go to Maceo's Lounge and talk to residents while they were researching *The Corner*.

Maceo's Lounge was a corner institution on Monroe Street in West Baltimore and it was not far from the Retreat Street stables where Scott and I filmed our documentary about "a-rabbers," the vendors who sold fruit and vegetables from horse-drawn carts.

The bar was everything the writers had described it to be with as much character and heart as the drug-ravaged neighborhood in its midst.

It was predominately African-American, poor, the rowhouses not maintained especially well. We felt distinctly that we were some of the few outsiders to come in and check the pulse of this area. And we were definitely being watched.

Yet despite the fact that the producers had suggested Maceo's, it was not close to any other area we were filming. The bar owners, however, loved *The Wire* and gave permission to use their upstairs offices to shoot other scenes, our trip to the Westside justified.

Over the course of several days, we would continue this process of seeing all of the different sides of Baltimore and deciding, along with

the tech team and the producers, what would best fit the show and shooting schedule.

And then production began.

Our big day came on the soundstage for the set of the *Baltimore Sun* newsroom. We had several cameras on hand to pick up reaction shots of the people gathered to hear Executive Editor Whiting's speech. In the crowd were several real reporters from David Simon's reporting days who were making cameos.

We moved the camera in on these faces, which had seen the impact the buyouts and budget cuts had already made on their industry. Their presence told us that they supported what was being said about the fate of the newspapers.

Clark Johnson, as City Editor Gus Haynes, was featured in the scene. Through Haynes, we could bring some humor to the seriousness of the moment. He added much more, however.

Season Five was about coming full circle, and Clark's appearance in the final episodes represented closure. He had directed the first episode of *The Wire*, the Season One pilot, and his choices in 2002, from casting to camera lens selection, were still present.

Clark had also been an advocate for Scott and me and our personal film projects over the years. His appearance on the set captured the journey *The Wire* had been on since the beginning, how far we had all come, how it would soon come to an end. It was a bittersweet moment on so many different levels.

Along the way, the show had lost a great producer, Robert Colesberry, and homage was paid to him at the beginning of our episode.

We revisited a scene from the pilot where, in the role of Detective Ray Cole, Colesberry tilted back in his chair and told McNulty, "Type quieter, asshole."

We recreated the original shot with Donald Worden, a retired Baltimore City homicide detective, who had been a good friend and source to Simon during his reporting days.

In each episode of the final season, similar "do-overs" would speak to the idea that the players may change, but some things remain the same.

Back on the streets of Baltimore, at an appliance store on the Eastside, we rehearsed a scene where Prop Joe, Marlo, Snoop, and Cheese discuss the bounty on Omar and his people.

Felicia Pearson, who played Snoop, asked us about the term "Memaw" – for grandmother – spoken in the scene.

Since I had used it in one of my scripts, I spoke to her about the word and was struck by this moment: two African-American women, from totally different backgrounds, standing on the set of a major American television show, doing something no one could have expected for either of us.

I came from a family of social workers and schoolteachers and accountants. Since pursuing a career in writing had been discouraged, I couldn't imagine directing as a possibility. Though raised by people who loved her, Snoop had grown up in the thick of the 'hood and had been to prison.

Yet here we were, defying all socio-economic odds. Because of a TV program.

The shoot for Episode 53 went at a steady clip and we finished in ten days. Fittingly, we wrapped at the soundstage and were able to say our thank-yous and goodbyes to the entire crew. And then we stepped out into the night air where a waiting van took us home.

Joy Kecken and Scott Kecken

episode
fifty-four

"TRANSITIONS"
"Buyer's market out there."
— TEMPLETON
Directed by Dan Attias
Story by David Simon & Ed Burns; teleplay by Ed Burns

Director Dan Attias, who directed four *Wire* episodes beginning with Season Two, won a Directors Guild of America award for this one.

In it, Michael and his crew are relaxing on their corner as cops Colicchio and "Truck" Carrick watch from theirs. Kenard shows up, ostentatiously hiding a paper bag under a set of steps.

When the officers go to make the arrest, they find the bag filled with dog shit. Losing his temper with a motorist stuck in the ensuing traffic jam, Colicchio pummels the man – a school teacher en route to work – to the cheers of the corner boys. Sergeant Carver will later write up Colicchio for his behavior, accepting whatever enmity it brings.

Face-to-face, Colonel Daniels tells Commissioner Burrell that he has not been gunning for his job which, if offered to him, he will decline. Burrell simply stares at him without comment. While Alma works a rumor that Burrell may be fired that day, Templeton works on his portfolio in advance of an interview at the *Washington Post*.

(At the *Post*, young Scottie will be told that his prose blushes purple and he needs more experience before he can step up.)

McNulty, needing bodies for his scheme, hears that a lot of homeless men are dying in the Southern District and, via Freamon, tries to find out who works the midnight shift there.

At the Southern, Freamon finds his old patrol partner – Officer Oscar Requer, named for the real-life "Bunk" – and asks him to give a holler when the next homeless body with little or no decomposition turns up. Requer agrees.

(In his own legit cases, Bunk Moreland is still having trouble getting lab work back – a good year later – on the 22 bodies found in the vacant houses.)

As Vondas compliments the pristine currency that Marlo has brought back to him, he also makes it clear that he doesn't want to be part of sloppy street business. Marlo will not be deterred. Vondas says that a future relationship, if there is one, will be viewed as an "insurance policy" against possible disruptions to business.

In the detail office, Freamon points out the fruit on a vine Sydnor deemed barren. Sydnor is discouraged to find out that $80,000 from Clay Davis's personal bank account went to repay a loan to the senator's mother-in-law.

But Lester calls it a "head shot," and a lucky break, later explaining to prosecutor Rhonda Pearlman that the $80k repayment falsifies Davis's loan application by proving a gift was actually a loan.

Such fraud could be punished under federal law with 30 years in jail and a million-dollar fine. But State's Attorney Rupert Bond continues to balk at turning the case over to the Feds; he'd rather keep it in his own backyard – four counts against Davis of stealing from his own charities – with the possibility of ten years on each count.

When it's Davis's turn to testify in front of the grand jury, he arrives as a hail-fellow-well-met until Pearlman begins connecting the dots of his money trail. He then recoils and takes the Fifth Amendment against self-incrimination.

Reviewing the list of favors that Carcetti owes the city's black ministers as a ramp up to firing Burrell, the mayor and his team decide that Rawls will serve as acting commissioner and a half-year later, Daniels will take over. Fighting back, Burrell tries to give Nerese Campbell some dirt on Daniels that goes way back, but is told that he cooked his own goose by turning in false crime statistics.

She does, however, offer him an out: go quietly and we'll find you a well-paying job in D.C. And takes the old files on Daniels with her.

With his lover Dante, Omar returns from Puerto Rico – where he wore Jimmy Buffet shirts and gave away candy to little kids – to get to the bottom of Butchie's death. It's not long before he finds out that Marlo was behind it. The same game that ended in Stringer Bell's death is on again.

Marlo also returns from the islands, with a fat check from his off-shore account. After a meeting of the Co-op, he asks Prop Joe for some advice on what to do with it.

When Rawls visits Burrell on Erv's last day, the outgoing commissioner tells his successor that it's a can't-win job; the City Hall rewrites its agenda from one day to the next and that won't change, regardless of who is charged with running the department.

Under the lash of "doing more with less," the City Desk tries to figure out how best to report Burrell's departure at the same time Clay Davis is leaving the Grand Jury inquiry, the latter missed by the paper and watched on TV.

Wanting to cut corners on a case that isn't real – to more or less just write reports out of thin air – McNulty is forced by Freamon to work a village of homeless people beneath the Hanover Street Bridge on the southside of town.

Too much at stake here, Freamon says, we have to approach it as we would a real case.

Finding a good corpse for their scheme, the partners in crime begin prepping the dead man to look like a murder victim as Freamon tells McNulty that serial killers begin crudely before moving toward more sophisticated work.

McNulty uses a set of false teeth, prepared by Freamon, to leave bite marks on the corpse and the pair debate over which one of them is sicker than the other.

Omar jacks up Slim Charles and, with a gun to his head, wants to know where he can find Prop Joe. Swearing that Joe had nothing to do with Butchie's murder, Charles begs Omar to "finish it." Instead, Omar releases him.

Prop Joe continues to school Marlo, introducing him to the well-known defense attorney for drug dealers, Maurice Levy. In Levy's office, Marlo recognizes Herc and asks if he ever found his camera. Herc, not amused, tells Stanfield that it cost him his job.

When Marlo and Levy sit down to talk in private, Herc and Prop Joe gossip about Burrell. Joe says he went to Dunbar with Burrell and that he was "stone stupid."

Omar, in the company of a colleague named Donnie (the real life stickup artist and ex-con Donnie Andrews whose street career informed Omar's character), watches Marlo's lair. The plan is to begin picking off Stanfield employees, beginning with Monk.

At his rowhouse in the Johnston Square neighborhood – not far from Green Mount Cemetery where the founder of the *Baltimore Sun*, Arunah S. Abell (1806–1888), is buried – Prop Joe packs a bag while his nephew Cheese stands by. Joe has decided to leave town now that Omar is back.

Cheese leaves and Marlo enters. Joe has been betrayed by his nephew and The Greek, who has given Marlo the okay to do what he has to.

"I treated you like a son," said Joe.

"Wasn't meant to play the son," Marlo answers, urging Joe to relax and close his eyes, it won't hurt none at all.

PROPOSITION JOE: SHOW-TUNE ENTHUSIAST

"Comedy is harder than drama ... Lucille Ball, John Ritter, Bill Cosby, and Richard Pryor ... they're my heroes ..."
— ROBERT F. CHEW

Robert Chew is not a murderous drug lord, but, boy, oh boy, does he play an especially insidious one on TV.

"It was a major surprise when I got the part because that's not my lifestyle," said Chew, whose demeanor as Proposition Joe Stewart is subtle yet unambiguous: I won't have you killed if I don't have to ... but if I have to, I will.

Not exactly Chew's beloved *I Love Lucy*, no matter how mad Ricky Ricardo got.

"That's the type of acting I really love, when the acting was right in your face," said Chew, a 1978 graduate of Baltimore's Patterson High School. "I like shows where everything is bigger than life, where if someone cries, tears are shed."

One glimpse of Chew's character as the man behind virtually all dope sold on the Eastside of Baltimore – "buy for a dollar and sell for two" – and you know that regardless of what Robert F. thinks, Prop Joe don't play that.

Preferring peace over mayhem, Joe first shows his moon face at the annual Eastside-Westside playground basketball game between drug factions from opposite sides of Crabtown.

He immediately persuades Avon Barksdale to double their wager on the game, sends in a ringer at the buzzer and collects when the Eastsiders win.

When Nicky Sobotka meets Joe for the first time to plead his cousin Ziggy's case over a drug debt in Season Two, Joe calmly lets the white boy from the docks know that if he weren't in the company of some heavy hitters associated with The Greek, he would be a "cadaverous motherfucker."

Proposition Joe Stewart is loosely based on a West Baltimore dealer of the same moniker but with the surname Johnson. Chew's portrayal is low-key, deadly serious, and at the same time, turn-of-the-phrase poetic.

Counseling Stringer Bell to keep a low-profile, he says: "Wanna know what kills more police than bullets and liquor?

"Boredom. They just can't handle that shit. You keep it boring, String. You keep it dead fucking boring."

Chew said he never met the real Prop Joe – shot to death in 1984 in a Northwest Baltimore after-hours club on Reisterstown Road – "but I hear he was charming, intelligent, and handsome, a real stylish player who liked the finer things.

"I didn't research it any more than that."

•

The great-grandson of a man who found his way to the States from Korea, Chew grew up in the heart of East Baltimore near Johns Hopkins Hospital, around the corner of Broadway and Eager Street. The house where he spent much of his childhood was torn down in the hospital's never-ceasing expansion and the nearby projects that he also called home for a while are gone as well.

Chew's father has been in prison on a manslaughter conviction since Robert was a kid. His mother was a social worker.

High school gave Robert a chance to sing, dance, and act in student theater as well as playing JV football and working on the school paper. In addition to watching *Gilligan's Island* in reruns and listening to the Captain & Tennille – "I liked anything that was over-the-top," said Chew – it kept young Robert out of trouble.

"When I played the villain in a school production of *Egad, What a Cad!* the whole school knew who I was," he said. "After high school I started appearing at the Arena Players."

Founded in someone's living room in 1953 by black Baltimoreans who wanted to put on plays, Arena is believed to be the oldest, continuously running, African-American community theater group in the nation.

At the Players' 300-seat theater at 801 McCulloh Street in West Baltimore, Chew has appeared in shows like *Five Guys Named Moe* and the Martin Luther King Jr. tribute *Gospel at Colonius*.

He has also taught young people drama and music there, showing them "how to open up . . . how to read music and understand tone."

He had small parts on the NBC series *Homicide* and appeared as a shoe salesman in 2000 on the HBO miniseries, *The Corner*.

Chew again worked for HBO in 2004 when he played a janitor in *Something the Lord Made*, in which Alan Rickman and Mos Def star as heart surgeons working at Johns Hopkins Hospital.

In *The Wire*'s debut season, Chew appeared in two episodes. One of the few gangsters to appear in all five seasons, he met his end in Episode Four – "Transitions" – of the final year.

"Close your eyes, Joe," says Marlo as Chris Partlow comes up behind the big man, betrayed by his nephew Cheese and seated at the dining room table of his grandfather's home, "the first colored man to own his own house in Johnston Square."

"Relax," says Marlo, with quiet respect for the man he is about to dispatch. "Breathe easy."

Prop Joe's final proposition – that he would simply get out of Marlo's way and disappear – is rejected and proven true in the moment that Marlo nods and Partlow pulls the trigger.

"From Robert's first scene, we knew we had a subtle, smart actor, and the role of Prop Joe acquired more and more authority as the writers felt comfortable writing bigger scenes for the character," said David Simon.

"He is clever and comic, but never in a way that detracts from the plot or goes bigger than the moment. Along with Jay Landsman's dialogue, what comes out of Joe's mouth is probably the most fun that the writers can have with dialogue."

Chew didn't see much of *The Wire* when it originally aired.

"I don't have HBO, but even if I did, I'm [hesitant] to watch because I don't want to become too critical of my work.

"I get recognized in the supermarket now, but that's not what I want. I want the acclamation you feel taking a bow onstage after a job well done."

episode
fifty-five

"REACT QUOTES"
"Just 'cause they're in the street don't mean they lack for opinion." - HAYNES
Directed by Agnieszka Holland
Story by David Simon & David Mills; teleplay by David Mills

Meeting Marlo at his favorite bench in Patterson Park, Vondas tells him that he was fond of Joe and then moves onto business: dependability is the ballgame.

He hands Marlo a cell phone and tells Marlo to use it to for legitimate phone calls to establish a pattern of normalcy for cops who are surely listening.

For business, Vondas shows Marlo how the device has covert functions. Leaving the meeting with Partlow, Marlo invites his lieutenant to celebrate with him in Atlantic City, but Chris is too concerned with security, noting that Omar is surely coming.

McNulty calls Alma for the latest scoop on his serial killer. He teases with a sexual angle to the murders but hangs up before answering her follow-up questions.

As Dukie Weems walks Bug home from school, discussing upcoming state tests with the boy, they pass Michael's corner. Kenard hits Dukie in the back with a drink and when Weems fights back, he's beaten by Spider.

Rubert Bond announces Clay Davis's indictment on the courthouse steps. Complaining to Rhonda Pearlman that the *Sun* never got a heads-up on the news, Bill Zorzi is told that Pearlman's office did call the paper. The reporter she tried to reach, Zorzi tells her, left the paper months ago.

Michael takes Dukie to Dennis "Cutty" Wise's, saying he will settle the score with Spider. Dukie turns the offer down and is instructed by Cutty to put on a pair of gloves.

Watching Dukie get worked over by a younger boy, Cutty tells Weems that just learning to fight won't keep bullies away, it's about something else.

He then explains that the rules of the street only apply to the street, that the world beyond the corner doesn't work that way.

When Dukie asks how he might get to that better place, Cutty doesn't have an answer.

Defense attorney Levy goes over the postponed weapons charges against Snoop and Chris Partlow with Marlo present and tells them it's nothing to worry about. Stanfield then hands Levy a check from his offshore account of laundered drug money and tells him to get in touch when he figures out what to do with it.

Templeton joins Alma Gutierrez when she goes to meet McNulty in a bar and tells Jimmy they need more "juice" to get the story better play. McNulty gives up a few more details and soon the juiciest of all: the killer has begun biting his victims. Templeton takes the info back to the desk in time to make the second edition.

On his way to work the next morning, McNulty sees his story on the front page. In the newsroom, Haynes assigns Alma to the police investigation of the serial killer with a taste for biting while Scott begins interviewing the homeless.

Searching for relatively sane homeless people proves difficult for Templeton, who mostly encounters crazy people and drug addicts.

At the Viva House Catholic Worker House of Hospitality – a soup kitchen established the same year in Baltimore as the riots following the assassination of the Rev. Martin Luther King, Jr. – the reporter finds that most of the guests represent the ever-growing class of working poor.

Carcetti presses Daniels for his strategy in catching the serial killer, which of course will take more resources and thus money. Carcetti approves unlimited overtime for two detectives. Nothing more.

Herc visits the Western and gives his old partner Carver Marlo's phone number, which he lifted from Levy's Rolodex. Naturally, Herc wants his camera in return.

When Clay Davis goes batshit in Nerese Campbell's office over his indictment – threatening to bring down other political associates with him – the City Council president gets right to the point.

He can take his lumps like a man or never work in Baltimore again. When Campbell uses Burrell as an example of how to go gently into the night – with a payback on the back end – Davis agrees.

At the rim shop, while Marlo eats Chinese take-out with his mentor Vinson, Snoop and O-Dog, Monk walks in with a bulletproof vest clearly visible beneath his shirt. And then Partlow arrives to say that Omar spent the night outside of Monk's apartment and is sure to return.

Michael takes Dukie for shooting lessons in the woods with a 9mm semi-automatic handgun. His uncoordinated friend is so green, however, he doesn't even know how to rack a load into the chamber.

The lesson disintegrates and Michael advises Dukie against carrying a gun: you will continue to be tested and if a gun is your defense against insult, you best be prepared and capable of using it.

Near desperate, Dukie bemoans the fact that he can neither shoot nor fight. Michael tries to buck him up by saying he has other worthwhile skills.

Kima Greggs is assigned to McNulty for his make-believe serial killer investigation. McNulty is disappointed – he was expecting surveillance equipment – but Bunk is livid that a working detective is being pulled off of real cases to assist Jimmy's bullshit.

Carver gives Marlo's cell number to Freamon at the detail office. When Lester calls the number with a food order, Marlo answers – bingo! – and hangs up.

Clay Davis takes his case directly to the people via a talk show hosted by Larry Young, a cameo role by a former Maryland State Senator named Larry Young, also indicted on ethics charges.

On deadline for the next day's update on the serial killer, Alma has nothing new from the cops; Mike Fletcher has compiled a profile of the victims and Templeton brings in a hearts-and-flowers tale (once known in the real *Baltimore Sun* newsroom as "pathos and shits") about a family of four living under the Hanover Street Bridge – the same area where Freamon and McNulty went fishing for bodies to dress up as murder victims.

Again Haynes presses Templeton for source info and again Templeton lies his ass off.

Trying to find a way to translate their serial killer case into a wiretap to use against Marlo, Freamon and McNulty come to the logical conclusion that the killer has to begin making phone calls. Before they do so, however, they agree a fresh body would help prime the pump.

Bubbles asks Walon to come with him to a clinic where he is going to be tested for HIV. He's afraid to go alone and Walon agrees. After a nurse finally draws blood from Bubble's addict-ravaged veins, good news arrives: he's negative. Instead of being relieved, Bubs is incredulous.

Walon tells him: "Shame ain't worth as much as you think. Let it go."

And shame doesn't seem to reside anywhere visible in Scott Templeton. Hell-bent for a ride on McNulty's serial killer story, he goes to a payphone with his notebook, dials his cell phone and begins taking notes.

Desperate for a way to hold onto the sober and considerate Jimmy McNulty who came home every night – a limited edition version now nowhere in sight – Beadie Russell talks to the detective's ex-wife by phone. And then she stops by homicide to talk to Bunk.

Although very angry with Jimmy about the serial killer charade, he winds up telling her nothing more profound than that he can't advise her how to play it.

Templeton is playing the homeless murder big, having concocted a call from the killer to the *Sun* and running with it. McNulty's scheme now has a surrogate mother in a renegade reporter. Realizing this is what he needs for the wiretap, Jimmy goes to the paper to discuss the situation with the editors. By the time he leaves, even Gus Haynes is on board.

With the wiretap up, the scheme is for McNulty to document no calls from the serial killer while Lester monitors calls to and from Marlo Stanfield. When calls reach Marlo's phone, however, all that can be heard is a click and a hiss.

When Omar and Donnie make their raid on Monk's apartment, they are ambushed by Partlow, O-Dog, Michael and Snoop.

Donnie is killed and Omar – out of rounds – crashes through a glass door and onto a balcony, where he leaps to the ground from a height sure to be fatal.

episode
fifty-six

"THE DICKENSIAN ASPECT"

"If you have a problem with this, I understand completely." — FREAMON

Directed by Seith Mann

Story by David Simon & Ed Burns; teleplay by Ed Burns

Taking in the height from which Omar jumped, Marlo cannot believe that his nemesis not only lived, but escaped. Yet Omar is nowhere to be found, including local hospitals. When the coast is clear, Omar hobbles out of a maintenance room at Monk's building, using a broomstick as a crutch.

Mayor Carcetti cuts a ribbon for his "New Westport Project" along a languishing stretch of the South Baltimore waterfront, following the advice of Democratic big wheels to get his name on something tangible.

Shoulder-to-shoulder with the mayor is the developer Andrew Krawczyk, the businessman who thought he was about to meet his maker on the day Omar killed Stringer Bell. As Carcetti wraps up his speech, a gang of stevedores heckle Krawczyk for carving up what is left of the working port.

As McNulty lounges at his desk in homicide, telling Bunk about the crazy shit Templeton is making up, Moreland goes back to old files on the murdered bodies found in the vacant houses. Real cases, he pointedly tells McNulty, who shrugs off the criticism and offers whatever help he can provide via extra funding sure to be on its way to catch the serial killer.

The big bosses at the paper congratulate Templeton on his work and approve his idea to spend the night with the homeless. Media from around the country want to interview Templeton, who is told by Whiting that the "Dickensian aspect" of homelessness will be his beat for the rest of the year. Stardust is being sprinkled and Alma wishes she'd kept the homeless killer story for herself.

Freamon tells Sydnor about the wiretap scheme – how it's unauthorized and off the radar – saying that if he has problems with it, he understands, but now is the time to walk away. Sydnor wants in and Freamon tells him that all of Marlo's phone conversations are routine except for five calls with half-minute stretches of little or no sound.

When McNulty comes in, Lester tells him they are going to need some manpower to follow Partlow and Monk. Jimmy responds with the morning news: the city is going to throw money at the serial killer. What does one have to do with the other? asks Sydnor. It's a long story, says Freamon.

Bunk wonders what Randy Wagstaff – one of the four schoolboy chums from Season Four – might have to say a year after the kid's name turned up in a murder file. Landsman trumps him with a folder of sealed indictments and confidential grand jury testimony found in Prop Joe's house after Joe's murder. The courthouse, obviously, has a significant leak.

(Bunk soon finds out how useful Randy might be when he visits the kid in a group home. Wagstaff is well calloused by now and dismisses Bunk and every other cop in the world: none of them can be trusted.)

About to give a press conference on the serial killer at police headquarters, Carcetti worries the ugly news will cancel whatever positive attention he got earlier in the day when announcing the new waterfront development.

The resentment carries over to the podium, Carcetti scolding the press for ignoring the Westport ribbon-cutting and focusing on the negative. But then he makes a U-turn in an off-the-cuff speech, saying that the powerful must be judged for how they tend to the city's most vulnerable.

The performance gets good reviews, the issue of homelessness seen in the mayor's inner circle as a horse strong enough, in light of the current governor's cuts in medical and housing aid, to ride to the winner's circle at the state house.

Bunk and Kima Greggs show up at the lab working – with the speed of a glacier – the tests on the bodies found in the vacant houses. When Bunk leans on the supervisor, the man admits that a temporary employee, hired in the midst of cuts in personnel, fucked up. The lab is now unsure what evidence came from which crime scene.

Back with the old files, tediously running names from Kima's case work through the crime database, Bunk gets a hit on Michael Lee and his murdered stepfather, Devar Manigault.

Meeting with the Co-op for the first time since Prop Joe's death, Marlo pins the death on Omar. He proceeds to say that he is now in control of the supply connection at the port and the Co-op is null and void. Cheese is promoted and the cost of the package has just gone up.

Templeton blows his own horn on television as a fearless reporter of the streets, and McNulty tells Lester they are going to need yet another body to force the city to release cash for the investigation.

After the meeting where Marlo dissolved the Co-op, Omar jumps Fat Face Rick, takes the gangster's gun and tells him to let Marlo know that he is waiting, out in the open, ready for a showdown. After agreeing, Rick asks Omar if he killed Pop Joe. Omar laughs and Rick says, "Didn't think so."

Visiting Michael Lee's junkie mother, Bunk accuses the woman of killing Manigault. She is uncooperative and Bunk threatens to lock her up. She then says it was her son, Michael, who probably killed Manigault along with Snoop and Partlow.

In the detail office, Freamon and Sydnor conclude that Marlo is communicating to his crew through photos sent as text messages.

Drunk before a statue of General George Armistead – commander of Fort McHenry when the British bombed Baltimore during the war of 1812 – McNulty screams his justifications for inventing a serial killer.

His conversation with the statue is interrupted by a call from Requer in the Southern saying there is another fresh body. By the time McNulty can get to it, however, cops and reporters are already there.

On the Westside, Omar carjacks a Stanfield SUV as it makes a cash pick-up. He shoots one guy in the knee and torches the vehicle and the money, telling the one with buckshot in his leg to make sure Marlo knows not only that he destroyed the money but he's not "man enough" to meet him in the street.

["Omar didn't want to rob Marlo, didn't want no big shoot out," said Michael Kenneth Williams. "He wanted Marlo to come out in the street, put his guns down and have an old-fashioned fight."]

During his night with the homeless, Templeton finds a veteran of the war in Iraq who tells him he wound up homeless after he returned home from combat.

McNulty has his own encounter with the homeless when he brings a damaged man he finds on the street to the detail office, takes his picture with a cell phone and lays out a new plan for Lester, who has been stymied by the one-step-ahead technology Marlo is using.

The scheme: McNulty will drive his pet homeless man – whom he calls "Mr. Bobbles" for the guy's spastic gait – to an out-of-the-way shelter and send a cell phone photo of him to Templeton with a note from the killer that there will be no more bodies, only photos of victims not yet killed.

Probable cause, says Freamon, for legal authority to begin surreptitiously collecting cell phone photos. McNulty then drives Mr. Bobbles to Richmond, supplies him with ID from a dead homeless guy and drops him off at a shelter.

WORLDS WITHIN WORLDS

CAMEOS AND STUNT CASTING

"Simon and Ed Burns send 'em over to read
and I do the best I can with 'em ... "
— PAT MORAN

ROBERT F. COLESBERRY AS DETECTIVE RAY COLE

Played by *The Wire*'s late executive producer, Robert F. Colesberry, Detective
Cole was a low-key piece of work, better suited, perhaps, to teaching high-
school history.

"It was a brave move on Bob's part to get out there on the floor with
the actors," said Pat Moran, "and he had that handsome, beleaguered look
of a homicide cop."

Even when there was something for him to cheer about, things never
got too good for Ray Cole, evidenced in the day he is all smiles because he
"got laid last night."

"Oh, yeah?" says Bunk. "Does your asshole still hurt?"

Cole's skills as an investigator are best shown in Episode 22, when he tries to pin a gun on Bodie after the shoot-out that killed a nine-year-old boy. He shares the scene with another ringer, former Baltimore police commissioner and Maryland State Police superintendent Ed Norris, playing a homicide detective of the same name.

"The thing is . . . you're unbelievably stupid," Norris says to Bodie. "I don't say that to upset you, just to state a fact."

When Bodie doesn't flinch, Norris says to Cole, "He doesn't think so."

"Nobody ever thinks they're stupid," says Cole. "It's part of the stupidity."

Cole then tells Bodie they not only have the guns used in the shooting – true – but he himself crosses over to the Continent of Stupidity by bluffing that they have his prints on one of them.

"Which one?" says Bodie.

Like a guy trying to remember which shell hides the pea, Cole guesses wrong, and Bodie – who will survive the corner by *not* being stupid until his pride gets the best of him – simply says: "Lawyer."

In the words of Dominic West: "It seemed this incredible inside joke to have the boss himself play this shambling, half-competent detective."

WILLIAM F. ZORZI AS BILL ZORZI

Season Five's political reporter was played with a cantankerous game face by Bill Zorzi, a respected *Baltimore Sun* journalist who filed hundreds of stories under the byline William F. Zorzi, Jr. before the idea of hitting a mark on a soundstage entered his cynical mind.

A man with an aversion to wearing socks, Bill was known at the *Sun* as "Zorzi" except to Peter Meredith, the paper's whimsical British weekend editor, who christened him "Zorz Babe."

Few outside the newsroom know that there were years in the late 1980s when Zorzi played it conservative by pulling back his bushy Irish-Italian mane in a ponytail.

At other times he was known to wear barrettes.

As a thespian, former City Desk colleagues of Zorzi said the Loyola High School graduate wasn't half bad.

But he's no Scott Shane.

EDWARD T. NORRIS AS DETECTIVE ED NORRIS

Edward T. Norris, a New Yorker brought to Baltimore to fight crime by Mayor Martin O'Malley, was the city police commissioner when *The Wire* debuted in 2002.

The then-commissioner's first line on the show was a nod to the department's rank and file.

"Show me the son of a bitch who can fix this department and I'll give back half my overtime."

By Season Two, Norris had jumped the O'Malley ship to become superintendent of the Maryland State Police. And before production began on Season Three, Norris had resigned after being indicted on federal tax and misappropriation charges on misuse of a quasi-public city police fund. He pleaded guilty in March of 2004.

Of Norris's acting chops, Simon said: "He says his lines and he doesn't walk into furniture."

Casting director Pat Moran was similarly impressed, but more so when he was the city's top cop: "When Ed Norris was city police commissioner, the drug corner in my neighborhood got cleaned up."

Norris held his own well enough to last through Season Five, when Bubbles goes into withdrawal in a police interrogation room and throws up on him.

LAURA LIPPMAN AND MICHAEL OLESKER AS THEMSELVES

Lippman, a longtime *Baltimore Sun* reporter and daughter of a *Sun* editorial writer, shared an early scene in Season Five with Michael Olesker, who wrote a local column for the paper for many years.

Together, they stand at a conference room window and watch smoke rise from a fire on the other side of town, sort of like a couple of kids trying to figure out what animals passing clouds look like.

Their reverie is broken when city editor Gus Haynes comes in and questions the heart of reporters who would watch a fire instead of chase one.

"David [Simon] approached me with a shyness totally out of character for him and asked if I'd mind doing a cameo," said Olesker. "Are you kidding? He's been a friend through good times and awful times, and from the moment I met him maybe 25 years ago, I realized this was a guy who was out to tell the truth."

Added Olesker: "Standing in that remarkable recreation of the *Sun* newsroom was like being transported back before newspapers started falling off the side of the earth."

JEFFREY FUGITT AS OFFICER CLAUDE DIGGINS, MARINE BOAT PILOT

Ahab to McNulty's Ishmael, Diggins was played by Officer Jeffrey Fugitt of the city marine unit, proving it's easier to teach a boatman to act than the other way around.

Fugitt's best line comes while watching in disbelief as McNulty tries to tie a line from the police boat to a pier piling: "Why don't you just do bunny ears?"

Said Moran, "I think he was more terrified of our cameras than plucking five floaters a day out of the harbor."

RETIRED BALTIMORE SUN REWRITE MAN DAVID MICHAEL ETTLIN AS HIMSELF

"I showed up to find my name taped on a cast trailer door, received a shirt and tie picked out by the costumers, enjoyed lunch with the extras, memorized my precious few seconds of dialogue in the script," said Ettlin, who spent 40 years working for his hometown newspaper.

"I had my recent haircut blessed by the stylist and a few years of wrinkles and blemishes removed from my face and walked up to the second floor of the production building for my first look at *The Wire*'s *Sun* newsroom.

"I was flabbergasted. Had I fallen asleep in the real newsroom and awakened on the set, I would have been very disoriented for the first minute or so . . . all so amazingly real."

Following his own, well-honed edict that the first rule of rewrite when an editor floats a story is to "shoot it down", Ettlin delivered this line – spoken in the real *Sun* newsroom more than a decade earlier – on his final screen appearance.

"Just because something happens doesn't mean it's news. There's always a salmonella outbreak somewhere. I don't see why we have to cover this one."

DE'ANDRE MCCULLOUGH AS LAMAR

Brother Mouzone's bodyguard is played by De'Andre McCullough, protagonist of David Simon's non-fiction narrative, *The Corner*.

A man of few words, Lamar delivers a mouthful with a subtle look when Mouzone sits with a pile of books – including *Love in the Time of Cholera* by Gabriel García Márquez – outside the Franklin Terrace high-rise.

"Do you know what the most dangerous thing in America is?" asks Mouzone, who has just run Cheese off the turf with a shot of ratgut to the shoulder. "A nigger with a library card."

Lamar and a fellow lieutenant share a look that says: How many times do we have to hear that one?

FORMER MARYLAND GOVERNOR ROBERT EHRLICH AS A STATE TROOPER WORKING STATE HOUSE SECURITY

To Mayor Carcetti, whom the fictional governor has kept waiting for more than an hour, Ehrlich says: ". . . the governor's office says he's ready to see you now."

BLUE EPPS AS A MAN AT BLIND BUTCHIE'S BAR ARGUING THE MERITS OF PORT VERSUS SHERRY

George "Blue" Epps, a real-life survivor of the corners of West Baltimore. Clean and sober for more than a decade, Epps works as a drug counselor in West Baltimore.

"A real corner guy who straightened himself out," said Moran. "He has a great face. You don't go through a war zone and escape with your life without some battle scars."

NATHAN "BODIE" BARKSDALE AS A RECOVERING ADDICT WHO REFUSES TO SIGN JUNKIE JOHNNY'S COURT SLIP IN SEASON ONE

Barksdale had only recently been released from the Maryland Correctional Institution in Jessup when this episode was filmed.

Although no specific character in *The Wire* was modeled on him, Simon and Burns were familiar with his status as a drug trafficker in the 1980s and used both his surname and street moniker in homage.

RETIRED BALTIMORE POLICE SERGEANT JAY LANDSMAN AS LIEUTENANT DENNIS MELLO

The real-life Sergeant Jay Landsman, a key player in David Simon's 1991 non-fiction narrative *Homicide*, and a friend to young police reporters, played Mello.

The bigger Robert Wisdom's role as Howard "Bunny" Colvin became, the larger Lieutenant Mello's screen presence. Mello was most prominent across the "Hamsterdam" arc of Season Three.

"He's got a great sense of humor, which is good, because if you're humor-impaired, making movies in Baltimore alleys is not the place to be," said Moran. "And he might have one of the thickest Baltimore accents going and he looks like a cop."

BOXING TRAINER MACK LEWIS AS HIMSELF

Lewis, now in his nineties, played the old trainer hanging on the ropes who gives Lester Freamon an old promotional poster of former Golden Gloves boxer Avon Barksdale. The scene was filmed in Lewis's East Baltimore gym where John Waters filmed the fight scenes in his 1977 film *Desperate Living*.

BALTIMORE TRIAL LAWYER BILLY MURPHY AS HIMSELF

William H. Murphy, Jr., was born into a prominent Baltimore family: an ancestor bought the fledgling *Afro-American* newspaper in the late 19th century and made it one of the most influential black papers in the country. His father was one of the first black judges in the State of Maryland.

The Murphy Homes housing projects on the Westside, which imploded like the fictional Franklin Terrace high-rise at the beginning of Season Three of *The Wire*, were named after his family.

On the show, Murphy plays an attorney accompanying state senator Clay Davis into a courthouse. Former Maryland state senator and local radio host Larry Young – whose career was not dissimilar to Davis's – plays a talk show host on *The Wire* who has Clay Davis as a guest.

Though one of the most successful attorneys in metropolitan Baltimore – he has successfully defended boxing promoter Don King and has said of his clients that they are ". . . a child of God and everyone else is a son-of-a-bitch" – Murphy's first love is jazz.

A drummer, his playing is about as subtle as his courtroom theatrics. If Keith Moon had lived to play jazz, it might sound like Billy Murphy on a good night.

CLIFTON GROSS, FORMER PRESIDENT OF THE INTERNATIONAL LONGSHOREMEN'S ASSOCIATION LOCAL NO. 333, AS A CARGO HANDLER

In Season Two, Gross helps Frank Sobotka unload a container in the scene where Sobotka – wracked with guilt over the way his best intentions on the docks turn to shit – works a ship to "get clean."

RICHARD PRICE AS A PRISON ENGLISH TEACHER

Richard Price, author of the novels *Clockers*, *Samaritan* and *Lush Life*, as well as the screenplay for *The Color of Money*, led a group study of *The Great Gatsby*.

In the class, D'Angelo Barksdale – having accepted the truth about his Uncle Avon – sees beyond Gatsby's glitter as well.

DAVID SIMON AS AN OBNOXIOUS REPORTER

Simon, notebook in hand, plays one of a number of anonymous reporters haranguing Frank Sobotka for a quote when the union leader leaves the longshoremen's headquarters after his arrest by the FBI.

Of the performance by the *Wire* creator, Pat Moran said, "He should stick to what he knows best."

episode
fifty-seven

"TOOK"

"They don't teach it in law school."
— PEARLMAN

Directed by Dominic West

Story by David Simon & Richard Price; teleplay by Richard Price

We all know that Jimmy McNulty likes action – whiskey, women, and wisecracks – and in this episode, Dominic West got the chance to call "ACTION!" in his directorial debut for *The Wire*. The story opens with reporter Scott Templeton taking a call in the newsroom from McNulty, who launches into a scripted rant, masquerading as the serial killer.

The killer tells Templeton to stop making up shit about him and putting it in the paper. Both incredulous and panicked, Templeton alerts his editors and tries to get McNulty on the phone, unaware that he's been on the line with the half-baked (and often pickled) detective all along.

Still on the phone with Templeton, Jimmy is starting to get a kick out of his experimental theatre and lays on a heavy "Bawlmer" accent.

McNulty/Serial Killer tells Templeton they won't be able to find the victims anymore and Freamon sends two pictures of Mr. Bobbles over the cell line.

Back in the detail listening room, Detective Vernon Holley – who is not in on the scheme – thinks he's got his first break in the serial killer wiretap. Cops begin to swarm the Inner Harbor, where they believe the call is coming from. Already there, Sydnor switches off the cell through which Freamon has placed McNulty's call, wraps it in aluminum foil and joins in the search for the killer.

In homicide, Landsman, Greggs, Detective Ed Norris, and Holley review the wire recording while McNulty meets Templeton and his editors on Calvert Street.

Gleefully putting Templeton on the spot, Jimmy asks the reporter if it sounded like the same guy. Assuring him it did (after some hesitation) Scott says he didn't remember such a heavy Baltimore accent the first time.

McNulty asks the editors not to publish the photo of the new victim and not to say where the cell call came from. Unable to resist needling Templeton one more time on his way out, McNulty tells the reporter that the killer is just using him. When the reporter finds that offensive, Jimmy says it shouldn't, since the whole thing has been a boon for him. Haynes clocks this and his suspicions regarding Templeton bloom anew.

In the wake of the phone call and photos from the serial killer, Judge Phelan signs an amended wiretap order, noting that this is all bad news for Carcetti – and his presumed run for governor – who ran for mayor on a law-and-order platform.

Carcetti, furious that the killer hasn't been caught yet, lifts the ban on overtime for the case and bitches out Rawls, who calls Daniels, who summons Landsman and Bunk Moreland to his office. Angry that McNulty's bogus horseshit is sucking up what little resources exist, Bunk refuses to go to the meeting.

On the corner, Michael is put in cuffs by Carver and Officer Baker and taken downtown. In the homicide interrogation room, Bunk shows Michael photos of his stepfather's brutally beaten body. The boy does not flinch and does not cooperate.

When Bunk criticizes McNulty and Freamon for the mess they've made, Lester says they're just a couple of weeks away at most from nailing Marlo.

And when Haynes tells Klebanow and Whiting that Templeton's prose style is over-the-top purple, Klebanow tells Gus he'll edit the story himself.

The FBI begins doing voice analysis of McNulty's fake phone call to Templeton. Freaked out, Jimmy pleads with Freamon to finish off Marlo as soon as possible.

While Bubbles serves guests at the Viva House soup kitchen on Mount Street – working alongside the real Brendan Walsh, who founded Viva House with his wife Willa Bickham – he recognizes *Sun* reporter Mike Fletcher.

Bubbles later takes Fletcher to a homeless village and tells the reporter to write it the way it feels.

Freamon and Sydnor intercept a photo from Marlo's phone: a picture of a clock reading 5:50 which is followed by a quick call to Monk. Sydnor heads out to tail Monk, who doesn't move for an hour and a half.

At Clay Davis's corruption trial, Rupert Bond questions Day-Day the driver about $40,000 he received as the executive director of a charity. Day-Day says he never saw any of the money; it all went back to Davis.

Defense attorney Billy Murphy points out that the driver has received immunity from prosecution in return for his testimony. He then gets Day-Day to admit that he was the one who cashed the checks for the charity salary and – even if it was supposed to go back to Davis – there's no proof the senator received it.

Meanwhile, McNulty has become the patron saint of OT in the homicide unit, doling it out to all of his begging colleagues from the serial killer account, promising to make the paperwork jive.

Haynes reads Templeton's published story, the one edited by Klebanow, and tosses the newspaper with disgust before heading to Kavanaughs, a cop bar, for a drink. There, he sees Major Mello from the Western and asks if it's possible that a woman could be processed through the court system on a fake ID. Mello says no, that judicial system IDs are linked to fingerprints and someone must be fucking with him.

On the street, Omar grabs Savino Bratton (played by Chris Clanton) and kills him with a bullet to the head, checking off another name on his list of Stanfield crew-members. At Michael's corner, he tells the boy that he's going to kill the rest of Marlo's muscle until Stanfield meets him in the street. Once he's gone, Michael is relieved that he wasn't recognized from the shootout at Monk's apartment.

When Lester tells McNulty they'll need more man hours and cars for surveillance to break Marlo's "clock code," Jimmy confesses to throwing OT hours around the office and Freamon warns that he's going to screw the whole thing up.

Seven or eight detectives are going to be necessary for the home stretch, says Lester, as he and McNulty try to think of people in the district stations whom they trust.

At City Hall, Carcetti is told that if the investigation of the serial killer lingers for even a month, he will be forced to lay off teachers. And that would be disaster for a candidate running for governor.

In court, Clay Davis gives the performance of his life. And the story is Robin Hood as Davis explains the reality of poor neighborhoods, that while the charity money did wind up in his bank account, he never kept a dime.

Cash and carry is the current of the 'hood, he says, that's how it works when people come to him directly for help with baby food and funerals.

When he's finished, the gallery erupts in applause, and Bond and Pearlman stand by, baffled.

episode
fifty-eight

CLARIFICATIONS
"A lie ain't a side of a story. It's just a lie."
— TERRY HANNING

Directed by Anthony Hemingway
Story by David Simon & Dennis Lehane; teleplay by Dennis Lehane

McNulty gives Mayor Carcetti a detailed report of his investigation thus far on the serial killer. Also present are Commissioner Rawls and his deputy, Cedric Daniels.

Asking for a budget for more surveillance, Jimmy adds that he'd like Sergeant Carver to head the team. And some decent undercover cars would also help. The mayor tells him to use rental cars.

Looking for a job, Dukie stops in at a shoe store where Poot – having had it with the corner after going to jail and seeing his homey Bodie murdered – is working.

["America," said Dennis Lehane,, who wrote this episode, "would very much not like to see gang-bangers humanized – it's too confusing."]

Poot recognizes Dukie from the neighborhood, tells him to hang in there a little longer and come back when he's older. Dukie's next job application is with a junk man collecting a derelict refrigerator on the street. He is hired on the spot.

When McNulty catches up with Carver, he tells him that he and Freamon will use the newly approved surveillance to chase Marlo Stanfield. Though suspicious that Lester's wiretap isn't kosher, Carver joins in.

Carcetti juggles conflicting priorities: how to avoid cuts in school funding, send extra money to the police department to catch the serial killer, and come out as undamaged as possible for a run at the governor's mansion?

Tommy will later float deals to potential opponents from suburban Washington to make sure the path is as clear as possible when the time comes.

In the swift trading of horses surrounding all of this, City Council president Nerese Campbell promises to support Carcetti any way she can if he endorses her for mayor. And the freshly exonerated Clay Davis promises fidelity in exchange for two seats on the liquor board.

Later, Freamon encounters Clay Davis charming a woman in a cocktail lounge. Lester tells Davis that it was he who amassed most of the evidence that Clay dodged at his corruption trial and wonders aloud if the senator could again be so fortunate.

Lester then gives Davis copies of the paper trail he's documented in regard to illegal loans and promises silence in exchange for future favors.

(Lester will tell a colleague: "When you show who gets paid behind all the tragedy and the fraud . . . when you show how the money routes itself, how we're all vested, all of us complicit, baby I could die happy.")

Carver's surveillance team – Dozerman, Brian McClarney, Bobby Brown, and Truck Carrick have a case worth working – one with unlimited OT and shiny new rental cars.

On the Guilford Avenue loading dock behind the newspaper, Gus Haynes speaks openly with other reporters about doubts regarding Templeton and the serial killer story. The editor is pretty sure Templeton is hyping it. No matter, it's real enough that they'll be writing column inches about homeless people through the end of the year.

Back in the newsroom, Haynes is told there's a homeless military vet in the lobby complaining that Templeton won't take his calls.

The vet – Terry Hanning – tells Gus that Templeton's story about the guy who came back from Iraq is riddled with bullshit, that a Marine would never embellish the details of combat.

The city editor's patience with Templeton has long given out, the most recent example of Scott's lack of integrity being his failure to own up to the errors in the seafood allergy story.

When Templeton tries to dismiss Hanning as a crackpot, Haynes orders him to track down other men from the unit and find out what happened near Fallujah. If there were errors, they will write a correction.

As Dozerman and Truck play with the bells and whistles on their undercover rental car, Omar approaches and lets them know where a couple of corner boys have stashed their dope.

In wake of the bust, Omar approaches, scattering a group of younger boys with his mere presence.

[Likewise proving who is boss to all the other kids on the tot lot, New Yorker Kate Porterfield outfits her toddler in a "onesie" that says: "Omar Don't Scare."]

Apparently, neither does Kenard (played by Thuliso Dingwall), who watches as the Bigfoot of Bawlmer – seldom seen but almost always fatal – tosses the drugs left behind by the corner boys.

["I made sure we kept a scene of Kenard looking at Omar for a second or two," said Kate Sanford, the film editor who cut this episode. "I wanted to make sure that moment existed for the record."

By the end of the hour, every viewer knows why.]

Omar then counts off several vacant rowhouses from the corner, and, in front of the fourth, announces that he will be "obliged" to come in if they don't behave accordingly.

In a moment, a trash bag of narcotics lands on the sidewalk, which Omar kicks toward the sewer opening in the curb, disposing of it.

He then shouts across the silent corner: "I'm out here in these streets everyday, me and my lonesome. Where he at? Huh? You put it in his ear – Marlo Stanfield is NOT a man for this town."

The stickup artist then goes to an Asian grocery to buy cigarettes through the revolving Plexiglas, paying no attention to the tinkling bell that announces the entry of the young hopper Kenard, who puts a bullet in the back of the big man's head.

When Bunk arrives to investigate, he finds a list of the Stanfield crew-members Omar was hunting among the dead man's belongings.

In the newsroom, Alma Gutierrez tells Gus of a Westside murder – no ID yet – and the editor tells her to write up a fire story instead.

[Said David Michael Ettlin, who spent 40 years on the City Desk of the real *Baltimore Sun* and appeared in the scene: "I tell Gus how much room he had for cop stories and he goes with the Charles County house fire with two dead and bags the sketchy homicide, thus consigning Omar Little's departure to news oblivion."]

What is not news at the newspaper, however, is big news in homicide as Bunk hands over Omar's handwritten hit-list to McNulty.

Bunk also tells Jimmy that the lab returned a positive match between Partlow and Michael Lee's dead stepfather, beaten to death in the alley. McNulty asks that Moreland hold off on the murder warrant as Lester Freamon is close to bringing down Marlo's house of cards. Bunk agrees.

But Lester is not as close as he thought. When Marlo receives a phone call, the surveillance teams reports that no one else in the Stanfield group has used a phone. There is someone else in the loop. When McNulty gives

Freamon Omar's hit-list, Lester sees Cheese's name on it and surmises that he must be the missing link in the Stanfield phone network.

Working with McNulty to catch the serial killer with the help of the FBI, Greggs digs into a mammoth pile of files on known sex offenders to compare them with what is known about the Baltimore predator. Unable to watch her do such tedious work for naught, McNulty comes clean, outing Freamon along with himself. Kima is flabbergasted.

Trying to find the location of a possible Marlo meet, Sydnor consults a Baltimore street map. Going over the coordinates, he has a Prez-like epiphany: Marlo's "clock code" is based on map coordinates.

Freamon deduces that each meeting likely takes place within an hour of receiving the clock code.

Back on Calvert Street, Gus tells Templeton he's cutting the lead to his homeless vigil story – at which Templeton makes an impassioned speech worthy of Clifford Odets – because he again used an unnamed source.

Templeton bristles and rants – in his immature way – at the suggestion he is lying, and managing editor Klebanow steps in to challenge Haynes. On his way out the door, the city editor says he is following the paper's policy on naming sources.

At home, McNulty unloads his conscience on Beadie, who is one straw away from kicking him out for good, and tells her about making up the serial killer and how it has spiraled beyond his control.

Beadie realizes that Jimmy could go to jail and she could be mixed into the prosecution. As a snapshot of Jimmy McNulty, beyond the chronic infidelity, drunkenness, and hubris, this may be his most selfish stunt of all.

episode
fifty-nine

LATE EDITIONS
"Deserve got nuthin' to do with it." – SNOOP
Directed by Joe Chappelle
Story by David Simon & George Pelecanos; teleplay by George Pelecanos

Sydnor and his team cover Marlo and his crew while Freamon tracks their coded cell phone images from the detail office. Noticing that a meeting is scheduled at a new and secluded spot, he surmises they are on to Stanfield's supplier. The surveillance teams are told to rally at a warehouse near the marine terminal.

A couple of blocks away, Freamon and Sydnor sit on the warehouse that Partlow has just entered. Lester tells the surveillance team that any Stanfield lieutenant leaving the warehouse is a target: pull them over, seize the dope and take their phones.

Inside, Partlow is told by a Greek deliveryman that there is more than 100 kilos of raw heroin inside a shipment of refrigerators. When Monk and Cheese leave the warehouse with the shipment, the cops are on them.

O-Dog meets with the shyster Levy, who arranges for the gangster to take the fall on weapons charges against Partlow and Snoop, a lesser version

of Wee-Bey Brice taking the rap for multiple murders within the Barksdale group. With no prior convictions, O-Dog is sure to get a relatively lenient sentence and will be well paid for his time. Though willing, he is not crazy about the idea.

At the paper, Gus Haynes welcomes back foreign correspondent Robert Ruby (played by Stephen Schnetzer and named for the former *Sun* reporter who covered the Middle East and authored the book *Jericho: Dreams, Ruins, Phantoms.*)

Ruby is back in Baltimore after the paper closed the London bureau. Gus asks him to look into Scott Templeton's reporting, as great an insult as exists in the newspaper world. Whiting surely won't like it, says Ruby, heading for the paper's library to pull clips of Templeton's work.

["I didn't envy 'my' character having to report on another reporter, but I was happy that he was the guy trusted enough to do the digging," said the real Ruby. "Plus, the guy with my name seemed like an adult without also being a dullard."]

Carcetti's chief of staff demands a ten percent drop in crime by the end of the quarter from Rawls and Daniels – more cops on the street, more arrests – to grease the mayor's run for governor.

Miffed that the mayor who promised an era of clean stats is no different from everybody else, Daniels finds Freamon waiting. Lester says he's just a few warrants away from locking up the entire Stanfield organization.

Happy to see some real police work bear fruit, particularly in the wake of political demands for faked improvements, Daniels calls Assistant State's Attorney Pearlman.

As police raid the warehouse and track Cheese, Partlow, and Marlo, Snoop and O-Dog rush to Michael's apartment, where the boy watches the big bust on the news: $16 million in seized heroin, a connection to the vacant rowhouse murders and the mayor trumpeting his department's fine work.

Marlo sits in Central Booking with Partlow, Cheese, and Monk, scrutinizing the documents that led to their arrests. Thinking there had to be a snitch – the paperwork mentions "information received" – Michael's name comes up. When Monk mentions that Omar has been calling out

Marlo by name in the streets, the boss shows a range of emotion – pure anger – not previously seen.

["Terrifying in every way," said the writer Malcolm Azania, who interviewed the actor Jamie Hector about his character. "Hector agreed when I asked if Marlo was a psychopath: devoid of the capacity for empathy, without restraint in exploitation and cruelty."]

Marlo demands to know what Omar said about him and orders his lieutenants to put out the word that he knew nothing of the challenge. As far as Michael goes, they can't afford any risks, says Stanfield.

The next day, far from the world in which his old friend Michael is now trapped, Namond Brice gives a passionate speech about fighting AIDS in Africa while Bunny Colvin and his wife look on like proud parents.

Visiting Marlo in jail, Levy and the drug lord try to figure out how the busts occurred. Only Snoop knew about it, and Marlo trusts her beyond doubt.

(All of this, deliciously, traced back to Herc's hard-on for Marlo in regard to the missing surveillance camera.)

Haynes meets Council President Nerese Campbell for lunch and though the conversation is about the upcoming mayor's race, he is hoping she sheds light on how factual Templeton's reporting has been.

(This is in light of Alma telling Haynes that Daniels refused to give a legitimate quote after the big drug bust, noting that he had been stung by anonymous, erroneous quotes when he spoke to the press after the Burrell/Carcetti flap hit the papers.)

Nerese concedes that Daniels's reputation for loyalty is solid and Haynes has confirmed his suspicions that the quote regarding the Burrell/Daniels rift was bogus.

Back in the newsroom, Haynes asks about the paperwork he ordered to fact-check the homeless Marine story and Templeton says it will take at least three weeks.

In the basement of his sister's house, Bubbles tells reporter Mike Fletcher the story of his colorful life as he comes up on a full year of continuous sobriety.

On Bubs's anniversary, Walon tells Fletcher that anything said at the NA meeting cannot leave the room, in keeping with the 12-step program's tradition which holds that anonymity must be maintained in regard to press, radio and film.

Although he is disappointed that his sister never shows up, Bubbles shares from the heart and speaks about the death of Sherrod. It's okay to hold onto grief, he says, as long as you make room for other things in life as well.

Threatening Clay Davis with a federal indictment, Freamon meets the senator Clay Davis at a bar, wanting to know who is in charge of laundering drug money in Baltimore.

Davis talks about Maurice Levy and other drug-connected defense attorneys and how they have side work sending money to developers and politicians, taking a cut at both ends.

As the final payment to be free of Lester, Davis tells him that Levy sells sealed grand-jury documents leaked to him by someone in the courthouse.

At Michael's corner, Snoop tells the soldier she needs his help on a hit ordered by the boss. He grows suspicious, however, when she tells him not to bring a gun.

Doing his homework, Michael watches Snoop and other Stanfield crew lay plans to set him up. When she comes back to the corner later on to pick him up for the job, Michael asks her to pull over so he can piss in an alley. When she stops, he pulls a gun from under his shirt and puts it to her head, saying he had nothing to do with the raids and arrests.

"You was never one of us," she tells him of his aloof and questioning nature. "Never could be."

When he racks the chamber, she looks in the side view mirror and says: "How my hair look, Mike?"

"Look good," he says, shooting her in the head.

[Kerry Ann Oberdalhoff, a lifelong Baltimorean and granddaughter of a *Sunpapers* delivery truck driver, was a devoted viewer of *The Wire* and not sad to see Snoop go. "I levitated in my chair when Snoop got it," said Oberdalhoff. "If only because I'd never have to hear that grating shit-in-her-mouth voice again. Man, I had a raging hate for her."]

Proving that a good editor never forgets how to ride a bike, Haynes interviews Sergeant Raymond Wiley, the Marine Templeton wrote about who lost his hands in the Iraq war.

While a therapist helps Wiley with his motorized prosthetic hands, the soldier tells Haynes that his buddies weren't exchanging fire the day he was wounded.

And his friend, Terry Hanning – who complained about the story – had no need to invent anything to impress Scott Templeton. Hanning had seen plenty of action and could have recounted stories on end. The *Sun*, says Wiley, must have lied.

At police headquarters, Greggs is on the warpath in regard to McNulty's manifold falsifications, confronting Carver about it and going to see Daniels, where she tells him about the made-up serial killer.

Daniels brings the news to Pearlman. Together they drive to evidence control to compare the serial killer's tapped number against Marlo's seized cell phone. When Rhonda dials the "killer's" number from a court document, Marlo's phone rings.

Having run from the SUV in which he murdered Snoop, Michael rushes into his apartment to gather up his little brother Bug and Dukie, who has been spending his time stealing junk metal with his a-rabber friends.

He drives his little brother to their aunt's house in Columbia and drops him off with a box full of cash, barely able to keep from breaking down.

Back in Baltimore, he takes Dukie to the a-rabber stables, where the cart-and-pony men are shooting dope by the light of fires burning in 50-gallon drums.

episode
sixty

-30-
'... the life of kings.'   – H.L. MENCKEN
Directed by Clark Johnson
Story by David Simon & Ed Burns; teleplay by David Simon

Mayor Carcetti learns that the Baltimore serial killer – the sick-o who liked to bite and murder homeless men – was a fairy tale.

Tommy is speechless for a moment before connecting all of the dots in the wake of McNulty's stunt: it has negated all of his political victories. If it goes public, he says, Rawls and Bond – and most likely Pearlman, too – will have to take the hit.

Rawls trades his silence on the McNulty/Freamon caper in exchange for a better job when and if Carcetti makes it to Annapolis as governor.

Freamon figures out that grand jury prosecutor Gary DiPasquale has lost three times his annual salary in Atlantic City in the past couple of years and tricks him into talking. In a matter of moments, DiPasqule becomes Lester's new informant.

When Lester gives his tape of DiPasquale's confession about selling grand jury documents to Pearlman, she gives him the hairy eyeball with a pointed comment that she knows what he and McNulty have been up to.

A very nervous Lester will soon share this info with Jimmy McNulty, and together they wonder why they haven't been arrested yet.

Why? Politics, of course. Between the upcoming election and the complications resulting from the Marlo Stanfield investigation, they figure they have more than enough chips to barter.

Robert Ruby reports to Haynes that his review of Templeton's published work shows it to be riddled with exaggerations, fake quotes, half-truths and manufactured sources. Gus puts Ruby's research in a drawer, not sure yet what to do.

As expected, Marlo Stanfield is denied bail and his attorney, Levy, says he's got to know how the cops figured out the clock code. The lawyer suspects a wire tap, but even then it doesn't all add up.

Crossing paths with Cheese after the meeting with Levy breaks up, Marlo tells his lieutenant to track down Michael once he is out on bail.

At the courthouse, Levy tells Pearlman he has figured out the weak spots in her case against Marlo and won't hesitate to exploit it in court. He suggests they meet somewhere and talk.

When they do, they hopscotch their way to a plea agreement deal. Pearlman plays the tape of Levy on the phone with DiPasquale. In exchange for not using it against him, she wants guilty pleas from Partlow, Cheese and Monk. Marlo, she says, can walk, as long as he stays off the street.

Curious as to why she is reluctant to bring her big evidence into an open courtroom, Levy can only conclude that the prosecutor must have some pretty big problems to hide.

Out of the loop, Jay Landsman keeps banging on McNulty to work the homeless murders harder, calling him about a man in a gray van who just tried to kidnap a homeless person. When Jimmy shows up he finds Templeton, who claims to have seen the crime outside of the *Sunpapers* building.

When Templeton leaves, another homeless man walks up to McNulty. It's an undercover cop who tells Jimmy that the reporter is full of shit: there was no gray van.

Reading over Mike Fletcher's profile of him, Bubbles still isn't sure he wants it published. His NA sponsor, Walon, tells Bubs he may just be afraid that people will think he's a good guy. Walon has brought Bubbles steamed crabs from the place where he works, and Bubbles, still on the fence about the story, takes them home to his sister.

Inside the paper, Haynes demands that Klebanow kill Templeton's gray van story, another tale without confirmed sources. You may win a Pulitzer with this guy, says Gus, but then you're going to have to give it back.

In South Baltimore, a call for a real killer of homeless men comes in: the case now has copycats picking up where McNulty left off.

McNulty shows up, saying that Daniels and Pearlman know the truth, and Bunk tells his old partner that he is responsible for the death of the man in the copycat murder.

Cornered in homicide by Rawls and Daniels, McNulty swears he had nothing to do with the fresh body in South Baltimore. The mayor knows what went on, says Rawls, and your best move is to solve the copycat murder and hope it all goes away.

Seeing a handful of business cards among the new victim's possession, Jimmy remembers a homeless man from his various visits to skid row having a box of business cards. When he shows up, he finds that the man also has a spool of red ribbon. In the midst of cops and a media circus, McNulty easily solves his own made-up case, mirrored back to him like some kind of Baltimore multi-verse.

In the newsroom, metro editor Steve Luxenburg tells Haynes that even though the evidence against Templeton is damning – and now includes the reporter's notebook on the serial killer, which is blank – making a stink about it may cost him his job.

Taking a deep breath, Haynes walks into Whiting's office, ready to make his case. They are joined by Klebanow.

Bunk and McNulty interview their red ribbon, business card-hoarding homeless suspect, who confesses to killing every victim publicized by McNulty.

As Jimmy leaves, he finds Templeton waiting for him in Landsman's office. Closing the door, McNulty goes off on the reporter, telling him he knows he lied because he made up the whole thing himself. With that, he sends a rattled Templeton back to his editors, knowing the guy can't share this truth with a soul.

Back in the interrogation room, McNulty refuses to manipulate the mentally ill homeless man into confessing to all six murders.

Carcetti tells the press that the killer of the homeless men has been arrested, charged with the two most recent ones and is suspected of the others. At the end of the press conference, the mayor publicly credits and congratulates Cedric Daniels on the arrest and the Stanfield case.

He then announces that Daniels is his new police commissioner.

Daniels, on the advice of his ex-wife, will resign from the department before his confirmation hearings begin. The move is to avoid being leveraged by City Hall with an old file alleging corruption when he worked the Eastern District. And to avoid staining the fresh political career of the former Mrs Cedric Daniels.

As his final official act in a very brief tenure as police commissioner, Daniels promotes Ellis Carver, his old protégé, to lieutenant.

Back in the homicide unit, Pearlman tells Jimmy and Lester that they won't be fired, but they won't be working street police anymore either. If they want to stay, it will be desk jobs or nothing.

It is not lost on McNulty and Freamon that both Levy and Marlo dodged prosecution, adding that they only have themselves to blame.

What is left of the New Day Co-op – Fat Face Rick, Slim Charles, and Clinton "Shorty" Buise – talk business with Marlo, who is auctioning his drug connection with The Greek.

Asking price: $10 million.

Later, when Cheese tries to throw in with the other Co-op dealers to buy the connection with him – saying it ain't about nostalgia or back in the day, it's just about selling dope – Slim Charles shoots him dead: "For Joe."

For their efforts to expose a crooked reporter, both Gus and Alma are demoted: he to the copy desk, she to a distant suburb. When Gus wonders why she was punished when she never brought up Templeton's empty notebook, Alma tells him that she told the editors about it herself in support of him.

Bubbles reads Mike Fletcher's profile of him while sitting on a curb, carefully folding it when he's done and putting it in his pocket.

At a downtown office party, Levy introduces Marlo – who had told his former drug compatriots that his next move would be "businessman" – to the real-estate elite of Baltimore, including the developer Andrew Krawczyk, whom one might think had had his fill of nouveau-riche drug dealers.

[Said Malcolm Azania: "Having won back his freedom from prison courtesy of another psychopath, Maurice Levy, Marlo has no grand vision of what to do with his millions won from addiction and death – no transformative lessons have been learned.

"Instead he leaves an elite gathering of Baltimore's powerful, in which he holds no sway, to return to his hunting grounds where he can feel alive and dominant by crushing teenagers with his fists.

"He is Milton's Satan, preferring to rule in hell than serve in heaven."]

As a group of drug dealers gather at Vinson's rim shop with their money, Michael steps out of the darkness with a shotgun, puts a load of buckshot in Vinson's leg and grabs a bag full of cash.

Michael don't scare.

At a wake for the careers of McNulty and Freamon at Kavanaugh's, Jimmy lays on the pool table, a stiff smirking at his own eulogies.

Holding forth, Landsman documents McNulty's history as a troublemaker, insubordinate and general all-round pain in the ass giver of grief.

He ends, however, with this: "If I was laying there dead on some Baltimore street corner, I'd want it to be you standing over me, catching the case.

"Because, brother, when you were good, you were the best we had."

THE DRUNKARD'S OPERA
Jimmy McNulty in Life and Letters

Most women have a Jimmy McNulty in their past. He's the guy you take home from the bar and never hear from again, the lover whose idea of a date is a drink-and-dial at midnight, the husband you divorce because you finally get fed up and too tired to care.

McNulty, of course, played all of those roles with various partners over the five seasons of *The Wire* and the performance resonated with female viewers who have tangled with his real-life counterparts.

"I've had McNultys in my past, have some in my present and am working assiduously to avoid having any in my future," says economic policy specialist Marceline White of Baltimore.

"He's the kind of guy I *loved* when I was in my twenties, but now I steer clear of," says Baltimore writer Laura Wexler. "They're totally attractive, but they're trouble."

Played with brutal charm by Dominic West, McNulty is not only a familiar real-life type but also an inspired mash-up of a long line of literary heroes stretching back to the 18th century, says Tita Chico, associate professor of British literature at the University of Maryland in College Park.

"The rakish hero has been a stock character type, simultaneously attractive and dangerous, trading on the currency of temptation, the thrill of adventure, and the promise – almost never, ever fulfilled – that he'll reform for the 'right' woman," says Chico.

"This kind of hero – the one who straddles the line between the criminal and the police, and who charms and betrays women left and right, but still seems to embody a true code of honor – lingers in all manner of crime and detective fiction today."

Dominic West tells a funny story that neatly encapsulates the allure, both sexual and literary, of the character he played with such gusto.

"I was walking down the street near my house one sunny evening and noticed an exceptionally beautiful woman walking towards me and laughing with her two friends, one of whom was reading aloud a newspaper article," he says.

"I remember thinking how sophisticated and exotic they seemed and what a beautiful sight they made in the twilight. Just as I was falling in love with her, she suddenly saw me and said 'Oh my God, I love you.'"

The woman, West soon realized, was the novelist Zadie Smith, acclaimed author of *White Teeth*, *On Beauty* and *The Autograph Man*. "She raved about *The Wire*," West recalls. "I spluttered something gauche like 'Oh . . . thanks very much, I love you too,' and hurried stupidly away."

McNulty, of course, would not have let such an opportunity pass without making a play for the beautiful writer, and it's that brazen hedonism, coupled with his professional chops, that male fans of *The Wire* find both compelling and slightly repugnant.

"He is both a cool guy and a messed-up jerk," says Baltimore novelist Michael Kimball. "Which one usually depends on how much he's had to drink or how deep he is into a case."

As with women, every man seems to have a McNulty in his life. "I've definitely had friends – exasperating ones – like McNulty. Fun to drink with, charming, self-destructive," says Random House book editor Jeff Alexander of New York.

"The kind of guy who wonders why you're not introducing your female friends to him, who doesn't quite understand that – as much as you like him – you'd never wish him upon someone you were close to."

McNulty is "the kind of guy you'd want at your bachelor party but you couldn't trust at the wedding reception."

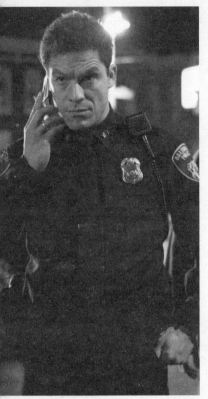

Alexander points out that the aspect of the character that makes McNulty and his story arc a more contemporary literary tradition is the narrative of addiction and recovery.

Smart, cocky, and hopelessly self-destructive, Jimmy McNulty is probably the most realistic functional alcoholic ever to appear on television. There is no sanctimony or sentimentality in *The Wire*'s depiction of McNulty's alcoholism, no "my name is Jimmy and I'm an alcoholic" moment.

But the series writers grant McNulty an epiphany in Season Five when FBI profilers deliver a capsule description of the serial killer menacing the city's homeless men:

"He is likely not a college graduate, but nonetheless feels superior to those with advanced education. He has a problem with authority, and a deep-seated resentment of those whom he feels have impeded his progress professionally. The subject has problems with lasting relationships and is possibly a high-functioning alcoholic."

McNulty's drunkard's pride and sense of superiority are the character's defining traits, a guy who always thinks he's the smartest guy in the room, David Simon has said.

But pride usually leads to a beat down, as Western civilization's oldest book points out, and that's especially true for the tribe of alcoholics.

McNulty hits bottom three times on the show and with each humiliation he comes progressively closer to the truth about himself, perhaps most crushingly when he loses a game of sexual politics to political consultant Teresa D'Agostino in Season Three.

After retreating to the more sympathetic arms of Amy Ryan's Beadie Russell in Season Four, he tries to sober up and wise up – only to relapse in Season Five.

"He's got to up the ante a bit because he's so in trouble with his job and so hateful of his bosses that he's got to go one step further with self-destruction before he can be free of his demons," West told *Flak Magazine* in 2008.

"He had to hit rock bottom, and I think this is what the serial killer angle does."

Near the end of the series, with his career in tatters, his closest friendships all but destroyed and his last-chance relationship about to fall apart, McNulty admits the truth to Beadie and to himself.

Trying to make sense of his behavior and the emotions behind it, he says: "I don't even know where the anger comes from. I don't know how to make it stop. Now that I've done all this, I watched myself do it, I can't even stand it."

It's as close as McNulty comes to a confession, paving the way for a tenuous happy ending.

In the end, the writers of *The Wire* offer McNulty the kind of absolution denied all but one other character, Bubbles, the recovering heroin addict whose journey most closely resembles his own.

Like McNulty, Bubs has grievously harmed not only himself but people he loves. His lonely mattress in the basement of his sister's house, a way station on the road to recovery, is the mirror image of McNulty's bare apartment post-divorce in Season One.

Both men need to go down into the depths before they can rise up to enjoy the fruits of normalcy – dinner in the kitchen with your family, the left-on porch light showing the way home.

Though he loses the job he both loves and hates, McNulty ends the series with his relationship and friendships intact, alive at his own wake, saluted by his fellow cops, even his longstanding nemesis Jay Landsman.

In evading the grim fate meted out to so many others, McNulty once again reveals his literary pedigree. He is a virtual ringer for the character of Macheath in John Gay's *The Beggar's Opera*, says literary scholar Chico.

In that "fierce satire of government and judicial corruption," she says, "Macheath is the ring leader of a criminal gang, and so on the other side of the law from McNulty, but is similar in his passion for wine and women and his strict sense of honor. In the face of true depravity – a government in cahoots with criminals – the Macheath hero is adored by all, charming and immune from being punished for any of his crimes."

Dominic West's ability to play this raw Baltimore Macheath so close to the bone has impressed even those familiar with his earlier theater work.

"I've seen Dominic playing quintessentially young English leads in plays like *The Seagull* on the London stage and I think his performance in *The Wire* is a revelation, it's like watching a different actor," says British theater and television director Edward Hall.

In London, where *Wire*-mania hit years after the series debut in the States, fans find his performance so convincing they have a hard time believing he is a fellow Brit.

"I didn't find out he was English until three seasons in," says musician Al English. "I so believed the character that it felt weird to watch him speaking with a British accent on YouTube.

"I saw a few clips of him in a period drama, and his English accent was really quite posh. It seemed like more of a put-on than his Baltimore accent."

The posh accent isn't fake. West is a public schoolboy, English version.

"One of my greatest pleasures is to watch Dominic playing an Irish-American cop so convincingly," says actor John Nettleton, who appeared with West in *The Voysey Inheritance* at the National Theatre in London.

"He is an Old Etonian, and usually it's hard for Etonians to change their accents; the role he plays in *The Wire* is a considerable achievement for anyone from that school."

Whatever the accent, there's clearly a bit of the hard-living McNulty in the actor who brought him so vividly to life.

While filming in Baltimore, the actor lived at Clipper Mill apartments, an upscale complex carved out of the shell of an old textile mill in North Baltimore.

West's next-door neighbor, Baltimore art dealer Jordan Faye Block, recalled the time the actor hosted a private party at the complex's pool at four a.m.

"He got crazy in the pool one night with a bunch of people he brought home with him," Block laughs. "They tried to punish him by taking away his pool provisions for a week."

McNulty would've been proud.

Deborah Rudacille
Sofia Alvarez in London contributed to this story.

AFTERWORD

HOMAGE TO THE QUIET MAN

"Bob's silences were more expressive than words ..."

– KAREN THORSON

It was god-awful news.

Bob, gone?

Trim, boyish, and seemingly fit as a fiddle, producer Robert F. Colesberry Jr. died at the age of 57 after complications from heart surgery. His death in New York City on February 9, 2004, knocked the wind out of *The Wire* family.

Each season of the show following his death would feature a photo of Bob in his on-screen role as Detective Ray Cole in the opening montage.

A man who often kept his own counsel, Bob was a silent type who listened more than he spoke. But his talent and commitment influenced every aspect of any project he had a hand in.

He learned from some of the film industry's most celebrated directors, many of whom came to regard Colesberry as an essential collaborator. Bertolucci embraced him. Scorsese credited him with helping to reinvigorate his career with *After Hours*. And Alan Parker told him that one day – his talents as a producer notwithstanding – he should direct.

"I never wanted to shoot another reel of film without Bob as my partner," said David Simon, who shared executive-producing duties on *The Wire* with Colesberry. "He was a consummate storyteller and a trusted friend."

Because the show must go on, "a triumvirate [Simon/Colesberry/Noble] had to be rethought and each of us took over some of what Bob had been to the show," said Simon in 2009.

Bob's widow "Karen pitched in ... so did Joe Chapelle and others. But the loss of Bob by necessity transformed Nina [Noble] from line producer to an executive producer. And she was ready."

Not by a long shot, however, was anyone ready for the death of Bob Colesberry.

A Philadelphia native who was once invited to minor-league camp as a second baseman by the Baltimore Orioles, Colesberry graduated from New York University, which established a scholarship in his name.

Over a long career not nearly long enough, he worked on films as diverse as *Fame*, *Mississippi Burning* and a CBS production of Arthur Miller's *Death of a Salesman*, starring Dustin Hoffman and John Malkovich.

During film school, he tended bar at Max's Kansas City in Manhattan – where the Velvet Underground played their last gigs with Lou Reed – and where Colesberry fell in with a coterie of young filmmakers surrounding Andy Warhol. Colesberry worked as an assistant director on several Warhol films.

On *Fame*, he served as first assistant to director Alan Parker, co-writing the B-side to the film's hit-single title song–a feat for which he continued to receive royalty checks years later.

"It was called 'Hot Lunch,'" said Parker. "Bob actually wrote the lyric, 'If it's blue, it must be stew.'"

Other directors who benefited from Colesberry's unwavering commitment include Ang Lee, Robert Benton, and Alan Pakula.

Pakula, who directed *The Parallax View* and *Sophie's Choice*, worked with Colesberry on the 1997 film *The Devil's Own* and died a year later in a freak car accident aged 70.

"Alan was somewhat of a father figure to Bob," said Karen Thorson, a post-production producer on *The Wire* to whom Colesberry was married for 12 years. "When Alan died, Bob withdrew.

"I don't think he contemplated his own death very much," Thorson said. "But prior to his [heart] surgery, he said, 'I have so much more to do with my life.'"

As the executive producer of HBO's *The Corner* – the project that first teamed him with Simon – Colesberry was honored with a Peabody Award and an Emmy for best miniseries.

He received Oscar and Golden Globe nominations for his work on *Mississippi Burning*, and Emmy nominations for both *Death of a Salesman* and HBO's *61** – about the race between Mickey Mantle and Roger Maris to break Babe Ruth's single-season home run record.

A devoted Yankees fan – much to the consternation of his Baltimore-centric crews on *The Corner* and *The Wire* – Colesberry jumped at the chance to work with director Billy Crystal on *61**.

At one point, when a friend called Colesberry to find out how the filming of *61** was going, Bob went into great length on the adventure of it all. He had the pleasure of eating lunch with Yogi Berra and stood at the plate in old Tigers Stadium, where the film was shot, trying to get some wood on knuckleballs thrown by former big-leaguer Tom Candiotti, who appeared in the movie.

"When it was announced that *61** had been nominated for an Emmy, [the film's director] Billy Crystal wrote Bob a note that said, 'Whether we win or not, it's how we played the game,'" said Thorson.

"After Bob died, I found a lot of little treasures like that."

•

At the time of his death, Colesberry was a longtime resident of both New York City and Amagansett, NY. To those who knew him in his early life outside of Philadelphia, his successful film career, or any career, was unexpected.

Friends from Germantown High School remembered a talented athlete who did little more than hang with the boys at the corner of Wayne and Tioga.

Outside of a lone loitering arrest and one notable attempted theft of a ceramic cow from the roof of a neighborhood steak house, young Bob didn't get into too much trouble. But, said a relative, "He was around the boys who did."

Jill Porter, a high school friend, recalled that Colesberry's academic career included spots on the varsity baseball and football teams and strict attendance at all four periods of lunch every day.

"He was nice and had this charm to him," she said. "But we all thought he was going absolutely nowhere."

An artillery lieutenant when discharged from the Army in 1968, Colesberry enrolled at Southern Connecticut State College, where, looking for easy courses, he tried drama.

It suited him. Elated, he found his calling and by his junior year had transferred to the Tisch School for the Arts at New York University, graduating in 1974 with a degree in film and television.

After stints as a location manager and first assistant director, he was – by the early 1980s – helping to produce such films as Barry Levinson's *The Natural* and Martin Scorsese's *The King of Comedy*.

In 1985, he worked on Scorsese's critically acclaimed dark comedy *After Hours*, which won the industry's Independent Spirit award and helped resurrect the director's career.

By the late 1980s, Colesberry had become a veteran, hands-on film producer, obsessed with every detail of the projects on which he labored. Passionate about authenticity, he reveled in stories rooted in reality.

Bob, said director Bill Forsyth, had a need "to believe utterly in what he was doing. But when that belief was intact, his dedication and loyalty were givens, always there."

His pre-production rituals were famous among those who worked with him. He filled reams of yellow legal pads, writing down every thought and phone call to be made, down to the smallest detail, creating shot lists and storyboards for every scene days ahead of time.

Colesberry would scout locations for filming with a discerning eye, firing off hundreds of still photos from a small digital camera that he carried everywhere. He was fearless in search of a shot, wandering with equal glee through Moroccan hillsides or Baltimore ghettos, camera in hand.

And he apparently saved everything. Friends remember crate upon crate of legal notepads, still photos, shot lists, casting tapes and directors' reels that would follow Colesberry from one project to the next.

Thorson has crew jackets, T-shirts and other mementos from more than two decades of work: State Police buttons from *Mississippi Burning*; a 1920s radio from *Billy Bathgate*; a crew photo from 1979's *Fame*.

Once, having left a favored crew sweatshirt from *The Corner* on a dangerous Baltimore corner, Bob went back alone, after wrap, to retrieve it.

"It was one of those crew shirts you get on film projects," said Thorson, who couldn't recall if Bob ever found it or not. "He kept those tokens because he was proud of the projects."

In addition to overseeing all of the visual aspects of *The Wire*, he also participated in story meetings with the writers.

And, at the urging of Simon and Noble, Colesberry directed the last episode of the show's second season and was slated to direct the first hour of the third season at the time of his death.

In May 2004, he posthumously received a second Peabody Award for his work on the show.

"He had spent a lifetime in film learning every aspect of his craft, in every way preparing himself to direct," recalled Simon. "When he finally did so, it all came to him naturally and beautifully. He understood everything about the process of telling a story visually, and he was utterly committed to that process."

•

As the team that Colesberry helped to assemble began meeting in Baltimore in March 2004 to begin filming the third season of *The Wire*, some of those who had worked closely with Bob gathered to talk about the man and his work.

They included Ed Bianchi, who directed three episodes of the drama; Uta Briesewitz, the show's director of photography in the first three seasons; and the late film editor Geraldine Peroni, who worked on the pilot episode of the series.

Joy Kecken, a director, independent filmmaker and writer for *The Wire*, served as a moderator.

JOY KECKEN: From a writer's point of view, I always thought it was amazing in some of the production meetings how Bob would come up with a certain look or how to complete the story without so much exposition.

ED BIANCHI: In my first tone meeting, the very first thing I was asking for was a crane. To do a crane shot. Bob got [the idea] immediately.

GERALDINE PERONI: Because he had a strong sense of story, he probably understood that the crane shot was part of telling the story rather than just being a fancy gimmick.

EB: Absolutely.

UTA BRIESEWITZ: I have a memory on that crane thing. Because Bob came up to me and said, "I saw the director Eddie Bianchi. The opening shot, he wants to do this really elaborate crane shot."

And I was thinking to myself – a crane shot, he's in trouble, he's not going to get a crane. Then Bob continues, in detail, completely describing the shot to me. I saw his fascination with it and how excited he was about you bringing this idea to the table. And halfway through it, I already knew it, he has his crane.

(*Laughter all around*)

JK: When I came here a few weeks ago for a story meeting, I was dreading having to pass Bob's office. I didn't want to see that it was empty.

UB: Wherever we were for the pilot or very often when you change locations, you walk into offices and they all look the same. They just have a computer or whatever, there's not much going on. You walk into Bob's office and it's completely . . .

EB: . . . dressed.

(*Laughter from all*)

UB: With all his little photos and his posters and his baseball stuff like he's been there for years. I always liked to come to his office.

He had little memorabilia from all the films that he'd done. And it always felt like home. It was like, "This is where production is now, this is my home, and this is where I love to be."

JK: How did Bob influence *The Wire*?

EB: The first day I met Bob he was with [David] Simon and I said it had the feeling of a movie. And David said, that's Bob. Bob wanted to approach it like it was a film rather than episodic television, and that always was a great jumping-off point for me because that's exciting.

UB: The whole aspect of making it look like a feature was mentioned from the very beginning. He always wanted to push me to make it look different or push the envelope a little bit.

That was very important to him as well – to move the camera. And then playing depth, foreground, middle ground, background, or longer lenses. For instance, the scene where D'Angelo explains how to play chess to Bodie and Poot. We started putting the camera on the dolly there as well and playing the long lens.

JK: It was great that he was willing to change the style midway through.

UB: I felt the show kept improving because Bob kept encouraging people at what they do and really encouraging them to put their talent into the show.

(*To Bianchi*) I remember you were the one to introduce music when Avon came to the projects when we did the slow-mo.

EB: We thought in editing that if we put the disc jockey a little bit ahead of the movement, we thought it would justify the sound, the music. But when they got into the editing room, Bob liked it and went with that despite it going against some things that they may have talked about before.

GP: Right. Because it almost worked as score. And there was the line that everything was source.

UB: And of course, I came back to Bob and said, "Can't we introduce music a little bit more?"

But we stuck to what our format was, which is a good thing. It's a most powerful tool to be as close to reality as possible.

JK: Bob was a producer as far back as [1988's] *Mississippi Burning*, but he was really a director at heart.

GP: It was the first season. I was living in Fells Point and I was driving home one evening. And I saw the crew trucks and everything and I got out and it turns out it was the second unit. It was the first time I saw Bob in his role as second unit director.

And he just looked like he was so happy to be there and to be directing. It was so apparent at that moment that he wanted to be out there doing that. In the editing room, we would get in tons and tons of footage because he would be so prepared and he would get so many angles.

When it came time for him to actually direct a whole episode, we were wondering how he was going to manage to get everything into the short amount of time, and he was prepared for that, too.

UB: I cannot agree more with you. When Bob directed the last episode, I've never seen him that happy. It just showed the passion he had. And also when I talked to Karen [Thorson] even before Bob passed away, I said you should have seen him, he was so happy.

And the whole crew was affected by it. We had a really, really fun, uplifting mood even though it was the last episode.

EB: In a way, I believed he used that second unit directing to prepare him for being a director on that last show.

GP: Oh, yeah.

EB: I thought he did a wonderful job. He was picking up, which I thought was really nice, these visual themes from the first episode, tying up everything that was started then, but the way he approached it visually, I thought – wow.

See, there's something that's very sophisticated. Certainly not a first-time-director kind of thing.

GP: [The episode] really turned out great. When David [Simon] and Nina [Noble] came up for the director's-cut screening, everyone was so excited because it really felt like a feature. And that was what he wanted and he accomplished that.

UB: I asked [Bob], "Why did you only start now? You should have done it years ago." He said to me, "I waited for 30 years to do that and I learned from the best."

So I think he was always the silent student behind all the famous directors that he worked with.

JK: He worked with Alan Parker . . .

UB: . . . Martin Scorsese . . .

JK: Let's talk about him as an actor.
  (*Laughter all around*)

EB: He got better the second year.
  (*More laughter*)

UB: Bob had a great sense of humor. He had very good style personally. He appreciated beautiful things. And he always dressed modern. The first time I saw him [as Ray Cole] I couldn't believe that he voluntarily dressed in these awful, nerdy clothes.

I was really impressed that he didn't protest, that he didn't say this is my time on the camera and I want to at least look as good as I look in real life, if not even better. So he totally took that part and we were poking fun at him. I just loved him for that already. But he was very often very nervous.

GP: He really was vulnerable there in front of the crew. So in a way it was really great that he was willing to allow the crew to see him in that way. I thought it was really interesting that he was willing to do that.

One of the things that was also interesting was how he liked to tell stories, but he never told stories where he turned out to be the hero.

But little by little, you'd find out these amazing things about him. Like at some point I found out he used to hang out at the Factory with Andy Warhol and all those guys. You'd get these little glimmers of his past that he would never just brag. He never bragged. He was very modest about all the people he worked with, which was very impressive.

UB: I think he wanted to be more part of the crew with everybody else than being the executive producer who would sit off by himself. You would see it when we would go out for a drink and Bob would come along.

I was sometimes too tired to do things, and I would hear the next day how Bob danced all night. It sounds so silly – like he was one of us, but he was really the glue to this whole crew.

EB: He came up that way. Bob came up as a crewmember, as an assistant director. That's who his friends were on movies. It's nice to keep though. A lot of people don't keep that part of themselves.

GP: People are very willing to shed it.

EB: He told his friend, his best friend, I don't recall his name, he came up to me at Bob's memorial. And he said Bob said I was still enthusiastic.

And I think that's what Bob was – still enthusiastic. He could have said that about himself. He was enthusiastic about his work and enthusiastic about the whole project. I think you kind of have to have an enthusiasm in order to dedicate yourself the way he dedicated himself to a project.

GP: It was definitely not a job.

UB: He was such a source of inspiration and energy. He will just be terribly, terribly missed. I can't even imagine how it's going to be not having him behind the monitor – a constant force and source of inspiration.

It's a big hole that can't really be closed.

A SCENE THAT WILL NEVER MAKE THE BONUS DISC

As serious an intellectual as they come – a brooding writer called "The Angriest Man in Television" in a cover story by the *Atlantic Monthly* – David Simon likes to fancy himself a prankster.

Simon routinely hid all of Bob Colesberry's New York Yankees memorabilia. He glued everything to director Clark Johnson's desk, creating a disorderly still life.

A year or so before *The Wire* went into production, Simon and I waited for fellow writer Bill Zorzi to join us for breakfast at the Blue Moon Café on Aliceanna Street in Fells Point. While waiting, Simon decided we should completely ignore Zorzi when he arrived, go on talking to one another as if Bill did not exist.

We did, to which Zorzi replied: "You assholes."

And then we ignored him for another two minutes.

When the "Backwash" episode in Season Two called for a practical joke to be played on Ziggy in retaliation for the goof having downloaded photos of his cock on another longshoreman's computer, Simon rejected all ideas about itching powder, laxatives and hair removing creams.

"We've seen enough of Ziggy jumping around," he said and set to write a scene in which the "legend of the docks" receives a letter from a law firm claiming he'd knocked up a woman who'd danced the cha-cha – at *least* once – with every guy in the neighborhood.

When his cousin Nicky suggests he call the number listed in the letter, a cell phone rings across the bar: it's Maui, the stevedore on whose computer Ziggy had placed a photo of "Pretty Boy."

All the while, "Love Child" by the Supremes plays over and over on the Clement Street Bar jukebox.

"He got ya, Zig," laughs Nick.

But Simon claims he never got anybody better than he got Dominic West and Wendell Pierce and the rest of the cast and crew of the show over the 2007 Labor Day weekend on the next-to-last day of filming five seasons of *The Wire*.

On that day, which was already looking to be an 18-hour marathon, one last script insert was delivered to the set. And this is what it said.

```
INT. INTERROGATION ROOM #1/HOMICIDE UNIT - NIGHT
BUNK, MCNULTY sit, worried. A long beat of frustrated
silence before MCNULTY leans back in his chair,speaks.
```

> MCNULTY
> If they were going to do me, I'd be done already.

> BUNK
> Now, later. They're gonna do you.

> MCNULTY
> I'm not so sure.

> BUNK
> You really think we need to discuss this some more? Whatever's gonna happen is gonna happen.

                              MCNULTY
                         What are you saying?

                               BUNK
              I'm not sure this conversation is going anywhere, Jimmy.

                    MCNULTY thinks on this, nods.

                               BUNK
        I'm sayin' this like that song by whatshersame, you know? Whatever the
                       fuck is gonna be is gonna be.

                              MCNULTY
                             Doris Day.

                               BUNK
                             Say what?

                              MCNULTY
                       Doris Day. Que sera, sera?

                               BUNK
                 The fuck are you going on about, motherfucker?

                              MCNULTY
            That's the song. "Que Sera, Sera", by Doris Day. Whatever will be,
                              will be.

                               BUNK
               The shit that's clogged up in your fuckin' head. Amazing.

                              MCNULTY
            You brought up the song, bitch. I'm here trying to figure out whether or
              not I'm gonna get done and you're talking in gay-ass clichés.

                               BUNK
                     You ain't goin' to get done.

                              MCNULTY
                         How do you know?

BUNK
How do I know?

MCNULTY
Yeah. Which god came down to Baltimore and gave you the power to see the motherfuckin' future. This is my life on the line here.

BUNK
Calm the fuck down.

MCNULTY
How can I?

BUNK
Look, you know the rest of the story.

MCNULTY
I do?

BUNK
Motherfucker, they done moved the whole script. And you read to the end of this shit, right?

MCNULTY
I know what it says so far, but all these fucking revisions. They're up to cherry-colored pages . . .

BUNK
Buff.

MCNULTY
What?

BUNK
Buff pages. Last revision was buff.

MCNULTY
Fuck buff. These pages right here are second white.

BUNK
That's what I'm sayin', Jimmy, we're far along in the process here.

MCNULTY
But they could still revise it more. Like this scene here . . .

BUNK
They ain't gonna shoot this bitch.

MCNULTY
You sure?

BUNK
Motherfucker, they lookin' at a seven-and-a-half-page day tomorrow
already. Simon tries to add this shit to that sked and the crew will bank
his white ass.

MCNULTY
I dunno. I think that cocksucker has been asking for impossible shit so
long, he just figures . . .

BUNK
He is a motherfucker, but, Jimmy, this one would go too far.

MCNULTY
So we're done?

BUNK
Done. These pages ain't gonna actually get shot, Jimmy.

MCNULTY
So we're just talking here.

BUNK
Talkin' shit about ourselves for ourselves. We a drunkass pair of meta-
motherfuckers right now.

MCNULTY
I love the way you say shit like that.

BUNK
Well, it's the script.

MCNULTY
But you make the shit sound good.

BUNK
I do.

MCNULTY
Profane, but poetic.

BUNK
Yeah, fuck.

MCNULTY
Motherfuck.

BUNK
Fuck me.

MCNULTY
Fuck fuck fuckity fuck fuck.

BUNK
Aw fuck.

MCNULTY
Yeah. Fuck, yeah.

On MCNULTY and BUNK, nodding in fucking affirmation
of just how fucking good The Wire crew is, just how
fucking grateful the writers are, how there is not
- we repeat, not - another scene remaining that we
could ask you to shoot,

FADE TO:

THE END

Appendix I
GLOSSARY

GLOSSARY

24-HOUR REPORT, or 24: Police report summarizing a major incident, prepared within the first 24 hours following the incident.

A-MATTER: Background or history of event/person/story being written about. In the pre-computer era of "hot-metal" typesetting, "A-matter" was often waiting in the composing room galley trays for a reporter to file the latest information for the top of the story.

A.M.E.: Assistant medical examiner.

APB: All points bulletin.

A.S.A.: Assistant state attorney, a city prosecutor.

AUSA: Assistant United States attorney, a federal prosecutor.

A TASTE: Slang term meaning a beer or drink or a hit of dope.

AIN'T UP: Not buying or using drugs.

ATTRIBUTION: Identification of source in reported information, as in: "Hamsterdam seemed like a good idea at the time," said Howard "Bunny" Colvin.

B OF I: Bureau of Identification, the unit that produces mug shots and other criminal intelligence material.

B&E: Breaking and entering.

BABY BOOKING: Juvenile intake unit for offenders under the age of majority.

BASER: A person who cuts cocaine in preparation for distribution.

BAWLMER: How many locals pronounce Baltimore.

BENNIES: Benefits.

BLOW THE BOX: Answering a question during a polygraph test in a way that causes the needle to soar, indicating a falsehood.

BODYMORE, MURDERLAND: Slang terms for Baltimore, Maryland, illustrating its high murder rate.

BPI: Baltimore Police Index. The city police computer.

BUG: A concealed microphone. Not to be confused with The Bug, which is AIDS, or Michael Lee's little brother, "Bug."

BULK CARGO: Shipping term for cargo that is stored in bulk in a ship's hold and does not utilize containers. At one time, almost all cargo was bulk; container technology has made it a relative rarity.

BUMP: Battle or fight.

BURNER: Pre-paid disposable cell phone.

BURNT: Cheated; short end of the stick; or in the case of sexual activity, given a dose of a venereal disease.

BUST A CAP: To fire a weapon.

BUYOUT: Corporate purchase of the remainder of a worker's employment, severing relationship with employee.

BYLINE: Name of reporter who wrote a newspaper story, appearing below the headline and before the text.

CI: Confidential informant.

CID: Criminal Investigation Division.

CAN: Slang term for a shipping container that can be detached from the chassis of a truck for loading onto a vessel, a railcar, or stacked in a container depot. Also known as a box.

CANVASS: Investigative interviews with residents and others in a particular geographic area.

CAP: Bullet; or, to shoot someone, you "put a cap in his ass".

CARRY WATER: To perform a duty, often unpleasant, for someone who would normally do it for themselves. At times, the work of a flunky.

CAUGHT THE CASE: When a police detective is assigned to investigate a crime/case.

CENTER PIECE: Feature story, illustrated by at least one large photograph, in the center of the front page of a section of a newspaper.

CHANNEL 3: The car-to-car frequency used by individual police units.

CHECKERS: Dockworkers who take an actual count of the goods (number of boxes, drums, bundles, pipes, etc.) versus the amount listed on the ship's manifest. Members of the longshoremen's checkers local will also note shortages, overages, or damage.

CITYWIDE: The main radio band for city police. All felony calls and announcements are broadcast on citywide.

CLEARANCE: A solved case. The clearance rate is the percentage of those crimes solved against the total reported.

CLOCKING: Dealing drugs.

CLUSTER-FUCK: A term of military origin used to describe a hopelessly screwed-up situation.

COLD PATCH TRUCK: City public works truck used to fix potholes.

CONTAINER: A truck trailer body that can be detached from the chassis for loading onto a vessel, a railcar, or stacked in a container depot. Also known as a can or box.

CONTRIB LINE: Short for contribution line, which lists writers who contributed material to the work of another reporter.

COOK THE BOOKS: To falsify information, usually statistics. Synonymous with "juke the stats."

CREW MEMBER: Someone belonging to a drug organization.

CUR: A dog who turns his head in a fight.

CUT HOUSE: Where a drug crew dilutes and packages product.

D WARD: Hospital detox.

DEU: Drug Enforcement Unit. The district-level drug squads in the nine Baltimore police districts. The Western DEU, for example, is the drug unit in the Western District.

DNR: Dialed-number recorder used to intercept the telephone numbers called from a phone and, if the caller ID is installed, to record incoming numbers. A preliminary step to any wiretap.

DSS: Department of Social Services.

DAP: Handshake between known associates that usually involves both hands being closed in a fist and then hit together, either knuckle to knuckle or bottom of hand to the top of the other person's hand.

DEPUTY OPS: The deputy commissioner of operations, the No. 2 man in the Baltimore police department, under the commissioner.

DETAIL: Team of law enforcement personnel assigned to a specific case.

DISTRICT: A police precinct in Baltimore. There are nine: the Central District, which encompasses downtown, and eight others named for compass directions surrounding the Central: Southern, Southwestern, Western, Northwestern, and so forth. Each district is commanded by a police major. The districts are home to the patrol force, small investigative contingents, and drug squads. The greater share of the Baltimore department's investigative capacity works out of police headquarters downtown.

DROP A DIME: To snitch on someone, to give up information to authorities.

DROPPED: Slang for someone being shot.

DUNKER: An easily solved case.

DUTY JUDGE: The judge on duty after hours, who can sign search or arrest warrants for detectives after court is closed.

DUTY OFFICER: The night commander for the police commander, appointed on a rotating schedule from the ranking commanders.

DWI: Driving While Intoxicated.

ECU: Evidence Control Unit.

ENFORCER: A gunman for a drug crew; a soldier, in street parlance.

EXHAUSTION: Investigative term. A legal requirement that the police prove that they have "exhausted" all other investigative strategies in a case, so that they are justified in requesting electronic intercepts.

EYEFUCK: A dirty look.

FIEND: Drug addict.

FIN: Five-dollar bill.

FIVE-O: An ancient slang term for police.

FLEX SQUAD: An extra squad of district plainclothesmen that can be used to target particular high-crime areas tactically.

FLIP: To cooperate with authorities and give evidence against criminal associates or superiors.

FLOATER: Dead body found in water.

GELCAP: A single dose of heroin, packaged in a pharmaceutical gelcap.

GLOCK: A make of semi-automatic weapon used by Baltimore police.

GO TO GROUND: When someone in flight stops running from police and hides.

G-PACK: One thousand vials of cocaine, prepackaged for sale.

GUMP: Nerd and/or wimp, from the movie *Forrest Gump*.

H-FILES: Homicide files.

HAND-TO-HAND: When an undercover narcotics officer buys drugs directly from a suspect.

HER-RON: Heroin.

HOMES: Term of affection. Homeboy may be grossly clichéd, but its abbreviated version is occasionally offered.

HOME FINAL: Final edition of paper delivered to residential subscribers.

HOOPTIE: Street slang for a knocked-around vehicle.

HOPPERS: Young kids, juveniles.

HOT BOX: A shipping container that is supposed to be off-loaded from a ship directly to a truck, rather than stored on the docks.

HOURS: Time working on a job or assignment.

HOUSECAT: Slang police term for an officer who works in the office, rather than on the street.

HUMBLE: An arrest based on weak or nonexistent evidence, such as disorderly conduct or loitering, used by street officers to humble an argumentative or provocative civilian.

I.I.D.: Internal Investigations Division. Investigates possible crimes/infractions involving police personnel.

IBS: *The Wire*'s fictional union, the International Brotherhood of Stevedores.

IN STIR: In prison.

IN THE WIND: Missing, lost, running from the law.

INDEPENDENCE CARD: State of Maryland "Electronic Benefits Transfer" (EBT). A debit card uploaded with food stamps and/or cash.

JOHN BLAZE: A fire, wild, strong.

JOHN DOE: Police investigation term used to describe an unidentified male dead body. An unidentified female is a Jane Doe.

JUVENILE INTAKE: Where juvenile criminals are taken after arrest to be processed for detention.

KGA: Code for the dispatcher on police radio calls.

KEL-LITE: A two-foot-long, metal-encased flashlight that can be used as a nightstick.

KEY: Kilogram of drugs.

LATENTS: Fingerprints found as evidence.

LAKE TROUT: Baltimore term for fried, breaded white fish, served on plain white bread with tartar sauce and hot sauce.

LAY IN THE CUT: To hide from a situation, not get involved.

LIZARD: Lesbian.

LOCK IN: To bring a witness before a grand jury, thereby locking in his testimony before he has a chance to reconsider and deny any knowledge of a crime.

LOOKOUT: Someone who works for the dealers, keeping an eye out for the police.

MANIFEST: A written document, signed by the captain of a ship, that lists the individual shipments constituting the ship's cargo.

MARYLAND SHIELD LAW: Statute protecting a reporter's privilege to protect sources.

MOPE: An ordinary street character, possibly guilty of crimes and possibly not, but certainly not a taxpayer.

MOUNT UP: Get your guns and get ready.

MSA: Maryland School Assessment. Standardized tests for reading, math and science administered in grades three through eight.

MULE: A drug courier who brings narcotics interstate.

MUSCLE: Those members of a drug crew responsible for enforcement and soldiering.

NADDIS: DEA's Narcotics and Dangerous Drugs Information System.

NCIC: The FBI's National Crime Information Center.

NAGRA: A wearable concealed recording device, now out of date.

No. 1: Police term used to describe a black or dark-skinned person.

No. 2: Police term used to describe a white or light-skinned person.

OIC: Officer in charge, either of a sector, a shift, or a unit.

OFF THE HOOK: Wild, crazed, out of control.

OFF-SITE: An office used to house a police detail that is apart from the regular police districts and established unit offices. Usually used for a single, complex case, such as a wiretap probe.

ON PAPER: On parole or probation. Not to be confused with having paper on you, which means you are wanted on an outstanding warrant.

ON THE SHELF: Desk work. Not working the beat.

ON THE WING: In flight from police, a fugitive.

ONE AND ONE: A single bag of heroin and a single vial of cocaine, suitable for mixing as a speedball, or an injected combination of both drugs.

ONE-PARTY CONSENT: Law regarding the recording of phone conversations in which only one party needs to give consent for the taping to be legal.

OUTTIE 5000: Exit phrase similar to "later."

PACECO: One of the tall cranes at the Baltimore port, named for its manufacturer.

PACKAGE: Bulk weight of drugs used to refresh a dealer's supply, or what a junkie calls his or her purchase from a dealer. However, saying someone has "the package" can also mean he has contracted HIV.

PAY LAWYER: Privately hired attorney.

PJs: The projects.

PLAYED: Taken for a fool.

PLAYER: One involved in the drug trade, or in any illegimate activity.

POINTS ON THE PACKAGE: Percentage of profits on sale of illegal drugs.

POLICE RADIO CODES:

> **10-1:** Communications check.
>
> **10-13 or SIGNAL 13:** Officer needs assistance.
>
> **10-2:** Loud and clear.
>
> **10-20:** Location. Also known in slang as simply a 20.
>
> **10-29:** Record check.
>
> **10-4:** Affirmative.
>
> **10-5:** Failed to acknowledge.
>
> **10-7:** Not available/out of service. Sometimes used by police to describe someone who is dead.
>
> **10-8:** Back in service.

POPO: Police.

PRO FORMA: Court rulings intended to expedite the cluttered judicial system.

PRODUCT: Drugs.

PUZZLE PALACE: Derogatory term for Baltimore City public school headquarters on North Avenue.

RAISE UP: As a lookout, to warn a drug crew of approaching police or stickup crews. Also, to provoke or confront someone.

RED BALL: An important, high-profile, or politically charged case.

RE-UP: Replenishment of drug supply to slingers, which is kept in the stash house.

REACT QUOTES: Quotes from various sources in response to a breaking news story.

READ OUTS: Police department info from recent crime reports.

ROLL SOMEONE UP: Impel a suspect to implicate a superior and cooperate in the prosecution of that superior.

ROLLER: Or harness roller. A uniformed patrol officer in a radio car.

RO-RO: Roll on/roll off. An ocean-cargo service using a vessel with ramps that allows wheeled vehicles to be loaded and unloaded without using cranes.

RUNNERS: Low-level workers, often juveniles, in the drug trade who retrieve the drugs once the customer has paid.

SECTOR: A patrol area under the command of a sergeant. There are three or four sectors in every Baltimore police district.

SERVE UP: To murder.

SHEET: Arrest history.

SHITBIRD: A negative term similar, but not quite as harsh, to calling someone an asshole.

SHOOTING GALLERY: Abandoned building where fiends go to shoot up or smoke crack.

SHORTY: Attractive female or young person of either sex. Alternatively, a half-pint of liquor.

SIGNIFYING: Street slang for hanging out, bearing witness, taking stock of a situation, or, more aggressively, presenting oneself as having some authority or right to be.

SKY OR SKY UP: Flee.

SLINGER: Low- to mid-level worker in the drug trade who sells drugs on the corner. Ranked above a runner, as he is allowed to handle drugs.

SLINGING: Dealing drugs.

SOLDIER: A rank-and-file player in the drug trade, and, more particularly, one capable of enforcement or warfare.

SPEEDBALL: An intravenous injection of both heroin and cocaine.

STASH HOUSE: The house where a dealer's drug supply is kept.

STEP ON IT: Cut drugs.

STEVEDORES: Companies provide equipment and hire workers to transfer cargo between ships and docks. Laborers hired by these firms are called stevedores or longshoremen.

STINGER: A police report that is bounced back because of clerical or technical problems.

STREET SWEEPS: A quick area raid and round-up of suspicious characters, loiterers, drug dealers, etc. by police.

SUCTION: Influence or power.

TAC: Short for tactical, which includes a variety of specialized police units, but is often used to refer to the heavily armored quick-response-team officers used on raids and in high-risk situations.

TAKE DOORS: Hit locations with search-and-seizure warrants.

TAP OUT: To run low on the current supply of narcotics.

TESTER: Free drug samples given to fiends to advertise the product.

THE BOARD: The black-and-red-lettered caseboard used in the homicide unit.

THE BOX: The police interrogation room.

THE BUG: The AIDS virus.

THE CUT: The House of Corrections in Jessup, south of Baltimore.

THE GAME: The drug trade.

THE HALL: City Hall.

THE OUT: In an interrogation, the excuse offered to a suspect that convinces him to admit guilt, albeit in such a way that the suspect believes his guilt is mitigated.

THE PIT: Slang term for the courtyard in the low-rise projects in West Baltimore where D'Angelo Barksdale was consigned.

THE POINT: Locust Point, in South Baltimore, home to many Polish stevedores and increasingly a yuppie haven.

THE ROTATION: The process by which homicide detectives catch murders, are given a basic amount of time to work those murders, and then must become available again for fresh cases.

THE VACANTS: Abandoned Baltimore rowhouses.

TIME OUT: What lookouts shout to alert a drug crew that the police or a stick-up crew has arrived.

TITLE III: Legal term for a federally sanctioned wiretap.

TOUT: A street-level slinger who announces what drugs are available and attracts customers.

TRIAL BALLOON: Information or idea sent out in order to observe reaction.

VIAL: The basic unit of street-sold cocaine, named for the small plastic, perfume-sample vials used as packaging. The vials have small, colored plastic tops, hence such brand names as Red Tops or Yellow Tops.

WALK AROUND MONEY: Money given to campaign workers on the street to get out the vote just before or on election day.

WALKING FOOT: Walking a beat as a foot patrolman.

WE BRACIN' UP: Getting ready to fight; getting guns and weapons.

WHIP: A nice vehicle.

WHISTLE: Handgun.

WHODUNIT: A hard-to-solve murder. The opposite of a dunker.

WIRE: A wiretap, or a concealed recording device on a person.

WIRED CI: Confidential informant who is wearing a concealed recording device.

WORD IS BOND: Short for "my word is bond," guaranteeing that what is being said is true.

YOU FEEL ME NOW?: Get it? Understand?

Appendix II
CAST & CREW

SEASON ONE CAST

DET. JAMES "JIMMY" MCNULTY .... Dominic West
DET. SHAKIMA "KIMA" GREGGS .... Sonja Sohn
LT. CEDRIC DANIELS .... Lance Reddick
DET. WILLIAM "BUNK" MORELAND .... Wendell Pierce
DET. THOMAS R. "HERC" HAUK .... Domenick Lombardozzi
DET. ELLIS CARVER .... Seth Gilliam
DET. LESTER FREAMON .... Clarke Peters
A.S.A. RHONDA PEARLMAN .... Deirdre Lovejoy
DEP. COMMISSIONER ERVIN H. BURRELL .... Frankie R. Faison
MAJ. WILLIAM A. RAWLS .... John Doman
SGT. JAY LANDSMAN .... Delaney Williams
D'ANGELO BARKSDALE .... Larry Gilliard Jr.
AVON BARKSDALE .... Wood Harris
STRINGER BELL... Idris Elba
BODIE .... J. D. Williams
BUBBLES .... Andre Royo
JOHNNY .... Leo Fitzpatrick
WEE-BEY .... Hassan Johnson
WALLACE .... Michael B. Jordan
POOT .... Tray Chaney
STINKUM .... Brandon Price
OMAR .... Michael K. Williams
SHARDENE .... Wendy Grantham
ORLANDO .... Clayton LeBouef
PROPOSITION JOE STEWART .... Robert F. Chew
DET. ROLAND "PREZ" PRYZBYLEWSKI .... Jim True-Frost
JUDGE DANIEL PHELAN .... Peter Gerety
DET. LEANDER SYDNOR .... Corey Parker Robinson
DET. RAY COLE .... Robert F. Colesberry
DET. MICHAEL SANTANGELO .... Michael Salconi
DET. PATRICK MAHONE .... Tom Quinn
DET. AUGUSTUS "AUGIE" POLK .... Nat Benchley
FBI SPECIAL AGENT TERRANCE FITZHUGH .... Doug Olear
MAJ. RAYMOND "RAY" FOERSTER .... Richard De Angelis
ELENA MCNULTY .... Callie Thorne
CHERYL .... Melanie Nicholls-King
MARLA DANIELS .... Maria Broom
BRIANNA BARKSDALE .... Michael Hyatt
DONETTE .... Shamyl Brown
BRANDON .... Michael Kevin Darnall
MICHAEL MCNULTY .... Tony Cordova

SEAN MCNULTY . . . . Eric Ryan
BIRD . . . . Fredro Starr
SAVINO . . . . Christopher J. Clanton
LITTLE MAN . . . . Micaiah Jones
CASSANDRA . . . . Sheena Barksdale
WILLIAM GANT . . . . Larry E. Hull
MAURICE "MAURY" LEVY . . . . Michael Kostroff
STATE SENATOR R. CLAYTON "CLAY" DAVIS. . . . . Isiah Whitlock Jr.
DAY-DAY. . . . . Donnell Rawlings
WALON . . . . Steve Earle
NAKEISHA LYLES . . . . Ingrid Cornell
STERLING . . . . Curtis Montez
A.S.A. ILENE NATHAN . . . . Susan Rome
DET. EDWARD NORRIS . . . . Edward Norris
INTERNAL INVESTIGATIONS DIVISION MAJOR REED . . . . Tony D. Head
A.M.E. RANDALL "DOC" FRAZIER. . . . . Eric Todd Dellums
DET. VERNON HOLLEY . . . . Brian Anthony Wilson
MAJ. STANISLAUS VALCHEK . . . . Al Brown
STATE TROOPER TROY WIGGINS . . . . Neko Parham
FBI SUPERVISOR AMANDA REESE . . . . Benay Berger
A.S.A. TARYN HANSEN . . . . Lucy Newman-Williams
A.U.S.A. NADIVA BRYANT . . . . Toni Lewis

SEASON ONE CREW

PRODUCERS

Executive Producer: Robert F. Colesberry
Executive Producer: David Simon
Producer: Nina K. Noble
Co-Producer: Karen L. Thorson
Assistant to Mr. Colesberry: Eric Morgan
Assistant to Mr. Simon: Amelia Cleary

DIRECTORS

Clark Johnson: Episodes 1, 2, 5
Peter Medak: Episode 3
Clement Virgo: Episodes 4, 12
Ed Bianchi: Episode 6
Joe Chappelle: Episode 7
Gloria Muzio: Episode 8
Milcho Manchevski: Episode 9
Brad Anderson: Episode 10
Steve Shill: Episode 11
Tim Van Patten: Episode 13

WRITING DEPARTMENT

Writer: David Simon (Episodes 1–4, 6, 8, 10, 13)
Writer: Rafael Alvarez (Episode 7)
Writer: Ed Burns (Episode 5)
Writer: Shamit J. Choksey (Episode 9)
Writer: George Pelecanos (Episode 12)
Writer: David H. Melnick (Episode 9)
Writer/Script Coordinator: Joy Lusco (Episode 11)
Writers' Assistant: Norman Knoerlein

PRODUCTION OFFICE

Production Coordinator: Peter Dodge Nichols
Assistant Production Coordinator: Ginny Galloway
Production Secretary: Kim Masimore
Office Production Assistant: Muna Otaru
Office Production Assistant: Tom Rappa

ACCOUNTING

Production Accountant: Marjorie Leder
1st Assistant Accountant: Elizabeth Guste
2nd Assistant Accountant: Kim Garman
Payroll Accountant: Alex Aubrey
Accounting Clerk: Jane Leslie Burka
Accounting Clerk: Ann Christman

ART DEPARTMENT

Production Designer: Vince Peranio
Art Director: Halina Gebarowicz
Art Department Coordinator: Ed Bellafiore

ADs/SET PAs

Assistant UPM: Alison Rosa
1st Assistant Director (Episodes 2, 4, 6, 8, 1 0, 12): Frank Ferro
1st Assistant Director (Episodes 3, 5): Ivan J. Fonseca
1st Assistant Director (Episodes 7, 9, 11, 13): Anthony Hemingway
2nd Assistant Director: Joseph Incaprera
2nd 2nd Assistant Director: Xanthus Valan
2nd Unit 1st Assistant Director: Michele "Shelley" Ziegler
2nd Unit 2nd Assistant Director: Julian Brain
Set Production Assistant: Timothy A. Blockburger
Set Production Assistant: Damond Gordon
Set Production Assistant: Stephanie Lovell
Set Production Assistant: Maureen McEvoy
Set Production Assistant: Melissa Morgan
Set Production Assistant: Shanalyna Palmer
Set Production Assistant: Drew Vandervelde
Set Production Assistant: Bobby Wilhelm

CAMERA

Director of Photography: Uta Briesewitz
Camera Operator: Andy Colvin
1st Assistant Camera: Boots Shelton
2nd Assistant Camera: Tom Schnaidt
Camera Loader: John Hamilton
Camera Intern: Goddey Asemota
B Camera/2nd Unit DP: Peter Mullett
B Camera/2nd Unit DP: Dave Insley
B Camera/2nd Unit DP: Richard Chisolm
B Camera Operator: Tom Loizeaux
B Camera/2nd Unit Camera Assistant: Kurt Parlow
B Camera/2nd Unit Camera Assistant: Doug Kofsky
B Camera/2nd Unit Camera Assistant: Lauren Schaub
Still Photographer: David Lee
Still Photographer: Paul Schiraldi

CASTING

Casting Director: Alexa L. Fogel, C.S.A.
Casting Director (Baltimore): Pat Moran, C.S.A.
Casting Associate (New York) (Episodes 1–5): Mercedes Kelso
Casting Associate (New York) (Episodes 6–12): Janice Wilde
Casting Associate (New York) (Episode 13): Brendan Mason
Casting Associate (Baltimore): John Strawbridge
Extras' Casting Assistant (Baltimore): Shamos Fisher

CATERING

Owner: Philippe Gallichet
Chef: John DeSarno
1st Assistant Caterer: Stephen Toth
2nd Assistant Caterer: Joshua Sayyeau

CLEARANCES

WB Clearances: Rebecca Thornell

CONSTRUCTION

Construction Coordinator: Randy G. Herbert
Lead Foreman: Scott Dunn
Details Set Foreman: Scott Pina
Details Set Gang Boss: Ted Lubonovich
Gang Boss: John Weiffenbach
Carpenter: Steve Blake

Carpenter: Joe Bukovsky
Carpenter: Jim Kelley
Carpenter: John Struss
Carpenter: Marc Braun
Carpenter: Bill Catania
Carpenter: Tom Cowen
Carpenter: F. Dale Davis
Carpenter: Tom Martin
Carpenter: Ted Nolan
Carpenter: Wes Goodwin
Carpenter: Ron Napier
Carpenter: Beau Seidel
Carpenter: Dan Yeager
Carpenter: Jim Doherty
Carpenter: Dale Swavely
Carpenter: Chris Southwick
Carpenter: Walter Wright Jr.
Shop Production Assistant: Dawson Nolley

CRAFT SERVICE
Craft Service: Elena Moscatt
Craft Service Assistant: Ellen Sara Popiel
Craft Service Assistant: Dena Cruz

DIALECT COACH
Dialect Coach: BettyAnn Leeseberg-Lange

ELECTRIC
Gaffer: Evans Brown
Best Boy Electric: Ted Ayd
Rigging Gaffer: Frank Caslin
Genny Operator: Jason Hubert
3rd Electric: Mark Hutchings
3rd Electric: Brian Johnson
3rd Electric: Phil Kathrens
3rd Electric: Trey Kistler
Additional Electric: Len Applefeld
Additional Electric: Chris Baker
Additional Electric: Kevin Campbell
Additional Electric: Ezra Picard
Additional Electric: Russ Wicks

FILM ELECTRONICS
Coordinator: Tom Farmer
Assistant: Thomas H. E. Scruggs

GRIP
Key Grip: Joe Kurtz
Best Boy Grip: Dave Wilkins
Grip: John Barber
Grip: Kenneth "Meat" Morton
Grip: Paul Thomas
Additional Grip: Chad E. Williams

HAIR
Key Hair: Janice Kinigopoulos
Hairstylist: Wyatt Belton
Hairstylist: Champaigne Lawrence

LOCATIONS
Location Manager: Adam Laws
Location Manager: Charley Armstrong
Assistant Location Manager: Chris Barber
Location Assistant: Doug Jones

MAKEUP
Key Makeup: Debi Young
Makeup Artist: Sandra Linn Koepper
Makeup Artist: Gina Wilgis Bateman

POST PRODUCTION
Post Production Supervisor: Leslie Jacobowitz
Post Production Coordinator (Baltimore)*:* Brian Cooper
Post Production Coordinator (New York)*:* Peter Phillips
Editor (Episodes 1, 2, 5, 8, 11): Geraldine Peroni
Editor (Episodes 3, 6, 9, 12): Thom Zimny
Editor (Episodes 4, 7, 10, 13): Kate Sanford
Assistant Editor: Michael Fay
Assistant Editor: Perri Pivovar
Assistant Editor: Carrie Puchkoff
Assistant Editor: Shelby Siegel

PROPS
Prop Master: Mike Sabo
Props Assistant: James McPherson
3rd Props Assistant: Bob Spore
Additional Props: Stephen Kicas

Scenic

Charge Scenic: Keith Weaver
Foreman: Suzanna Glattly
Gangboss: Jennie Bell
Scenic: Anthony Ladd Brennan
Scenic: Rick Crandall
Scenic: Fran Gerlach
Scenic: James Hastings
Scenic: Lucy Pealer
Scenic: Craig Schuman
Scenic: Tracy Shusta

Script Supervisor

Script Supervisor: Christine Moore

Security

Security Supervisor: Perry Blackmon
Assistant Security Supervisor: William "B.J."
   Spencer

Set Dressing

Set Decorator: Bill Cimino
Leadman: John Millard
Assistant Set Decorator/Set Buyer: Rebecca
   Weidner
On Set Dresser: Brook Yeaton
Swing Gang: Patrick Eagan
Swing Gang: Cris Hastings
Swing Gang: Clark Hospelhorn

Sound

Production Sound Mixer: Bruce Litecky
Boom: Lorenzo Millan
Utility: Carol Everson
Utility: Ivan Hawkes

Stunts

Stunt Coordinator (Episodes 2–5): Doug
   Crosby
Stunt Coordinator (Episodes 6–13): Jeff
   Gibson

Teacher

Teacher: On Location Education

Technical Advisor

Technical Advisor: Major Gary D'Addario

Transportation

Transportation Coordinator: Foard Wilgis
Captain: Ronnie Smith
Co-Captain: Tony Raimondo
Driver: Chuck Bauer
Driver: Rick Cochin
Driver: James Hubbard
Driver: Albert Hamilton
Driver: Greg Jacobs
Driver: Michael Luckeroth
Driver: Bob Phillips
Driver: Charles Plantholt
Driver: Steve Pollock
Driver: Frank Matkins
Driver: Sal Raimond
Driver: John Simms
Driver: Gerard Titus
Driver: Doug Walk
Driver: John Watkins
Driver: Jennifer Weiland
Driver: Bob Wilhem Sr.
Driver: Mark Wiesand
Driver: Walter "Pete" Wright
Driver: Wayne Wright
Driver: Bruce Zamzow
Driver: Kenneth Ziegler Jr.

Video

Video Assistant: Alex Applefeld

Wardrobe

Costume Designer: Alonzo Wilson
Costume Supervisor: Mara Majorowicz
Assistant to Costume Designer: Amanda
   Johnson
Key Costumer: Dona Gibson
Set Costumer: Da'Juan T. Prince
Additional Costumer: Annabelle MacNeal

SEASON TWO CAST

OFC. JAMES "JIMMY" MCNULTY .... Dominic West
LT. CEDRIC DANIELS .... Lance Reddick
DET. SHAKIMA "KIMA" GREGGS .... Sonja Sohn
DET. WILLIAM "BUNK" MORELAND .... Wendell Pierce
DET. LESTER FREAMON .... Clarke Peters
DET. THOMAS R. "HERC" HAUK .... Domenick Lombardozzi
SGT. ELLIS CARVER .... Seth Gilliam
DET. ROLAND "PREZ" PRYZBYLEWSKI .... Jim True-Frost
OFC. BEATRICE "BEADIE" RUSSEL .... Amy Ryan
COMMISSIONER ERVIN H. BURRELL .... Frankie R. Faison
COL. WILLIAM A. RAWLS .... John Doman
A.S.A. RHONDA PEARLMAN .... Deirdre Lovejoy
AVON BARKSDALE .... Wood Harris
STRINGER BELL .... Idris Elba
D'ANGELO BARKSDALE .... Larry Gilliard Jr.
OMAR .... Michael K. Williams
FRANK SOBOTKA .... Chris Bauer
NICK .... Pablo Schreiber
ZIGGY .... James Ransone
SPIROS "VONDAS" VONDOPOULOS .... Paul Ben Victor
THE GREEK .... Bill Raymond
BODIE .... J. D. Williams
POOT .... Tray Chaney
BUBBLES .... Andre Royo
JOHNNY .... Leo Fitzpatrick
MAJ. STANISLAUS VALCHEK .... Al Brown
SGT. JAY LANDSMAN .... Delaney Williams
OFC. CLAUDE DIGGINS .... Jeffrey Fugitt
A.M.E. RANDALL "DOC" FRAZIER .... Eric Todd Dellums
BRIANNA BARKSDALE .... Michael Hyatt
CHERYL .... Melanie Nicholls-King
AIMEE .... Kristin Proctor
MARLA DANIELS .... Maria Broom
ELENA MCNULTY .... Callie Thorne
DONETTE .... Shamyl Brown
LOUIS SOBOTKA .... Robert Hogan
JOAN SOBOTKA .... Elisabeth Noone
MICHAEL MCNULTY .... Tony Cordova
SEAN MCNULTY .... Eric Ryan
ASHLEY .... Lauren Godwin
HORSEFACE .... Charley Scalies

JOHNNY FIFTY . . . . Jeffrey Pratt Gordon
OTT . . . . Bus Howard
NATHANIEL "NAT" COXSON . . . . Luray Cooper
LA-LA . . . . Kelvin Davis
DELORES . . . . Jill Redding
LITTLE BIG ROY . . . . Richard Pelzman
NEW CHARLES . . . . Stan Stewart
BIG ROY . . . . Doug Lory
CHESS . . . . J. Valenteen Gregg
MOONSHOT . . . . Harold L. Able Sr.
MAUI . . . . Lance Irwin
BRUCE DIBIAGO . . . . Keith Flippen
RINGO . . . . Jon Garcia
ANDREW KRAWCZYK . . . . Michael Willis
PROPOSITION JOE STEWART . . . . Robert F. Chew
MAURICE "MAURY" LEVY . . . . Michael Kostroff
STATE SENATOR R. CLAYTON "CLAY" DAVIS . . . . Isiah Whitlock Jr.
DANTE . . . . Ernest Waddell
TOSHA . . . . Edwina Findley
KIMMY . . . . Kelli R. Brown
SERGEI "SERGE" MALATOV . . . . Chris Ashworth
GEORGE "DOUBLE–G" GLEKAS . . . . Ted Feldman
ETON . . . . Lev Gorens
ILONA . . . . Gordana Rashovich
SHAMROCK . . . . Richard Burton
COUNTRY . . . . Addison Switzer
PUDDIN . . . . DeRodd Hearns
BROTHER MOUZONE . . . . Michael Potts
MOUZONE'S SECOND . . . . DeAndre McCullough
BUTCHIE . . . . S. Robert Morgan
CHEESE . . . . Method Man
WEE-BEY . . . . Hassan Johnson
CORRECTIONAL OFC. DWIGHT TILGHMAN . . . . Antonio D. Charity
FROG . . . . Gary "D. Reign" Senkus
DIRT . . . . Brandon DiLeonardi
FBI SPECIAL AGENT TERRANCE FITZHUGH . . . . Doug Olear
FBI SQUAD SUPERVISOR AMANDA REESE . . . . Benay Berger
A.S.A. ILENE NATHAN . . . . Susan Rome
JUDGE DANIEL PHELAN . . . . Peter Gerety
DET. EDWARD NORRIS . . . . Edward Norris
DET. VERNON HOLLEY . . . . Brian Anthony Wilson

SEASON TWO CREW

PRODUCERS
Executive Producer: Robert F. Colesberry
Executive Producer: David Simon
Co-Executive Producer: Nina K. Noble
Co-Producer: Karen L. Thorson
Assistant to Mr. Colesberry: Ugboaku Opara
Assistant to Mr. Simon: Amelia Cleary
Assistant to Ms. Noble: Muna Otaru

DIRECTORS
Ed Bianchi: Episodes 14, 15
Elodie Keene: Episodes 16, 17
Steve Shill: Episodes 18, 19
Thomas J. Wright: Episode 20
Daniel Attias: Episode 21
Tim Van Patten: Episode 22
Rob Bailey: Episode 23
Ernest Dickerson: Episode 24
Robert F. Colesberry: Episode 25

WRITING DEPARTMENT
Writer: David Simon
Story Editor: Ed Burns
Story Editor: George Pelecanos
Staff Writer: Rafael Alvarez
Staff Writer: Joy Lusco Kecken
Script Coordinator: Cheri Taylor
Researcher: Norman Knoerlein
Writers' Assistant: Laura A. Schweigman

PRODUCTION OFFICE
Production Supervisor: Marlis Pujol
Assistant Production Coordinator: Ann
  Christman
Production Secretary: Jackie Sawiris
Office Production Assistant: Thomas "Toby"
  Hessenauer
Office Production Assistant: Melissa DeMino

ACCOUNTING
Production Accountant: Peter Tolle
1st Assistant Accountant: Siobhan Hegarty

2nd Assistant Accountant: Kim Garman
Payroll Accountant: Molly Proctor
Accounting Clerk: Renee Fischer

ART DEPARTMENT
Production Designer: Vince Peranio
Art Director: Halina Gebarowicz
Art Department Coordinator: Ed Bellafiore

ADs/SET PAs
*1st Assistant Director (Episodes 14, 15, 18,
  19, 21, 23, 25):* Anthony Hemingway
*1st Assistant Director (Episodes 16, 17, 20,
  22, 24):* Michele "Shelley" Ziegler
Key 2nd Assistant Director: Joe Incaprera
2nd 2nd Assistant Director: Xanthus Valan
2nd Unit 1st Assistant Director: Frank
  Ferro
2nd Unit Key 2nd Assistant Director:
  Alison Rosa
Set Production Assistant: Timothy
  Blockburger
Set Production Assistant: Douglas Jones
Set Production Assistant: Heather Ingegneri
Set Production Assistant: Maureen McEvoy
Set Production Assistant: Brendan Walsh

CAMERA
Director of Photography: Uta Briesewitz
Camera Operator: Tom Schnaidt
1st Assistant Camera: Boots Shelton
2nd Assistant Camera: Kurt Parlow
Loader: Charlie Newberry
2nd Unit Director of Photography: Peter
  Mullett
2nd Unit Director of Photography: David
  Insley
B Camera Operator: Richard Chisolm
B Camera Operator: Thomas Loizeaux
Still Photographer: Larry Riley

CASTING
Casting Director (New York): Alexa L. Fogel, C.S.A.
Casting Director (Baltimore): Pat Moran, C.S.A.
Casting Associate (New York): Heather Baird
Casting Associate (Baltimore): John Strawbridge
Extras' Casting: Shamos Fisher

CATERING
Owner: Philippe Gallichet
Chef: Mike Bowers
1st Assistant Caterer: Michael J. Filosa
2nd Assistant Caterer: W. Griffin Giles

CLEARANCES
WB Clearances: Rebecca Thornell

CONSTRUCTION
Construction Coordinator: Randy G. Herbert
Lead Foreman: Scott Dunn
Gang Boss: John Weiffenbach
Gang Boss: John Struss
Carpenter: Shawn Baron
Carpenter: Jim Doherty
Carpenter: Pat Hendrick
Carpenter: Mike Key
Carpenter: Tom Lombardi
Carpenter: Patrick Pirrone
Carpenter: Garry Snyder
Carpenter: Scott Wallace
Shop Production Assistant: Zack Schwartz

CRAFT SERVICE
Craft Service: Elena Moscatt
Craft Service Assistant: Dena Cruz

DIALECT COACH
Dialect Coach: BettyAnn Leeseberg-Lange

ELECTRIC
Gaffer: Jennifer "Jenna" Perkins
Rigging Gaffer: Frank Caslin
Best Boy Electric: Ted Ayd

Rigging Best Boy: James Brian Johnson
Genny Operator: Jason Hubert
3rd Electric/2nd Unit Gaffer: Mark Hutchings
3rd Electric: Russell Wicks
3rd Electric: Kevin "Vinnie" Campbell
3rd Electric: James Brian Johnson
3rd Electric: Trey Kistler
3rd Electric: Philip Kathrens
3rd Electric: Ezra Picard
Additional Electric: Todd Norton
Additional Electric: Don Aros
Additional Electric: Franz Wise
Additional Electric: Ryan Gallo
Additional Electric: Alex Pacheco

FILM ELECTRONICS
Coordinator: Tom Farmer
Electronics Assistant: Thomas H. E. Scruggs

GRIP
Key Grip: Joe Kurtz
Best Boy Grip: Dave Wilkins
Dolly Grip/2nd Unit Key: Kenneth "Meat" Morton
Grip: John Barber
Grip: Paul William Thomas
Grip: John-Anthony Gargiullo
Additional Grip: William Crest
Additional Grip: John Eboigbe
Additional Grip: Chad Williams

HAIR
Key Hair: Janice Kinigopoulos
Hairstylist: Wyatt Belton
2nd Unit Key Hair: Ardis Cohen
2nd Unit Hairstylist: Lydia Benaim

LOCATIONS
Location Manager: Charley Armstrong
Assistant Location Manager #1: Christopher Roe
Assistant Location Manager #2: Patrick Burns
Location Assistant: Evan Guilfoyle
Location Assistant: Bob Bernard

MAKEUP
Key Makeup: Debi Young
Makeup Artist: Sandra Linn Koepper
2nd Unit Key Makeup: Annabelle MacNeal
2nd Unit Makeup Artist: Lorraine Boushell

MARINE
Marine Coordinator: Christopher S. Wrzosek

MEDIC
Medic: Jeff Johnson

POST PRODUCTION
Post Production Supervisor: Leslie Jacobowitz
Post Production Coordinator (Baltimore)*:*
   Robert Zorella
Post Production Coordinator (New York)*:*
   Daniel Wagner
Music Editor/Music Supervisor: Blake Leyh
Broadcast Scripts: Marc Dworkin
Editor (Episodes 14, 15, 20, 23): Kate Sanford
Editor (Episodes 16, 17, 21, 24): Thom
   Zimny
Editor (Episodes 18, 19): Allyson Johnson
Editor (Episodes 22, 25): Geraldine Peroni
Assistant Editor: Shelby Siegel
Assistant Editor: James Mastracco
Assistant Editor/Baltimore: Shelly
   Westerman
Post Production Production Assistant (New
   York)*:* Zachary MacDonald

PROPS
Prop Master: Mike Sabo
Props Assistant: James McPherson
3rd Props Assistant: Bob Spore
Additional Props Assistant: Alison Haygood

SCENIC
Charge Scenic: Keith Weaver
Foreman: Claire Sharp
Gangboss: Silvija L. Moess
Scenic: Lucy Pealer
Scenic: Craig Schuman
Scenic: Bobby Raber

SCRIPT SUPERVISOR
Script Supervisor: Christine Moore

SECURITY
Director of Security: Perry Blackmon
Assistant Director of Security: William
   "B.J." Spencer

SET DRESSING
Set Decorator: Barbara Haberecht
Leadman: John Millard
Assistant Set Decorator/Set Buyer:
   Dawson Nolley
On Set Dresser: Brook Yeaton
Set Dressing Foreman: Patrick
   Eagan
Swing Gang: Clark Hospelhorn
Swing Gang: Norman Thurston Jr.
Swing Gang: Jaclyn M. Riedel

SOUND
Sound Mixer: Bruce Litecky
Boom: Lorenzo Millan
Utility: Ivan Hawkes

STUNTS
Stunt Coordinator: Jeff Gibson

TEACHER
Teacher: On Location Education

TECHNICAL ADVISOR
Technical Advisor: Major Gary D'Addario

TRANSPORTATION
Transportation Coordinator: Foard Wilgis
Captain: Ronnie Smith
Co-Captain: Tony Raimondo
Driver: Charles Bauer
Driver: Richard B. Cochin
Driver: Donald Davis
Driver: Duane S. Kelly
Driver: Vincent Guariglia Jr.
Driver: Daniel A. Hirsch
Driver: James Hubbard

Driver: Greg Jacobs
Driver: Frank Matkins
Driver: Franklin G. Metts Sr.
Driver: Robert W. Phillips
Driver: Charles B. Plantholt Sr.
Driver: George Moon
Driver: Steve Pollock
Driver: Larry Sinclair
Driver: Steven E. Truckenmiller
Driver: John Watkins
Driver: Jennifer Weiland
Driver: Bart Wright
Driver: Kenny Ziegler Jr.

VIDEO
Video Assistant: Alex Applefeld

WARDROBE
Costume Designer: Alonzo Wilson
Costume Supervisor: Alice Daniels
Costume Supervisor: Carl V. Curnutte III
Costume Supervisor: Mara Majorowicz
Assistant to Costume Designer: Amanda Johnson
Key Costumer: Tamara Wilson
Tailor: Dona Adrian Gibson
Costumer: Linda M. Boyland

SEASON THREE CAST

DET. JAMES "JIMMY" MCNULTY . . . . Dominic West
LT. CEDRIC DANIELS . . . . Lance Reddick
DET. SHAKIMA "KIMA" GREGGS . . . . Sonja Sohn
DET. WILLIAM "BUNK" MORELAND . . . . Wendell Pierce
DET. LESTER FREAMON . . . . Clarke Peters
SGT. ELLIS CARVER . . . . Seth Gilliam
DET. THOMAS R. "HERC" HAUK . . . . Domenick Lombardozzi
DET. ROLAND "PREZ" PRYZBYLEWSKI . . . . Jim True-Frost
MAJ. HOWARD "BUNNY" COLVIN . . . . Robert Wisdom
STRINGER BELL . . . . Idris Elba
AVON BARKSDALE . . . . Wood Harris
BODIE . . . . J. D. Williams
WEE-BEY . . . . Hassan Johnson
POOT . . . . Trey Chaney
PUDDIN . . . . De' Rodd Hearns
OMAR . . . . Michael K. Williams
BUBBLES . . . . Andre Royo
PROPOSITION JOE STEWART . . . . Robert F. Chew
CHEESE . . . . Method Man
MARLO STANFIELD . . . . Jamie Hector
DENNIS "CUTTY" WISE . . . . Chad L. Coleman
A.S.A. RHONDA PEARLMAN . . . . .Deirdre Lovejoy
COUNCILMAN THOMAS "TOMMY" CARCETTI . . . . Aidan Gillen
MAYOR CLARENCE V. ROYCE . . . . Glynn Turman
COUNCILMAN ANTHONY GRAY . . . . Christopher Mann
STATE DEL. ODELL WATKINS . . . . Frederick Strother

STATE SEN. R. CLAYTON "CLAY" DAVIS .... Isiah Whitlock, Jr.

MAURICE "MAURY" LEVY .... Michael Kostroff

THERESA D'AGOSTINO .... Brandy Burre

ANDREW KRAWCZYK .... Michael Willis

COMM. ERVIN H. BURRELL .... Frankie Faison

DEP. COMM. OPS. WILLIAM A. RAWLS .... John Doman

COL. RAYMOND "RAY" FOERSTER .... Richard DeAngelis

MAJ. STANISLAUS VALCHEK .... Al Brown

LT. DENNIS MELLO .... Jay Landsman

SGT. JAY LANDSMAN .... Delaney Williams

DET. LEANDER SYDNOR .... Corey Parker Robinson

DET. EDWARD NORRIS .... Ed Norris

DET. VERNON HOLLEY .... Brian Anthony Wilson

OFC. CAROLINE MASSEY .... Joilet F. Harris

OFC. KENNETH DOZERMAN .... Rick Otto

OFC. MICHAEL SANTANGELO .... Michael Salconi

OFC. ANTHONY COLICCHIO .... Benjamin Busch

OFC. LLOYD "TRUCK" CARRICK .... Ryan Sands

OFC. LAMBERT .... Nakia Dillard

OFC. BAKER .... Derek Horton

OFC. AARON CASTOR .... Lee Everett Cox

CHIEF OF STAFF COLEMAN PARKER .... Cleo Reginald Pizana

EASTERN DISTRICT COMMANDER .... Barnett Lloyd

COMMUNITY RELATIONS SERGEANT .... R. Emery Bright

A.M.E.RANDALL "DOC" FRAZIER .... Erik Todd Dellums

I.I.D. MAJ. BOBBY REED .... Tony D. Head

SPECIAL AGENT TERRANCE FITZHUGH .... Doug Olear

MARLA DANIELS .... Maria Broom

CHERYL .... Melanie Nicholls-King

ELENA MCNULTY .... Callie Thorne

MICHAEL MCNULTY .... Tony Cordova

SEAN MCNULTY .... Eric Ryan

BRIANNA BARKSDALE .... Michael Hyatt

DONETTE .... Shamyl Brown

JENNIFER CARCETTI .... Megan Anderson

CARCETTI'S DAUGHTER .... Nikki Lusk

LITTLE BUNK .... De'Juan Anderson

GRACE .... Dravon James

CUTTY'S GRANDMOTHER .... Sarallen

BUTCHIE .... S. Robert Morgan

BROTHER MOUZONE .... Michael Potts

VINSON .... Norris Davis

DEACON .... Melvin Williams

SHAMROCK .... Richard Burton

COUNTRY .... Addison Switzer

```
SLIM CHARLES ............................................... Anwan Glover
TANK ....................................................... Jonathan Wray
DANTE ..................................................... Ernest Waddell
TOSHA ..................................................... Edwina Findley
KIMMY ..................................................... Kelli R. Brown
JOHNNY .................................................... Leo Fitzpatrick
GERARD (f/k/a SOLDIER #1) ...................................... Mayo Best
PERRY (f/k/a SOLDIER #2) ................................... Perry Blackmon
RICO (f/k/a SOLDIER #3) ....................................... Rico Welchel
SAPPER (f/k/a SOLDIER #4) ................................. Brandan T. Tate
BERNARD ............................................... Melvin Jackson, Jr.
SQUEAK ..................................................... Mia Chambers
CHRIS PARTLOW ......................................... Gbenga Akinnagbe
SNOOP .................................................... Felicia Pearson
FRUIT ..................................................... Brandon Fobbs
JAMAL ................................................... Melvin T. Russell
JUSTIN ..................................................... Justin Burley
BOO .......................................................... Esley Tate
DINGER (f/k/a GANGSTER #1) ........................... Terrence Whitehurst
```

SEASON THREE CREW

PRODUCERS

Executive Producer: David Simon
Executive Producer: Nina K. Noble
Co-Executive Producer: Joe Chappelle
Producer: Edward Burns
Producer: George Pelecanos
Producer: Karen Thorson
Assistant to Mr. Simon: Laura A.
  Schweigman
Assistant to Ms. Noble: Thomas "Toby"
  Hessenauer
Producers/Writers Assistant: Derrick
  Washington

DIRECTORS

Ed Bianchi: Episode 26
Steve Shill: Episode 27
Rob Bailey: Episode 28
Ernest Dickerson: Episodes 29, 37
Dan Attias: Episode 30
Leslie Libman: Episode 31
Tim Van Patten: Episode 32
Agnieszka Holland: Episode 33

Alex Zakrzewski: Episode 34
Christine Moore: Episode 35
Joe Chappelle: Episode 36

WRITING DEPARTMENT

Writer: David Simon
Story Editor/Writer (Episodes 30, 35):
  Edward Burns
Story Editor/Writer (Episodes 29, 36):
  George Pelecanos
Writer (Episode 31): Rafael Alvarez
Writer (Episode 32): Joy Lusco Kecken
Writer (Episode, 27, 33): Richard Price
Writer (Episode 28): Dennis Lehane
Staff Writer: Bill Zorzi
Script Coordinator: Chris Collins
Researcher: Anne Hefley

PRODUCTION OFFICE

Unit Production Manager: Dana Kuznetzkoff
Production Supervisor (Episodes, 26–31):
  Marlis Pujol

Production Supervisor (Episodes, 32–37):
  David Price
Assistant Production Coordinator: Ann
  Christman
Production Secretary: Heather Walker
Office Production Assistant: Allison C. Heaps
Office Production Assistant: Ryan McCracken

ACCOUNTING
Production Accountant: Ira Friedlander
1st Assistant Accountant: David Muscatine
2nd Assistant Accountant: Kim Garman
Payroll Accountant: Molly Proctor
Accounting Clerk: Duane Cipollini

ART DEPARTMENT
Production Designer: Vince Peranio
Art Director: Halina Gebarowicz
Art Department Coordinator: Ed Bellafiore

ADs/SET PAs
1st Assistant Director (Episode 26): Michele
  "Shelley" Ziegler
1st Assistant Director (Episodes 27, 29, 31,
  33, 35, 37): Anthony Hemingway
1st Assistant Director (Episodes 28, 30, 32,
  34, 36): Eric Henriquez
Key 2nd Assistant Director: Joe Incaprera
2nd 2nd Assistant Director: Xanthus Valan
Set Production Assistant: Timothy
  Blockburger
Set Production Assistant: Amanda Faison
Set Production Assistant: Scott Foster
Set Production Assistant: Douglas Jones
Set Production Assistant: Asa McCall
Set Production Assistant: Brendan Walsh

CAMERA
Director of Photography (Episodes 26–29):
  Uta Briesewitz
Director of Photography: Eagle Egilsson
Camera Operator: David Insley
Additional Camera Operator: Tom Schnaidt
Additional Camera Operator: Richard
  Chisolm

1st Assistant Camera: Boots Shelton
2nd Assistant Camera: Ian L. Axilrod
Loader: Joe Wagner
Still Photographer: Paul Schiraldi

CASTING
Casting Director: Alexa L. Fogel, CSA
Casting Director (Baltimore): Pat Moran,
  CSA
*Casting Associate (*New York): Andrew J.
  Fox
Casting Associate (Baltimore): John
  Strawbridge
Extras' Casting: Shamos Fisher
Casting Assistant (Baltimore): Emily
  Eyre

CATERING
Owner: Philippe Gallichet
Chef: Mike Bowers
1st Assistant: Tommy Huston

CLEARANCES
HBO Clearances: Rebecca Thornell

CONSTRUCTION
Construction Coordinator: Randy G.
  Herbert
Lead Foreman: Scott Dunn
Gang Boss: John Weiffenbach
Gang Boss: John Struss
Carpenter: Howard J. Boyer
Carpenter: Michael Key
Carpenter: Thomas F. Lombardi
Carpenter: Garry W. Snyder
Carpenter: Dale V. Swavely
Shop PA: Jesse Rose-Smith

CRAFT SERVICE
Craft Service Key: Elena Moscatt
Craft Service Assistant: Donna Kurtinecz

DIALECT COACH
Dialect Coach: BettyAnn Leeseberg-Lange

ELECTRIC

Gaffer (Episodes 26–29): Jennifer Perkins

Gaffer/2nd Unit DP (Episodes 30–37):
  Evans Brown

Rigging Gaffer: Frank Caslin

Best Boy Electric: Theodore J. Ayd

Rigging Best Boy: Chris Henry

Generator Operator/2nd Unit Gaffer:
  Mark Hutchings

*Dimmer Operator/2nd Unit Gaffer (Episodes
  30–34):* Kevin "Vinnie" Campbell

Generator Operator: Jason Hubert

Set Lighting Technician: Philip E. Kathrens

Set Lighting Technician: Todd Norton

Set Lighting Technician: Wade Tyree

Additional Set Lighting Technician: Russell
  A. Wicks

Additional Set Lighting Technician: Aaron
  Johnson

Additional Set Lighting Technician:
  Jonathan Moore

Additional Set Lighting Technician:
  Jonathan Hilton

Additional Set Lighting Technician: Mike
  Pearce

Additional Set Lighting Technician: Basil
  "Chip" Tydings

Additional Set Lighting Technician: Jason
  Remeikis

Additional Set Lighting Technician: Franz Wise

Additional Set Lighting Technician: Elliot Snell

FILM ELECTRONICS

Coordinator: Tom Farmer

Electronics Assistant: Thomas H.E. Scruggs

GRIP

Key Grip: Joseph Kurtz

Best Boy Grip: David Wilkins

Dolly Grip: Rodney G. French

Grip/2nd Unit Key: John Barber

Grip: Paul William Thomas

Grip: Michael Gearheart

Grip: William Crest

Grip: Michael James Marqua

Grip: Jason Dunn

Grip: John-Anthony Gargiullo

Grip: Julilan Sternthal

HAIR

Key Hair: Janice Kinigopoulos

Hairstylist: Wyatt Belton

LOCATIONS

Location Manager: Charley Armstrong

Assistant Location Manager: Patrick Burn

Assistant Location Manager: Michael
  Faulkner

Locations Scout: Eric Bannat

Locations Assistant: Peter Gottlieb

Locations Assistant: Octavius Lee
  Johnson

MAKEUP

Key Makeup: Debi Young

Makeup Artist: Sandra Linn Koepper

Additional Makeup: Ngozi Olandu

MEDIC

Medic: Jeff Johnson

POST PRODUCTION

Associate Producer: Simon Egleton

Associate Producer: Leslie Jacobowitz

Post Production Coordinator (New York):
  Eliza Tuli Pierson

Post Production PA (New York): Richard Grant

Post Production Coordinator (Baltimore):
  Jonathan Schultz

Editor (Episodes 26, 31, 34, 37): Thom
  Zimny

Editor (Episodes 27, 30, 33): Kate Sanford

Editor (Episodes 28, 32, 35): Michael
  Berenbaum

Editor (Episodes 29, 36): Deborah Moran

Assistant Editor (New York): Mike Fay

Assistant Editor (New York): Shelby Siegel

Assistant Editor (New York, Baltimore): Eric
  Lorenz

Props

Prop Master: Mike Sabo
2nd Props Assistant: Bob Spore
3rd Props Assistant: Teri Garner

Scenic

Charge Scenic: Keith Weaver
Scenic Foreman: Claire Sharp
Gang Boss: Craig Lee Schuman
Scenic Painter: Silvija L. Moess
Scenic Painter: Lucinda E. Pealer
Scenic Painter: Bobby Raber
Scenic Painter: Toad Brennan

Script Supervisor

Script Supervisor: Christine Moore
Script Supervisor (Episodes 34, 35): Jane Burka
Script Supervisor (Episode 11): Seth Copans

Security

Director of Security: Perry Blackmon
Assistant Director of Security: William "B.J." Spencer
Assistant Director of Security: Rico Whelchel
Stage Security Coordinator: Johnny "J.W." Weaver

Set Dressing

Set Decorator: John Millard
Assistant Set Decorator/Set Buyer: Brook Yeaton
On Set Dresser: Lester Poser
Leadman: Clark Hospelhorn
Set Dressing Foreman: Patrick Eagan
Swing Gang: Jim Doherty
Swing Gang: Albert W. Ford Jr.
Swing Gang: Norman Thurston Jr.
Swing Gang: Jaclyn M. Riedel
Swing Gang: Dawson Nolley

Sound

Production Sound Mixer: Bruce Litecky
Boom: Lorenzo Millan
Utility: Ivan Hawkes

Special Effects

Special Effects Coordinator: Conrad F. Brink
Special Effects: Hank S. Atterbury

Stunts

Stunt Coordinator: Jeff Gibson

Technical Advisor

Technical Advisor: Dep. Maj James Rood

Transportation

Transportation Coordinator: Foard Wilgis
Captain: Ronald B. Smith
Co-Captain: Tony Raimondo
Driver: Charles Bauer
Driver: Vincent Guariglia Jr.
Driver: Albert Hamilton
Driver: James Hubbard
Driver: Greg Jacobs
Driver: Frank Matkins
Driver: Robert W. Phillips
Driver: Charles B. Plantholt, Sr.
Driver: Sal Raimond
Driver: Gerald Titus
Driver: Doug Walk
Driver: John Watkins
Driver: Tony Wisnom
Driver: Bart Wright
Production Office Driver: Foard "Joe" Wilgis Jr.

Video

Video Assistant: Alex Applefeld
Assistant Video Assistant: Ben Watson

Wardrobe

Costume Designer: Alonzo Wilson
Assistant Costume Designer: Amanda Johnson
Costume Supervisor: Dona Adrian Gibson
Uniform Specialist: Bebe Ferro
Key Costumer: Mary Anne Creamer
Costumer (Episodes 27, 29, 31, 33, 35, 37): Allecia A. Davis

Costumer (Episodes 26, 28, 30, 32, 34, 36):
  Kim Chewning
Costumer: Molly Cashman
Tailor: Mary F. Miles

2ND UNIT

1st Assistant Director: Jeffrey T. Bernstein
1st Assistant Director: Frank W. Ferro
1st Assistant Director: Christopher Surgent
2nd Assistant Director: Jennifer Truelove

2nd Assistant Director: Kurt Uebersax
1st AC: Kurt Parlow
2nd AC: Tim Hennessy
Key Hair: Ardis F. Cohen
Key Makeup: Annabelle Macneal
Prop Master: Kristina M. Kilpe
Script Supervisor: Janis Hopper Sanders
Sound Mixer: C. Peter Thomas
Boom Operator: Mark Brunner
Video Assistant: Rob Coughlin

SEASON FOUR CAST

OFC. JAMES "JIMMY" MCNULTY	Dominic West
COL. CEDRIC DANIELS	Lance Reddick
DET. SHAKIMA "KIMA" GREGGS	Sonja Sohn
DET. WILLIAM "BUNK" MORELAND	Wendell Pierce
DET. LESTER FREAMON	Clarke Peters
SGT. ELLIS CARVER	Seth Gilliam
SGT. THOMAS R. "HERC" HAUK	Domenick Lombardozzi
ROLAND "PREZ" PRYZBYLEWSKI	Jim True-Frost
DET. LEANDER SYDNOR	Corey Parker Robinson
A.S.A. RHONDA PEARLMAN	Deirdre Lovejoy
HOWARD "BUNNY" COLVIN	Robert Wisdom
OFC. BEATRICE "BEADIE" RUSSELL	Amy Ryan
MAYOR THOMAS "TOMMY" CARCETTI	Aidan Gillen
MAYOR CLARENCE V. ROYCE	Glynn Turman
NORMAN WILSON	Reg E. Cathey
BODIE	J. D. Williams
OMAR	Michael K. Williams
WEE-BEY	Hassan Johnson
BUBBLES	Andre Royo
PROPOSITION JOE STEWART	Robert F. Chew
POOT	Tray Chaney
SPIROS "VONDAS" VONDOPOULOS	Paul Ben Victor
MARLO STANFIELD	Jamie Hector
MICHAEL LEE	Tristan Wilds
NAMOND BRICE	Julito McCullum
RANDY WAGSTAFF	Maestro Harrell
DUQUAN "DUKIE" WEEMS	Jermaine Crawford
DENNIS "CUTTY" WISE	Chad L. Coleman
SLIM CHARLES	Anwan Glover

CHRIS PARTLOW	Gbenga Akinnagbe
SNOOP	Felicia Pearson
CHEESE	Method Man
DEACON	Melvin Williams
BUTCHIE	S. Robert Morgan
KIMMY	Kelli R. Brown
WALON	Steve Earle
COMM. ERVIN H. BURRELL	Frankie Faison
DEP. COMM. OPS. WILLIAM A. RAWLS	John Doman
DEP. COMM. STANISLAUS VALCHEK	Al Brown
COL. RAYMOND FOERSTER	Richard DeAngelis
I.I.D.. MAJ. BOBBY REED	Tony D Head
LT. DENNIS MELLO	Jay Landsman
LT. CHARLES MARIMOW	Boris McGiver
LT. JAMES ASHER	Gene Terinoni
SGT. JAY LANDSMAN	Delaney Williams
DET. VERNON HOLLEY	Brian Anthony Wilson
DET. EDWARD NORRIS	Ed Norris
DET. MICHAEL CRUTCHFIELD	Gregory L. Williams
OFC. MICHAEL SANTANGELO	Michael Salconi
OFC. KENNETH DOZERMAN	Rick Otto
OFC. CAROLINE MASSEY	Joilet F. Harris
OFC. ANTHONY COLICCHIO	Benjamin Busch
OFC. LLOYD "TRUCK" CARRICK	Ryan Sands
OFC. EDDIE WALKER	Jonnie Louis Brown
OFC. BAKER	Derek Horton
OFC. AARON CASTOR	Lee Everett Cox
OFC. BOBBY BROWN	Bobby Brown
A.S.A.. ILENE NATHAN	Susan Rome
PRINCIPAL CLAUDELL WITHERS	Richard Hidlebird
ASSISTANT PRINCIPAL MARCIA DONNELLY	Tootsie Duvall
GRACE SAMPSON	Dravon James
SCHOOL SECRETARY	Tyreeka Freamon
UM. PROFESSOR DAVID PARENTI	Dan Deluca
MS. DUQUETTE (f/k/a TEACHER)	Stacie Davis
BRIANNA BARKSDALE	Michael Hyatt
ELENA MCNULTY	Callie Thorne
CHERYL	Melanie Nicholls-King
JENNIFER CARCETTI	Megan Anderson
DE'LONDA	Sandi McCree
MICHAEL MCNULTY	Tony Cordova
SEAN MCNULTY	Eric Ryan
LITTLE BUNK	DeJuan Anderson
MISS ANNA	Denise Hart
CARCETTI'S DAUGHTER	Nikki Lusk

CARCETTI'S SON . . . . Cole Berger & Dean Berger
ELIJAH . . . . Elijah Grant Johnson
JUDY PRYZBYLEWSKI . . . . Stephanie Burden
STATE DEL. ODELL WATKINS . . . . Frederick Strother
STATE SEN. R. CLAYTON "CLAY" DAVIS . . . . Isiah Whitlock, Jr.
COLEMAN PARKER . . . . Cleo Reginald Pizana
COUNCILMAN ANTHONY GRAY . . . . Christopher Mann
MAURICE "MAURY" LEVY . . . . Michael Kostroff
MARLA DANIELS . . . . Maria Broom
THERESA D'AGOSTINO . . . . Brandy Burre
ANDREW KRAWCZYK . . . . Michael Willis
STATE'S ATTORNEY STEPHEN E. DEMPER . . . . Doug Roberts
JERILEE BENNETT . . . . Karen Vicks
MAYOR'S SECRETARY . . . . Tamieka Chavis
COUNCIL PRESIDENT NERESE CAMPBELL . . . . Marlyne Afflack
BUDGET DIRECTOR . . . . David Goodman
CHIEF OF STAFF . . . . Neal Huff
DONUT . . . . Nathan Corbett
KENARD . . . . Thuliso Dingwall
KEVIN . . . . Tyrell Baker
FRUIT . . . . Brandon Fobbs
TOTE . . . . Terrance Whitehurst
JUSTIN . . . . Justin Burley
SPIDER . . . . Edward Green
MONK (f/k/a LIEUTENANT #1) . . . . Kwame Patterson
SHERROD . . . . Rashid Orange
RENALDO . . . . Ramon Rodriguez
OLD FACE ANDRE . . . . Alfonso Christian Lover
FIEND . . . . Armando Cadogan Jr.
BUG . . . . Keenon Brice

SEASON FOUR CREW

PRODUCERS
Executive Producer: David Simon
Executive Producer: Nina K. Noble
Co-Executive Producer: Joe Chappelle
Producer: Edward Burns
Producer: Karen Thorson
Consulting Producer: Eric Overmyer
Assistant to Mr. Simon: Laura A. Schweigman
Assistant to Ms. Noble: Thomas "Toby"
  Hessenauer
Producers' & Writers' Assistant: Ailene
  Staples

DIRECTORS
Joe Chappelle: Episodes 38, 49
Christine Moore: Episode 39
Seith Mann: Episode 40
Jim McKay: Episode 41
David Platt: Episode 42
Dan Attias: Episode 43
Anthony Hemingway: Episode 44
Agnieszka Holland: Episode 45
Alex Zakrzewski: Episode 46
Ernest Dickerson: Episodes 47, 50
Brad Anderson: Episode 48

WRITING DEPARTMENT

Writer (Episode 46): Kia Corthron
Writer (Episode 41): Dennis Lehane
Writer (Episode 39): David Mills
Writer (Episode 49): George Pelecanos
Writer (Episode 40): Richard Price
Story Editor: Bill Zorzi
Staff Writer/Script Coordinator: Chris Collins
Researcher: Anne Hefley

PRODUCTION OFFICE

Unit Production Manager: Nina K. Noble
Assistant Unit Production Manager: Joseph Incaprera
Production Office Coordinator: Elizabeth J. Nevin
Assistant Production Office Coordinator: Ann Christman
Production Secretary: Ryan Mccracken
Office Production Assistant: Stephen Hartzell
Office Production Assistant: Darrell Davis

ACCOUNTING

Production Accountant: LaDonna Conard
1st Assistant Accountant: Christine Sanders
2nd Assistant Accountant: Emilianos Hurmuziou
Payroll Accountant: Gai Loper
Accounting Clerk: Duane Cipollini

ART DEPARTMENT

Production Designer: Vince Peranio
Art Director: Halina Gebarowicz
Art Department Coordinator: Ed Bellafiore

ADS / SET PAS

1st Assistant Director: Anthony Hemingway
1st Assistant Director: Shelley Ziegler
1st Assistant Director (Episode 43): Frank Ferro
1st Assistant Director (Episode 44): Eric Henriquez
Key 2nd Assistant Director: Xanthus Valan
2nd 2nd Assistant Director: Greg Gilman

Set Production Assistant: Scott Foster
Set Production Assistant: Niko Godfrey
Set Production Assistant: Amanda Faison
Set Production Assistant: Patrick Pfupauena
Set Production Assistant: Dana Lewis
Set Production Assistant: Asa McCall

CAMERA

Director of Photography: Russell Lee Fine
Camera Operator: Tom Schnaidt
1st Assistant Camera: Boots Shelton
2nd Assistant Camera: Ian Axilrod
Loader: Sarah Brandes
2nd Unit Director of Photography/ B Camera Operator: Dave Insley
Still Photographer: Paul S. Schiraldi

CASTING

Casting Director (New York): Alexa L. Fogel, CSA
Casting Associate (New York): Lois J. Drabkin
Casting Director (Baltimore): Pat Moran, CSA
Casting Associate (Baltimore): Megan Lewis
Casting Assistant (Baltimore): Shamos Fisher
Casting Assistant (Baltimore): Sareva Racher
Intern: Lauren Klemm

CATERING

Owner: Philippe Gallichet
Chef: Mike Bowers
1st Assistant: Tommy Huston
2nd Assistant: Christopher Hamilton
2nd Assistant: Shafton Gabb

CLEARANCES

HBO Clearances: Rebecca Thornell

CONSTRUCTION

Construction Corrdinator: Randy G. Herbert
Lead Foreman: Scott Dunn
Gang Boss: John Weiffenbach

Gang Boss: John Struss
Carpenter: Michael Key
Carpenter: Thomas F. Lombardi
Carpenter: Erik Rudolph
Carpenter: Michael Smith
Shop PA: Jesse Rose-Smith

CRAFT SERVICE
Craft Service Key: Elena Moscatt
Craft Service Assistant: Maryann Mack
Craft Service Assistant: R. Bailey Witt

DIALECT/ACTING COACH
Dialect Coach: BettyAnn Leeseberg-Lange
Acting Coach: Robert Chew

ELECTRIC
Gaffer: Evans Brown
Rigging Gaffer: Ted Ayd
Best Boy: Aaron Johnson
Rigging Best Boy: Chris Baker
Generator Operator: Phil Kathrens
Dimmer Operator: Kevin "Vinnie" Campbell
House Electrician: Jason Hubert
Set Lighting Technician: Todd Norton
Set Lighting Technician: Wade Tyree
Set Lighting Technician: Len Applefeld
Set Lighting Technician: Eliott Snell
Additional Set Lighting Technician: Jonathan Hilton

FILM ELECTRONICS
Coordinator: Tom Farmer
Electronics Assistant: Alex Perkins

GRIP
Key Grip: Rodney G. French
Best Boy Grip: David Wilkins
Dolly Grip: Dean Citroni
Key Rigging Grip: Michael Gearhart
Grip: Shawn C.H. Baron
Grip: Michael "MJ" Marqua
Grip: John C. Barber
Additional Grip: Paul William Thomas

Additional Grip: Michael G. DiGiovanni
Additional Grip: Mike Miller
Additional Grip: William Iversen
Additional Grip: Jason Remeikis
Additional Grip: Rick Strodel

HAIR
Key Hair: Janice Kinigopoulos
Hairstylist: Wyatt Belton

LOCATIONS
Location Manager: Charley Armstrong
Assistant Location Manager: Felicia Dames
Assistant Location Manager: Michael Faulkner
Locations Scout: Eric Bannat
Locations Assistant: Octavius Lee Johnson
Location Assistant: Brandi Washington

MAKEUP
Key Makeup: Debi Young
Makeup Artist: Sandra Linn Koepper
Makeup Artist: Ngozi Olandu

MEDIC
Set Medic: Jeff Johnson

POST PRODUCTION
Associate Producer: Simon Egleton
Associate Producer: Leslie Jacobowitz
Post Production Coordinator: Lee Meyer
Post Production Coordinator (Baltimore): Kyle Russell
Editor (Baltimore) *(Episodes 38, 41, 44, 47):* Kate Sanford
Editor (Baltimore) *(Episodes 39, 43, 49):* Meg Reticker
Editor (Episodes 42, 46, 48): Alex Hall
Editor (Episode 50): John Chimples
Assistant Editor (New York): Agnes Challe Grandits
Assistant Editor (New York): Craig Cobb
Assistant Editor (Baltimore): Matthew Booras
Apprentice Editor (Baltimore): De'Rodd Hearns

Post Production Production Assistant:
  Lance Edmands

PROPS
Prop Master: Mike Sabo
Assistant Prop Master: Bob Spore
Assistant Props: Dawson Nolley

SCENIC
Charge Scenic: Keith Weaver
Scenic Foreman: Claire Sharp
Gang Boss: Lucy Pealer
Scenic Painter: Craig Lee Schuman
Scenic Painter: Rachel Sitkin

SCRIPT SUPERVISOR
Script Supervisor: Claire Cowperthwaite

SET DRESSING
Set Decorator: John Millard
Assistant Set Decorator: Brook Yeaton
Leadman: Clark Hospelhorn
On Set Dresser: Lester Poser
Set Dressing Foreman: Patrick Eagan
Swing Gang: Jim Doherty
Swing Gang: William Depaola
Swing Gang: Norman Thurston Jr.
Swing Gang: Jaclyn M. Riedel

SPECIAL EFFECTS
Special Effects Coordinator: Conrad Brink
Special Effects: Henry S. Atterbury

SOUND
Sound Mixer: Bruce Litecky
Boom Operator: Lorenzo Millan
Sound Utility: Ivan Hawkes

STUNTS
Stunt Coordinator: Jeff Gibson

TEACHER
Teacher: On Location Education

TECHNICAL ADVISOR
Technical Advisor: Dep. Major James Rood

TRANSPORTATION
Transportation Coordinator: Foard Wilgis
Transportation Captain: Ronald Smith
Transportation Co-Captain: Tony
  Raimondo
Driver: Franklin G. Metts Sr.
Driver: Bart Wright
Driver: Victor Gray
Driver: Frank Matkins
Driver: Robert W. Phillips
Driver: Ronald G. Bohn Sr.
Driver: Mike Luckeroth
Driver: Jeff Cash
Driver: Tony Wisnom
Driver: Vincent J. Guariglia, Jr.
Driver: James Hubbard
Driver: Larry Sinclair
Driver: Donald G. Sauter
Driver: Robert A. Kidd
Driver: Billy Ellis
Office Van Driver: James "Jimbo" R.
  Hulson, Jr.
Driver: Raymond Hirsch
Driver: Howard M. Johnson

VIDEO
Video Assistant: Alex Applefeld
Assistant Video Assistant: Ben Watson

WARDROBE
Costume Designer: Alonzo Wilson
Assistant Costume Designer: Amanda
  Johnson
Costume Supervisor: Dona Adrian Gibson
Key Costumer: Mary Ann Creamer
Costumer: Allecia A. Davis
Costumer: Molly Cashman
Tailor: Minerva Diann Savoy

SEASON FIVE CAST

DET. JAMES "JIMMY" MCNULTY .... Dominic West
COL. CEDRIC DANIELS .... Lance Reddick
DET. SHAKIMA "KIMA" GREGGS .... Sonja Sohn
DET. WILLIAM "BUNK" MORELAND .... Wendell Pierce
DET. LESTER FREAMON .... Clarke Peters
SGT. ELLIS CARVER .... Seth Gilliam
ROLAND "PREZ" PRYZBYLEWSKI .... Jim True-Frost
THOMAS R. "HERC" HAUK .... Domenick Lombardozzi
DET. LEANDER SYDNOR .... Corey Parker Robinson
A.S.A. RHONDA PEARLMAN .... Deirdre Lovejoy
MAYOR THOMAS "TOMMY" CARCETTI .... Aidan Gillen
EX-MAYOR CLARENCE V. ROYCE .... Glynn Turman
COMM. ERVIN H. BURRELL .... Frankie Faison
DEP. COMM. OPS. WILLIAM A. RAWLS .... John Doman
CITY EDITOR AUGUSTUS "GUS" HAYNES .... Clark Johnson
SCOTT TEMPLETON .... Tom McCarthy
ALMA GUTIERREZ .... Michelle Paress
AVON BARKSDALE .... Wood Harris
OMAR .... Michael Kenneth Williams
WEE-BEY .... Hassan Johnson
BUBBLES .... Andre Royo
MARLO STANFIELD .... Jamie Hector
MICHAEL LEE .... Tristan Wilds
NAMOND BRICE .... Julito McCullum
RANDY WAGSTAFF .... Maestro Harrell
CHRIS PARTLOW .... Gbenga Akinnagbe
PROPOSITION JOE STEWART .... Robert F. Chew
SPIROS "VONDAS" VONDOPOULOS .... Paul Ben-Victor
THE GREEK .... Bill Raymond
SERGET "SERGE" MALATOV .... Chris Ashworth
MAURICE "MAURY" LEVY .... Michael Kostroff
DUQUAN "DUKIE" WEEMS .... Jermaine Crawford
DENNIS "CUTTY" WISE .... Chad L. Coleman
SLIM CHARLES .... Anwan Glover
SNOOP .... Felicia Pearson
WALON .... Steve Earle
BUTCHIE .... S. Robert Morgan
POOT .... Tray Chaney
OFC. BEATRICE "BEADIE" RUSSELL .... Amy Ryan
SGT. JAY LANDSMAN .... Delaney Williams
DET. EDWARD NORRIS .... Ed Norris

OFC. MICHAEL SANTANGELO . . . . Michael Salconi
DET. VERNON HOLLEY . . . . Brian Anthony Wilson
DET. MICHAEL CRUTCHFIELD . . . . Gregory L. Williams
OFC. KENNETH DOZERMAN . . . . Rick Otto
DET. FRANK BARLOW . . . . Michael Stone Forrest
OFC. ANTHONY COLICCHIO . . . . Benjamin Busch
MAJ. DENNIS MELLO . . . . Jay Landsman
LT. JAMES ASHER . . . . Gene Terinoni
OFC. LLOYD "TRUCK" CARRICK . . . . Ryan Sands
OFC. AARON CASTOR . . . . Lee Evertt Cox
OFC. BOBBY BROWN . . . . Bobby Brown
OFC. BRIAN MCLARNEY . . . . Brian E. McLarney
ROOKIE DETECTIVE . . . . Dennis Hill
DET. AUGUSTUS "AUGIE" POLK . . . . Nat Benchley
OFC. OSCAR REQUER . . . . Roscoe Orman
DET. JOHN MUNCH . . . . Richard Belzer
SPECIAL AGENT TERRANCE FITZHUGH . . . . Doug Olear
SQUAD SUPERVISOR AMANDA REESE . . . . Benay Berger
STATE SEN. R. CLAYTON "CLAY" DAVIS . . . . Isiah Whitlock, Jr.
DEP. COMM. ADMIN. STANISLAUS VALCHEK . . . . Al Brown
NORMAN WILSON . . . . Reg E. Cathey
COUNCIL PRESIDENT NERESE CAMPEELL . . . . Marlyne Afflack
CHIEF OF STAFF MICHAEL STEINTORF . . . . Neal Huff
MARLA DANIELS . . . . Maria Broom
STATE'S ATTORNEY RUPERT BOND . . . . Dion Graham
JUDGE DANIEL PHELAN . . . . Peter Gerety
STATE DEL. ODELL WATKINS . . . . Frederick Strother
HOWARD "BUNNY" COLVIN . . . . Robert Wisdom
U.S. ATTORNEY . . . . Joseph Urla
ANDREW KRAWCZYK . . . . Michael Willis
MANAGING EDITOR THOMAS KLEBANOW . . . . David Costabile
EDITOR-IN-CHIEF JAMES WHITING III . . . . Sam Freed
ROGER TWIGG . . . . Bruce Kirkpatrick
JEFF PRICE . . . . Todd Scofield
STATE EDITOR TIM PHELPS . . . . Tom McCarthy
METRO EDITOR STEVEN LUXENBERG . . . . Robert Poletick
REGIONAL AFFAIRS EDITOR REBECCA CORBETT . . . . Kara Quick
REWRITE MAN JAY SPRY . . . . Donald Neal
BILL ZORZI . . . . Bill Zorzi
MIKE FLETCHER . . . . Brandon Young
SCOTT SHANE . . . . Scott Shane
REWRITE MAN DAVE ETTLIN . . . . Dave Ettlin
LONDON BUREAU CHIEF ROBERT RUBY . . . . Stephen Schnetzer
JENNIFER CARCETTI . . . . Megan Anderson
ELENA MCNULTY . . . . Callie Thorne

MICHAEL MCNULTY . . . . Tony Cordova
SEAN MCNULTY . . . . Eric Ryan
JACK . . . . Connor Aikin
KARI . . . . Sophia Ayoud
CHERYL . . . . Melanie Nicholls-King
ELIJAH . . . . Elijah Grant Johnson
ASSISTANT PRINCIPAL MARCIA DONNELLY . . . . Tootsie Duvall
NICK SOBOTKA . . . . Pablo Schreiber
LITTLE BIG ROY . . . . Richard Pelzman
NATHANIEL "NAT" COXSON . . . . Luray Cooper
JOHNNY FIFTY . . . . Jeffrey Pratt Gordon
HUNGRY MAN . . . . Duane Rawlings
FATFACE RICK . . . . Troj Marquis Strickland
PHLL BOY . . . . Sho "Swordsman" Brown
KENARD . . . . Thuliso Dingwall
BUG . . . . Keenon Brice
HUCKLEBUCK . . . . Gil Deeble
CHEESE . . . . Method Man
DAY-DAY . . . . Donnell Rawlings
MONK . . . . Kwame Patterson
RAE . . . . Eisa Davis
O-DOG . . . . Darrell Britt-Gibson
SAVINO . . . . Christoper J. Clanton
SPIDER . . . . Edward Green
DONNIE . . . . Larry Andrews
VINSON . . . . Norris Davis
BIG GUY . . . . Derrick Purvey
DEACON . . . . Melvin Williams
TERRY HANNING . . . . Aubrey Deeker
MR. BOBBLES . . . . William Joseph Brookes
SHARDENE . . . . Wendy Grantham
MICHAEL'S MOTHER . . . . Shamika Cotton
BRENDAN WALSH . . . . Brendan Walsh
HOMELESS MAN #2 . . . . Ptolemy Slocum
A-RABBER . . . . Reggie A. Green

SEASON FIVE CREW

PRODUCERS/ASSISTANTS

Executive Producer: David Simon
Executive Producer: Nina K. Noble
Co-Executive Producer: Joe Chappelle
Co-Executive Producer: Edward Burns
Producer: Karen Thorson

Producer (Episode 56): George Pelecanos
Assistant to Mr. Simon: Laura A. Schweigman
Assistant to Ms. Noble: Ailene Staples
Producers' & Writers' Assistant: April Jones

DIRECTORS

Joe Chappelle: Episodes 51, 59
Ernest Dickerson: Episode 52
Joy Kecken & Scott Kecken: Episode 53
Dan Attias: Episode 54
Agnieszka Holland: Episode 55
Seith Mann: Episode 56
Dominic West: Episode 57
Anthony Hemingway: Episode 58
Clark Johnson: Episode 60

WRITING DEPARTMENT

Writer (Episode 55): David Mills
Writer (Episode 57): Richard Price
Writer (Episode 58): Dennis Lehane
Writer (Episode 59): George Pelecanos
Executive Story Editor/ Writer (Episode 52): Bill Zorzi
Story Editor/ Writer (Episode 53): Chris Collins
Script Coordinator: Joshua Luxenberg
Researcher: Chris Yakaitis

PRODUCTION OFFICE

Unit Production Manager: Nina K. Noble
Unit Production Manager: Joseph Incaprera
Production Office Coordinator: Ellen Gannon
Assistant Production Office Coordinator: Chris Menke
Special Projects Coordinator: Thomas "Toby" Hessenauer
Office Production Assistant: Amy Beth Barnes
Office Production Assistant: Pierre M. Coleman
Wrap Coordinator: Cathleen Clarke Kurtz

ACCOUNTING

Production Accountant: Ira Friedlander
1st Assistant Accountant: Michael Roccuzzo
Co-1st Assistant Accountant: Kim Garman
Payroll Accountant: Sally Douglass
Accounting Clerk: Duane Cipollini
Accounting PA: Shenia Hatchett

ART DEPARTMENT

Production Designer: Vince Peranio
Art Director: Halina Gebarowicz
Art Department Coordinator: Eric Huffman

ADs / SET PAs

1st Assistant Director (Episodes 51, 53, 55, 57, 59): Shelley Ziegler
1st Assistant Director (Episodes 52, 54, 56, 58, 60): Eric Henriquez
Key 2nd Assistant Director: Xanthus Valan
2nd 2nd Assistant Director: Tim Blockburger
Key Set Production Assistant: Doug Jones
Set Production Assistant: Amanda Faison
Set Production Assistant: Scott Foster
Set Production Assistant: Steve Lafferty
Set Production Assistant: Dana Lewis
Set Production Assistant: D'Arcy Rossiter

CAMERA

Director of Photography (Episodes 51–56): Russell Lee Fine
Director of Photography (Episodes 57–60): Dave Insley
Camera Operator: Niels Alpert
1st Assistant Camera: Boots Shelton
2nd Assistant Camera: Ian Axilrod
Loader: Sarah Brandes
Still Photographer (Episodes 51–55): Paul S. Schiraldi
Still Photographer (Episodes 56–60): Nicole Rivelli
B Camera Operator: James Ball
B Camera 1st Assistant: Kurt Parlow
B Camera 2nd Assistant: Jason David Foster

CASTING

Casting Director (New York): Alexa L. Fogel, CSA
Casting Associate (New York): Christine Kromer
Casting Director (Baltimore): Pat Moran, CSA

Casting Associate (Baltimore): Meagan
   Lewis
Casting Assistant (Baltimore): Shamos Fisher
Extras Casting Coordinator: Sareva Racher
Extras Casting Intern: Lauren Klemm

CATERING
Owner: Paul Kuzmich
Chef: W. Stanley Pratt
1st Assistant: Dorian Alvarez
Prep Cook / Server: Victor Martinez

CLEARANCES
Senior Script Clearance Analyst HBO:
   Rebecca Thornell

CONSTRUCTION
Construction Coordinator: Randy G.
   Herbert
Lead Foreman: Scott Dunn
Gang Boss: John Weiffenbach
Gang Boss: John Struss
Key Carpenter: Michael Key
Key Carpenter: Thomas F. Lombardi
Carpenter: Michael P. Conner
Shop PA: Brad Willard

CRAFT SERVICE
Craft Service Key: Elena Moscatt
Craft Service Assistant: Kim Bogues

DIALECT/ACTING COACH
Acting Coach/Dialect: Robert Chew

ELECTRIC
Gaffer: Ted Ayd
Rigging Gaffer: Kevin "Vinnie"
   Campbell
Best Boy: Aaron Johnson
Rigging Best Boy: Eliott Snell
Dimmer Operator: Len Applefeld
House Electrician: Chris Baker
Genny Operator: Todd Norton
Set Lighting Technician Shop Steward:
   Wade Tyree

Set Lighting Technician: Andy Vallerie
Set Lighting Technician: Philip E. Kathrens

FILM ELECTRONICS
Coordinator: Tom Farmer
Electronics Assistant: Thomas H.E. Scruggs
Additional Electronics Assistant: Clayton
   Barrow
Additional Electronics Assistant: Beau Seidel

GRIP
Key Grip: Rodney G. French
Best Boy Grip: David Wilkins
Key Rigging Grip: Michael Gearhart
Dolly Grip: John C. Barber
B-Camera Dolly Grip: Shawn C. H. Baron
Grip: Will Iversen
Grip: Richard J. Fortkiewicz
Grip: Dale V. Swavely
Grip: Eddie Hohman
Grip: Jeff Callow

HAIR
Key Hair (Episodes 51–58): Janice
   Kinigopoulos
Hairstylist (Key Hair Episodes 59–60):
   Wyatt Belton
Hairstylist (Episodes 59–60): Kim Hart

LOCATIONS
Location Manager: Charley Armstrong
Assistant Location Manager: Michael
   Faulkner
Assistant Location Manager: Patrick Burn
Locations Scout: Eric Bannat
Locations Assistant: Marvin Ruffin
Locations Assistant: Ethan Yang

MAKEUP
Key Makeup: Debi Young
Makeup Artist (Episodes 57–58): Sandra
   Linn Koepper
Makeup Artist (Episodes 59–60): Annabelle
   Macneal
Makeup Artist: Ngozi Olandu

MEDIC

Set Medic: Jeff Johnson

POST PRODUCTION

Associate Producer: Simon Egleton

Associate Producer (Episodes 51–55): Shannon Fogarty

Associate Producer (Episodes 56–60): Leslie Jacobowitz

Post Production Coordinator: Lee Meyer

Post Production Coordinator (Baltimore): Kyle Russell

Editor (Episodes 51, 53, 57, 60): Kate Sanford

Editor (Episodes 54, 56, 59): Alex Hall

Editor (Episodes 52, 55, 58): John Chimples

Assistant Editor: Victoria Lang

Assistant Editor (Episodes 51–56): Agnes Challe-Grandits

Assistant Editor (Episodes 57–60): Laura Weinberg

Assistant Editor: Matthew Booras

Apprentice Editor: De'Rodd Hearns

Post Production P.A. (Episodes 51–56): Gina Sansom

Post Production P.A. (Episodes 57–60): Gabe Kolodny

Music Supervisor: Blake Leyh

Supervising Sound Editor / ADR and Loop Group Supervisor: Jennifer Ralston, MPSE

SFX Editor: Rachel Chancey

Dialogue Editor (Episodes, 51–54): David Briggs

Dialogue Editor (Episodes 55–60)

Background Editor: Igor Nikolic

Foley Supervisor: Matt Haasch

Foley Editor (Episodes 51–54): Alex Soto

Foley Artists: Jay Peck

Foley Engineer: Ryan Collison

Re-Recording Mixer Studio B: Andrew Kris

ADR Mixer: Bobby Johnson

ADR Mixer: Dave Boulton

Editorial Rental Manager: Irwin Simon

Billing Studio Managers: Jay Rubin

Billing Studio Managers: Jim Gardner

ADR Scheduler: Mike Howells

ADR Scheduler: Tom O'Bryon

PROPS

Prop Master: Mike Sabo

Assistant Prop Master: Bob Spore

Assistant Props: Dawson Nolley

Assistant Props: MJ Marqua

SCENIC

Charge Scenic: Keith Weaver

Scenic Foreman: Claire Sharp

Gang Boss: Lucy Pealer

Scenic Painter: Craig Lee Schuman

Scenic Painter: Bobby Raber

SCRIPT SUPERVISOR

Script Supervisor (Episode 51): Jan Sanders

Script Supervisor (Episodes 52–58): Claire Cowperthwaite

Script Supervisor (Episodes 59–60): W. Thom Rainey

SET DRESSING

Set Decorator: John Millard

Assistant Set Decorator: Jaclyn M. Riedel

Leadman: Clark Hospelhorn

On Set Dresser: Chad Williams

Set Dressing Foreman: Patrick Eagan

Swing: Ted Lubonovich

Swing Gang (Episodes 51–56): Eric Boring

Swing Gang (Episodes 51–56): John Fulcher

Swing Gang (Episodes 57–60): Rachel Sitkin

Swing Gang (Episodes 57–60): Robert Scott Trieschman

SPECIAL EFFECTS

Special Effects Coordinator: Conrad Brink

Special Effects: Henry S. Atterbury

SOUND

Sound Mixer: Bruce Litecky, CAS

Boom Operator: Lorenzo Millan

Sound Utility: Ivan Hawkes

STUNTS
Stunt Coordinator: Jeff Gibson

TEACHER
Teacher: On Location Education

TECHNICAL ADVISOR
Technical Advisor: Dep. Major James Rood

TRANSPORTATION
Transportation Coordinator: Foard Wilgis
Transportation Captain: Tony Raimondo
Transportation Co-Captain: Gerry Titus
Driver: Frank Matkins
Driver: Sal Raimond
Driver: Robert W. Phillips
Driver: Ronald G. Bohn Sr.
Driver: Vincent J. Guariglia, Jr.
Driver: James Hubbard
Driver: Albert Hamilton Sr.
Driver: Charles E. Bauer
Driver: Bruce "Bubbles" Zamzow
Driver: Jeffrey L. Cash
Driver: Robert Freedenburg
Driver: Robert A. Kidd
Driver: Larry O'Connell
Driver: Michael Salamone
Driver: George Zimnoch
Driver: Donald G. Sauter
Driver: Bart Wright
Driver: Raymond Taylor
Driver: Todd Dunklebarger
Office Van Driver: James "Jimbo" R. Hulson, Jr.

VIDEO ASSIST
Video Assistant: Alex Applefeld
Assistant Video: Matt Grube
Assistant Video: Ben Watson

WARDROBE
Costume Designer: Alonzo Wilson
Assistant Costume Designer: Amanda Johnson

Costume Supervisor: Dona Adrian Gibson
Key Costumer (Episodes 51–56, 58–60): Linda Boyland
Key Costumer (Episode 7): Helen L. Simmons
Costumer (Episodes 51–55): Da' Juan T. Prince
Costumer (Episodes 56–60): Michael N. Simon
Additional Costumer: Constance Harris
Uniforms Specialist: Molly Cashman
Tailor: Minerva Diann Savoy

SECOND UNIT
2nd Assistant Director: Kurt Uebersax
Camera Operators: Sheila Smith; Jeff Schmale
1st Assistant Camera: Wayne Arnold
2nd Assistant Camera: Doug Kofsky
Loaders: Nick Huynh; Jared Roybal
Craft Service: Sarah Fales
Gaffer: Stewart Stack
Key Grip: Dave Noble
Dolly Grip: Dean Citroni
Key Hair: Ardis F. Cohen; Charmaine Henninger
Key Makeup: Annabelle Macneal
Script Supervisors: Laura A. Schweigman; Robb Foglia; Jane Burka
On Set Dresser: Eddie Hohman
Sound Mixer: Dennis Towns
Boom Operator: Ben Watson
Video Assistant: Sam Insley

ACKNOWLEDGMENTS

I am in debt to many folks who helped make this book possible, including Canongate editor Nick Davies and his able assistant, Dan Franklin; my literary agent, Rebecca Oliver; HBO's Bree Conover; Laura Schweigman of good 'ole Bawlmer; Charley "CB" Allen of Hollywood via the Pelican State; Jen Ralston, Fran Boyd, Susan Allenback, Toots Duvall, and the rest of the "loop group" crew who gathered for steamed crabs at Jimmy's Famous Seafood on Holabird Avenue in Dundalk; Pat Moran and Vince Peranio; film editor Kate Sanford.

And David Simon, who graciously gave me this assignment and next to whom I once sat in the "Ego Row" section of the *Baltimore Sun* newsroom when we were young.

Rafael Alvarez
May 24, 2009
Los Angeles

NOTE ON THE CONTRIBUTORS

Victor Paul Alvarez is an editor for the East Bay newspapers in Providence, Rhode Island. He began his career as a copy boy in the newsroom of the *Baltimore Sun*.

Michael A. Fletcher covered City Hall for the *Baltimore Sun* before leaving for the *Washington Post*, where he currently covers the Obama White House.

Greg Garland is an investigative reporter for the Baton Rouge (Louisiana) *Advocate*. Before that, he was a general assignment state reporter for the *Baltimore Sun*.

Nick Hornby's latest novel is *Juliet, Naked*. His interview with David Simon was first published in the *Believer*.

Joy Lusco Kecken graduated from Towson State University in Baltimore and wrote for the first three seasons of *The Wire*. She is a writer/director living in Los Angeles.

Laura Lippman was a reporter for 20 years, including 12 years at the *Baltimore Sun*. She is the author of 15 novels, many featuring the reporter turned sleuth Tess Monaghan.

Ann LoLordo, a poet, worked for the *Baltimore Sun* for 30 years, covering everything from cops and robbers to a posting as the paper's Jerusalem correspondent.

George Pelacanos is the author of 15 crime novels set in and around Washington, D.C. He has been nominated for an Emmy for his writing on *The Wire*.

Deborah Rudacille, a lifelong Baltimorean, holds a masters degree in science writing from Johns Hopkins University. She is the author of *The Riddle of Gender: Science, Activism, and Transgender Rights*, published in 2005 by Pantheon.

Tom Waldron is a Baltimore writer and author. He played a state delegate in Season Two of *The Wire*.

Anthony Walton is the author of *Mississippi: An American Journey*.

William F. Zorzi is a journalist and screenwriter. He worked at the *Baltimore Sun* for almost 20 years and covered politics for the majority of his career.

PHOTO CREDITS

TEXT PERMISSIONS

INDEX